Elisabeth Schüssler Fiorenza is the Krister Stendahl Professor at Harvard Divinity School, a founding editor of the *Journal of Feminist Studies in Religion,* past president of the Society of Biblical Literature, and author of many important and influential works, among them *In Memory of Her* (1984), *Bread Not Stone* (1985), *Jesus: Miriam's Child, Sophia's Prophet* (1995), *The Power of the Word: Scripture and the Rhetoric of Empire* (Fortress Press, 2007), and *Transforming Vision: Explorations in Feminist The*logy* (Fortress Press, 2011). She is editor of *Searching the Scriptures,* a feminist introduction and commentary (two vols., 1993, 1994).

CHANGING HORIZONS

Explorations in Feminist Interpretation

Elisabeth Schüssler Fiorenza

Fortress Press
Minneapolis

CHANGING HORIZONS
Explorations in Feminist Interpretation

Cover image: George Tjungurrayi, *The Dancing Women at Nyuminga*, 1976. Copyright © 2012 George Tjungurrayi, licensed by Aboriginal Artists Agency Ltd, National Museum of Australia.

Cover design: Laurie Ingram

Library of Congress Cataloging-in-Publication Data
Schüssler Fiorenza, Elisabeth, 1938-
Changing horizons : explorations in feminist interpretation /
Elisabeth Schüssler Fiorenza.
p. cm.
Includes bibliographical references.
ISBN 978-0-8006-9807-2 (alk. paper) — ISBN 978-1-4514-2641-0 (ebook)
1. Bible—Feminist criticism. 2. Bible—Hermeneutics. I. Title.
BS521.4.S37 2013
220.6082–dc23   2012035109

The paper used in this publication meets the minimum requirements of American National Standard for Information Sciences — Permanence of Paper for Printed Library Materials, ANSI Z329.48-1984.

Manufactured in the U.S.A.

In memoriam Jane Schaberg

Feminist biblical scholar and pathmaker

Contents

Preface

Many people have been involved in producing this collection of essays and many thanks are in order. I am grateful to the editors and publishers who originally edited and published these articles; many of them were written by a young, emerging scholar. As the senior editor of the *Journal of Feminist Studies in Religion*, I am well aware of how much care and work such editing takes. Although I did my best to avoid overlaps and cut pages, it is in the nature of a collection of essays such as this that ideas and arguments are repeated. While the individual essays were written for variegated audiences, their collection and order in a single volume changes their context and rhetoric.

I am very grateful for the help I have received in preparing the manuscript. My faculty assistants, Ms. Hayfa Abdul Jaber and Ms. Robin Lee, not only contacted publishers for reprint permissions but also worked hard to scan articles not available in digital format. I am also greatly indebted to my research assistants, without whom this work could not have been completed. Ms. Young Ra Rhee labored hard to convert the scanned texts into editable documents, and Ms. Kelsi Morrison-Atkins carefully proofread the manuscript. To both a heartfelt thanks. Without their capable support I would not have found the time and energy to start and finish this book.

Changing Horizons is the second volume of a three-volume project. While the first volume, *Transforming Vision*, gathered my feminist the*logical essays, this volume assembles some of my exegetical and hermeneutical work. I am grateful to Fortress Press and especially its former editor-in-chief Michael West for his enthusiastic support of this project. I am also indebted to acquiring editor Neil Elliott for his assistance, Susan Johnson, former managing editor at Fortress Press, for working out contractual issues, Marissa Wold for coordinating all aspects of the production and manufacturing process, and Josh Messner and Jo Quanbeck for their careful editing of the manuscript.

I also want to thank my colleague Dr. Linda Maloney for her initial translation of the chapter titled "The*logy as Rhetoric, Ethic, and Critique of Ideology," first published in my book *Grenzen überschreiten: Der theoretische Anspruch feministischer Theologie. Ausgewählte Aufsätze*. Her work allowed me to prepare a revision for this chapter.

Last but not least, as always I am deeply grateful to my partner, Francis Schüssler Fiorenza, and to Chris Miryam Schüssler-Fiorenza for their support, love, and friendship. I also want to thank the members of my fall 2011 seminar on feminist biblical interpretation for their spirited discussions, thoughtful contributions, and critical challenges.

This book is dedicated to a leading feminist biblical scholar who has departed too early from us. Jane Dewar Schaberg's pathbreaking scholarship on Mary of Magdala and her book *The Illegitimacy of Jesus* have not only greatly shaped the field of feminist biblical studies but also have had great public impact. Jane's friendship and vision will be missed greatly. Although already very ill, Jane graciously accepted the dedication of this book in honor of her work. She consulted with me also on her own collection of essays, on which she worked with professor Holly E. Hearon during the last months of her life. Unfortunately, Jane will not be able to see the publication of this collection of essays. I am glad that she was able to complete her own collection, entitled *The Death and Resurrection of the Author and Other Feminist Essays on the Bible*.

When asked in one of her last interviews by a student what she hoped for the future of her own work, Jane responded: "I would like to see my work remembered and myself as a good scholar—not just for being attacked— and a feminist." We all need to ensure that what Jane and other feminist biblical scholars who have passed on "have done, will be told"—not just their transforming scholarship but also their feminist struggles.

Acknowledgments

The following chapters were first published in other places, as follows. I thank the publishers for their permission to reprint these essays here.

Introduction, "Claiming the Authority of Biblical Interpretation," *Revista Alternativas* 15 (2008): 15–32.

Chapter 1. "Interpreting Patriarchal Traditions," in *The Liberating Word: A Guide to Nonsexist Interpretation of the Bible*, edited by Letty Russell, 39–61 (Philadelphia: Westminster 1976).

Chapter 2. "Toward a Feminist Biblical Hermeneutics: Biblical Interpretation and Liberation Theology," in *The Challenge of Liberation Theology: A First World Response*, edited by B. Mahan and D. Richesin, 91–112 (Maryknoll: Orbis, 1981).

Chapter 3. "Feminist Interpretation and New Testament Studies," *Journal for the Study of the Old Testament* 22 (1982): 32–46.

Chapter 4. "The Will to Choose or to Reject: Continuing Our Critical Work," in *Feminist Interpretation of the Bible*, edited by Letty Russell, 125–36 (Philadelphia: Westminster John Knox, 1985).

Chapter 5. "For the Sake of the Truth Dwelling among Us: Emerging Issues in Feminist Biblical Interpretation," in *Christian Feminism: Visions of a New Humanity*, edited by Judith Weidman, 33–54 (New York: Harper & Row, 1984).

Chapter 6. "Feminist Hermeneutics," in *Anchor Bible Dictionary*, edited by David N. Freedman et al., 783–91. Vol. 2 (New York: Doubleday, 1992).

Chapter 7. "Unterscheidung der Geister: Schriftauslegung als Ideologiekritik, Theologische Rhetorik und Interpretationsethik," in Adrian Holderegger and Jean-Pierre Wills, eds., *Interdisziplinäre Ethik: Grundlagen, Methoden, Bereiche—Festgabe für Dietmar Mieth* (Freiburg: Herder, 2001), 149–64.

Chapter 8. "Disciplinary Matters: A Critical Rhetoric and Ethic of Inquiry." In *Rhetoric, Ethic, and Moral Persuasion in Biblical Discourse: Essays from the 2002 Heidelberg Papers*, edited by Tom H. Olbricht and Anders Eriksson, 9–32 (New York: T&T Clark, 2005).

Chapter 9. "Escritura como retorica do Imperio," in *A teia do Conhecimento*, edited by Ana Maria Tepedino and Alessandro Rocha, 19–36 (Sao Paulo: Paulinas, 2008).

Chapter 10. "To Set the Record Straight: Biblical Women's Studies," *Horizons* 10 (1983): 111–21.

Chapter 11. Biblical Interpretation and Critical Commitment," *Studia theologica* 43, no. 1 (1989): 5–18.

Chapter 12. "The Politics of Otherness: Biblical Interpretation as a Critical Praxis for Liberation," in *The Future of Liberation Theology: Essays in Honor of Gustavo Gutiérrez*, edited by Marc Ellis and Otto Maduro, 311–25 (Maryknoll: Orbis, 1989).

Chapter 13. "'Waiting at Table': A Critical Feminist Theological Reflection on Diakonia," in *Diakonia*, edited by Norbert Greinacher and Norbert Mette, 84–94, Concilium 198 (Edinburgh: T&T Clark, 1988).

Chapter 14. "The Twelve and the Discipleship of Equals," in *Changing Women, Changing Church*, edited by L. M. Uhr, 109–21 (Newtown: Millennium, 1992).

Chapter 15. "Resisting Violence-Engendering Easter," in Elisabeth Schüssler Fiorenza, *The Open House of Wisdom: Critical Feminist Theological Explorations*, edited and translated by Satoko Yamaguchi (Tokyo: Shinkyo Shuppansha, 2005).

Chapter 16. "Liberation, Unity and Equality in Community: New Testament Case Studies," in *Beyond Unity-in-Tension: Unity, Renewal, and the Community of Women and Men*, edited by Thomas F. Best, 58–74 (Geneva: WCC Publications, 1988).

Chapter 17. "Bread/Rice of Wisdom: Biblical Interpretation for Liberation," *Ewha Journal of Feminist Theology* 2 (1997): 101–25.

Chapter 18. "Invitation to Dance: In the Open House of Wisdom: Feminist Study of the Bible." In *Engaging the Bible: Critical Readings from Contemporary Women*, edited by Choi Hee An and Katheryn Pfister Darr, 81–104 (Minneapolis: Fortress Press, 2006).

Chapter 19. "The Power of the Word: Charting Critical Global Feminist Biblical Studies," in *Feminist New Testament Studies: Global and Future Perspectives*, edited by Kathleen O'Brien Wicker, Althea Spencer Miller, and Musa W. Dube, 43–62 (New York: Palgrave MacMillan, 2005).

Introduction

CLAIMING THE AUTHORITY OF BIBLICAL INTERPRETATION

Fifty years ago feminist biblical studies was not yet born. Today it is a growing, developing, and stimulating field of study.[1] I am often asked: With whom did you study feminist the*logy? And I unfailingly answer: When I studied the*logy[2] in the 1960s, feminist the*logy and feminist studies in religion did not exist. Hence, we had to invent it. Since the history of feminist biblical studies still remains to be written,[3] this collection of essays on feminist biblical hermeneutics seeks both to trace the emergence of feminist biblical studies and my participaton in it. It does so not only in a chronological but also in a topological[4] way that circles around the key *topoi* of feminist hermeneutics.

THE STORY AND SITE OF FEMINIST BIBLICAL HERMENEUTICS

I remember that in the late 1960s, when the so-called "second wave" of the wo/men's[5] movement first emerged on the scene, I devoured everything that was published on any wo/men's or feminist topic. In the 1970s, I could still read anything that appeared in the area of feminist the*logy or feminist studies in religion. In the 1980s, I was no longer able to keep informed and to read everything that appeared in feminist critical studies, but I could still keep abreast of most of the publications in my own area of expertise, biblical studies. In the 1990s, I have had a difficult time to keep up and to read the literature appearing in my field of specialization, Christian (New) Testament Studies. In the first decade of this century, feminist biblical studies have been joined by other voices—such as queer studies, postcolonial studies, masculinity studies, or ideological biblical criticism—and it is impossible to read and integrate all these different approaches. This impossibility, however, is not a depressing fact but rather exhilarating, because it documents that feminist biblical studies has developed into a rich and variegated area of study.

Indeed, this enormous proliferation of critical feminist intellectual work in general and in biblical studies in particular is ground for celebration. Feminist hermeneutics has been established as a legitimate site of biblical hermeneutics. It brings a chorus of new voices to biblical hermeneutics. The variegated intellectual voices of feminist biblical studies have aptly been characterized with the metaphor of heteroglossia, "speaking in other, different tongues." This expression alludes to the biblical notion of glossolalia (speaking in tongues) as a gift of the Divine Spirit. Without question, in the last thirty years feminist biblical studies has been established as a new field of study with its own publications. It is taught in schools, colleges, and universities and is practiced by many scholars in different parts of the world.

However, to tell the story of the emerging field of feminist biblical studies as a success story obscures the fact that it is for the most part the success story of white Euro-American Christian scholarship. While Jewish feminist biblical scholarship has greatly increased in the 1990 and 2000s, Muslim feminist biblical scholarship is in its beginnings. While the presence and work of womanist/black feminist, Latina, and Asian feminist biblical scholars arrived on the scene of biblical studies in the 1980s and 1990s, only very few African American, Latina, or Asian wo/men scholars have graduate level positions in biblical studies. Celebrating the success story of feminist biblical interpretation must not overlook that articles and books by African, Latin American, Australian, Chinese, Korean, Indian, Native American, Maori, and other Indigenous feminist scholars around the globe are still scarce because only a very few wo/men of the Two-Thirds World have gained access to biblical academic studies and have the status and means to publish their work.

This dire situation is not due, however, to the racism and elitism of white feminist scholars, as is often alleged, but due to the fact that academic institutions have not changed their kyriarchal ethos and because global capitalism is built on the exploitation of wo/men. Hence, because of the societal, cultural, and religious structures of domination, very few wo/men of disadvantaged groups or countries achieve access to the*logical education and higher biblical studies.

Moreover, even in the white European and North American academy where one finds a good number of highly educated wo/men, feminist biblical interpretation is often still not widely recognized as an important field of study. If one, for instance, looks at and searches through introductions to the Bible or to specific areas of biblical studies, one very rarely will find even a mention of feminist biblical studies as a formal area of inquiry.[6] Many collections of essays in the field still are published without any feminist contributions to the topic. Feminist scholars are still daily written out of history and our work is consigned to the margins. This is not due to the self-ghettoization of feminist biblical scholars as some have suggested. Rather it is due to the kyriarchal structures and ethos of the field.

Applicants often are still not selected for ministerial or doctoral programs if they express interest in a feminist studies approach. Scholars still have a difficult time to receive tenure or ecclesiastical approval if they have published in the area of feminist biblical studies or feminist the*logy. Students are still told not to write their dissertation on a feminist topic if they want to be serious scholars. Senior scholars are put down rather than honored because they have done feminist work. In short, the marginalizing and silencing tendencies of kyriocentric academic and religious structures that have barred wo/men from higher education and the study of the*logy in the past are still in place, but they are now directed against feminists and not against wo/men who support the academic system of exclusion and subordination.

I have here frequently used the f-word "feminist," although this expression is still in most of the world a negative word and in many audiences it calls forth an array of complex emotions, negative reactions, and harmful prejudices. Since the word also evokes a host of different understandings, I hasten to explain how I understand it. My preferred definition of feminism is expressed by a well-known bumper sticker that with tongue in cheek asserts, "feminism is the radical notion that wo/men are people." This definition accentuates that feminism is a radical concept and at the same time ironically underscores that at the beginning of the twenty-first century feminism should be a common-sense notion. It asserts: wo/men are not ladies, wives, sex-objects, handmaids, seductresses, or beasts of burden, but wo/men are full decision-making citizens.

This definition of "feminism" alludes to the democratic assertion "We, the people" and positions feminism within radical democratic discourses, which argue for the rights of all the people who are wo/men. It evokes memories of struggles for equal citizenship and decision-making powers in society and religion.[7] According to this political definition of feminism, men can advocate feminism just as wo/men can be antifeminist. Feminism is not just concerned about gender but also about race, class, heterosexism and imperialism. It is concerned about kyriarchal power relations of domination.

Hence, I have proposed early on to replace the category of "patriarchy" with the neologism *kyriarchy*, which is derived from the Greek words *kyrios* (lord/slavemaster/father/husband/elite/propertied/educated man) and *archein* (to rule, dominate).[8] In classical antiquity, the rule of the *kyrios* to whom disenfranchised men and all wo/men were subordinated is best characterized as *kyriarchy*.

Kyriarchy is best theorized as a complex pyramidal system of interlocking[9] multiplicative[10] social and religious structures of superordination and sub-ordination, of ruling and oppression. Kyriarchal relations of domination are built on elite male property rights as well as on the exploitation, dependency, inferiority, and obedience of wo/men who signify all those subordinated. Such kyriarchal relations are still today at work in the multiplicative intersection-ality[11] of class, race, gender, ethnicity, empire, and other structures of dis-crimination. In short, kyriarchy is constituted as a sociocultural and religious system of dominations by intersecting multiplicative structures of oppression. The different sets of relations of domination shift historically and produce a different constellation of oppression in different times and cultures. The structural positions of subordination that have been fashioned by kyriarchal relations stand in tension with those required by radical democracy.

Rather than identifying kyriarchy with the patriarchal and racial binary male over female, black over white, Western over colonialized peoples, it is best to understand it in the classical sense of antiquity. Modern democracies are still structured as complex pyramidal political systems of superiority and inferiority, of dominance and subordination. As kyriarchal democracies, they are stratified by gender, race, class, religion, heterosexism, and age; these are *structural positions* that are assigned to us more or less by birth. However, how we live these structural kyriarchal positions is determined not simply by these structural positions, but also by the *subject positions* through which we live our structural kyriarchal positions. Whereas an essentialist approach assigns to people an "authentic" identity that is derived from our *structural position,* our *subject position* becomes coherent and compelling through political discourse, interpretive frameworks, and the development of theoretical horizons regarding domination.

Thus, a critical intersectional analytic does not understand kyriarchy as an essentialist ahistorical system. Instead, it articulates kyriarchy as a heuristic (derived from the Greek, meaning "to find") concept, or as a diagnostic, analytic instrument that enables investigation into the multiplicative interdependence of hetero-normativity, gender, race, class, and imperial stratifications, as well as into their discursive inscriptions and ideological reproductions. Moreover, it highlights that people inhabit not only one but several *structural positions* of race, sex, gender, class, disability, and ethnicity. If one position becomes privileged, it constitutes a nodal point. While in any particular historical moment class may be the primary modality through which one experiences gender, colonialism, and race, in other circumstances gender may be the privileged position through which one experiences sexuality, race, colonialism, and class. Consequently, feminist biblical interpretation is best conceptualized in terms of wo/men's struggles to free ourselves from kyriarchal domination and mind-sets, our struggles for survival, self-determination, and well-being, our struggles to become fully entitled and responsible citizens in society and religion.

THE ROOTS OF FEMINIST BIBLICAL STUDIES IN EMANCIPATORY STRUGGLES

Feminist studies in general and feminist biblical studies in particular, I argue, do not owe their existence and inspiration to the academy but to social movements for change. Most of the social movements for change in modernity have been inspired by the dream of radical democratic equality and equal human rights. Since the democratic idea promises equal participation and equal rights to all but in actuality has restricted rights and equality to a small group of elite men, the subalterns, who have been deprived of their human rights and dignity, have struggled to transform their situations of oppression and exclusion. Such radical democratic struggles are not just a product of modernity, nor is their ethos and vision of radical equality a product restricted to the West.

These struggles for wo/men's self-determination, equal rights, decision-making power, human dignity and radical democratic equality provide the context of a critical feminist interpretation for liberation. They do so not only by articulating ever new sites of struggle but also by providing ever more sophisticated categories for the analysis of domination as well as by articulating visions of liberation. Since the Bible has been used in most of these struggles either for legitimating the status quo of the kyriarchal order of domination *or* for challenging dehumanization, feminist biblical interpretation is best articulated as an integral part of wo/men's struggles for authority and self-determination.

If the Bible has been used against and for wo/men in our diverse struggles, then the goal of biblical interpretation cannot just be *to understand* biblical texts and traditions. Rather, its goal must be *to change* western idealist hermeneutical frameworks, individualist practices, and sociopolitical relations. Hence liberation the*logies of all colors take the experience and voices of the oppressed and marginalized, of those wo/men traditionally excluded from articulating the*logy and shaping communal life, as the starting point of biblical interpretation and the*logical reflection. In reclaiming the authority of wo/men as religious-the*logical subjects for shaping and determining biblical religions, the act of biblical interpretation becomes a moment in the global struggles for liberation.

Long before postmodern theories, liberation the*logies have not only recognized the perspectival and contextual nature of knowledge and interpretation but have also asserted that biblical interpretation and the*logy are—knowingly or not—always engaged for or against the oppressed. Intellectual neutrality is not possible in a historical world of exploitation. However, such a position does not assume the innocence and purity of the oppressed. Neither does it see them purely as victims but rather understands them as agents for change. Such a shift from a modern western malestream to a critical liberationist frame of reference engenders a fourfold change: a change of interpretive assumptions and goals, a change of methodology and epistemology, a change of individual and collective consciousness, and a change of social-ecclesial institutions and cultural-religious formations.

Consequently, a critical interpretation for liberation does not commence by beginning with the text and by placing the Bible at the center of its attention. Rather it begins with a reflection on wo/men's experience in the struggles for justice and our sociopolitical religious location. For such a reflection it utilizes a critical systemic analysis of the structures of domination that shape our lives and are inscribed in biblical texts and interpretations. In reading biblical texts, a "feminist standpoint" must be taken that remains focused on wo/men who struggle at the bottom of the kyriarchal pyramid of domination and exploitation. This is necessary, because their struggles reveal both the fulcrum of dehumanizing oppression threatening every wo/man and the power of Divine Wisdom at work in our midst.

Christian identity that is shaped by the Bible must in ever new readings be deconstructed and reconstructed in terms of a global praxis for the liberation of all wo/men. Equally, cultural identity that is shaped by biblical discourses must be critically interrogated and transformed. Hence, one needs to reconceptualize the traditional spiritual practice of discerning the spirits as a critical hermeneutic-ethical-political practice. As interpreting subjects, biblical readers need to learn how to claim their spiritual authority to assess both the oppressive as well as the liberating imagination of particular biblical texts and their interpretations.

By deconstructing the rhetorics and politics of inequality and subordination that are inscribed in the Bible, we are able to generate new possibilities for the ever new articulation of radical democratic religious identities and emancipatory practices. In order to do so, a critical ethical-political interpretation does not subscribe to one single reading strategy and interpretive method but employs a variety of exegetical and interpretive methods for understanding the Bible as public discourse.

Feminists have used different rhetorical metaphors for naming such an emancipatory method and hermeneutical process; "Making visible," "hearing into speech," and "finding one's voice," are just a few. I myself have favored metaphors of movement such as "turning," "dance," "ocean waves," or "struggle." One could also think of biblical interpretation as cooking a stew, utilizing different herbs and spices that season the rice, meats, and carrots equally and when stirred together combine into a new and different flavor.

Whether one thinks of biblical interpretation as a "stew" or a "dance," crucial "spices" or "moves" in a critical feminist emancipatory interpretation are experience and conscientization, a critical analytic of domination, suspicion rather than trust, assessment and evaluation in terms of a feminist scale of values, reconstruction or re-membering, (re)imagination and ritualization, and the goal of transformation and action for change. These strategies of a critical feminist emancipatory interpretation, however, are not to be construed simply as successive independent steps of inquiry or simply as discrete methodological rules or recipes. Rather they must be understood as interpretive moves or strategies of seasoning that interact with each other simultaneously in the process of reading a particular biblical or any other cultural text in light of the globalization of inequality.

These movements in the hermeneutical "dance" of liberation work on two different levels of interpretation: on the level of the language-systems, ideological frameworks, and sociopolitical-religious locations of contemporary readers in kyriarchal contexts of domination, on the one hand, and on the level of the linguistic and sociohistorical systems of biblical texts and their effective histories of interpretation, on the other. In such a critical feminist hermeneutical dance we continue to turn and to move, beginning at the end, circling back to the beginning. Like the tides of the ocean, Divine Wisdom-Sophia always moves and returns, but with a difference. If feminist biblical interpretation moves and changes in the direction of the divine it might glimpse a vision of Her all-embracing justice and enveloping well-being. As Karen Baker-Fletcher has seen Her ceaseless motion:

> When I watch the wind tease and urge into dance the waves of the ocean, when I feel the moon's pull on the waters and on the cycles of my own body, I often think of the deep powerful waters of the ocean dancing with the spirit of G*d . . . Creation is born out of a loving, creative dance between Spirit and the elements of the cosmos. We humans are ādām (which means "earth creature" in Hebrew), dependent on all the elements of water, earth, air, sun. Our own nativity and the birth of our children's children is dependent on this power of life.[12]

If the Scriptures were seen to be like the "deep powerful waters of the ocean dancing with the Spirit of G*d," feminist biblical interpretation could then be understood as articulating and participating in "the creative dance between the Spirit and the elements" of the biblical traditions. In the hermeneutical movements of the dance of critical feminist interpretation, biblical discourses could become Divine power and food for life again.

Such a complex interactive model of a critical interpretation for liberation challenges both the academy and the churches in order to transform them in the interest of all non-persons struggling in neocolonial situations for human dignity, justice, and well-being. It seeks to recast interpretation not in positivist but in rhetorical terms. It does not deny but recognizes that religious texts are rhetorical texts, produced in and by particular historical debates and struggles.

A critical feminist emancipatory interpretation insists on the hermeneutical priority of feminist struggles in order to be able not only to disentangle the ideological (religious-the*logical) practices and functions of biblical texts for inculcating and legitimating the kyriarchal order but also to identify their potential for fostering justice and liberation.

A critical interpretation for liberation that reads the Bible with a feminist lens in the context of wo/men struggling to change oppressive kyriarchal structures of religious, cultural, and societal texts and institutions, must be distinguished from both a Christian "apologetic" biblical interpretation by women and dualistic academic gender studies. Popular and academic biblical readings *by women*, reading the Bible *as a woman and from the perspective of woman*, as well as biblical interpretation in terms of *gender* are not simply identical with a *critical feminist interpretation for liberation*, insofar as these modes of reading do not question the religious and cultural gender lens of interpretation and their goal is not change and transformation.

In short, a critical feminist interpretation for liberation does not derive its lenses from the modern individualistic understanding of religion and the Bible. Rather it seeks to shift attention to the politics of biblical studies and its sociopolitical contexts of struggle. Hence, it places wo/men as subjects and agents, as full decision-making citizens at the center of attention. To that end it favors not only a deconstructive but also a reconstructive approach to interpretation. It struggles to elucidate the ways in which religious doctrines, symbols, practices, and biblical texts function in the creation and maintenance of ideas about sex/gender, race, colonialism, class, and religion. It also examines how such social constructions have influenced and shaped theoretical frameworks, the*logical formulations, biblical interpretations, and our own self-understanding.

Feminist Biblical Interpretation as a Site of Struggle

Feminist biblical interpretation is thus best understood as a site of struggle over meaning rather than as a means to provide definite interpretations of biblical texts. A major site of struggle is the struggle over *the authority* to interpret the Bible. Not only wo/men but also feminists often have internalized that they do not have either the ecclesial or the academic authority of interpretation. Readers of biblical texts early on learn to develop strategies of textual valorization and validation rather than hermeneutical skills to critically interrogate and assess scriptural interpretations and texts along with their visions, values, and prescriptions. If the literary canonization of texts in general places a work outside of any further need to establish its merits, the canonization of Sacred Scriptures in particular brings even more sympathy and uncritical acceptance. Canonization compels readers to offer increasingly more ingenious interpretations, not only in order to establish "the truth of the text itself" or "a single sense" correct meaning of the text. It also does so in order to sustain affirmation of and submission to the authority of the Bible either as sacred scripture or as a cultural classic.

Many students have expressed the anxiety that they have experienced in challenging and evaluating biblical texts in feminist terms. A widespread fear exists that critical scrutiny of one's religious tradition will automatically engender a form of cultural relativism that believes that all religions are equally good and thereby weakens allegiance to one's own religious community. Such anxiety is even greater when one critically approaches the Bible. This unease is articulated in the following group reflection from one of my classes: "This led to a discussion of how we feel a sense of great uneasiness at the thought of denying scriptural authority altogether for biblical texts that preach violence. For those of us from faith traditions, it was particularly difficult for us to go against what has been deeply ingrained in us. As a group we seemed to have many problems with identifying a text as kyriarchal. But we had even more problems to reenvision the text. This seems to be an ongoing struggle for our group and its members—giving ourselves the authority to go beyond critiquing and actually rewriting the text, especially in the sense of reimagining it without 'historical facts' to support our ideas."[13]

Hence, some feminist scholars have rejected a critical feminist approach to biblical texts that demystifies biblical texts and readings that advocate power over and violence. They argue one should not reject such texts out of respect for the "meaning making" of conservative wo/men who derive self-worth and solace from reading kyriocentric biblical texts. This attempt to claim the reading of conservative wo/men as a feminist reading overlooks one of the key insights of a liberation hermeneutics. The Brazilian educator Paolo Freire pointed out a long time ago that the oppressed have also internalized oppression and are divided in and among themselves. I quote him: "The oppressed, having internalized the image of the oppressor and adopted his guidelines, are fearful of freedom. Freedom would require them to eject this image and replace it with autonomy and responsibility. Freedom . . . must be pursued constantly and responsibly."[14]

Since both the oppressed and their oppressors are, according to Freire, "manifestations of dehumanization,"[15] the methodological starting point of a critical emancipatory hermeneutics cannot be simply the "common sense" experience and the interpretation done by wo/men. Rather such a starting point must be systemically analyzed and reflected experience. Since wo/men also have internalized worldviews of domination and are shaped by kyriarchal "common sense" mind-sets and values, the hermeneutical starting point of a critical feminist interpretation is not simply the experience of wo/men. Rather it is wo/men's experience of injustice that has been critically explored with a hermeneutics of suspicion in the process of "conscientization."

Insofar as biblical interpretations of conservative women do not start with a critical consciousness and a critical feminist analysis of kyriarchal sociopolitical and ecclesial-religious subordination and second class citizenship, they tend to construe respect and dignity for women in terms of their internalized cultural ideological frameworks of femininity and true womanhood or in terms of the dominant ideology of the "white Lady." Consequently such conservative readings cannot but keep the ideological structures of wo/men's self-alienation in place and internalize them further.

By continuing to insist that such readings are not feminist or liberationist and by disagreeing with their often antifeminist interpretations, one does not deny agency and respect to individual women. Rather, because of respect for them, one needs to insist on a reading strategy that interrupts rather than reinforces their religious self-alienation. Focus on the theory and practice of wo/men's struggles for transforming kyriarchal relations of domination and subordination remains a normative principle for a critical feminist hermeneutics of liberation.

However, I agree with one point of this argument for conservative wo/men's reading very strongly. I have argued for quite some time that biblical interpretation must shift its attention from the kyriocentric text to the ways wo/men read authoritative texts. Hence, we need to develop strategies of reading that allow wo/men to become conscious of the ways our readings and self-understandings are determined and shaped by kyriarchal institiutions and interests. As long as Scripture is used not only against women struggling for emancipation and in support of kyriarchy[16] but also for shaping women's self-understandings and lives, we need to encourage wo/men to engage kyriocentric biblical and other texts critically, to reclaim our spiritual authority for adjudicating what we read, and to value the process of biblical readings as a process of conscientization.

Closely connected with the struggle for wo/men's authority of interpretation is *the struggle over scriptural authority*. At least since the last century feminists have intensified the crisis of biblical authority brought about by scientific biblical criticism insofar as they have pointed out that the Bible has not only been written by human hand but by elite men. It is not only the product of kyriarchal past cultures but also has been used to instill the dehumanizing violence of such cultures as "word of G*d." Particularly Protestant the*logical interpretation, with its emphasis on *sola scriptura*, faces this problem of how to articulate the authority of Scripture. As Mary Ann Tolbert has pointed out: "For Protestants, the central and unavoidable problematic posed by the role of scripture is its *authority*, but exactly what that authority entails varies from denomination to denomination and indeed is often a hotly contested issue within denominations. . . . Scripture, then, for Protestants becomes the primary medium of communication with G*d."[17]

If for Protestants the Bible is "not primarily a source of knowledge about" G*d[18] but "rather a source for *experiencing*, hearing, G*d or G*d-in-Jesus in each present moment in life,"[19] then the question of criteria for judging the truth claims of such experiences becomes especially pressing. Yet this question is not just a problem for Protestantism.

Although traditional Roman Catholic the*logy has insisted that the teaching authority of the hierarchy defines biblical norms and criteria, such an assertion does not provide a way out of the problem because the teaching authority of the hierarchy remains bound to the norms of Scripture. Hence, both Protestant and Catholic the*logical hermeneutics had to develop a different approach to the hermeneutical problem raised by the insight into the historicity and linguisticality of Scripture.[20] Approaches to the question of biblical authority vary not only in terms of confessional dogmatism but also in terms of sociopolitical interests.

A CRITICAL FEMINIST HERMENEUTICS

Different hermeneutical approaches have been developed by Christian feminist the*logians to address this problem. If one takes Jewish and Muslim feminist hermeneutics into account, the whole debate becomes even more complex and variegated. Like feminist studies in general, so also feminist biblical hermeneutics does not have a homogeneous perspective but advocates a variety of sometimes conflicting approaches.

The *hermeneutics of loyalty* argues that only biblical interpretations—not biblical texts—promote wo/men's discrimination.

The *hermeneutics of scientific interpretation* claims to be able to say with certainty which biblical texts are true and which are not if the proper methods are used.

The *hermeneutics of rejection* argues that the Bible is completely and thoroughly sexist and patriarchal. Hence feminists must reject it as totally oppressive.

The *hermeneutics of desire* in turn reinvents the Bible rather than abandoning it. It uses it as a language to express its own visions of well-being and happiness.

The *hermeneutics of revision* understands the patriarchal word of the Bible as a wrapping or covering that contains the word of G*d as a non-patriarchal kernel, core, or essence. Feminist biblical interpretation has thus the task of separating the core from the human patriarchal wrappings.

The *cultural hermeneutic approach* in turn reads the Bible not as religious text but as a cultural classic that has greatly shaped and influenced Western cultures.

The *hermeneutics of the Divine Feminine* searches the Bible for traces of matriarchal religions and G*ddess traditions.

The *hermeneutics of liberation* seeks to assess the oppressive or liberating functions of biblical texts in the lives and struggles of wo/men.

A *critical emancipatory hermeneutics* finally calls for transformative and engaged biblical readers who may or may not be professional interpreters or Christian believers.

CHANGING HORIZONS

This collection of essays seeks to trace in a prismatic way the development of a critical emancipatory hermeneutics. The notion of hermeneutics derives from the Greek word *hermeneuein* and means "to interpret, exegete, explain, or translate." It owes its name to Hermes, the messenger of the g*ds, who has the task to mediate the announcements, declarations, and messages of the Gods to mere mortals. His proclamation, however, is not a mere communication and mediation but always also an explication of divine commands in such a way that he translates them into human language so that they can be comprehended and obeyed.

According to Gadamer, hermeneutics—like Hermes—has the task of translating meaning from one "world" into another.[21] Like Hermes, the messenger of the Gods, hermeneutics not only communicates knowledge but also instructs, directs, and enjoins. Hermeneutics thus has affinities to manticism and prophecy. It conveys revelation and interprets signs and oracles. It is a matter of practical understanding, which involves the Aristotelian virtue of *phronesis*—practical judgment and adjudication—which is not secured by an a priori method but only in the process of understanding.

Since a critical feminist interpretation is primarily interested in the emancipatory interests of knowledge production, I have argued in *Transforming Vision*[22] that "hermeneutics," as it is traditionally understood, seems to be a misnomer for the method used to pursue such emancipatory interests. Relying on a critical theory of language and the insights of liberation movements, I have sought to develop a feminist hermeneutics as a critical feminist *metic* of liberation and transformation. Such a critical hermeneutical theory attempts to articulate interpretation both as a complex process of reading and reconstruction and as a cultural-religious praxis of resistance and transformation. It moves from the traditional understanding of "hermeneutic" to a form of interpretation that can best be described as *metic*.

It is not the myth of Hermes but the myth of Metis and Athena that articulates the task of a critical feminist hermeneutic and rhetoric. Athena, the patron Goddess of the classic Athenian city-state, was not only the patron of the arts and technological and scientific knowledge, but also was a war Goddess. According to Hesiod, she came fully grown and armored from the head of her father Zeus. However, she only appears to be motherless. Her real mother is the Goddess Metis, the "most wise woman among Gods and humans."[23]

According to the myth, Zeus, the father of the Gods, was in competition with Metis. He duped her when she was pregnant with Athena because he feared that Metis would bear a child who would surpass him in wisdom and power. Hence he changed Metis into a fly. But this was not enough! Zeus swallowed the fly Metis wholesale in order to have her always with him and to benefit from her wise counsel. This mythical story of Metis and Zeus reveals not only the father of the Gods' fear that the child of Wisdom would surpass him in knowledge, but it also lays open the conditions under which wo/men in kyriarchal cultures and religions are able to exercise wisdom and to produce knowledge.

Read with a hermeneutics of suspicion, the myth of Metis and Athena shows that kyriarchal systems of knowledge and power objectify wo/men and swallow them up in order to co-opt their wisdom and knowledge for their own interests of domination. Wo/men's or gender studies remains, therefore, an ambiguous notion since it has wo/men or gender, rather than structures of domination, as objects of its research. Critical emancipatory feminist studies, in contrast, seek to empower wo/men by encouraging them to recognize and change such knowledge and structures of marginalization and oppression.

Since for the hermeneutic theory of Gadamer as well as for a critical feminist emancipatory hermeneutics, the notion of "horizon" is central, this collection of essays on a critical feminist interpretation is titled "*Changing Horizons.*" To quote Gadamer:

> Every finite present has its limitations. We define the concept of "situation" by saying that it represents a standpoint that limits the possibility of vision. Hence an essential part of the concept of situation is the concept of "*horizon.*" The horizon is the range of vision that includes everything that can be seen from a particular vantage point . . . A person who has no horizon is a man who does not see far enough and hence overvalues what is nearest to him. On the other hand, "to have an horizon" means not being limited to what is nearby, but being able to see beyond it. . . . [W]orking out of the hermeneutical situation means the achievement of the right horizon of inquiry for the questions evoked by the encounter with tradition.[24]

The well-known "hermeneutical circle" means that understanding can only take place if we situate a phenomenon in a larger context, that is, the parts of some larger reality can only be grasped in terms of the whole. In this "to and fro" of the hermeneutical circle or spiral, we can fuse or broaden our horizon with that which we seek to understand. However, whereas Gadamer understands the hermeneutical event as a fusion of horizons (*Horizontver-schmelzung*), a critical emancipatory hermeneutic seeks to deconstruct the kyriarchal horizon of biblical texts and our own in order to change both horizons, since the dominant cultural and religious horizon of the past and the present has been exclusive of wo/men as subjects of knowledge and understanding. Gadamer is correct that people, both wo/men and men, are embedded in the history and culture that has shaped them. Feminists agree but point out that cultural and religious history has been distorted insofar as wo/men were excluded from the articulation and the production of knowledge in society and religion. Hence, a critical feminist hermeneutics intends to change this kyriarchal horizon and our own that is defined by it.

CONCEPTUALIZING "CHANGING HORIZONS"

Since the term *hermeneutics* covers both the *theory* and the *art* of interpretation,[25] I have divided the book into a first part that addresses theory and a second part that attempts to display my practices of the art of interpretation. Central to both sections is not only the question "what will the text do to us if we submit to its world of vision?" but also how to refuse "submission" if the sacred text's world of vision is not suffused by the desire for justice and well-being for all without exception?

The first part of the book seeks to trace the theoretical development of such a critical feminist emancipatory hermeneutics chronologically through my contributions to it, whereas the second part explores the practices of interpreting early Christian canonical texts that are displayed in my essays. While I have tried to edit out repetitions, it is impossible to avoid overlaps of both parts in such a collection of essays, as well as overlaps in the arguments of different chapters. Positively understood, such overlaps and repetitions, I hope, will help the reader to see the multifaceted prism of a critical feminist hermeneutics for liberation and well-being.

The chapters in the first part of the book advance chronologically to indicate the development of a critical feminist interpretation of liberation. However, the first part moves not only chronologically but also topologically. It seeks to document the theoretical struggles for articulating my theoretical approach. To enable readers to follow these struggles, I did not change the use of terms such as "patriarchy," "God," "theology," or "women" in the earlier chapters of this part to my present way of indicating hermeneutical problems through my lettering. However, a chronological-topological review also shows that a critical feminist interpretation and the*logy was from its very beginnings not only concerned with gender—as is often alleged—but also with the multiplicative structures of domination, sex, gender, race, class, or imperialism.

While I used the term "patriarchy" until the late 1980s to name the pyramid of dominations, I did not understand *patriarchy* in dualistic terms as domination of men over wo/men but rather in intersectional terms, although the term *intersectionality* was introduced only in the 1990s.[26] As far as I recall, I presented this pyramidal understanding of *patriarchy* for the first time at a conference on *Women and Religion in Hawaii* in 1978. However, many hearers and readers continued to understand *patriarchy* in dualistic terms. Hence, in order to make my pyramidal understanding of *patriarchy* clearer, I coined the term *kyriarchy*, which seeks to name the multiplicative interstructuring and intersectionality of dominations, and began to use it in the late 1980s.

Black American feminists, as well as Two-Thirds World feminists, have problematized the interpretation of wo/men's oppression solely in terms of gender or racial dualism. On the one hand, they have pointed out that wo/men are oppressed not only by heterosexism, but also by racism, classism, and colonialism. On the other hand, they have rejected an essentializing definition of gender and patriarchy that holds that all men are oppressors and all wo/men are their victims. The same critique of dualistic essentializing constructions applies to race, class, and postcolonial theories.

Instead, critical intersectional theorists have argued consistently that wo/men of subordinated races, nations, and classes are often more oppressed by elite white wo/men than by the men of their own class, race, culture, or religion. As a result of this contradiction in wo/men's lives, the interconnection between the exclusion of wo/men and all other "subordinates" from citizenship has not been given sufficient attention. The same is true for its ideological justifications in the form of reified "natural" sexual/racial/class/cultural differences.

Consequently, intersectional theorists usually conceptualize such social and ideological structures of domination as *hierarchical*, in order to map and make visible the complex interstructuring of the conflicting status positions of different wo/men. However, I believe that the label *hierarchy* for such a pyramidal system is also a misnomer, since the term only targets one specific, religiously sanctioned form of domination. Hence, it is necessary to replace the categories of *patriarchy* or *hierarchy* with the neologism *kyriarchy* to characterize the sociopolitical structures of domination that determine wo/men's second- or third-class citizenship.

The second part of the book seeks to display the art and practice of a critical feminist hermeneutics by seeking to make conscious *kyriarchal* structures of domination inscribed in Scripture in the process of interpretation. To interpret early Christian text with a critical feminist lens means to make conscious such kyriarchal inscriptions and to point to alternative visions and possibilities also inscribed in Scriptures. Hence, I analyze particular Christian (New) Testament texts that shape not only wo/men's religious but also our cultural self-understandings. I also seek to show how the practices of a critical feminist hermeneutics are embedded and shaped by their contexts and the questions raised in different sociopolitical-religious locations. Most of these chapters have their origins in lectures and conferences. By exploring how my arguments work in different socioreligious locations, I seek to document how a critical feminist hermeneutics is articulated in interaction with general and scholarly audiences from different parts of the globe. While a critical gender approach[27] is primarily situated in the academy, a critical feminist hermeneutics of liberation has its roots in and seeks to contribute to the struggles of wo/men for the*logical and intellectual authority and self-determination by using the tools of the academy to foster conscientization and a change of horizons.

NOTES

[1] Part of this material has appeared in "Claiming the Authority of Biblical Interpretation," *Revista Alternativas* 15 (2008): 15–32.

[2] Carol Christ has argued that *theology* should be replaced with *thealogy* in feminist discourses because theology proclaims the masculine whereas thealogy expresses the feminine notion of G*d. To avoid such a gendered definition of the divine, I am writing G*d and the*logy with an * so that readers have to think twice and have to decide how to understand G*d.

[3] I am in the process of editing a collection of essays called *Feminist Biblical Studies in the Twentieth Century*, which will appear in the series The Bible and Women: An Encyclopaedia of Exegesis and Cultural History, published in four languages. This collection indicates how much work needs to be done on the history of feminist biblical studies.

[4] Topological is derived from the Greek word *topos*, meaning "place," from *tópos koinós*, common place; *pl. topoi*; in Latin, *locus* (from *locus communis*). The technical term *topos* is variously translated as "topic," "line of argument," or "commonplace." I understand it here in terms of "line of argument."

[5] In order to lift into consciousness the linguistic violence of so-called generic male-centered language, I write the term wo/men with a slash in order to use the term "wo/men" and not "men" in an inclusive way. I suggest that whenever you read "wo/men," you need to understand it in the generic sense. Wo/man includes man, she includes he, and female includes male. Feminist studies of language have elaborated that Western, kyriocentric—that is, master-, lord-, father-, male-centered language systems—understand language as both generic and as gender specific. Wo/men always must think at least twice, if not three times, and adjudicate whether we are meant or not by so-called generic terms such as "men, humans, Americans, or professors." To use "wo/men" as an inclusive generic term invites male readers to learn how to think twice and to experience what it means not to be addressed explicitly. Since wo/men always must arbitrate whether we are meant or not, I consider it a good spiritual exercise for men to acquire the same sophistication and to learn how to engage in the same hermeneutical process of thinking twice and of asking whether they are meant when I speak of wo/men. Since, according to Wittgenstein, the limits of our language are the limits of our world, such a change of language patterns is a very important step toward the realization of a new feminist consciousness.

[6] See, however, the excellent review article by Hal Taussig, "The End of Christian Origins? Where to Turn at the Intersection of Subjectivity and Historical Craft?" *Review of Biblical Literature* 13 (2011): 1–46.

[7] See my book *Democratizing Biblical Studies: Toward an Emancipatory Educational Space* (Louisville: Westminster John Knox, 2009).

[8] For the first development of this concept, see my book *But She Said: Feminist Practices of Biblical Interpretation* (Boston: Beacon, 1993), 103–32.

[9] Patricia Hill Collins, *Black Feminist Thought: Knowledge, Consciousness, and the Politics of Empowerment* (Boston: Unwin Hyman, 1990).

[10] See Deborah K. King, "Multiple Jeopardy, Multiple Consciousness: The Context of Black Feminist Ideology," *Signs* 14 (1988): 42–72.

[11] See my introduction to Laura Nasrallah and Elisabeth Schüssler Fiorenza, eds., *Prejudice and Christian Beginnings: Investigating Race, Gender, and Ethnicity in Early Christian Studies* (Minneapolis: Fortress Press, 2009).

[12] Karen Baker-Fletcher, *Sisters of Dust, Sisters of Spirit: Womanist Wordings on God and Creation* (Minneapolis: Fortress Press, 1998), 27.

[13] Group Reflection, Womanist Theology Group (Fall Semester, 1999).

[14] Paolo Freire, *Pedagogy of the Oppressed* (New York: Seabury, 1973), 31.

[15]Freire, 33.

[16]Elizabeth Cady Stanton, ed., *The Woman's Bible*. 2 vols. (1884/1888), Seattle: Coalition Task Force on Women and Religion (1984).

[17]Mary Ann Tolbert, "Protestant Feminists and the Bible," in Alice Bach, ed., *The Pleasure of Her Text: Feminist Readings of Biblical and Historical Texts* (Philadelphia: Trinity, 1990), 11.

[18]To the consternation of previous copyeditors, I have again changed my writing of G-d, which I advocated in *But She Said* and *Discipleship of Equals*, since such a spelling recalls for many Jewish feminists a fundamentalist orthodox mind-set. My new way of spelling G*d seeks to indicate that G*d is "in a religious sense unnamable" and belongs to the "realm of the ineffable." God is not G*d's "proper name." See Rebecca S. Chopp, *The Power to Speak: Feminism, Language, God* (New York: Crossroad, 1989), 32.

[19]Tolbert, 12.

[20]For a discussion of diverse hermeneutical discourses and a critique of the method of correlation, see Francis Schüssler Fiorenza, "The Crisis of Hermeneutics and Christian Theology," in *Theology at the End of Modernity*, ed. Sheila Greeve Davaney (Philadelphia: Trinity, 1991), 128–30; see also his earlier article "The Crisis of Scriptural Authority: Interpretation and Reception," *Interpretation* 44, no. 4 (1990): 353–68.

[21]See Richard Bernstein, "What Is the Difference That Makes a Difference? Gadamer, Habermas, and Rorty," in *Hermeneutics and Modern Philosophy*, ed. Brice R. Wachterhauser (Albany: SUNY Press, 1986), 343–76.

[22]Elisabeth Schüssler Fiorenza, *Transforming Vision: Explorations in Feminist The*logy* (Minneapolis: Fortress Press, 2011), 55–78.

[23]See my article, "Der 'Athenakomplex' in der the*logischen Frauenforschung," in *Für Gerechtigkeit streiten: Theologie im Alltag einer bedrohten Welt*, ed. Dorothee Sölle (Gütersloh: Kaiser, 1994), 103–11.

[24]Hans-Georg Gadamer, *Truth and Method* (New York: Continuum, 1997), 302.

[25]Bjorn Ramberg and Kristin Gjerdal, "Hermeneutics," in *Stanford Encyclopedia of Philosophy*.

[26]See Kimberlé W. Crenshaw, "Mapping the Margins: Intersectionality, Identity Politics, and Violence against Women of Color," in Martha Albertson Fineman and Roxanne Mykitiuk, eds., *The Public Nature of Private Violence* (New York: Routledge, 1991), 93–118; see Nina Lykke, *Feminist Studies: A Guide to Intersectional Theory, Methodology, and Writing* (New York: Routledge, 2010), and Helma Lutz, Maria Teresa Herrera Vivar, and Linda Supik, eds., *Fokus Intersektionalität: Bewegungen und Verortungen eines vielschichtigen Konzeptes* (Wiesbaden: Verlag für Sozialwissenschaften, 2010) for an overview of the discussion.

[27]See Todd Penner and Caroline Vander Stichele, eds., *Mapping Gender in Ancient Religious Discourses* (Atlanta: SBL, 2007).

PART I

Charting Critical Feminist Biblical Hermeneutics

1

Interpreting Patriarchal Traditions

The Hebrew and Christian Scriptures originated in a patriarchal society and perpetuated the androcentric (male-centered) traditions of their culture. Today, feminist analyses have uncovered the detrimental effects of these traditions on women's self-understanding and role in society and in the churches. Christians, both women and men, consequently face a grave dilemma. On the one hand they seek to remain faithful to the life-giving truth of the biblical revelation and on the other hand they seek to free themselves from all patriarchal traditions and sexist concepts that hinder their human and Christian liberation. The interpretation and understanding of the androcentric traditions of the Bible are therefore major theological tasks for all Christians today. This task cannot be accomplished by putting down the feminist critique as "unscholarly," "somewhat uninformed," or "excessive," but only by taking seriously the fact that the Hebrew and Christian Scriptures share in the concepts and ideologies of their patriarchal culture and age.

In order to accomplish this task we have to take into account the methods of historical-critical scholarship, the results of the discussion of methods of interpretation, and the insights of feminist analysis.[1] Historical-critical scholarship has taught us that it is necessary to understand the historical setting, the cultural environment, the literary forms, and the specific language of a text if we interpret and teach or preach the Bible. Discussion of interpretation has underlined that a value-free, objectivistic historiography is a scholarly fiction. All interpretation of texts depends upon the presuppositions, intellectual interests, politics, or prejudices of the interpreter, historian, or theologian. Scholars are always committed, whether they realize it or not. Feminist analyses have, therefore, pointed out that the biblical texts were not only recorded from an androcentric point of view but were also consciously or unconsciously interpreted by exegetes and preachers from a perspective of cultural male dominance. Several biblical texts that were throughout the centuries quoted to support women's inferiority and submission do not have in their original intent and context a misogynist slant. The study of androcentric traditions in the Bible has thus to observe not only the original intention of the texts but also their androcentric history of interpretation. Biblical history, just like history on the whole, has become "his story"[2] recorded and interpreted from an androcentric point of view.

This chapter discusses a sampling of patriarchal texts and androcentric interpretations of the Bible in order to demonstrate how a reading of the Bible from a feminist perspective could contribute to a better and deeper understanding of the biblical message. Insofar as this discussion singles out for interpretation androcentric and patriarchal scriptural texts, it might appear at first glance one-sided and overly critical. Insofar as it uncovers sexist presuppositions and biases of modern exegetes and preachers, it will provoke emotional reaction and controversy. Yet such a study might also recover in some seemingly androcentric texts a tacit criticism and transcendence of patriarchal and androcentric values. Moreover, a feminist interpretation can show that some texts, even though recorded from an androcentric perspective, refer to a historical situation in which women had more authority and influence than is usually attributed to them.

ANDROCENTRIC TRADITIONS OF THE OLD TESTAMENT

Although some texts of the Old Testament[3] might reflect a matriarchal or matrilineal society, the patriarchal character of Hebrew culture is undisputed. Spanning nearly a millennium and embracing a variety of religio-cultural contexts, the Hebrew Scriptures clearly espouse male priority and superiority in the national as well as in the religious community.[4] *Patriarchal Texts:* Israel as a nation and as a religious community was constituted by male-dominated families, and full membership in it was reserved to the adult male. It is true that Israel had this patriarchal fabric in common with all the surrounding Near Eastern cultures and religions. Yet the legal and social position of women was often lower in Israel than in the neighboring countries.[5] In Hebrew patriarchal society, women were totally dependent on their fathers and husbands. Numbers 30:2-12, for example, demonstrates the complete dependency and subordination of a daughter or a wife, not only in familial-cultural affairs but also in religious matters. The vows of a daughter or a wife were not considered valid if the father or the husband vetoed them.

> But when her husband makes them null and void on the day that he hears them, then whatever proceeds out of her lips concerning her vows, or concerning her pledge of herself, shall not stand: her husband has made them void, and the Lord will forgive her. (Num. 30:12)

The main values of patriarchal society were the perpetuation of the family and the clan, as well as the protection of property. Since sons prolonged the family line and preserved the family's fortunes, they were highly desired.

Daughters were less valued, because they would leave the family when they married. A daughter was the property of her father and could even be sold as a slave if the purchaser intended to make her his own or his son's concubine (Lev. 21:7-11). In early Hebrew society the future husband had to pay a bride-price as a compensation to the bride's family. Well known in this regard is the story of Leah and Rachel (Gen. 29:16-30), who complained that their father, after having sold them, had used the money paid for them (Gen. 31:15). Less known but even more drastic is the story of David, Saul, and Michal (1 Sam. 18:20-27).

That a daughter was at the disposal of her father is apparent in the story of Lot and his daughters. In Gen. 19:1-11[6] two strangers accept the invitation of Lot to stay in his home. When the men of the town want to abuse them sexually, Lot offers his own daughters instead: "Behold, I have two daughters who have not known man; let me bring them out to you, and do to them as you please; only do nothing to these men, for they have come under the shelter of my roof" (Gen. 19:8). Although the daughters are not ravished, the sacredness of hospitality is clearly the greater value in the story. The incident cannot be explained as an example of "bargaining by the unacceptable alternative," in which the offer is so shocking that no one would dream of accepting it. This becomes apparent when we consider the very similar tale in Judg. 19:22-30. As in Gen. 19:1-11, a father offers his virgin daughter and his guest's concubine to the men of the town for sexual abuse in order to protect the male guest of his house. When the men did not listen to him, the guest "seized his concubine, and put her out to them; and they knew her, and abused her all night until the morning" (Judg. 19:25). Because the woman dies from their violence, Israel rallies to warfare against the offending town of the Benjaminites, "for they have committed abomination and wantonness in Israel" (Judg. 20:6). However, there is uttered no word of criticism of the husband who saved his own life by offering his concubine for rape and abuse.

The extent to which women were in the power of men is also demonstrated in the conclusion of this narrative cycle. After the Israelites have defeated the Benjaminites, they feel compassion for them. "One tribe is cut off from Israel this day. What shall we do for wives of those who are left, since we have sworn by the Lord that we will not give them any of our daughters as wives?" (Judg. 21:6-7).

When the congregation finds out that no one from Jabesh-Gilead had taken this oath, they decide to kill all inhabitants of the city except for four hundred virgins whom they gave as wives to the surviving Benjaminites (Judg. 21:12). Since there were still some men without wives, the elders of the congregation decide to obtain more women through "highway" robbery. When, at the occasion of the yearly festival, the daughters of Shiloh came out to dance in the vineyards, the Benjaminites abducted them, and the elders of Israel were prepared to defend this action against the complaining fathers or brothers of the women (Judg. 21:20-23). The virgin daughters are clearly the possession of their fathers. The women themselves have nothing to say throughout all these events. Just as at the beginning of the narrative cycle hospitality was more highly valued than the lives of women, so at the end the survival of the tribe of Benjamin justifies the brutal violence against them.[7]

In a patriarchal family structure the daughter is dependent upon her father or brother and the wife becomes totally reliant on her husband. Thus, the woman remains all her life a minor. The Decalogue includes a man's wife among his possessions, along with his house and land, his male and female slaves, his ox and his ass (Exod. 20:17; Deut. 5:21). The root meaning of the Hebrew verb "to marry a wife" is "to become master" (ba'al, see Deut. 21:13; 24:4). The wife, therefore, calls her husband master (ba'al, see Exod. 21:4, 22; II Sam. 11:26) and lord ('adōn, Gen. 18:12; Judg. 19:26; Amos 4:1). Even after the wife is widowed, her father-in-law retains authority over her (Gen. 38:24).

The wife's primary task in life is to bear children, and her greatest honor is motherhood. Barrenness was, therefore, seen as misfortune and divine punishment (Gen. 11:30; 30:1; Exod. 23:26; 1 Sam. 1:6; Hos. 9:14).[8] In Hebrew society, polygyny was legally recognized, the husband could take a concubine, and divorce was a male prerogative (Deut. 24:1-4). Whereas woman's sexual misconduct was severely punished, infidelity on the part of the man was penalized only if he violated the rights of another man. Since sexual intercourse with a betrothed virgin or a married woman offended the property rights of the patriarch, it was severely punished and provoked even Yahweh's intervention. A good example is the story of Abraham and Sarah, which we find with variations three times in Genesis: Gen. 12:10 to 13:1; 20:1-18; 26:6-11 (Isaac and Rebekah).

According to the Yahwist's (J) account (Gen. 12:10 to 13:1), in order to save his own life Abraham persuades his beautiful wife Sarah to pass as his sister in Egypt. She is taken into the harem of Pharaoh, but Yahweh intervenes on her behalf. Pharaoh reproaches Abraham for not telling him the truth and extradicts him and his company. The Yahwist's account tells the marvelous preservation of the future mother of the heir of promise. Abraham is at fault.

Even though location and names are different, the Elohist's (E) story (Gen. 20:1-18) materially corresponds in detail to the Yahwistic account. Yet the story clearly now has a different theological tendency. The author takes pains to justify, theologically, Abraham's selfish action. This androcentric shift becomes clear from the following points: First, Yahweh has to castigate Abimelech because Sarah is another man's wife (v. 3). Abraham's property rights are violated. Second, the story stresses that Sarah herself says that she is the sister of Abraham (v. 5). Third, it is emphasized that Abimelech does not touch Sarah (v. 6c). Fourth, Abraham justifies himself, giving as his motive theological reasons ("There is no fear of God at all in this place," v. 11b). Fifth, Sarah is indeed Abraham's sister because they have the same father, but a different mother (vv. 12, 16). Finally, Abimelech takes care to honor Abraham, to restore Sarah to him, and to vindicate her publicly. Abraham in turn prays for Abimelech and his house, and the wrath of Yahweh is taken from them. The Elohist's story thus glorifies Abraham and exonerates King Abimelech. Sarah comes into view solely as Abraham's compliant wife who remained untouched by another man because of Yahweh's intervention on behalf of her husband's rights. The story clearly exhibits patriarchal values and pictures its characters from an androcentric point of view.

In prophetic times, the patriarchal marriage relationship becomes theologized insofar as it becomes a model for the covenant relationship between Yahweh and Israel. This theological model not only divinely authorizes the superiority of the husband but also theologically sanctions the inferior role of women in the patriarchal marriage relationship. Further, the image of the marriage between Yahweh and Israel eliminates female imagery and symbolism from the divine realm insofar as Yahweh has no divine female consort but only a human bride to love and to serve him.[9] The oracle of salvation in Hos. 2:19 does not project divine equality between Yahweh and Israel for the future, but solely announces that "Israel will not just respect Yahweh somewhat reluctantly, since he is its legal lord, but it knows itself to be placed into a completely new, loving relationship with him."[10]

The prophets, moreover, often use the image of Israel or Jerusalem as a woman or wife in a negative way in order to censure Israel for its apostasy to the cults and mythologies of Canaan. Through the marriage metaphor, Israel's apostasy and idolatry become identified with the adultery, fornication, and whoredom of women. This theological language and imagery associates women not only with sexual misconduct but also with unfaithfulness and idolatry.

> Plead with your mother, plead— for she is not my wife, and I am not her husband— that she put away her harlotry from her face, and her adultery from between her breasts; lest I strip her naked and make her as in the day she was born. (Hos. 2:2-3)

The theological image of Yahweh as the loving husband and Israel as the unfaithful wife has in the history of theology perpetuated the subordinate role of women and associated them with whoredom and adultery as well as with apostasy and idolatry.

ANDROCENTRIC INTERPRETATION

The Yahwistic creation story—Genesis 2 and 3—is an example used throughout Christian history by theologians and preachers both to teach that woman is according to God's intention derivative from man and to characterize her as the temptress of man and the one through whom sin came into the world.[11] More recent feminist studies, however, have convincingly shown that, far from being "sexist," the Genesis story maintains the coequality of woman and man, although Gen. 2:18 clearly indicates that the story is told from the male point of view since *'ādām* (Genesis 2) not only is a generic term but also communicates that the first individual human being was male.[12]

The narrative follows an ancient pattern of creation myths in which the gods at first attempt a trial creation before they accomplish the perfect creation.[13] The creation of the animals follows this trial-creation pattern insofar as the animals are not coequal beings with *'ādām*. Only the woman who is taken from *'ādām* is coequal with him and the perfect creation. The linguistic consonance of the terms "man" (*'īsh*) and "woman" (*'ishsha*) underlines this co-equality. The statement of the narrator in Gen. 2:24 summarizes the intention of the creation story (Gen. 2:4b-24). It explains that man leaves his parents in order to become one flesh with a woman. This summarizing statement of the Yahwist interestingly enough does not presuppose the patriarchal family model, according to which the woman leaves her family to become part of the male clan, but states exactly the opposite.

As Genesis 2:4b-24 attempts to explain the coequality and unity of man and woman in marriage, so Genesis 3 attempts to come to terms with Israel's experience of the oppressive human reality in which man and woman find themselves. Along with ch. 2, the narrative in ch. 3 forms a unit that is not prescriptive but is a story that tries to make sense out of man's and woman's present existence. It explains why woman lives now under patriarchy and suffers from childbearing, and why man has to toil and wrestle his livelihood from the earth from which he is taken. Whereas before the Fall the husband left his family to become one flesh with his wife, now the woman is tied into a relationship of domination by her desire for her husband. In consequence of this desire, her childbearing increases and, moreover, causes her great pain and suffering. The penalties in 3:14-19 reflect the culturally conditioned situation of man and woman in a nomadic and agricultural society. Man's domination of woman is a consequence of sin and transgression. Yahweh did not intend this patriarchal domination of woman, but had created her as coequal to man.

The Priestly writer (P) grasped this point of the Yahwistic creation account when he summarized God's intention in the creation of humans:

> God created humankind (*'ādām*) in his own image . . . ; male (*zākār*) and female (*neqēbā*) he created them. (Gen. 1:27)

Far from being the androcentric or sexist story as it is often misunderstood, the Yahwistic creation account implies a criticism of the patriarchal relation-ship between man and woman. The domination of the wife by the husband is interpreted as a consequence of sin.

ANDROCENTRIC TRADITIONING

If we wish to understand biblical texts, we have not only to ask whether a tradition of androcentric interpretation has veiled their original intention but also to question whether the original narrator or author in an androcentric way has told history that was not androcentric at all. A good example of such a male-centered tradition process is, in my opinion, provided by the scattered references to the prophet Miriam. Exegetes generally agree that Miriam originally was an independent leader in Israel and was made a sister of Aaron and Moses only in the later traditions of the Old Testament (see Num. 26:59 [P]). According to Exod. 15:20 (J), Miriam was a prophet who proclaimed the triumph of Yahweh over the Egyptian Pharaoh. Her song is the oldest extant praise of Yahweh in the Old Testament. The prophetic tradition knows Miriam as a leader of Israel during the exodus, coequal with Moses and Aaron (Micah 6:4). Numbers 20:1 mentions Kadesh as her burial place.

Numbers 12 (JE) represents one of the oldest and most interesting traditions related to Miriam. The text does not yet know that Miriam, Aaron, and Moses are siblings. The story begins with the rebellion of Miriam and Aaron against the superiority and authority of Moses. They not only reproach Moses for having married a non-Israelite wife, but they also maintain that Yahweh has not revealed things solely through Moses: "Has the Lord indeed spoken only through Moses? Has he not spoken through us also?" With these words, Miriam and Aaron claim to be equal with Moses as recipients and mediators of divine revelation. The rest of the story is told in order to reject this claim of Miriam and Aaron.

The narrative not only betrays a bias for Moses but also repudiates Miriam much more severely than Aaron. Whereas the text mentions Miriam first, as leader of the rebellion, the answer of Yahweh addresses first Aaron and then Miriam (v. 5). Yahweh stresses that Moses is the authentic revelation bearer to whom God speaks "mouth to mouth, clearly, and not in dark speech" (v. 8). Although the speech of Yahweh is described as first addressing Aaron and Miriam, the Lord punishes Miriam but not Aaron.

The punishment of the rebellious woman is the main theme of this androcentric text. The narrative stresses her dependence on the goodwill of Aaron and Moses. When she is afflicted with leprosy (see also Deut. 24:9), Aaron begs Moses to intercede and Moses prays for her to God. Yet Yahweh behaves like a stern patriarch. Miriam is punished in the same way as if she were a girl whose "father had but spit in her face." Therefore, she is "shamed seven days" (v. 14). The story clearly establishes Moses' superiority and accords Miriam the same relationship to Yahweh as a girl had in a patriarchal family. The narrative, however, presupposes the knowledge that Miriam competed with Moses for the prophetic leadership of Israel and argues against such an aspiration by a woman.

In dealing with this story of an "uppity woman," modern male comment-ators are helpless. They speculate about jealousy between siblings[14] or the displeasure of the "prima donna" of the women's choir[15] over God's preference for Moses. Even such a scholar as Martin Noth[16] attempts to explain away Miriam's exceptional role by asserting that as the only female figure around Moses she led the case against the Cushite women, but in claiming equal prophetic status with Moses she was only following Aaron. According to Noth, the point of the story is the mild punishment of Miriam, who actually should have been afflicted with permanent leprosy for revolting against the great servant of Yahweh.

Just like the first recorder, so modern commentators on the story cannot conceive of Miriam as an independent leader in Israel, but only as the jealous and rebellious sister of Moses with whom Yahweh deals as a patriarchal father would handle his uppity daughter. The story of Miriam's rebellion in its present form functions to repudiate Miriam's leadership claim and to extol Moses' superiority. A careful reading of the story, however, detects elements of a tradition that knew that Miriam was a leading figure in Israel's past.

With these few examples I have attempted to show that a feminist reading of various Old Testament texts uncovers their patriarchal and androcentric character. Yet such an interpretation can also liberate biblical texts from an androcentric bias and misunderstanding by demonstrating that certain narratives, which are often misunderstood by an androcentric interpretation, indirectly protest against their patriarchal cultural values (see Genesis 2 and 3), or that they reflect a stage in the tradition that was relatively free from such a bias (see Genesis 12). Such a feminist reading might furthermore be able to recover traces of the lost "her-story" of great women in the Old Testament.

ANDROCENTRIC TRADITIONS IN THE NEW TESTAMENT

It is quite remarkable that the canonical literature of the New Testament does not transmit a single sexist story of Jesus,[17] although he lived and preached in a patriarchal culture and society.[18] Studies of the sociocultural conditions of the early Christian movement have shown that it was a socially and religiously deviant group similar to other sectarian Jewish groups of the first century. In distinction to the sect of Qumran, for instance, the Jesus movement was not an exclusive group but was rather inclusive. Jesus did not call into his discipleship righteous, pious, and highly esteemed persons but invited tax collectors, sinners, and women to be his followers and friends. He rejected the primacy of the cultic purity laws and therefore could include in his community of disciples the outlaws and nonpersons of the Jewish religion and society.[19] In the fellowship of Jesus, women apparently did not play a marginal role, even though only a few references to women disciples have survived the androcentric tradition and redaction process of the gospels.

Women accompanied Jesus as disciples in his ministry in Galilee, Judea, and Jerusalem (Mark 15:40 and parallels) and witnessed his execution as a criminal [by the Romans] on the cross. They were not afraid to be known as his followers. Moreover, women were, according to all criteria of historical authenticity, the first witnesses of the resurrection, for this fact could not have been derived from contemporary Judaism[20] or invented by the primitive church. That the tradition did not leave these women disciples anonymous, but identified them by name, suggests that they played an important role in the Christian group in Palestine. Their most outstanding leader appears to have been Mary Magdalene,[21] since all four Gospels transmit her name, whereas the names of the other women vary. Thus, according to the Gospel traditions, women were the primary apostolic witnesses for the fundamental data of the early Christian message: they were the witnesses of Jesus' ministry, his death, his burial, and his resurrection.

A closer examination of the Gospel accounts, however, discloses the androcentric tendency to play down the women's roles as witnesses and apostles of the Easter event. This trend is apparent in Mark's Gospel, which stresses that the women "said nothing to anyone, for they were afraid" (Mark 16:8). It is also evident in Luke's comment that the words of the women seemed to the Eleven and those with them "an idle tale, and they did not believe them," but instead went to see for themselves (Luke 24:11). In Acts 1:21, Luke excludes the apostleship of women when he stresses that only a man was eligible to replace Judas. This androcentric bias is also reflected in the Lukan confessional statement: "The Lord has risen indeed, and has appeared to Simon!" (Luke 24:34).

This Lukan androcentric confessional formula corresponds to that of the pre-Pauline creedal tradition quoted in 1 Cor. 15:3, which mentions Cephas and the Eleven as the principal witnesses of the resurrection, but does not refer to the witness of the women.[22] The androcentric proclivity to play down the first witness of the resurrection by women is also apparent in the editing of the Fourth Gospel, which takes pains to ensure that the beloved disciple, not Mary Magdalene, was the first believer in the resurrection (John 20:1-18). Most contemporary commentators show the same androcentric inclination to suppress the significance of the women as primary witnesses to the resurrection when they stress that their witness had only a preliminary function, since according to Jewish law women were not competent to witness.

Patriarchalization of the Early Church. Scholars generally agree that Jesus did not leave his followers a blueprint for the organization and structuring of the Christian church. In Paul's time, leadership roles were still diversified and based on charismatic authority. The process of solidification and institutionalization set in only gradually during the last part of the first century. The pastoral epistles provide evidence that the Christian community and its offices were perceived and patterned after the patriarchal family structures of the time. Church authority was vested in elders, deacons, and bishops. Criteria for their election from the male members of the community were that they must be husbands of one wife and must have demonstrated their ability to rule the community by the proper ordering of their households and the successful upbringing of their children (1 Tim. 3:1-13; Titus 1:5-9).

From a sociological perspective, the gradual institutionalization and adaption of the Christian movement to the patriarchal societal structures of the time was unavoidable if the Christian community was to expand and to survive. At the same time, this structural solidification meant a patriarchalization of the Christian leadership functions that gradually eliminated women from roles of leadership and relegated them to subordinate feminine roles. The more Christianity became a genuine part of the patriarchal Jewish or Greco-Roman society and culture, the more it had to relegate women's leadership to fringe groups or to limit it to women's functions. In gnostic as well as catholic groups, "maleness" became the standard for being a full Christian. The recently discovered Coptic Gospel of Thomas states:

> Simon Peter said to them [the disciples]: Let Mary [Magdalene] go away from us, for women are not worthy of life. Jesus said: Lo, I shall lead her so that I may make her a male, that she too may become a living spirit, resembling you males. For every woman who makes herself a male will enter the kingdom of heaven. (Log. 114)

The androcentric emphasis of the Pauline tradition stresses the subordination of women on theological grounds and reflects the reactionary patriarchal evolution of the Christian community. Whether or not Paul himself initiated this patriarchal reaction is discussed by scholars.[23] Certainly, however, the theological justification of the patriarchalization of the Christian community expressed in 1 Cor. 11:2-16 and 14:33b-36 was able to claim the authority of Paul without being challenged.

In the context of his discussion of Christian enthusiasts Paul addresses, in his first letter to the Corinthians, the question of women's behavior in the Christian congregation. In both cases when Paul speaks about women he is concerned not with women's rights or the role of women in the church in general but with their concrete behavior in the Christian worship assembly in Corinth. In 1 Cor. 11:2-16, Paul does not deny that women can prophesy; he only demands that they should be appropriately dressed. In this debate, Paul adduces different arguments that he derived from nature, custom, and Scripture.

According to Paul, the order of creation is hierarchical: God-Christ-Man-Woman (v. 3). The Corinthian women still live in this order of creation and they ought to behave accordingly (vs. 4-6). Verse 7 theologically justifies the inferiority and dependence of woman: Man is the image and glory of God, whereas woman is only the glory of man, a prolongation and manifestation of his authority and power. With his reference to Gen. 2:18-23 in vs. 8-9, Paul demonstrates that man is prior to woman in the order of creation, and in v. 10 he adduces a further theological argument, namely, the presence of the angels in the worship assembly. Verses 11-12 assert that Paul does not wish to negate the reciprocity of man and woman in Christ. Yet, at stake in the Corinthian discussion is not the theological coequality of Christian women and men but the propriety of women's conduct (vs. 13-15). In his last sentence, Paul points to the universal practice of the churches and to his own apostolic authority. It is clear that for him the issue is one of contentiousness and party spirit (v. 16).

Similarly, the passage 1 Cor. 14:33b-36, which is widely held to be a post-Pauline interpolation, addresses the question of order and competition within the community (see v. 40). For the sake of order, 1 Cor. 14:33b-36 explicitly forbids women to speak in the assembly and directs them to their husbands for religious instruction. The main argument here is decency: "For it is shameful for a woman to speak in church."

The so-called household code texts of the later Pauline literature uphold the patriarchal family order of the time and therefore demand the subordination of the wife to the husband. Their rules of conduct for women, children, and slaves are not specifically Christian, but are a part of the Jewish and Greco-Roman culture of the time.[24] These culturally conditioned injunctions are, however, theologized or, better, Christologized in Ephesians, so that the model after which the Christian patriarchal marriage ought to be patterned is the relationship between Christ and the church.

It is true that the husbands are admonished to imitate Christ's love for the church in their love of their wives. Nevertheless, the author does not demand equal love and subordination of husband and wife, but decidedly preserves the patriarchal order in a Christian context. Just as Christ loves the church, which is clearly subordinated to him, so a husband should love his wife, who is required to be subordinated to him in everything (Eph. 5:24) and to pay him his due respect (Eph. 5:33). The subordination of the wife to the husband is, as in 1 Corinthians 11, justified with the theological rationale that the husband is the head of the wife as Christ is the head of the church (Eph. 5:23).

The household code of 1 Peter 3:1-7 may be considered an extension of Pauline patriarchal emphasis, inasmuch as the first letter of Peter is widely considered to represent Pauline theology and tradition. The author points to the example of the holy women of the Old Testament, especially of Sarah, in order to justify his stance that women best practice their Christian mission in submitting to the societal patriarchal order. In doing so, they might win over their husbands to Christianity without saying a word. The recommendation to the husbands in turn asks that they live considerately with their wives and bestow honor unto them.

The author stresses that husband and wife are "joint heirs of the grace of life," but considers woman to be the "weaker vessel" (KJV). As elsewhere in the New Testament, here again the term "weak" refers to physical, moral, or spiritual and intellectual inferiority. The expression "vessel" derogatorily describes woman as an object. Since this mode of characterizing woman is based on Jewish as well as Hellenistic sentiment, the author maintains the natural weakness of woman in accordance with the androcentric definitions of his time.

First Timothy 2:9-15 combines both the household code tradition and the silence in church tradition of the Pauline androcentric emphasis. Concerned with the proper behavior at worship, the author demands that men lift up their hands when they pray and that women not wear braided hair, jewelry, and expensive dress. They are, moreover, to be quiet and to learn with all submissiveness. They may on no account presume to teach or to have authority over men (v. 12). The author theologically justifies his androcentric injunctions with a reference to Genesis 2 and 3: Eve is not only second in the order of creation but she is also first in the order of sin. Woman's task is childbearing, and her salvation is dependent on this task (v. 15). Christian women were to conduct themselves according to contemporary patriarchal role definitions.

The author appears to formulate his patriarchal theology and ethics in order to counter the influence of a rival Christian group. This group seems to have had great success among women (2 Tim. 3:6), probably because it accorded women teaching and leadership functions and did not limit them to their societal patriarchal roles. In opposition to this Christian theological understanding of women's role, the author stresses that women are not to behave in an unusual way by wanting to teach or to have authority in the community. They are rather to be silent (stressed twice!), submissive, and modest.

ANDROCENTRIC TRADITIONING

At the end of the first century, a Christian prophet, who was the head of a prophetic group or school, exercised great leadership in the community of Thyatira (Rev. 2:19-23). The authority of this prophet must have been well established in the community, since the author of the book of Revelation criticizes the congregation for not having actively opposed her, and her influence must have been far-reaching and threatening to him. In labeling her "Jezebel" he insinuates that, like the Old Testament queen, the prophet promoted idolatry and achieved her goals through seductive power and malevolent scheming.

The author characterizes her activity with language gleaned from the imagery and language of the Old Testament prophets, describing the lapses of Israel into idolatry and apostasy as adultery, whoredom, and gross immorality. Despite this attack by the author of Revelation, the text still communicates that the prophet was not the head of an already heretic group, since she still exercised her leadership within the community of Thyatira.[25] Her impact must have been lasting, because Thyatira became in the second century a center of the Montanist movement in which female prophets were prominent (Epiphanius, *Heresies*51.3).

Although we no longer know the real name of the prophet of Thyatira, the text of Revelation furnishes us with an example showing that even at the end of the first century women exercised prophetic leadership in the Christian community. In addition, this text provides a paradigm of how patriarchal and androcentric theologizing and polemics distorted the contribution of women in the early church. A feminist history of the first centuries of the Christian church could uncover the struggle between those women who were inspired by the Christian vision expressed in Gal. 3:28 and the androcentric leadership of the church that attempted to force Christian women back into their limited cultural, patriarchal roles.

Suggestions for Interpreting Androcentric Texts of the Bible

The methods for the interpretation of historical texts, as well as those of feminist studies, enable us to approach the androcentric passages of the Bible with the following insights and guidelines:

1. Historical texts have to be understood and evaluated in their historical setting, language, and form. Since the biblical texts have their origin in a patriarchal culture, they reflect the androcentric situations, conditions, and values of this patriarchal culture. They appear to be, therefore, an excellent tool for the consciousness-raising of women and men in preaching and teaching.

2. Since biblical texts are rooted in a patriarchal culture and recorded from an androcentric point of view, a careful analysis from a feminist perspective might unearth traces of a genuine "her-story" of women in the Bible. It is very important that teachers and preachers point out these instances of a genuine "her-story" again and again, so that women in the church become conscious of their own "her-story" in the biblical patriarchal history.

3. Since biblical androcentric texts are recorded and told from a patriarchal point of view, it will be helpful to retell the androcentric biblical stories from the woman's point of view. As the Elohist retold the story of Abraham and Sarah from Abraham's point of view, so we should attempt to retell it from Sarah's perspective. An example of the retelling of Genesis 2 and 3 is Judith

Plaskow's "The Coming of Lilith."[26] Such a retelling of biblical stories is not a feminist invention. Throughout the centuries we have examples of parallel elaborations such as the apocryphal infancy stories or our Christmas legends.

4. Biblical texts are not only recorded but also translated and interpreted from an androcentric perspective since most exegetes are not aware of a feminist perspective. We have therefore to be cautious in adopting standard scholarly translations and interpretations of texts and to screen such interpretations for their androcentric or sexist presuppositions or prejudice.

5. Biblical revelation and truth about women are found, I would suggest, in those texts that transcend and criticize their patriarchal culture and religion. Such texts should be used to evaluate and to judge the patriarchal texts of the Bible. A biblical interpretation that is concerned with the *meaning* of the Bible in a post-patriarchal culture has to maintain that solely the nonsexist traditions of the Bible present divine revelation if the Bible should not become a tool for the oppression of women. Such an interpretation does not suggest a "modernizing" of ancient texts,[27] but is a necessary corrective if we do not want to give the impression that we worship a sexist God and thus an idol who is made in the image of males.

NOTES

[1] For a more thorough discussion, see my article "Feminist The*logy as a Critical The*logy of Liberation," *Theological Studies*, 36, no. 4 (1975): 611, and the excellent article by J. Lambert, "Un-Fettering the Word: A Call for Coarcial Interpretation of the Bible," *Covenant Quarterly* (May 1974): 3–26.

[2] The feminist use of "his story" or "her story" is *not* an etymological explanation but a wordplay to point out the male bias of all history and historiography. To quote Henry Adams: "The study of history is useful to the historian by teaching him his ignorance of women; and the mass of this ignorance causes one who is familiar enough with what is called historical sources to realize how few women have ever been known. The woman who is only known through a man is known wrong." See Mary R. Beard, *Woman as Force in History* (Macmillan, 1971), 219.

[3] Today, I would write "Hebrew Bible."

[4] In writing this section, I found extremely helpful Phyllis Bird's article "Images of Women in the Old Testament," in Ruether, ed., *Religion and Sexism*, 41–88.

[5] Roland de Vaux, *Ancient Israel: Its Life and Institutions* (McGraw-Hill, 1961), 40. Here I unwittingly reproduce the Christian prejudice that Hebrew society was more patriarchal than its surrounding cultures. This was written before the feminist anti-Judaism discussion that underscored that such malestream Christian prejudices were unwittingly also reproduced by Christian feminists.

[6] Gerhard von Rad, *Genesis: A Commentary*, rev. ed., OTL (Westminster, 1973), 215–22. Von Rad pleads that the text "must not be judged simply by our Western ideas" (218).

[7] Hans Wilhelm Hertzberg, *Das Buch der Richter* (ATD), 9, no. 19: 3rd ed. (Göttingen: Vandenhoeck and Ruprecht, 1965), 254–56, points out that the final redactional remark in Judg. 21:25 attributes the events to the fact that Israel had no king at the time. But Hertzberg argues that the actions against the women were justified because the survival of an Israelite tribe was endangered.

[8] See L. Blagg Harter, "The Theme of the Barren Woman in the Patriarchal Narratives," *Concern* (Nov. 1971): 20–24, (Dec. 1971): 18–23.

[9]See "Images of Women in the Bible," *Women's Caucus Religious Studies Newsletter*, vol. 2, no. 3 (1974): 1–6; J. C. Williams, "Yahweh, Women, and the Trinity," *Theology Today*, vol. 32, no. 3 (Oct. 1975): 234–42; and the unpublished paper of Phyllis Bird, "Masculinity and Monotheism: An Inquiry into the Limitation of the Feminine in Old Testament Representation of the Deity with Attention to Its Sources and Consequences," delivered at the Southwest Regional Meeting of the Society of Biblical Literature, March 1975.

[10]Hans Walter Wolff, *Hosea*, Hermeneia (Minneapolis: Fortress Press, 1974), 14, 24.

[11]This tendency is still found in the most recent scholarly Old Testament lexicon, where the Fall is attributed to the fact that the first woman distanced herself from her husband and acted without him (Gen. 3:1-6). See G. Johannes Botterweck and Helmer Ringgren, *Theologisches Wörterbuch zum Alten Testament* (Stuttgart: Kohlhammer, 1971), col. 244 (N. Bratsiottis).

[12]See Phyllis Bird, "Images of Women in the Old Testament," in Ruether, ed., *Religion and Sexism*, 87, who contests the argument that *'ādām* is understood as an androgynous being. See Phyllis Trible, "Depatriarchalization in Biblical Interpretation," *JAAR* 41 (1973), 35.

[13]Claus Westermann, *Genesis*, Biblischer Kommentar: Altes Testament (Neukirchen: Vluyn, 1970), 245.

[14]Herbert Lockyer, *The Women of the Bible* (Zondervan, 1967), 113.

[15]Michael Cardinal von Faulhaber, *Women of the Bible*, ed. Brendan Keogh (Newmans, 1955), 50.

[16]Martin Noth, *Das vierte Buch Mose: Numeri*, ATD 7 (Göttingen: Vandenhoeck and Ruprecht, 1966), 84.

[17]For a more detailed argumentation, see my article "The Role of Women in the Early Christian Movement," *Concilium* 7 (1976).

[18]Leonard Swidler, "Is Sexism a Sign of Decadence in Religion?" in Judith Plaskow and Joan A. Romero, eds., *Women and Religion*, rev. ed. (Scholars, 1974), 170.

[19]I would replace the distancing "the" with "his" Jewish society and religion.

[20]Again, this rule of New Testament Historical Jesus research is dubious in light of the anti-Judaism discussion in the intervening years.

[21]See my book *Der vergessene Partner, Grundlagen, Tatsachen und Möglichkeiten der Mitarbeit der Frau in der Kirche* (Düsseldorf: Patmos, 1964), 57–59, 125–27.

[22]In my sermon "Mary Magdalene, Apostle to the Apostles," *UTS Journal*, April 1975, 22, I pointed out that, according to the Pauline and Lukan criteria of apostleship, Mary Magdalene and the other women were apostles, since they accompanied Jesus and had seen the resurrected Lord. R. E. Brown accepts this suggestion but then plays down this insight: "The priority given to Peter in Paul and in Luke is a priority among those who became *official* [italics mine] witnesses to the Resurrection. The secondary place given to the tradition of an appearance to a woman or women probably reflects the fact that women did not serve at first as official preachers of the church—a fact that would make the creation of an appearance to a woman unlikely." See Brown's article "Roles of Women in the Fourth Gospel," *Theological Studies* 36, no. 4 (1975): 692n12. I do not understand what the qualification "official" means in a situation where church offices were in the stage of development and when we know that women had leading roles as prophets, apostles, and missionaries in the early Christian communities. It is problematic to project later church institutional forms back into the early church.

[23]Scroggs, "Paul and the Eschatological Woman," 5–17; W. A. Meeks, "The Image of the Androgyne," *History of Religion* 13 (1974): 165–208; W. Munro, "Patriarchy and Charismatic Community," in Plaskow and Romero, eds., *Women and Religion*, 189–98; W. O. Walker, "1 Corinthians 11:2-16 and Paul's View Regarding Woman," *Journal of Biblical Literature* 94 (1975): 94–110.

[24]J. E. Crouch, *The Origin and Intention of the Colossian Haustafel* (Göttingen: Vandenhoeck and Ruprecht, 1972). John Howard Yoder, *The Politics of Jesus* (Grand Rapids: Eerdmans, 1972), 163–92, however, argues that the concept of subordination is a specific Christian concept. See his argument against Krister Stendahl's position, *The Bible and the Role of Women: A Case Study in Hermeneutics* (Fortress Press, 1966): "What if, for instance, the sweeping, doctrinaire egalitarianism of our culture, which makes the concept of the 'place of woman' seem laughable or boorish and makes

that of 'subordination' seem insulting, should turn out really (in the 'intent of God' or in long-run social experience) to be demonic, uncharitable, destructive of personality, disrespectful of creation, and unworkable?" (177n22).

[25] For the wider context, see my article "Apocalyptic and Gnosis in the Book of Revelation and Paul," *JBL* 92 (1973): 565–81.

[26] Judith Plaskow, "The Coming of Lilith," in Rosemary Radford Ruether, ed., *Religion and Sexism*, 341–43.

[27] See Katherine D. Sackenfeld, "The Bible and Women: Bane or Blessing?" *Theology Today* 32, no. 3 (October 1975): 228. Sackenfeld speaks about the danger of searching for "timeless truth" that "seems to transcend the normally expected cultural biases of the author" because new biases about what is "timeless" are often introduced. Although revelation occurs within the human sphere and it is not possible to make absolute identification of such "truths," it is possible to look for points at which the liberating Word of God seems to have broken through cultural patterns on behalf of the oppressed.

2

Toward a Christian Feminist Biblical Hermeneutics

Biblical Interpretation and Liberation Theology

To discuss the relationship between liberation theology and biblical interpretation in general, and to ask for the function of the Bible in the struggle of women for liberation in particular, is to enter an intellectual and emotional minefield. One must detect and lay bare the contradictions between historical exegesis and systematic theology, between value-neutral scientific inquiry and "advocacy" scholarship, between universal-objectivist preconceptions of academic theology and the critical partiality of liberation theologies. To attempt this in a short paper entails, by necessity, a simplification and typologization of a complex set of theological problems.

To raise the issue of the contemporary meaning and authority of the Bible from a feminist theological perspective, and to do this from the marginalized position of a woman in the academy,[1] is to expose oneself to triple jeopardy. Establishment academic theologians and exegetes will reject such an endeavor as unscientific, biased, and overly conditioned by contemporary questions, and therefore unhistorical, or they will refuse to accept it as a serious exegetical or theological question because the issue is raised by a woman. Liberation and political theologians will, at best, consider such a feminist theological endeavor as one problem among others, or at worst, label it as "middle class" and peripheral to the struggle of oppressed people. After all, how can middle-class white women worry about the ERA or the sex of God, when people die of starvation, are tortured in prisons, or vegetate below poverty level in the black and Hispanic ghettos of American cities?

However, such an objection against feminist theology and the women's liberation movement overlooks the fact that more than half of the poor and hungry in the world are women and children dependent on women.[2] Not only do women and children represent the majority of the "oppressed," but poor and third world women suffer the triple oppression of sexism, racism, and classism. If liberation theologians make the "option for the oppressed" the key to their theological endeavors, then they must become conscious of the fact that "the oppressed" are women.

Feminist theology, therefore, not only challenges academic theology to take its own intellectual presuppositions seriously, but it also asks other liberation theologies to concretize their option for the oppressed. Finally, the feminist theologian challenges not only the supposedly value-neutral and objective stance of the academic theologian, but she also must qualify the definition of the advocacy stance of liberation theology as "option for the oppressed." Her involvement in liberation theology is not "altruistic," but it is based on the acknowledgment and analysis of her own oppression as a woman in sexist, cultural, and theological institutions. Having acknowledged the dimensions of her own oppression, she can no longer advocate the value-neutral, detached stance of the academy. In other words, feminist theologians' experience of oppression is different from those of Latin American male liberation theologians, who generally do not belong to the poor, but have made the cause of the oppressed their own.[3] Such an emphasis on the differences in the approaches of different liberation theologies is important. Robert McAfee Brown has pointed out, "What we see depends on where we are standing."[4]

Moreover, the Native American theologian Vine Deloria[5] has cautioned that one way of co-opting liberation theology is to classify all minorities as oppressed and in need of liberation. Christian theologians often add to this that we are all under sin and therefore all equally oppressed: male and female, black, white, and red. In co-opting the terms "oppression," and generalizing it so much that it becomes meaningless, the liberal establishment successfully neutralizes specific analyses of oppression and prohibits oppressed groups from formulating their own goals and strategies for liberation. Therefore, it seems to be methodologically inappropriate to speak in generalized terms about oppression or about liberation theology in the singular.

THE "ADVOCACY" STANCE OF LIBERATION THEOLOGIES

This insight has far-reaching consequences for the methodological approach of this chapter. Instead of asking for the scriptural *loci* of liberation theology in general, or critically evaluating their approach from a "superior" methodological historical-critical point of view, I have decided to concentrate on one specific issue of contention between so-called academic theology and all forms of liberation theology. The basic insight of liberation theologies and their methodological starting-point is the insight that all theology knowingly or not is by definition always engaged for or against the oppressed. Intellectual neutrality is not possible in a historical world of exploitation and oppression. If this is the case, then theology cannot talk about human existence in general, or about biblical theology in particular, without identifying whose human existence is meant and about whose God biblical symbols and texts speak.

This avowed "advocacy" stance of all liberation theologies seems to be the major point of contention between academic historical-critical or liberal-systematic theology on the one side and liberation theology on the other side. For instance, in many exegetical and theological circles a feminist interpretation of the Bible or the reconstruction of early Christianity is not the proper substantive historical and theological subject matter for serious academic theology. Since such a feminist interpretation is sparked by the women's movement and openly confesses its allegiance to it, academic theologians consider it to be a popular "fad" and judge it not to be a serious historical theological problem for historical-critical scholarship.[6] Since this interpretative approach is already prejudiced by the explicit advocacy position of the inquiring scholar, no value-neutral scientific inquiry is possible. Therefore, no one publicly identified with the "feminist cause" in theology and society can be considered to be a "serious" scholar. Or as one of my colleagues remarked about a professor who wrote a rather moderate article on women in the Old Testament: "It's a shame! In writing this article she may have ruined her whole scholarly career."

The ideal of historical-critical studies that all exegetical inquiry should be a value-neutral and objective historical description of the past overlooks the fact that biblical studies as "canonical" studies are already "engaged," insofar as the Bible is not just a document of past history, but functions as Holy Scripture in Christian communities today.[7] The *biblical* exegete and theologian, in distinction from the historian of antiquity, never searches solely for the historical meaning of a passage, but also raises the question of the Bible's meaning and authority for today. The argument that the "hermeneutical privilege of the oppressed"[8] or the feminist interest in the role of women in the New Testament is too engaged or biased pertains, therefore, to all biblical inquiry *qua* biblical inquiry, and not only to the study and use of the Bible by liberation theologians. Insofar as biblical studies are "canonical" studies, they are related to and inspired by their *Sitz im Leben* in the Christian church of the past and the present. The feminist analysis of the Bible is just one example of such an ecclesial contextuality and of the theological commitment of biblical studies in general.

This fact is recognized by Schubert Ogden, who nevertheless objects to the "advocacy" stance of liberation theology. He argues that all existing liberation theologies are in danger of becoming ideologies in the Marxist sense, insofar as they, like other traditional theological enterprises, are "the rationalization of positions already taken."[9] Rather than engaging in a critical reflection on their own positions, liberation theologies rationalize, with the help of the Bible, the positions of the oppressed instead of those of the oppressors. Insofar as they attempt to rationalize the prior claims of Christian faith and their own option for the oppressed, they are not theologizing but witnessing. Theology as a "second act" exists, according to Latin American liberation theologians, not "for its own sake," but for the sake of the church's witness, its liberating praxis.

One must, however, question whether this statement adequately characterizes the "advocacy" stance of liberation theologians. Ogden suggests that the only way theology—be it academic or liberation theology—can become emancipated is by conceiving its task as that of a critical reflection on its own position. He then proceeds to work out a "still more adequate theology of liberation than any of them has as yet achieved."[10] However, he not only fails to reflect critically on the political standpoint and implications of his own process theology, but he also goes on to talk about "women's theology" and to explore the "being of God in himself" as if he had never studied feminist theology.

While Ogden accuses liberation theologians of too "provincial an understanding of bondage," James Cone insists to the contrary that the option for the oppressed should become the starting point of all theology: "If Christian theology is an explication of the meaning of the gospel for our time, must not theology itself have liberation as its starting point or run the risk of being, at best, idle talk, and at worst blasphemy?"[11] Such a provocative formulation should not, however, be classified as mere "rhetoric,"[12] but must be seen as an indicator of serious theological differences in the understanding of the task and function of theology.

This disagreement about the function and goal of theology has serious implications for the way theologians understand the task of biblical interpretation. As a feminist theologian I have taken the "advocacy" position, but do not think that this option excludes "critical reflection" on my own feminist position. Such a critical reflection must not only be applied to the "advocacy" position of liberation theologies, but it must also be extended to the ways exegetes and theologians have construed the relationship between the biblical past and its meanings, and explicated the claim of Christian theology that the Bible has authority and significance for Christians today.

Such a critical reflection indicates *first* that biblical and theological interpretation has always taken an advocacy position without clearly reflecting upon it. Such an advocacy position is not unique to liberation theologies.

Second, in order to reflect critically on the function of liberation theologians' explicit advocacy position in the process of biblical theological interpretation, I have chosen to discuss two concrete examples of liberation theological hermeneutics. This is necessary because it is methodologically incorrect to reduce every advocacy stance and every analysis of concrete structures of oppression by liberation theologies to one common level. I will argue that liberation theologies, because of their option for a specific group of oppressed people—for example, women or Native Americans—need to develop, within the overall interpretative approach of a critical theology of liberation, more adequate heuristic interpretative models appropriate to specific forms of oppression. In short, the biblical interpretation of liberation theologians is to become more concrete, or more "provincial," before an "interstructuring" of different interpretative models, and a more universal formulation of the task of a critical theology of liberation can be attempted.

The hermeneutical discussion is concerned with the meaning of biblical texts. While one direction of hermeneutics seeks to discover the synchronic ontological, atemporal, ideal, noematic meaning of written texts by separating it from the diachronic, temporal, communicative, personal, and referential speech-event, another direction does not concentrate so much on the linguist-icality of the text as on the involvement of the interpreter with the text. The interpreter always approaches the text with specific ways of raising questions, and thus with a certain understanding of the subject matter with which the text is concerned.[13]

The hermeneutic circle conceives of the relationship between the contemporary interpreter and the historical text as a continuous dialogue that corrects the presuppositions of the interpreter and works out the true meaning of the text. At this point, it becomes clear that in this third paradigm dialogical interpretation is the governing model. While form and redaction criticism show that early Christian communities and "authors" were in constant dialogue with the tradition and the living Lord authorizing this tradition, the hermeneutic circle continues this dialogic endeavor in the act of interpretation. Therefore, this hermeneutic understanding can be combined with the neoorthodox theological enterprise. Or as Schillebeeckx points out: "The apparent point of departure is the presupposition that what is handed down in tradition and especially the Christian tradition, is always meaningful, and that its meaning must only be deciphered hermeneutically and made actual."[14]

The hermeneutic-contextual discussion is interested in the "continuation" of the tradition, and therefore advocates as a position in line with neoorthodox theology, a "hermeneutics of consent."[15] The explicit advocacy position, however, of liberation theologies threatens to uncover the hidden political interests of existing biblical interpretative paradigms. This may be one of the main reasons why established theology refuses to reflect critically on its own societal-ecclesial interests and political functions.

LIBERATION THEOLOGY AND BIBLICAL INTERPRETATION

The second part of this chapter will attempt to explore critically the position of a theology of liberation within the existing paradigms of biblical interpretation. I will do this by discussing two different hermeneutical approaches of liberation theologies. As case studies, I have chosen the hermeneutical model of Juan Luis Segundo as one of the more sophisticated proposals in contemporary theology, and have placed in contrast to it Elizabeth Cady Stanton's approach in proposing the *Woman's Bible*. Both examples indicate that liberation theologies have worked out a distinctive approach to biblical interpretation that leads to a redefinition of the criteria for public theological discourse. Instead of asking whether an approach is appropriate to the Scriptures and adequate to the human condition,[16] one needs to test whether a theological model of biblical interpretation is *adequate* to the historical-literary methods of contemporary interpretation and *appropriate* to the struggle of the oppressed for liberation.

The Interpretative Model of Juan Luis Segundo

While the hermeneutic-contextual approach advocates the elimination of all presuppositions and pre-understandings for the sake of objective-descriptive exegesis, existential hermeneutics defines pre-understanding as the common existential ground between the interpreter and the author of the text.[17] Political theologians have challenged this choice of existential philosophy, while liberation theologians maintain a hermeneutics of engagement instead of a hermeneutics of detachment. Since no complete detachment or value-neutrality is possible, the interpreter must make her/his stance explicit and take an advocacy position in favor of the oppressed. To truly understand the Bible is to read it through the eyes of the oppressed, since the God who speaks in the Bible is the God of the oppressed. For a correct interpretation of the Bible, it is necessary to acknowledge the "hermeneutical privilege of the oppressed" and to develop a hermeneutics "from below."

Since theology is explicitly or implicitly intertwined with the existing social situation, according to Segundo the hermeneutic circle must begin with an experience or analysis of the social reality that leads to suspicion about our real situation. In a second step we apply our ideological suspicion to theology and to all other ideological superstructures. At a third level we experience theological reality in a different way, which in turn leads us to the suspicion that "the prevailing interpretation of the Bible has not taken important pieces of data into account."[18] At a last stage we bring these insights to bear upon the interpretation of Scripture. However, only active commitment to the oppressed and active involvement in their struggle for liberation enable us to see our society and our world differently, and give us a new perspective for looking at the world. This perspective is also taught in the New Testament, if the latter is interpreted correctly.

Segundo acknowledges that James Cone has elaborated such a liberation theological interpretation for the black community. He admits his indebtedness to Bultmann, but he reformulates the hermeneutic circle to include action: "And the circular nature of this interpretation stems from the fact that each new reality obliges us to interpret the word of God afresh, to *change* reality accordingly, and then go back and reinterpret the Word of God again and so on [emphasis mine]."[19]

It is apparent that Segundo cannot be accused of rationalizing a previously taken position. He does not operate within the interpretative tradition of the doctrinal paradigm. He also clearly distinguishes his own theological interpretation from that of academic historical-critical scholarship by rejecting the biblical revelation-contemporary application model. According to him biblical interpretation must reconstruct the second-level learning process of biblical faith. Faith is identical with the total process of learning in and through ideologies, whereas the faith responses vis-à-vis certain historical situations are ideologies. Therefore, faith should not be defined as content or *depositum fidei*, but as an educational process throughout biblical and Christian history. Faith expresses the continuity and permanency of divine revelation, whereas ideologies document the historical character of faith and revelation. "Faith then is a liberative process. It is converted into freedom for history, which means freedom *for ideologies*."[20] It is obvious that Segundo does not understand ideology as "false" consciousness, but as historical-societal expression.

According to Segundo, Christian faith is also not to be defined as content, doctrine, or principle, but as an educational process to which we willingly entrust ourselves. "In the case of . . . the Bible we learn to learn by entrusting our life and its meaning to the historical process that is reflected in the expressions embodied in that particular tradition."[21] It is thus clear that Segundo does not work within the overall approach of either the doctrinal or historical value-free paradigms, but proposes an interpretative model within the hermeneutic-contextual paradigm. He shares with neoorthodoxy the hermeneutical presupposition that scriptural traditions are meaningful, and that they can therefore claim our obedience and demand a "hermeneutics of consent." In distinction from neoorthodox theology, Segundo does not claim that it is the content of Scripture that is reflected in the Bible as meaningful and liberative. It is, rather, in the process of learning how to learn that meaning and liberation are seen.

However, this assumption does not take into account the fact that not only the content of Scripture but also this second-level learning process can be distorted. Segundo must, therefore, either demonstrate that this is not the case, or formalize this learning process to such a degree that the "advocacy" becomes an abstract principle not applicable to the contents of the Bible. In other words, Segundo's model does not allow for a critical theological evaluation of biblical ideologies as "false consciousness." One must question whether historical content and hermeneutic learning can be separated. Such a proposal also does not allow us to judge whether a text or interpretation is appropriate and helpful to the struggle of the oppressed for liberation. The failure to bring a critical evaluation to bear upon the biblical texts and upon the process of interpretation within Scripture and tradition is one of the reasons why the use of the Bible by liberation theologians often comes close to "proof texting." To avoid such an impression, liberation hermeneutics must reflect on the fact that the process of interpretation of Scripture is not necessarily liberative.

The Hermeneutics of the Woman's Bible

While liberation theologians affirm the Bible as a weapon in the struggle of liberation, and they claim that the God of the Bible is a God of the oppressed, feminist writers since the inauguration of the women's movement in the last century have maintained, to the contrary, that the Bible and Christian theology are inherently sexist and thereby destructive of women's consciousness. A revisionist interpretation of Scripture and theology, therefore, will either subvert women's struggle for liberation from all sexist oppression and violence, or it will be forced to re-interpret Christian tradition and theology in such a way that nothing "Christian" will remain.

Feminist theology as a critical theology of liberation must defend itself against two sides: while liberation theologians are reluctant to acknowledge that women are exploited and oppressed, radical feminist thinkers claim that feminist consciousness and Christian faith are contradictions in terms. The question that feminist theologians must face squarely is thus a foundational theological problem: Is being a woman and being a Christian a primary contradiction that must be resolved in favor of one to the exclusion of the other? Or can both be kept in creative tension so that my being a Christian supports my struggle for liberation as a woman, while my being a feminist enhances and deepens my commitment to live as a Christian?[22]

Insofar as feminist theology as a Christian theology is bound to its charter documents in Scripture, it must formulate this problem also with reference to the Bible and biblical revelation. Since the Bible was and is used against women's demand for equality and liberation from societal, cultural, and ecclesial sexism, it must conceive of this task first in critical terms before it can attempt to formulate a hermeneutics of liberation. While the danger of liberation theology is "proof texting," the pitfall to be avoided by feminist theology is apologetics, since such an apologetics does not take the political implications of scriptural interpretation seriously.

The debate surrounding the *Woman's Bible*,[23] which appeared in 1895 and 1898, may serve here as a case study for the *political* conditions and implications of feminist biblical interpretation as well as for the radical critical impact of feminist theology for the interpretative task. In her introduction to the *Woman's Bible*, Elizabeth Cady Stanton, the initiator of the project, outlined two critical insights for a feminist theological hermeneutics. The Bible is not a "neutral" book, but it is a political weapon against women's struggle for liberation. This is so because the Bible bears the imprint of men who never saw or talked with God.

First: Elizabeth Cady Stanton conceived of biblical interpretation as a political act. The following episode characterizes her own personal conviction of the negative impact of Christian religion on women's situation. She refused to attend a prayer meeting of suffragists that was opened by the singing of the hymn "Guide Us, O Thou Great Jehovah" by Isabella Beecher Hooker. Her reason was that Jehovah had "never taken any active part in the suffrage movement."[24] Because of her experience that Yahweh was not on the side of the oppressed, she realized the great political influence of the Bible. She, therefore, proposed to prepare a revision of the Bible that would collect and interpret (with the help of "higher criticism") all statements referring to women in the Bible. She conceded, however, that she was not very successful in soliciting the help of women scholars because they were "afraid that their high reputation and scholarly attainments might be compromised by taking part in an enterprise that for a time may prove very unpopular. Hence we may not be able to get help from that class."[25]

And indeed, the project of the *Woman's Bible* proved to be very unpopular because of political implications. Not only did some of the suffragists argue that such a project was either not necessary or politically unwise, but the National American Woman's Suffrage Association formally rejected it as a political mistake. In the second volume, which appeared in 1898, Cady Stanton sums up this opposition by saying: "Both friend and foe object to the title." She then replies with biting wit to the accusation of a clergyman that the *Woman's Bible* is "the work of women and the devil," saying: "This is a grave mistake. His Satanic Majesty was not to join the Revising Committee that consists of women alone. Moreover, he has been so busy of late years attending Synods, General Assemblies and Conferences, to prevent the recognition of women delegates, that he has no time to study the languages and 'higher criticism.'"[26]

Although the methods and theological presuppositions of the "higher criticism" of the time are rather outdated today, the political arguments and objectives of a feminist biblical interpretation remain valid. They are outlined by Cady Stanton in her introduction to the first volume. She gives three reasons why such an objective scientific feminist revision and interpretation of the Bible is politically necessary:

1. Throughout history and especially today the Bible is used to keep women in subjection and to hinder their emancipation.

2. Not only men but especially women are the most faithful believers in the Bible as the Word of God. Not only for men, but also for women, the Bible has a numinous authority.

3. No reform is possible in one area of society if it is not advanced also in all other areas. One cannot reform the law and other cultural institutions without also reforming biblical religion that claims the Bible as Holy Scripture. Since "all reforms are interdependent," a critical feminist interpretation is a necessary political endeavor, though perhaps not opportune. If feminists think they can neglect the revision of the Bible because there are more pressing political issues, then they do not recognize the political impact of Scripture upon the churches and society, and also upon the lives of women.

Second: Elizabeth Cady Stanton advocated such a revision of the Bible in terms of "higher criticism." Her insights, therefore, correspond with the results of historical biblical studies of her time. Over and against the doctrinal understanding of the Bible as Word of God, she stresses that the Bible is written by men and reflects patriarchal male interests. "The only point in which I differ from all ecclesiastical teaching is that I do not believe that any man ever saw or talked with God."[27] While the churches teach that such degrading ideas about patriarchal injunctions against women come from God, Cady Stanton maintains that all these degrading texts and ideas emanated from the heads of men. By treating the Bible as a human work and not as a magic fetish, and by denying divine inspiration to the negative biblical statements about women, she claims that her committee has shown more reverence and respect for God than does the clergy or the church. She concedes that some teachings of the Bible, such as the love-command or the golden rule, are still valid today. Since the teachings and lessons of the Bible differ from each other, the Bible cannot be accepted or rejected as a whole. Therefore, every passage on women must be carefully analyzed and evaluated for its impact on the struggle for the liberation of women.

In conclusion: Although the idea of a *Woman's Bible* consisting only of the biblical texts on women must be rejected today on methodological grounds,[28] biblical scholarship on the whole has proven accurate Cady Stanton's contention that the Bible must be studied as a human work, and that biblical interpretation is influenced by the theological mind-set and interests of the interpreter. Contemporary feminist interpreters, like some of Cady Stanton's suffragist friends, either reject biblical interpretation as a hopeless feminist endeavor because the Bible is totally sexist, or they attempt to defend the Bible in the face of its radical feminist critics. In doing so they follow Frances Willard, who argued against the radical critique of the *Woman's Bible* that not the biblical message but only its patriarchal contemporary interpretation preaches the subjugation of women: "I think that men have read their own selfish theories into the book, that theologians have not in the past sufficiently recognized the progressive quality of its revelation nor adequately discriminated between its records as history and its principles of ethics and religion."[29]

The insight that scholarly biblical interpretations need to be "de-patriarchalized" is an important one. However, this critical insight should not be misunderstood as an apologetic defense of the non-patriarchal character of the Bible's teachings on ethics and religion. It was exactly Elizabeth Cady Stanton's critical insight that the Bible is not just misunderstood, but that its contents and perspectives can be used in the political struggle against women. What Gustavo Gutiérrez says about human historiography in general must also be applied to the writing of the Bible: "Human history has been written by a white hand, a male hand from the dominating social class. The perspective of the defeated in history is different. Attempts have been made to wipe from their minds the memory of their struggles. This is to deprive them of a source of energy, of an historical will to rebellion."[30]

If we compare Cady Stanton's hermeneutical stance with that of Segundo, we see that she could not accept his understanding of a liberative second-level learning process within Christian history exactly because she shares his "advocacy stance for the oppressed." Cady Stanton cannot begin with the affirmation that the Bible and the God of the Bible are on the side of the oppressed because her experience of the Bible's use as a political weapon against women's struggle for suffrage tells her otherwise.

The subsequent reaction to the *Woman's Bible* also warns liberation theologians that a biblical interpretation that resorts too quickly to the defense of the Bible could misconstrue its advocacy stance for the oppressed. The task of liberation theologians is not to prove that the Bible or the church can be defended against feminist or socialist attacks. Only when we critically comprehend how the Bible functions in the oppression of women or the poor can we prevent its misuse for further oppression. Otherwise, liberation theology is in danger of succumbing to proof-texting. The advocacy stance of liberation theology can only be construed as a rationalization of preconceived ecclesial or dogmatic positions if it does not fully explore the oppressive aspects of biblical traditions. Because of their advocacy stance for the oppressed, feminist theologians must insist that theological-critical analysis of Christian tradition should not only begin with the time of Constantine, but it also must apply itself to the Christian charter documents themselves.

Because of its allegiance to the "defeated in history," a feminist critical theology maintains that a "hermeneutics of consent" that understands itself as the "actualizing continuation of the Christian history of interpretation" does not suffice. Such a hermeneutics overlooks the fact that Christian Scripture and tradition are not only a source of truth, but also of untruth, repression, and domination. Since the hermeneutic-contextual paradigm seeks only to *understand* biblical texts, it cannot adequately take into account the fact that the Christian past, as well as its interpretations, has victimized women. A critical theology of liberation,[31] therefore, must work out a new interpretative paradigm that can take seriously the claim of liberation theologians that God is on the side of the oppressed. Such a paradigm must also accept the claim of feminist theologians that God has never "taken an active part in the suffrage movement," and that therefore the Bible can function as a male weapon in the political struggle against women's liberation.

Toward a Feminist Interpretive Paradigm of Emancipatory Praxis

A critical theology of liberation cannot avoid raising the question of the truth-content of the Bible for Christians today.[32] If, for instance, feminist theologians take fully into account the androcentric language, misogynist contents, and patriarchal interests of biblical texts, then we cannot avoid the question of the "canon," or the criterion that allows us to reject oppressive traditions and to detect emancipatory traditions within biblical texts and history.

First: Such a need for a critical evaluation of the various biblical texts and traditions has always been recognized in the church. While the doctrinal paradigm insisted that Scripture must be judged by the *regula fidei*, and can only be properly interpreted by the teaching office of the church, the historical-critical paradigm evaluated the theological truth of biblical texts according to their historicity. The hermeneutic-contextual paradigm has not only established the canon as the pluriform root-model of the Christian community, but it has also underlined the fact that the Bible often includes various contradictory responses to the historical situation of the Israelite or Christian community.

Since not all these responses can equally express Christian revelation, biblical scholarship has attempted to formulate theological criteria to evaluate different biblical traditions. Such a "canon within the canon" can be formulated along philosophical-dogmatic or historical-factual lines. Some theologians distinguish between revelatory essence and historical expression, timeless truth and culturally conditioned language, or constant Christian tradition and changing traditions.

When such a canon is formulated along the lines of the hermeneutic-contextual paradigm, scholars juxtapose Jesus and Paul, Pauline theology and early Catholicism, the historical Jesus and the kerygmatic Christ, or Hebrew and Greek thought. Whereas, for example, Ogden accepts as such a canon the

Jesus-traditions of Marxsen,[33] Sobrino emphasizes the Jesus of history as the criterion for liberation theology. Segundo, on the other hand, is methodologically most consistent when he insists that no contentual biblical statement can be singled out as such a criterion because all historical expression of faith is ideological. In line with the hermeneutic-contextual paradigm, he insists that not the content but the process of interpretation within the Bible and Christian history should be normative for liberation theology. Yet such a proposal does not allow for the insight that this process of expressing faith in a historical situation can also be falsified and serve oppressive interests.

Therefore, a critical feminist theology of liberation cannot take the Bible or the biblical faith defined as the total process of learning in and through ideologies as *norma normans non normata*[34] but must understand them as sources alongside other sources. This point was already made by James Cone, who pointed out that the sources of theology are the Bible as well as our own political situation and experience. However, the norm for black theology is "Jesus as the Black Christ who provides the necessary soul for black liberation." "He is the essence of the Christian gospel."[35]

I would be hesitant to postulate that Jesus as the feminist Christ is the canonical norm, since we cannot spell out concretely who this feminist Christ is if we do not want to make Christ a formalized *chiffre* or resort to mysticism. This is the argument of Jon Sobrino, who in turn postulates that the historical Jesus is the norm of truth since "access to the Christ of faith comes through our following of the historical Jesus."[36] However, such a formulation of the canonical norm for Christian faith presupposes that we can know the historical Jesus and that we can imitate him, since an actual following of Jesus is not possible for us. Moreover, a feminist theologian must question whether the historical man Jesus of Nazareth can be a role model for contemporary women, since feminist psychological liberation means exactly the struggle of women to free themselves from all male internalized norms and models.

Second: I would suggest that the canon and norm for evaluating biblical traditions and their subsequent interpretations cannot be derived from the Bible or the biblical process of learning within and through ideologies, but can only be formulated within and through the struggle for the liberation of women and all oppressed peoples. It cannot be "universal," but it must be specific and derived from a particular experience of oppression and liberation. The "advocacy stance" of liberation theologies must be sustained at the point of the critical evaluation of biblical texts and traditions. The personally and politically reflected experience of oppression and liberation must become the criterion of "appropriateness" for biblical interpretation.

A hermeneutical understanding that is not only oriented toward an actualizing continuation of biblical history, but also toward a critical evaluation of it, must uncover and denounce biblical traditions and theologies that perpetuate violence, alienation, and oppression. At the same time, such a critical hermeneutics also must delineate those biblical traditions that bring forward the liberating experiences and visions of the people of God. Such a hermeneutics points to the eschatological vision of freedom and salvation, and maintains that such a vision must be historically realized in the community of faith.

The "advocacy stance" demands that oppressive and destructive biblical traditions cannot be accorded any truth and authority claim today.[37] Nor did they have such a claim at any point in history. Such a critical hermeneutic must be applied to *all* biblical texts and their historical contexts. It should also be applied to their subsequent history of interpretation in order to determine *how* much these traditions and interpretations have contributed to the patriarchal oppression of women. In the same vein, such a critical feminist hermeneutics must rediscover those biblical traditions and interpretations that have transcended their oppressive cultural contexts even though they are embedded in patriarchal culture. These texts and traditions should not be understood as abstract theological ideas or norms, but as faith-responses to concrete historical situations of oppression. For instance, throughout the centuries Christian feminism has claimed Gal. 3:28 as its magna carta, while the patriarchal church has used 1 Corinthians 14 or 1 Timothy 2 for the cultural and ecclesial oppression of women.[38]

Third: The insight that the Bible is not only a source of truth and revelation but also a source of violence and domination is basic for liberation theologies. This insight demands a new paradigm of biblical interpretation that does not understand the Bible as archetype, but as prototype. "A dictionary definition reveals the significant distinction between the words. While both archetype and prototype 'denote original models,' an archetype is 'usually construed as an ideal form that establishes an unchanging pattern.' . . . However . . . a prototype is not a binding, timeless pattern, but one critically open to the possibility, even the necessity of its own transformation. Thinking in terms of prototypes historicizes myth."[39]

Since the hermeneutic-contextual paradigm has as a goal the appropriation of biblical truth and history, but not its ideological critique, liberation theologians must develop a new critical paradigm of biblical interpretation. T. S. Kuhn has pointed out that such a new scientific paradigm must also create a new scientific ethos and community.

The hermeneutic-contextual historical paradigm allows for the "advocacy stance" within the hermeneutical circle as a presupposition from which to raise questions, but objects to it as a conviction or definite standpoint. However a new critical paradigm must reject such a theory as ideological. It must, in turn, insist that all theologians and interpreters of the Bible stand publicly accountable for their own position. It should become methodologic-ally *mandatory* that *all* scholars explicitly discuss their own presuppositions, allegiances, and functions within a theological-political context, and especially those scholars who, in critiques of liberation theology, resort to an artificially construed value-neutrality.

Scholars no longer can pretend that what they do is completely "detached" from all political interests. Since we always interpret the Bible and Christian faith from a position within history, scholarly detachment and neutrality must be unmasked as a "fiction" or "false consciousness" that serves definite political interests. Further, theological interpretation must also critically reflect on the political presuppositions and implications of theological "classics" and dogmatic or ethical system. In other words, not only the content and traditioning process within the Bible, but the whole of Christian tradition should be scrutinized and judged as to whether or not it functions to oppress or liberate people.

Finally, the "advocacy stance" as a criterion or norm for evaluating biblical texts and their political functions should not be mistaken as an abstract, formalized principle. The different forms of a critical theology of liberation must construct specific heuristic models that adequately analyze the mechanisms and structures of contemporary oppression and movements for liberation. On the one hand, too generalized an understanding of oppression and liberation serves the interests of the oppressive systems that cannot tolerate a critical analysis of their dehumanizing mechanisms and structures. At the same time it prevents the formulation of very specific goals and strategies for the liberation struggle.

On the other hand, too particularized an understanding of oppression and liberation prevents an active solidarity among oppressed groups, who can be played against each other by the established systems. The "advocacy stance" as the criterion or norm for biblical interpretation must, therefore, develop a critical theology of liberation that promotes the solidarity of all oppressed peoples, and at the same time has room enough to develop specific heuristic theological models of oppression and liberation.[40]

Liberation theologians must abandon the hermeneutic-contextual paradigm of biblical interpretation and construct, within the context of a critical theology of liberation, a new interpretative paradigm that has as its aim emancipatory praxis. Such a paradigm of political praxis has, as a research perspective, the critical relationship between theory and practice, between biblical texts and contemporary liberation-movements. This new paradigm of emancipatory praxis must generate new heuristic models of interpretation that can interpret and evaluate biblical traditions and their political function in history in terms of their own canons of liberation.

NOTES

[1] See Adrienne Rich, "Toward a Woman-Centered University," in *Women and the Power to Change*, ed. Florence Howe (New York: McGraw-Hill), 15–46; and my analysis in "Toward a

Liberating and Liberated Theology: Women Theologians and Feminist Theology in the United States," *Concilium* 115 (1979) 22–32.

[2] See, for example, Lisa Leghorn and M. Roodkowsky, *Who Really Starves? Women and World Hunger* (New York: Friendship, 1977); Diane E. Nichole Russel and N. Van de Ven, eds., *Crimes against Women: Processings of the International Tribunal* (Millbrae: Les Femmes, 1976); Susan Hill Lindley, "Feminist Theology in a Global Perspective," *Christian Century* 96 (April 25, 1979): 465–69.

[3] See, for instance, Gustavo Gutiérrez, *A Theology of Liberation* (Maryknoll: Orbis, 1973), 204–5: "A spirituality of liberation will center on a *conversion* to the neighbor, the oppressed person, the exploited social class, the despised race, the dominated country. Our conversion to the Lord implies this conversion to the neighbor." Compare the description of feminist conversion by Judith Plaskow, *Sex, Sin, and Grace: Women's Experience and the Theologies of Reinhold Niebuhr and Paul Tillich* (Washington, DC: University Press of America, 1980), 171–72: "The woman who, having seen the non-being of social structures, feels herself a whole person, is called upon to become the person she is in that movement. . . . The experience of grace is not the experience of the sole activity of God, but the experience of the emergence of the 'I' as cocreator. . . . Relatedness to God is expressed through the never-ending journey toward self-creation within community, and through the creation of ever wider communities, including both other human beings and the world."

[4] Robert McAfee Brown, *Theology in a New Key: Responding to Liberation Themes* (Philadelphia: Westminster, 1978), 82.

[5] Vine Deloria, "A Native American Perspective on Liberation," in *Mission Trends 4: Liberation Theologies*, ed. Gerald H. Anderson and Thomas F. Stransky (New York: Paulist, 1979), 261–70.

[6] See my article, "Women in Early Christianity: Methodological Considerations," in *Critical History and Biblical Faith in New Testament Perspectives*, ed. T. J. Ryan (Villanova: Catholic Theology Society Annual Publications, 1979), 30–58.

[7] See my article, "For the Sake of Our Salvation . . . Biblical Interpretation as The*logical Task," in *Sin, Salvation, and the Spirit*, ed. Daniel Durken (Collegeville: Liturgical, 1979), 21–39, for a more extensive discussion of the literature.

[8] See Lee Cormie, "The Hermeneutical Privilege of the Oppressed: Liberation Theologies, Biblical Faith, and Marxist Sociology of Knowledge," *Proceedings of the Catholic Theological Society of America* 32 (1977); D. Lockhead, "Hermeneutics and Ideology," *Ecumenist* 15 (1977): 81–84.

[9] Schubert M. Ogden, *Faith and Freedom: Toward a Theology of Liberation* (Nashville: Abingdon, 1979), 116.

[10] Ibid., 32.

[11] James H. Cone, *God of the Oppressed* (New York: Seabury, 1975), 51–52.

[12] See Charles H. Strain, "Ideology and Alienation: Theses on the Interpretation and Evaluation of Theologies of Liberation," *JAAR* 45 (1977): 474.

[13] See T. Peters, "The Nature and Role of Presupposition: An Inquiry into Contemporary Hermeneutics," *International Philosophical Quarterly* 14 (1974): 209–22; Frederick Herzog, "Liberation Hermeneutic as Ideology Critique," *Interpretation* 27 (1974): 387–403.

[14] Edward Schillebeeckx, *The Understanding of Faith* (New York: Seabury, 1974), 130.

[15] See especially Peter Stuhlmacher, *Historical Criticism and Theological Interpretation of Scripture: Toward a Hermeneutics of Consent* (Philadelphia: Fortress Press, 1977), 83.

[16] For these criteria, see Ogden, *Faith and Freedom*, 26, and especially David Tracy, *Blessed Rage for Order: The New Pluralism in Theology* (New York: Seabury, 1975), 72–79.

[17] This whole section is based on an analysis of Juan Luis Segundo, *The Liberation of Theology* (Maryknoll: Orbis, 1976).

[18] Ibid., 9; see also José Míguez Bonino, *Doing Theology in a Revolutionary Situation* (Philadelphia: Fortress Press, 1975), 86–105, who accepts Professor Casalis's reformulation of the "hermeneutical circle" as "hermeneutical circulation" (102).

[19] Segundo, *The Liberation of Theology*, 8.

[20] Ibid., 110.

[21] Ibid., 179.

[22] See my article, "Feminist Spirituality, Christian Identity and the Catholic Vision," in *Womanspirit Rising: A Feminist Reader in Religion*, ed. Carol Christ and Judith Plaskow (New York: Harper and Row, 1979), 136–48.

[23] Elizabeth Cady Stanton, *The Woman's Bible*, American Women Series: Images and Realities, 2 vol.; reprint of 1895 ed. (New York: Arno).

[24] Barbara Welter, "Something Remains to Dare: Introduction to the Woman's Bible," in *The Original Feminist Attack on the Bible (The Woman's Bible)*, E. Cady Stanton, facsimile ed. (New York: Arno, 1974), xxii.

[25] Cady Stanton, *The Woman's Bible*, I:9.

[26] Ibid., II:7.

[27] Ibid., I:12.

[28] See, however, Marie Fortune and Joann Haugerud, *Study Guide to the Woman's Bible* (Seattle: Coalition Task Force on Women and Religion, 1975) for a contemporary application; and Leonard Swidler, *Biblical Affirmations of Woman* (Philadelphia: Westminster, 1979), who basically follows the same principle.

[29] Cited in Cady Stanton, *The Woman's Bible*, II:200.

[30] Gustavo Gutiérrez, "Where Hunger Is, God Is Not," *The Witness* 59 (April 1976): 6.

[31] For the conceptualization of feminist the*logy as such a critical the*logy of liberation, see my article, "Feminist Theology as a Critical Theology of Liberation," in *Woman: New Dimensions*, ed. Walter Burkhardt (New York: Paulist, 1977), 19–50.

[32] See the pathbreaking article of Francis Schüssler Fiorenza, "Critical Social Theology and Christology: Toward an Understanding of Atonement and Redemption as Emancipatory Solidarity," *Proceedings of the Catholic Theological Society of America* 30 (1975): 63–110.

[33] Ogden, *Faith and Freedom*, 44, and his article, "The Authority of Scripture for Theology," *Interpretation* 30 (1976): 242–61.

[34] For this expression, see David Tracy, "Theological Classics in Contemporary Theology," *Theology Digest* 25 (1977): 347–55.

[35] James H. Cone, *Liberation: A Black Theology of Liberation* (Philadelphia: Lippincott, 1970), 80.

[36] Jon Sobrino, "The Historical Jesus and the Christ of Faith," *Cross Currents* 27 (1977/78): 460.

[37] Such a proposal should not be misunderstood in the sense of the *Woman's Bible* approach that has singled out for discussion biblical texts on women. The criterion has to be applied to all biblical texts insofar as they claim authority for today. Such a the*logical evaluation must also be distinguished from a reconstruction of early Christian history in a feminist perspective. While a feminist reconstruction of early Christian history asks for women's history and heritage, a feminist biblical hermeneutics evaluates the truth-claims of biblical texts for today. Thus both approaches are interdependent but quite distinct.

[38] See my analysis in "Word, Spirit, and Power," in *Women of Spirit*.

[39] Rachel Blau DuPlessis, "The Critique of Consciousness and Myth in Levertov, Rich, and Rukeyser," *Feminist Studies* 3 (1975): 219.

[40] Rosemary Radford Ruether, *New Woman/New Earth: Sexist Ideologies and Human Liberation* (New York: Seabury, 1975), 115–32, has called for an "interstructuring" of various models of alienation/liberation.

3

Feminist Interpretation and New Testament Studies

In reconstructing the past, exegetes and theologians construct the world. What we live in is not an objectified reality but an intellectual universe that we create socially and imaginatively. Our ideas, values, social institutions, belief-systems, and theological convictions together produce a sense of life and reality, a perception of the way things are. To anyone living in a total cultural and ideological matrix, this matrix appears reality-like and objective. But reality is something we construe in the context of the social conditions in which we live. The reconstruction of history and the interpretation of texts depend to a large extent on our sense of our historical selves and our perception of our contemporary world, and vice versa. Oppressed people do not have a written history. They remain invisible in the reality-construction of those in power.

The feminist movement as an agent for cultural and societal change has not only engendered Women's Studies as an academic discipline as well as a wide range of feminist theory in all areas of scholarship,[1] but it has also influenced women in the churches and in theology. Most importantly, it has shattered our unreflected assumption that the universe is androcentric-male centered. For the Western understanding and linguistic expression of reality, male existence has become the paradigm of human existence and humanity. As Simone de Beauvoir has elucidated, man is the historical subject, the absolute; woman is the "other" defined in relationship to man. Our linguistic and scientific structures define women as secondary to men and therefore as not significant in the making of human culture, religion, and history. This androcentric perception of being human in the world has determined the reality constructions and scholarly interpretations not only of men but also of women. In such an androcentric worldview women are historically and culturally marginal. Feminist scholars have challenged this widely accepted and almost "common sense" androcentric perception of reality and history in order to arrive at a more adequately human scholarly interpretation and construction of the world.

Feminist theologians have developed different approaches to the interpretation of religion in general and of the Bible in particular. This panel presents a variety of such approaches and methods. I myself have sought to develop feminist theology as a critical theology of liberation that shares the critical impulses of historical-critical scholarship, on the one hand, and the theological goals of liberation theologies on the other hand. It challenges not only the androcentric reality construction in language but seeks to move from androcentric texts to patriarchal-historical contexts. Whereas androcentrism characterizes a "mind-set," patriarchy represents a sociocultural system in which a few men have power over other men, women, children, slaves, and colonized people. Feminist theology as a critical theology of liberation, therefore, seeks to develop not only a textual-biblical hermeneutics but also a historical-biblical hermeneutics of liberation. Fundamentally, it challenges textual interpretations and historical reconstructions, especially in the following areas.

Scholarly Pre-Understandings and Frameworks

Feminist theology as a critical theology of liberation challenges the scholarly pretense of value-neutrality and objectivity as well as its androcentric perspectives and theoretical frameworks. The basic methodological insight of liberation theologies is the recognition that all theological interpretation and historical scholarship is engaged for or against marginal and oppressed people. Intellectual neutrality is not possible in a historical world of oppression. Feminist theology shares this perspective of liberation theology insofar as it challenges the assumption of women's cultural marginality and religious subordination.

Feminist theologians therefore have challenged their colleagues to reflect critically also on their own unconscious assumptions and institutional interests within the academy or the church. All interpreters and theologians of the Bible must stand publicly accountable for the hermeneutical presuppositions and "political functions" of their own scholarship. It is methodologically mandatory that all scholars explicitly discuss their own presuppositions, allegiances, and functions, and especially those who in critique of feminist theology resort to the value-neutrality of historical-critical scholarship. Since we always interpret the Bible from a position within history, scholarly detachment and objectivist historicism is unmasked as a unconscious "fiction" or a "false consciousness."

Scholarly objections to the intellectual engagement of feminist theology and historiography overlook the fact that interpretations and reconstructions of the past are always already defined by contemporary questions and horizons. The interest in assessment and legitimization as well as in the opening up of the future is always also a major motif in the interpretation of the New Testament and the reconstruction of early Christian history. As James Robinson writes: "New Testament scholarship as an intellectual activity is a modern science reflecting as well as molding the modern understanding of reality. . . . Every scholar or scientist who deals with a subject matter from the past does so in terms of his present grasp of reality and the results of his research in turn flow into the current body of knowledge from which the continual modification of our understanding of reality emerges."[2]

If this assessment of New Testament scholarship is correct—and I believe it is—then one must ask whether the resistance of established scholars to a feminist biblical interpretation is more rooted in the refusal to modify our present view of reality rather than in the legitimate concern for the integrity of biblical interpretation. Scholars assume—because of their own androcentric worldview and theology of the church—that the "early church" was a "man's church" and that women were marginal in it. They, therefore, cannot do justice to the sources that speak of the leadership of women in early Christianity. Moreover, because of their androcentric model of reality, scholars understand the biblical injunctions for women's subordination as descriptive and not as prescriptive attempts to reestablish patriarchal reality.

Since historical knowledge is inferential (Collingwood), exegetes and historians have to construct some frame of reference or theoretical model in the context of which they discuss the available textual or historical evidence.[3] Because of the unquestioned assumption of androcentrism, scholars understand the early church as a genuine segment of its patriarchal culture in which women were insignificant. Therefore the role of women in early Christian beginnings and texts is also considered to be trivial or marginal to the academic interpretation of the Bible and the reconstruction of early Christian history. Seen as a "women's issue," the problem can be raised in articles or panel discussions on "women," but it does not affect the overall theoretical framework of New Testament interpretation or early Christian historiography. Anyone identified with the "feminist cause" is ideologically suspect and professionally discredited, while scholars who do not articulate their theoretical pre-understandings and political allegiances are "objective" exegetes—free from bias, non-partisan, and absolutely scientific.

The debate between a feminist critical hermeneutics of liberation and mainline androcentric biblical scholarship indicates a shift in interpretative paradigms. The academic field of Women's Studies not only seeks to make "women's agency" a key interpretative category but also to transform androcentric scholarship and knowledge into truly human scholarship and knowledge. The shift from an androcentric to a feminist interpretation of the world and of religion therefore is, in the words of T. S. Kuhn, "a shift in scientific paradigms"[4] that has far-reaching ramifications not only for the interpretation of human history but also for that of biblical texts and history.

Since paradigms determine how scholars see reality and how we conceive of theoretical problems, the shift from an androcentric to a feminist paradigm implies the transformation of the scientific imagination. Such an "intellectual conversion" engenders a shift in perspective and intellectual commitment that allows us to see old "data" and texts in a new light. The "woman's issue" is no longer a marginal topic unworthy of much exegetical or historical attention, but instead it challenges our perception of Christian reality today and in the first centuries.

Androcentric Texts and Translations

The issue of masculine-biased language has received much attention in the last years, as Professor Sakenfeld has pointed out. While I agree completely with her elaborations, I should like to point to another aspect of androcentric language that is not just important for contemporary translations and God-language but has hitherto unexplored ramifications for our understanding of biblical texts and sources. A historically adequate translation has to take into account the interpretative implications of androcentric language that functions as "inclusive" language in a patriarchal culture. Such androcentric "inclusive" language mentions women only and when their presence has become in any way a problem or when they are "exceptional," but it does not mention women in a so-called "normal" situation. For instance, even today the minutes of an exegetical conference will still read, "professor so and so . . . and he said," although women scholars might have been present at the conference. Only if a woman is exceptional or makes a presentation might the minutes identify her as a woman. Moreover, before the issue of androcentric language was made conscious, even women scholars referred to themselves with the pronoun "he." In other words, androcentric language is inclusive of women but does not mention them explicitly. Such androcentric inclusive language functions in the same way in biblical texts as today; it mentions women only when a problem existed or when they are exceptional individuals.

Scholars understand and interpret such androcentric language in a twofold way: as generic and as gender specific. Although many exegetes would refuse to translate the Pauline address "brothers" with "brothers and sisters," they nevertheless assume that the Christian communities to which Paul writes consisted of "brothers and sisters." Since they do not usually claim that early Christianity was a male cult like the Mithras-cult, exegetes understand grammatically masculine terms such as "elect, saints, brother, sons" as generic language designating men and women. They do not apply to male Christians only, designating them over and against female Christians, but they apply to all members of the Christian community. Grammatically masculine language with respect to community membership is not understood in a gender-specific but in an "inclusive," generic way. However, whenever scholars discuss leadership titles—as, for example, apostles, prophets, or teachers—they *eo ipso* assume that these terms apply to men only, although we have clear instances in the New Testament where such grammatically masculine titles as a matter of fact are applied to women also. For example, Rom. 16:1 characterizes Phoebe with the grammatically masculine form of the Greek term *diakonos* and Titus 2:3 applies the grammatically masculine title *kalodidaskalos* to women.

If exegetes seriously took into account the issue of androcentric language as generic language, then they would maintain that any interpretation and translation claiming to be historically adequate to the language character of its sources must understand, and they would translate, New Testament androcentric language on the whole as inclusive of women until proven otherwise. The passages of the New Testament that directly mention women do so because they were exceptional women or because their actions had become a problem. These texts cannot be taken as providing all the available information on women in early Christianity. We no longer can simply assume, for instance, that only 1 Corinthians 11:2-16 speaks about women prophets whereas the rest of chapters 11–14 refers to male charismatics and to male prophets. The opposite is the case: 1 Corinthians 11–14 speaks about the worship of all Christians, men and women, and singles out women only because their behavior constituted a special problem for Paul. Thus, a historically adequate translation and interpretation must not take just the inclusiveness of androcentric language into account but also must acknowledge the limitations of the topical approach to "women in the New Testament."

ANDROCENTRIC SOURCES AND TRADITIONS

One could reject such a methodological analysis and argue that the historical marginality of women is not created simply by contemporary exegesis or the silence of androcentric texts but by the fact that women were marginal in the discipleship of Jesus and in the earliest Christian churches. Jesus was a man, the apostles were men, the twelve were men, and early Christian prophets, teachers, and missionaries were men. According to church tradition, all New Testament writings were written by men and express early Christian male experience. Women seemed not to have any significance in the early church; they were not allowed any leadership or teaching functions. The Christian marginality of women has its historical roots in the patriarchal beginnings of the church and in the androcentrism of Christian revelation.

Feminist theology, however, as a critical theology of liberation here challenges historical-critical scholarship to take its own critical insights and methods more seriously in reconstructing early Christian beginnings. Form-, source-, and redaction criticism have shown, for instance, that early Christian writings are not at all objectivistic, factual reports or descriptive transcripts but are pastorally and theologically engaged writings. Early Christian writers have selected, redacted, and reformulated their traditions and sources according to their own theological-pastoral intentions and objectives. None of the early Christian writings is free from "theological tendencies." All early Christian writings, even the Gospels and Acts, intend to speak to actual problems and situations of early Christian communities and individuals.

We must maintain that these critical insights, engendered by the historical methods of biblical interpretation, apply equally to traditions and sources on "women" in the discipleship of Jesus and in the earliest churches. We have to distinguish methodologically, therefore, between early Christian countercultural beginnings and the gradual adaption of the early Christian movement to its patriarchal culture that is reflected in androcentric traditions and texts. Such a methodological distinction can still be made because the New Testament does not only transmit stories or injunctions reflective of its patriarchal culture and religion but also texts that are critical of such patriarchal structures. Studies of the social world of early Christianity have indicated that early Christian community and life did not from its very beginnings conform to the patriarchal religion and culture of the Jewish or Greco-Roman world.

Studies of the Jesus-movement in Palestine and the early Christian missionary movement in the Greco-Roman cities have elucidated that the earliest Christian communities were, sociologically speaking, a culturally and religiously deviant group similar to other sectarian groups in Judaism or the Greco-Roman world.[5] The circle of Jesus' followers did not belong to the Jewish political or religious establishment. They were a group of outsiders who did not accept their own patriarchal cultic institutions and values but stood in opposition to them. Jesus and his disciples did not live an ascetic life-style as John the Baptist and his group did. They rejected the purity laws and attracted those who for various reasons were ostracised from their religious community. In distinction to the Qumran or Pharisaic communities, the Jesus-movement was not an exclusive group but was an inclusive one. Jesus invited into his discipleship the outcasts and those who did not belong: tax collectors, sinners, cripples, and women. He promised God's empire not to the rich, the pious or the learned but to the poor, the destitute, and the prostitutes. This inclusive character of the Jesus-movement allowed women to become disciples as well as leading members of the missionary churches.

Paul's letters indicate that women like Prisca, Mary, Tryphena, Tryphosa, Persis, Euodia, or Syntychē were missionary coworkers before or with Paul.[6] There is no indication that they were dependent on Paul or subordinated to him. The Pauline letters apply the missionary leadership-titles—for example, colaborer, *diakonos*, brother/sister, and apostle—to women as well as men. Women had an important role, moreover, in the founding, sustaining, and leading of house-churches. Since the house-churches were the place where the Christian community gathered, preached the gospel, and celebrated the Lord's Supper, we must assume that women as leaders of house-churches also presided at the worship gatherings of the community. Paul takes it for granted that women were praying in the assembly and speaking as prophets, glossolalists, or charismatics in the congregation. According to Rom. 16:1, Phoebe was such an official minister and leader of the whole church at Cenchreae and well deserved the respect of the Christian communities. Even at the end of the first century a woman was the head of a prophetic group or school in Thyatira. The author of Revelation attacks her for her teachings but not for being a woman prophet. In the second and third centuries Christians were still slandered for basing their faith on the words of women and being ruled by women.

Such leadership by women in the earliest Christian churches is rooted in their theological understanding of baptism and community, as is referred to in Galatians 3:28. This pre-Pauline baptismal formula[7] expresses the self-understanding of the newly initiated over and against the societal-religious stratifications commonplace in the Greco-Roman world. Like other religions from the East, especially Judaism and the cult of Isis, the early Christians accepted socially powerless people like slaves and women as full members into their religion. Like these religious groups, Christians had to face accusations that they upset the Roman social order by breaking up the patriarchal household. Whenever Christians made converts, especially among slaves and wealthy women, they could be accused of corrupting the Greco-Roman patriarchal structures and thus undermining the social-patriarchal order.[8] Because of the economic independence of wealthy women, their conversion implied an even greater threat.

Since Christians were named after one who was executed for insurrection by the Romans, their situation was politically even more precarious. This situation produced a missionary-apologetic tendency that is already found in the Pauline letters. It also can be found in the redactional attempts of the Gospels to downplay Roman responsibility for the execution of Jesus. Such political apologetics also sought, on the one hand, to adapt the Christian community to the patriarchal structures of the Greco-Roman world and, on the other, to downplay women's role in the beginnings of Christianity. The "household-code-trajectory" indicates that the gradual patriarchalization of the household engendered the gradual patriarchalization of ecclesial church structures. The Pastoral Epistles not only forbid women to have authority over men but also assert that the bishop is capable of presiding over the church as the household of God only if he has proven himself to be an excellent *pater familias.* Yet the injunctions of the Pastoral Epistles are not descriptive but prescriptive, arguing against a different practice in the churches of Asia Minor.

It is therefore important to note that the redaction and composition of the Gospels and of Acts happened at a time when this patriarchalization process was well underway. Since for various reasons the New Testament authors were not interested in extolling women's and slaves' participation and leadership in the early Christian movement, we can assume that they transmit only a fraction of the possibly rich traditions of women's contributions to the early Christian movement. Many of the data and traditions about the activity of women in the beginnings of Christianity are irretrievable because the patriarchal transmission and redaction process considered these stories and materials either as insignificant or as a threat to the gradual patriarchalization of the Christian movement. A study of the redactional tendencies of the Lukan work, for example, could easily show how such a gradual androcentric redaction took place.[9] Moreover, the inconsistencies between different New Testament writings indicate also such an androcentric transmission and redaction of early Christian materials on women. Therefore most of women's early Christian heritage is probably lost and has to be sifted out from androcentric early Christian records. Finally, since the Gospels were written at a time when other New Testament authors clearly attempted to adapt the role of women within the Christian community to that of patriarchal society and religion, it is the more remarkable that not one story or statement is transmitted in which Jesus demanded the cultural patriarchal adaptation and submission of women.

PATRIARCHAL CANONIZATION AND CENSURE

While the androcentric transmission and redaction of early Christian traditions can be partly attributed to an early Christian cultural-political apologetics, the canonization of early Christian writings takes place at a time when different parts of the church are engaged in a bitter struggle against women's leadership engendered by the gradual patriarchalization of the church. The textual and historical marginalization of women is also a by-product of the "patristic" selection and canonization process of Scripture. Hence, feminist studies in religion challenge the patristic interpretative model that identifies heresy with women's leadership and orthodoxy with patriarchal church structures.

The classic understanding of heresy presupposes the temporal priority of orthodoxy. According to Origen all heretics were first orthodox but then erred from the true faith. Heresy is, then, not only a freely chosen defection but also an intended mutilation of the true faith. Jesus founded the church and gave his revelation to his apostles who in turn proclaimed his teachings to the whole world. The Orthodox Church preserves the continuity of revelation with Jesus Christ and establishes this continuity by maintaining the apostolic succession. All early Christian groups shared this understanding of early Christian beginnings and the importance of unbroken continuity with it.[10] They sought to demonstrate that their own form of being Christian was in apostolic continuity with Jesus and the first disciples. Montanism, gnostic groups of various persuasions, and "patristic" groups claimed apostolic tradition and succession in order to legitimate their own authenticity. Both parties, the advocates as well as the opponents of the ecclesial leadership and ordination of women, claimed apostolic origin and succession for such a leadership.[11] Since the process of scriptural canonization occurred at the same time, it also was affected by the polemics and struggles concerning the leadership of women in the church.

The acid polemic of the so-called Fathers against the ecclesial leadership of women, against their teaching and their writing of books, indicates that the patriarchalization of church structures still was not yet accomplished in the second and third centuries. It also documents that the progressive patriarchalization of church office did not happen without opposition but had to overcome an early Christian theology and tradition that acknowledged women's leadership claims. We owe to this polemic the few surviving bits of information about women's role in various Christian groups of the early church. They do not give us historically adequate and theologically appropriate information but as the outcome of bitter polemic, they indicate the theological-patriarchal climate in which early Christian writings were selected and became "Holy Scripture." We have, therefore, to broaden the sources and information that we use as a historical and theological basis for the reconstruction of early Christian beginnings and for formulating the meaning of being church. Early Christian history and theology has to become ecumenical, that is, inclusive of all Christian groups. All early Christian groups and texts have to be tested as to how much they preserve and transmit the apostolic inclusivity and equality of early Christian beginnings and revelation.

The canonization process of early Christian writings has not only preserved the patriarchalizing texts of the New Testament but also those earliest Christian traditions and texts that still allow us a glimpse of the egalitarian-inclusive practice and theology of the early Christians. These texts are like the tip of an iceberg, indicating a possibly rich heritage that we have lost but can still glimpse. Thus, we have to stop interpreting the women's passages in the New Testament in isolation from their historical-ecclesial-social context. What is necessary is a systemic interpretation and historical reconstruction that can make the submerged rest of the iceberg "visible." Moreover it becomes necessary to understand not just the canonical texts but also their subsequent history of interpretation and ecclesial praxis. While the so-called patriarchalizing texts always are used to bolster a patriarchal system and the subordination of women in church or society, the so-called egalitarian texts of the New Testament throughout the centuries have sparked a non-patriarchal Christian vision and praxis.

Scriptural Authority and Feminist Hermeneutics

The historical-theological insight that the New Testament is not only a source of revelatory truth but also a resource for patriarchal subordination and domination demands a new paradigm of biblical hermeneutics and theology.[12] This paradigm not only has to shed its historicist pretense of disinterestedness but also its doctrinal essence-accidence interpretative model. Patriarchal oppressive texts on the one hand and non-androcentric liberative texts on the other hand cannot be separated according to the interpretative model of timeless revelatory essence and historical-cultural accidence. There is no theological essence of revelation that could be once and for all distilled from its culturally conditioned and patriarchally tinged language. All early Christian texts are formulated in an androcentric language and conditioned by their patriarchal milieus and history. Biblical revelation and truth are not found in an ahistorical essence that could be construed as an Archimedean point in the sea of cultural pluriformity, but are given only in those texts and interpretative models that transcend their patriarchal frameworks and allow for a vision of Christian women as historical and theological subjects and actors.

A feminist theological hermeneutics of the Bible that has as its canon the liberation of women from oppressive sexist texts, structures, institutions, and internalized male values maintains that solely those traditions and texts of the Bible that transcend their patriarchal culture and time have the theological authority of revelation if the Bible should not continue to be a tool for the patriarchal oppression of women. The "advocacy stance" of liberation theologies cannot accord any revelatory authority claim to any oppressive and destructive biblical text or tradition. Nor did they have any such claim at any point in history. Such a critical measure must be applied to all biblical texts, their historical contexts, and theological interpretations and not just to biblical texts on women.

This measure should also be applied to the subsequent history of interpretation in order to determine *how much* and *why* these traditions and interpretations have contributed to the patriarchal deformation of Christian faith and community as well as to the oppression of women and all other subjected people. In the same vein, such a critical feminist hermeneutics needs to test how much some biblical traditions have transcended their cultural patriarchal context and contributed to the liberation of people, especially women, although these texts and traditions were embedded in a patriarchal culture and preached by a patriarchal church. These texts of the New Testament, however, should not be misunderstood as abstract, timeless theological ideas or norms but as faith-responses to concrete historical situations.

Feminist theology, therefore, challenges biblical theological scholarship to develop a paradigm of biblical hermeneutics that does not understand the

New Testament as an archetype but as a prototype. Both archetype and prototype, according to the dictionary definition, denote original models. However, an archetype is an ideal form that establishes an unchanging timeless pattern, whereas a prototype is not a binding timeless pattern or principle. A prototype is thus critically open to the possibility of its own transformation. "Thinking in terms of prototype historicizes myth."[13] A hermeneutical understanding of Scripture as prototype has not only room for but requires the transformation of its own models of Christian faith and community. It demands a critical exploration of the historical-social-theological dynamics operative in the formulation and canonization of the New Testament as Scripture, as well as an integration of biblical history and theology.

A feminist critical hermeneutics of the Bible seeks to develop theoretical interpretative models that can integrate the so-called countercultural, heretical, and egalitarian traditions and texts into its overall reconstruction of scriptural theology and history. Although the canon preserves only a few remnants of the nonpatriarchal early Christian ethos, these remnants allow us still to recognize that the patriarchalization process is not inherent in Christian revelation and community but progressed only slowly and with difficulty. A feminist biblical hermeneutics then reclaims early Christan theology and history as our own theology and history. Women had the power and authority of the Gospel. They were central in the early Christian movement. The church is built on women prophets and apostles.

Such a feminist critical hermeneutics of liberation carefully analyzes the theological and structural patriarchalization of the New Testament and "patristic" churches without too quickly resorting to biblical apologetics or to an ahistorical disinterest. It seeks to become conscious of the interrelationships of ecclesial-cultural patriarchy and theological texts and traditions. It elucidates the fact that a misogynist theology is always engendered by the attempt of the patriarchal church to marginalize women and to displace us as ecclesial and theological subjects.

Women as church have a continuous history and tradition that can claim Jesus and the praxis of the earliest church as its biblical root-model or prototype that is open to feminist transformation. A feminist Christian theology in my opinion has as a primary task to keep alive the *memoria passionis*[14] of Christian women and to reclaim our religious-theological heritage. This theological heritage is misrepresented, however, when it is understood solely as the history of oppression. It also must be reconstituted as a history of liberation. The history and theology of women's oppression perpetuated by patriarchal biblical texts and a clerical patriarchy must be understood for what it is. This history and theology must not be allowed to cancel out the history and theology of the struggle, life, and leadership of Christian women who spoke and acted in the power of the Spirit. In the last analysis the effects of Women's Studies on Biblical Studies depend on whether or not we as women scholars will be able to reclaim intellectually early Christian theology and history as "our own affair."

NOTES

[1] See especially the contributions in *Feminist Studies, Signs: Journal of Women in Culture and Society*, and the international quarterly *Women's Studies*, a multidisciplinary journal for the rapid publication of research communications and review articles in *Women's Studies*.

[2] James M. Robinson and Helmut Köster, *Trajectories through Early Christianity* (Philadelphia: Fortress Press, 1971).

[3] See, for example, G. Leff, *History and Social Theory* (New York: Doubleday, 1971); N. Brox "Fragen zur 'Denkform der Kirchengeschichtswissenschaft,"' *ZKG* 90 (1979): 1–21.

[4] T. S. Kuhn, *The Structure of Scientific Revolutions* (Chicago: Chicago University Press, 1971).

[5] See the reviews of works on the social world of early Christianity by W. A. Meeks in *CSR* Bulletin 6 (1975); J. G. Gager in *GSR* 5 (1979): 174–79; D. J. Harrington, "Sociological Concepts and the Early Church: A Decade of Research," *Theological Studies* 41 (1980): 181–90; and especially Gerd Theissen's work and its critical review by W. Stegemann, "Wanderradikalismus im Urchristentum? Historische und theologische Auseinandersetzung mit einer interessanten These," in W. Schottroff, *Der Gott der kleinen Leute* (München: Kaiser, 1979): 94–120.

[6] See my article "Women in the Pre-Pauline and Pauline Churches," *USQR* 33 (1978): 153–66, for a more extensive discussion of the literature.

[7] See especially H. D. Betz, *Galatians*, Hermeneia (Philadelphia: Fortress Press, 1980), 180–20, for an extensive discussion of the literature on the passage.

[8] For such an interpretation and documentation, see D. Balch, *Let Wives be Submissive* (Ann Arbor: University Microfilm, 1974).

[9] See my article "Apostleship of Women in Early Christianity," in L. and A. Swidler, eds., *Women Priests* (New York: Paulist, 1976), 114–22, 135–40.

[10] See W. Bauer, *Orthodoxy and Heresy in Earliest Christianity* (Philadelphia: Fortress Press, 1971); Jaroslav Pelikan, *The Emergence of the Catholic Tradition* (Chicago: Chicago University Press, 1971).

[11] See now also Elaine Pagels, *The Gnostic Gospels* (New York: Random, 1979), who, however, seems to reverse the the*logical judgment of heresy, without also critically discussing Gnosticism.

[12] See my contributions, "For the Sake of Our Salvation . . . Biblical Interpretation as Theological Task," in D. Durken, ed., *Sin, Salvation, and the Spirit* (Collegeville: Liturgical, 1979), 21–39; and "Toward a Feminist Biblical Hermeneutics: Biblical Interpretation and Liberation Theology," see chapter 2.

[13] R. Blau duBlessis, "The Critique of Consciousness and Myth in Levertov, Rich, and Rukeyser," *Feminist Studies* 3 (1975): 219.

[14] For such a theological conceptuality, see Johann B. Metz, *Faith in History and Society* (New York: Seabury, 1980), 100–18.

4

For the Sake of the Truth Dwelling among Us

Emerging Issues in Feminist Biblical Interpretation

The second letter of John—the only writing of the New Testament addressed to a woman—was written "for the sake of the truth that dwells among us and will be with us forever." Biblical interpretation as theological interpretation is concerned with the divine presence dwelling among the people of God in the past and in the present. Feminist Christian biblical interpretation makes explicit that such divine truth and revelatory presence is also found among women who are the "invisible" part of the people of God. It makes explicit that the receivers and proclaimers of such revelation are not solely men but also women. It thus seeks to interrupt the theological silence and ecclesial invisibility of women so that God's grace and truth may reveal itself among us in its fullness.

The critical rereading of the Bible in a feminist key and from women's perspectives is uncovering lost traditions and correcting mistranslations, peeling away layers of androcentric scholarship, and rediscovering new dimensions of biblical symbols and theological meanings. In Bible study groups, sermons, and seminars, women are rediscovering our biblical heritage, realizing that this heritage is part of our power today. Feminist scholars seek to explore systematically the theological questions and hermeneutical issues raised by women in biblical religion. Such a rediscovery of women's biblical heritage on a popular and academic level is made possible by two basic shifts in how we see the world and reality and in how we see the function of biblical texts and interpretations. Such paradigm shifts are, on the one hand, the shift from an androcentric to a feminist perception of the world and, on the other hand, the shift from an apologetic focus on biblical authority to a feminist articulation of contemporary women's experience and struggle against patriarchal oppression in biblical religion.

From an Androcentric to a Feminist Interpretive Framework

The resurgence of the women's movement in the sixties revived not just women's political struggle for civil rights and equal access to academic institutions but also brought forth feminist studies as a new intellectual discipline. In all areas of scientific and intellectual knowledge, courses and research projects have developed that seek to expand our knowledge of women's cultural and historical contributions, as well as to challenge the silence about us in historiography, literature, sociology, and all the human sciences. Such feminist scholarship is compensatory as well as revolutionary. It has inaugurated a scientific revolution that engenders a scholarly paradigm shift from an androcentric—male centered—worldview and perspective to an inclusive feminist comprehension of the world, human life, and history.

While androcentric scholarship takes *man* as the paradigmatic human being, feminist scholarship insists on the reconceptualization of our intellectual frameworks in such a way that they become truly inclusive of all human experience and articulate male experience as just one particular experience and perception of reality. Feminist scholarship therefore throws into question our dominant cultural mind-set articulated in male generic language, classical texts, scholarly frameworks, and scientific reconstructions that make invisible and marginalize women. This androcentric mind-set perpetuates the worldview and consciousness that women's experiences and cultural contributions are less valuable, less important, or less significant than men's. Feminist studies challenge male symbolic representations, androcentric language, and the habitual consciousness of two sex classes as a "naturally given" and classificatory fact in our language and thought-world. They point to the interaction between language and society, sexual stereotypes and culture, gender and race, as social constructs and political legitimizations. Sexism, racism, imperialism, and militarism constitute different aspects of the same language of oppression in our society.

However, it must be noted that feminist studies articulate the feminist paradigm in different ways and with the help of varying philosophical perspectives. While liberal scholarship, for example, often seeks to show that women were and are equal to men without critically reflecting on the male-centered framework underlying such an argument, feminists coming from an existentialist or a sociology of knowledge approach use as their main heuristic category androcentrism or phallocentrism. While socialist feminists use as their key analytical category the relationship between social class and gender as determinant of women's condition in society, third world feminists insist on the relationship between racism, colonialism, and sexism as defining women's oppression and struggle for liberation. Such a variety of emphases and approaches results in different conceptions and frameworks of feminism, women's liberation, and of being human in the world.

Such diversity in approach and polyphony in feminist intellectual articulations is also found among feminists in biblical religion and feminist theologians. There exists not one feminist theology or *the* feminist theology but many different expressions and articulations of feminist theology. These articulations share not only in the diverse presuppositions and perspectives of feminist studies, but also work within the frameworks of divergent theological perspectives, such as neoorthodoxy, evangelical theology, liberal theology, liberation theology, process theology, or various confessional theological perspectives. As theological articulations, they are rooted in the ecclesial visions and political situations of the Christian or Jewish communities to whom they are committed.

Yet feminist theologies introduce a radical shift into all forms of traditional theology insofar as they insist that the central commitment and accountability for feminist theologians is not to *the* church as a male institution but to women in the churches, not to *the* tradition as such but to a feminist transformation of Christian traditions, not to *the* Bible on the whole but to the liberating word of God coming to articulation in the biblical writings. Feminist theologians who see our work and ourselves as members of the women's movement in the churches and define our allegiances not just in terms of the women's movement in society and culture, tend to articulate our theology also with respect to the religio-political goals, the spiritual needs, and the communal problems of women in biblical religion. The theological discussions on an inclusive translation of the Bible or on the question of God-language are situated in such a context within organized biblical religion.

Those of us who do not understand ourselves as members of biblical communities, but are committed to the religious quest of women in different cultures and religions, tend to formulate our questions and theological perspectives more in terms of a religious studies approach. In such a history of religions approach, the situation of women in the Bible or in early Christianity is studied as a part of the Oriental or Greco-Roman world and religion to which the biblical writings belong. Such research has had significant results with respect to women in Egypt, Rome, or Judaism and has shattered the apologetic assumption that biblical religion has emancipated ancient women.

Jewish feminists in turn have pointed out that a Jewish feminist biblical interpretation has to wrestle with a different set of theological problems and hermeneutical frameworks than Christian feminist scholarship of the Bible. Not only do Christians claim the New Testament and the Hebrew Bible as their own holy scriptures, but they also often perpetrate the anti-Judaism codified in the New Testament. Moreover, Judaism has developed quite distinct exegetical methods and hermeneutical traditions. The following must thus clearly be understood as written from a feminist Christian theological perspective. I have defined this perspective as a feminist critical theology of liberation. Such articulation of my own feminist theological perspective has grown out of my experience as a Roman Catholic Christian woman and is indebted to historical-critical scholarship, critical theory, and political as well as liberation theologies.

At this point it becomes necessary to explicate my understanding of feminism and of patriarchal oppression. Feminism is not just a theoretical worldview or perspective but a women's liberation movement for societal and ecclesial change. Likewise patriarchal oppression is not identical with androcentrism or sexism. It is not just a "dualistic ideology" or androcentric world-construction in language but a sociopolitical system and societal structure of graded subjugations and oppressions. Although this patriarchal[1] system has undergone significant changes throughout its history, it has prevailed as the dominant sociopolitical structure in the last five thousand years or so. Its classical expression is found in Aristotelian philosophy, which has decisively influenced not only Christian theology but also Western culture and political philosophy.[2]

Patriarchy defines not just women but also subjugated peoples and races as the "other" to be dominated. Moreover, it defines women not just as the "other" of men but also as subordinated to men in power insofar as it conceives of society in analogy to the patriarchal household that was sustained by slave labor. Women of color and poor women are doubly and triply oppressed in such a patriarchal societal system. Therefore a critical feminist theology of liberation does not speak of male oppressors and female oppressed, of all men over and against all women, but about patriarchy as a pyramidal system and hierarchical structure of society and church in which women's oppression is specified not only in terms of race and class but also in terms of marital status. The patriarchal victimization and dehumanization of the "poorest and most despised women on earth"[3] exhibits the full death-dealing powers of patriarchy, while their struggles for liberation and their survival expresses the fullest experience of God's grace and power in our midst. Such a universal understanding of feminist liberation was already articulated by black activist Anna Cooper in 1892:

> Let women claim to be as broad in the concrete as in the abstract.
> We take our stand on the solidarity of humanity, the oneness of
> life, and the unnaturalness and injustice of all special favoritism,
> whether of sex, race, country, or condition. . . . The colored woman
> feels that women's cause is one and universal; and that not till the
> image of God, whether in parian or ebony, is sacred and inviolable;
> not till race, color, sex, and condition are seen as accidents, and not
> the substance of life; not till the universal title of humanity to life,
> liberty, and the pursuit of happiness is conceded to be inalienable
> to all; not till then is woman's cause won—not the white woman's,
> nor the black woman's, nor the red woman's, but the cause of

every man and every woman who has writhed silently under a mighty wrong. Woman's wrongs are thus indissolubly linked with all undefended woe and the acquirement of her "rights" will mean the final triumph of all right over might; the supremacy of the moral forces of reason, and justice, and love in the government of the nations of earth.[4]

A feminist hermeneutic of liberation must remain first and foremost a critical theology of liberation as long as women suffer the injustice and oppression of patriarchal structures. It explores the particular experiences of women struggling for liberation from systemic patriarchy and at the same time indicts all patriarchal structures and texts, especially those of biblical religion. Such a hermeneutic seeks to name theologically the alienation, anger, pain, and dehumanization of women engendered by patriarchal sexism and racism in society and church. At the same time it seeks to articulate an alternative vision of liberation by exploring women's experiences of survival and salvation in their struggle against patriarchal oppression and degradation, as well as by assessing Christian texts, traditions, and communities in terms of such liberation from patriarchal oppression.

Such a critical feminist hermeneutic of liberation does not advocate the co-optation of women's religious powers of interpretation by ecclesiastical patriarchy nor the feminist abandonment of biblical vision and community. Its feminist heuristic key is not a dual theological anthropology of masculine and feminine, nor the concept of the complementarity of the sexes, nor a metaphysical principle of female ascendancy. Its formulations are based on the radical assumption that gender is socially, politically, economically, and theologically constructed, and that such a social construction serves to perpetuate the patriarchal exploitation and oppression of all women that is most fully expressed in the fate of the "poorest and most despised women on earth."

A feminist critical hermeneutic of liberation seeks to enable Christian women to explore theologically the structural sin of patriarchal sexism, in a feminist conversion to reject its spiritual internalizations, and to become in such a conversion the *ekklesia* of women, women-church. In exorcising the internalized structural evil of patriarchal sexism, as well as in calling the whole church to conversion and repentance, Christian feminism and feminist theology reclaim the right and power to articulate our own theology, to reclaim our own spirituality, and to determine our own and our sisters' religious life. As the church of women we celebrate our religious powers and ritualize our visions for change and liberation.

We bond together in struggling with all women for liberation, and we share our strength in nurturing each other in the full awareness and recognition that the church of women is always the ekklēsia *reformanda*, the church on the way in need of conversion and "revolutionary patience" with our own failures as well as with those of our sisters. Concern for reconciliation is pivotal for such a process of becoming "a people of God." We need to listen to each other's experiences, to cease speaking for all women, and to overcome in solidarity and support our guilt reactions.

To advocate as the hermeneutical center of a feminist critical theology of liberation the women's liberation movement in biblical religions—to speak of the "church of women"—does not advocate a separatist strategy but underlines the visibility of women in biblical religion and safeguards our freedom from spiritual male control. Just as we speak of the church of the poor, of an African or Asian church, or Presbyterian, Episcopalian, or Roman Catholic churches without relinquishing our theological vision of the universal catholic Christian church, so it is also justified to speak of the *church of women* as a manifestation of this universal church. Since all Christian churches suffer from the structural evil of patriarchal sexism and racism in various degrees, the Christian feminist movement transcends all traditional "manmade" denominational lines. Its commitment and mission is defined by the solidarity with the most despised women suffering from the triple oppression of sexism, racism, and poverty. A feminist biblical interpretation of the Bible that develops within the framework of a critical theology of liberation must be situated within the feminist community of women in biblical religion.

THE BIBLE AS THE BOOK OF THE *Ekklēsia* OF WOMEN

Taking as our hermeneutical criterion the authority of women's experience struggling for liberation, we must ask whether and how the Bible as the product of a patriarchal culture and expressed in androcentric language can also be the sacred scripture for the church of women. This is a difficult question since the Bible has been used to halt the emancipation of women, slaves, and colonized peoples. Elizabeth Cady Stanton has eloquently summed up this use of the Bible against women's demand for political and ecclesial equality: "From the inauguration of the movement for woman's emancipation the Bible has been used to hold her in the 'divinely ordained sphere' prescribed in the Old and New Testaments. . . . Creeds, codes, Scriptures and statutes are all based on this idea."[5]

Whenever women protest against political discrimination, economic exploitation, sexual violence, or our secondary status in biblical religion, the Bible is invoked against such claims. At the same time the Bible has not only served to justify theologically the oppression of women, slaves, or the poor, but it also has provided authorization for Christian women and men who rejected slavery, poverty, and patriarchal sexism as against God's will.

While in the last century clergymen invoked the Bible in order to bar women from speaking in public and in this century from becoming ordained to the priesthood, women have pointed to other biblical texts and insisted on the right interpretation of the Bible in order to legitimize their claim to public speaking and the ministry. While many feminists reject the Bible as totally oppressive and patriarchal, others have attempted to show that the Bible, correctly interpreted, preaches the emancipation of women. While Christian apologists argue that only feminist ignorance or misunderstanding leads to the rejection of the Bible, Christian biblicists maintain that feminism is a perversion of God's word and godless humanism. While Christian feminists seek for a "usable past," Christian conservatives claim that women can find happiness only by living out the scriptural injunctions to submission.

In this political-religious controversy, the women-passages in scripture are used as proof-texts for justifying one's own political-ecclesial interests. Central to this apologetic debate is the interest in legitimizing one's own position with reference to biblical authority. The detractors as well as the defenders of women's liberation refer to the Bible because of its ecclesial authority and societal influence. The focal point of this political apologetics is the Bible, but not the experience of women insofar as both sides seek to prove or disprove the patriarchal character of certain biblical texts.

However, postbiblical feminists do not challenge just certain passages and statements of the Bible; they reject the Bible as a whole as irredeemable for feminists. Recognizing that androcentric language and patriarchal traditions have erased women from biblical texts and made us "nonbeings" in biblical history, they argue that the Bible is not retrievable for feminists who are committed to women's struggle for liberation. The Bible ignores women's experience, speaks of God in male language, and sustains women's powerlessness in society and church. It legitimizes women's societal and ecclesial subordination and second-class status as well as male dominance and violence against women, especially against those caught in patriarchal marriage relationships. Because of its androcentric-patriarchal character, feminists cannot but reject the authority of the Bible. Revisionist interpretations are at best a waste of time and at worst a co-optation of feminism for patriarchal biblical religion.

Christian apologists as well as postbiblical feminists not only overlook the experiences of women in biblical religion but also assume that the Bible has authority independently of the community to which it belongs. Insofar as this apologetic debate either seeks to salvage or to reject the religious authority of the Bible for women today, it understands the Bible as a mythical archetype rather than as a historical prototype open to feminist theological transformation. As mythical archetype the Bible can only be either accepted or rejected, but not critically evaluated. A mythical archetype takes historically limited experiences and texts and posits them as universals that become authoritative and normative for all times and cultures. For instance, many scriptural texts speak of God as a male, patriarchal, all-powerful ruler. Therefore, it is argued, feminists have to accept the patriarchal male language and God of the Bible, or they have to reject the Bible and leave behind biblical religion.

By giving universal ramifications to specific historical texts and cultural situations, the mythical archetype establishes an ideal form for all times that represents unchanging patterns of behavior and theological structures for the community in which it functions as sacred scripture. The Bible as archaic myth therefore constitutes the enduring order and perspective of biblical religion, reflecting unchangeable ontological patterns and perennial models for human behavior and communal life. Since biblical texts as the Word of God are formulated in androcentric language and are products and reflections of patriarchal cultures, they express a patriarchal system and androcentric worldview valid for all times.

Insofar as the Bible is stamped by patriarchal oppression but claims to be the Word of God, it perpetuates an archetypal oppressive myth that cannot but be rejected by feminists on the one hand and must be maintained over and against feminism by biblical religion on the other hand. However, the archetypal myth of the Bible as the Word of God has been challenged by historical-critical scholarship and has undergone significant modifications in the last centuries. Although biblical and theological scholarship is well aware of the difficulties raised by such an archetypal understanding of the Bible, ecclesiastical authority and popular preaching have not quite accepted the challenge of historical-critical scholarship to the archetypal definition of biblical inspiration.

In the dominant paradigm of biblical interpretation, three hermeneutical models are interrelated, but can be distinguished.

First, the doctrinal model of interpretation centers around the teachings and creeds of the church and refers to the Bible in order to prove and substantiate patriarchal teachings and symbolic structures. For instance, the debate on whether Paul teaches the subordination of women or allows for the full equality of women in the church, and therefore for women's ordination, is situated within the ambience of this doctrinal model. This model subscribes fully to the archetypal understanding of the Bible, especially if it understands it in a literalist way and conceives of biblical revelation as verbal inspiration. Although evangelical feminism modifies this doctrinal model, it seeks to remain within the boundaries set by it in order to remain faithful to biblical revelation.

The *second* model in biblical interpretation could be termed the historical-factual model. It was developed over and against the doctrinal model and often identifies biblical truth and authority with historical or textual facticity. The Bible must be understood as a collection of historical writings that are more or less true, that is, historically reliable. However, the canonical collection of early Christian writings is not comprehensive, and therefore historical-critical scholarship must study all early Christian writings that are still extant today. The truth of biblical religion resides in those traditions and texts that are historically reliable, that is, tell us what actually happened. Biblical authority is understood in terms of historical facticity. If, for instance, scholars can prove that the "empty tomb stories" in the New Testament are secondary legends of the community, then they cannot accord historical reliability and theological significance to the resurrection witness of Mary Magdalene and the women disciples. Or, if Jesus chose only men and not women as his followers, then he established a pattern for all times and women cannot become apostolic successors and be ordained as priests. This model thus establishes the archetypal significance of the Bible through historical verification.

The *third* model of biblical interpretation could be termed the dialogic-pluralistic model of form and redaction criticism that seeks to recover *all* the canonical texts and traditions and to understand them as theological responses to their historically communal situations. The Bible becomes a kaleidoscope mirroring and reflecting the pluralistic and multifaceted life and faith of biblical communities in their historical-cultural circumstances.

However, the Bible contains not only a variety of texts but also many contradictory or even oppressive texts and symbols that cannot all have the same theological authority for communities today. While this dialogic-pluralistic model moves away from the archetypal understanding of the Bible in its historical-critical interpretations, it resorts again to the archetypal paradigm in its theological evaluations and normative claims whenever it seeks to identify God's voice in the polyphony of biblical voices. Acknowledging the pluriform theological character of the canon, it must establish a "canon within the canon," a theological criterion and measuring rod with which to assess the truth and authority of the various biblical texts and traditions. This "measure" is derived from the canon, which is the collection of biblical writings acknowledged by Christians as sacred scriptures. This attempt to define a "canonical" criterion began with Marcion in the second century CE and has become especially important for the dialogic-pluralistic understanding of the Bible.

In response to the factual-historical model, the neoorthodox "canon within the canon" debate attempts to theologically identify those texts and traditions of the Bible that can serve as measuring rods for evaluating the pluralistic collection of canonical writings as to their truth-claims. This neoorthodox model no longer understands the whole Bible as archetypal myth but only those texts and traditions that are judged "canonical," that is, as expressing the Word of God. It identifies such a "canon" either along historical-factual lines (for example, the authentic Jesus-traditions, the *ipsissima verba* of Jesus, or the earliest traditions of the apostolic church), along doctrinal lines (the gospel message; the Pauline doctrine of justification by faith; the creed) or along philosophical lines of argument (for example, revelatory essence and historical accidental statements; timeless truth and culturally conditioned language; universal revelation and historical expression; constant tradition and changing traditions; the liberating impulses of the biblical vision and its oppressive patriarchal articulations).

Such a search for a fixed point of revelation or a normative tradition in the shifting sand of cultural-historical pluralism is also found in feminist theology. For instance, Rosemary Radford Ruether has proposed the distinction between the liberating prophetic critique or biblical religion and its cultural deformations,[6] whereas Letty Russell has reformulated her distinction of Tradition and traditions with reference to the eschatological future of God's liberation: "The Bible has authority because it witnesses to God's liberating action on behalf of God's creation."[7] However, the attempt to derive a universal principle or normative tradition from particular historical texts and specific cultural situations indicates that such a feminist theological hermeneutics still adheres to the archetypal biblical paradigm that establishes universal principles and normative patterns. Since it is impossible for feminist theologians to accept *all* canonical texts and traditions, they must claim that certain texts or traditions are not deformed by androcentrism and patriarchy if they want to reclaim the Bible as normative and authoritative for feminists in biblical religion.

However, such a feminist hermeneutics should take into account more seriously the androcentric character of biblical language, on the one hand, and the patriarchal stamp of all biblical traditions, on the other hand. By distinguishing language and content, patriarchal expression and liberating tradition, androcentric text and feminist "witness," it relies on an untenable linguistic-philosophical position that divides form and content, linguistic expression and revelatory truth. By choosing one tradition, text, or biblical trajectory, it advocates a reductionist method of theological critique that relinquishes the historical richness of biblical experience.

A feminist critical interpretation of the Bible, I would therefore argue, cannot take as its point of departure the normative authority of the biblical archetype, but must begin with women's experience in their struggle for liberation. In doing so it subjects the Bible to a critical feminist scrutiny and to the theological authority of the church of women that seeks to assess the oppressive or liberative dynamics of all biblical texts and their function in the contemporary feminist struggle for liberation. Just as Jesus, according to the gospels, realized freedom toward scripture and tradition for the sake of human well-being and wholeness (Mark 2:27), so also a feminist critical hermeneutics seeks to assess the function of the Bible in terms of women's liberation and wholeness. It follows Augustine, Thomas, and the Second Vatican Council[8] in formulating a criterion or canon that limits inspired truth and revelation to matters pertaining to the salvation, freedom, and liberation of all, especially of women.

However, it derives such a "canon" *not* from the biblical writings but from the contemporary struggle of women against racism, sexism, and poverty as oppressive systems of patriarchy and from its systemic explorations in feminist theory. It can do so because it does not understand the Bible as unchanging archetype but as historical prototype or as formative root-model of biblical faith and life. Its vision of liberation and salvation is informed by the biblical prototype but not derived from it. It places biblical texts under the authority of feminist experience insofar as it maintains that revelation is ongoing and takes place "for the sake of our salvation." It does not seek for identification with certain biblical texts and traditions, but for solidarity with women in biblical religion. As the church of women, we are not called to reproduce biblical structures and traditions, but to remember and transform our biblical heritage.

The understanding of the Bible as a historical prototype rather than as a mythical archetype allows the church of women to make connections with our own experiences, historical struggles, and feminist options in order to create visions for the future out of these interconnections between women's struggle for liberation and biblical religion. It enables us to make choices between oppressive and liberative traditions of the Bible without having to accept or reject it as a whole. In such a process of feminist critical evaluation and assessment, the Bible functions no longer as authoritative source but as a multifaceted resource for women's struggle for liberation. Insofar as the Bible is the formative root-model of Christian life and community, a feminist critical interpretation has to explore *all* dimensions of the biblical text and tradition as well as its contemporary functions in order to assess their structural impact and religious-cultural influence on women today, whether they are members of the church of women or not. Such a feminist paradigm of critical interpretation is not based on a faithful adherence to biblical texts or obedient submission to biblical authority, but on the solidarity with the women of the past and of the present whose lives and struggles are touched by the biblical trajectory in Western culture.

Toward a Feminist Model of Biblical Interpretation

To make the systematically articulated feminist experience of the *ekklēsia* of women central to biblical interpretation and theological reflection requires a paradigm shift in biblical interpretation, a shift from the understanding of the Bible as archetypal myth to its understanding as a historical prototype. In the context of such a paradigm shift, a feminist model of critical interpretation is emerging that is committed to the church of women and women's struggle for liberation. As far as I can see, this interpretive model of a critical feminist theology of liberation is in the process of developing four structural elements constitutive for a feminist biblical interpretation.

Since all biblical texts are formulated in androcentric language and reflect patriarchal societal structures, a feminist critical interpretation begins with a *hermeneutics of suspicion* rather than with a hermeneutics of consent and affirmation. It develops a *hermeneutics of proclamation* rather than a hermeneutics of historical factuality because the Bible still functions as holy scripture in Christian communities today. Rather than reduce the liberating impulse of the Bible to a feminist principle or one feminist biblical tradition, it develops a *hermeneutics of remembrance* that moves from biblical texts about women to the reconstruction of women's history. Finally, a feminist model of critical interpretation moves from a hermeneutics of disinterested distance to a *hermeneutics of creative actualization* that involves the church of women in the imaginative articulation of women's biblical story and its ongoing history and community.

First: A *hermeneutics of suspicion* does not presuppose the feminist authority and truth of the Bible but takes as its starting point the assumption that biblical texts and their interpretations are androcentric and serve patriarchal functions. Since most of the biblical writings are ascribed to male authors and most of the biblical interpreters in church and academy are men, such an assumption is justified. Just as the woman in the parable sweeps the whole house in search of her lost coin, so feminist critical interpretation searches for the lost traditions and visions of liberation among its inheritance of androcentric-biblical texts and their interpretations. In order to unearth a "feminist coin" from the biblical tradition, it critically analyzes contemporary scholarly and popular interpretations, the tendencies of the biblical writers and traditioning processes themselves, and the theoretical models underlying contemporary biblical-historical and theological interpretations.

In the past years feminist scholarship has cleared away many androcentric mistranslations, patriarchal interpretations, and one-sided reconstructions of biblical scholars. Among the "coins" found are the maternal God-language of the Old Testament, which especially Phyllis Trible has rediscovered; women's apostleship and leadership in the early Christian movement, which I have underlined; and the leadership of women in the ancient synagogue, which Bernadette Brooten has retrieved from male scholarly prejudice.[9] Feminist critical scholarship has also pointed to the androcentric tendencies and patriarchal interests of biblical writers and of the canonization process in the so-called patristic period. Such tendencies can be traced in, for example, the different Old Testament references to the prophet Miriam, or in the way Luke plays down the apostleship of women and the writer of the Pastoral Epistles reintroduces a patriarchal model of biblical community, or in the canonical exclusion of traditions of so-called heretical movements.

A feminist hermeneutics of suspicion also questions the underlying presuppositions, androcentric models, and unarticulated interests of contemporary biblical interpretation. Feminist scholarship has questioned the unreflected androcentric worldview and patriarchal interpretive models presupposed by biblical scholarship. The very fact that we study only the statements of biblical writers about women, but not about men, reflects an androcentric theoretical-cultural paradigm that understands man as the paradigmatic human being and woman as the "other," the exception but not the rule. Biblical scholarship thus reproduces the effects of androcentric biblical language that generally subsumes woman under the generic "man" and "he." Because scholars do not recognize the dynamics of this interpretive model of androcentrism, they do not understand that all androcentric language must be understood as generic language until proven otherwise. All androcentric biblical texts must therefore be assumed to speak about men and women unless women and female aspects are explicitly excluded.

Such a hermeneutics of suspicion has therefore far-reaching consequences for the question of biblical translation, which has received much intention in recent years. The mass media have dubbed the search for an inclusive translation of the Bible as the "castration" of the Bible, whereas the political right sees it as one of the gravest aberrations of the National Council of Churches. The emotional reactions to the proposal of inclusive translation indicate the political importance of this issue. Since language shapes our self-understanding and worldview, the problem of inclusive biblical translation is not a trivial issue. If it is true that "the limits of our language are the limits of our world," then androcentric biblical language and its translation becomes a feminist issue of utmost importance. Such language not only marginalizes women but also makes us invisible in the written classics of our culture, among which the Bible is preeminent.

An adequate biblical translation must render androcentric language differently at a time when androcentric language no longer is understood as generic language. Faithfulness to the biblical texts means to translate those texts that are patriarchal with grammatically masculine language, and those texts that are not with grammatically feminine and masculine terms with generic human words. Therefore such a critical translation requires a feminist critical assessment and evaluation of the patriarchal oppressive or generic liberative dynamics of individual texts. A historically adequate translation must not either further patriarchalize biblical generic texts, on the one hand, or veil their patriarchal character and impact in generic language, on the other. Feminist linguists have given us some guidelines for recognizing when language functions in a sexist way: Sexist language creates the linguistic invisibility or marginality of women; it describes women as dependent and as derived from men; it characterizes women in stereotypical roles and images; it ridicules women and trivializes their contributions; it mentions women only when they are the exceptions or present a problem; and it singles them out from the collective—for example, blacks, Jews, third world peoples—as if women did not belong to each of these groups. A hermeneutics of suspicion must test not just the original biblical texts but also contemporary translations as to how much they succumb to linguistic sexism.

Second: While a historically adequate translation of the Bible has to bring to the fore the sexist-patriarchal as well as the feminist inclusive character of biblical texts, a *hermeneutics of proclamation* has to assess its theological significance and power for the contemporary community of faith. Faithfulness to the struggle of women for liberation requires an evaluative theological judgment and insistence that oppressive patriarchal texts and sexist traditions cannot claim the authority of divine revelation. Such oppressive texts and traditions must be denounced as androcentric articulations of patriarchal interests and structures. Such texts must be tested not only with respect to their sexism but also with respect to their racism and colonial militarism. Such a historical-critical assessment must be complemented by a political-critical feminist evaluation that seeks to assess the interaction of patriarchal biblical texts with contemporary culture. Rather than to free women from cultural stereotypes and oppression, patriarchal texts reinforce cultural stereotypes and patriarchal submission. They do so not because they are misinterpreted but because they are formulated in order to legitimate patriarchal oppression.

Yet not only historical patriarchal texts but also from a historical point of view, feminist-neutral or even feminist-positive texts of the Bible can function to reinforce patriarchal structures if they are proclaimed or taught in order to assure patriarchal behavior and inculcate oppressive values. If, for example, a battered woman is told to take up her cross and to suffer as Jesus did in order to save her marriage, then such feminist-neutral biblical motives are used for reinforcing patriarchal submission. Similarly, in our culture that socializes primarily women into altruism and selfless love, the biblical commandment of love and call for service can be culturally misused to sustain women's patriarchal exploitation. A feminist hermeneutics of proclamation must therefore critically analyze the intersection of biblical texts with contemporary patriarchal culture and values.

In conclusion, a feminist hermeneutics of proclamation has, on the one hand, to insist that all texts that are identified as sexist or patriarchal should not be retained in the lectionary and be proclaimed in Christian worship or catechesis. On the other hand, those texts that in a feminist critical process of evaluation are identified as transcending their patriarchal contexts and as articulating a liberating vision of human freedom and wholeness should receive their proper place in the liturgy and teaching of the churches. In short, a feminist critical translation of the Bible must be complemented by a careful theological evaluation of biblical texts and their oppressive or liberative impact in specific cultural situations.

Third: Such a feminist hermeneutics of proclamation must be balanced by a critical *hermeneutics of remembrance* that recovers *all* biblical traditions through a historical-critical reconstruction of biblical history from a feminist perspective. Rather than relinquishing androcentric biblical texts and patriarchal traditions, a hermeneutics of remembrance seeks to utilize historical-critical analysis in order to move beyond the androcentric text to the history of women in biblical religion.[10] If feminist identity is not based on the experience of biological sex or on essential gender differences, but on the common historical experience of women as collaborating or struggling participants in patriarchal culture and biblical history, then the reconstruction of early Christian history in a feminist perspective is not just a historical-critical but also a feminist-theological task. Feminist meaning cannot only be derived from the egalitarian surplus of androcentric texts, but must also be found in and through androcentric texts and patriarchal history.

Rather than abandon the memory of our foresisters' sufferings and hopes in our patriarchal Christian past, a hermeneutics of remembrance *reclaims* their sufferings and struggles in and through the subversive power of the "remembered past." If the enslavement and colonialization of peoples becomes total when their history is destroyed and the solidarity with the dead is made impossible, then a feminist biblical hermeneutics of remembrance has the task of becoming a "dangerous memory"[11] that reclaims the visions and sufferings of the dead. Such a "subversive memory" not only keeps alive the sufferings and hopes of women in the biblical past, but also allows for a universal solidarity of sisterhood among women of the past, present, and future. The continuing challenge of the victims of religious patriarchy is not met by the denial of their self-understanding and religious vision as mistaken or as ideological self-deception, but only in and through engaged solidarity and committed remembrance of their hopes and despairs in the church of women.

Such a feminist hermeneutics of remembrance proposes theoretical models for historical reconstructions that place women not on the periphery but in the center of biblical community and theology. Insofar as androcentric biblical texts not only reflect their patriarchal-cultural environment but also allow a glimpse of the early Christian movements as the discipleship of equals, the reality of women's commitment and leadership in these movements precedes the patriarchal injunctions of the New Testament. Although the canon preserves only remnants of such a non-patriarchal Christian ethos, these remnants still allow us to recognize that such a patriarchalization process is not inherent in Christian community but progressed only slowly and with difficulty. Therefore, a feminist hermeneutics of remembrance can reclaim early Christian theology and history as our own theology and history. Women as church have a continuous history and tradition that can claim the discipleship of equals as its biblical roots.

In short, a feminist hermeneutics of remembrance has as its primary task to keep alive the *memoria passionis* of biblical women, as well as to reclaim our biblical heritage. However, this heritage is misrepresented when it is understood solely as a history of patriarchal oppression. It also must be reconstituted as a history of liberation and religious agency. The history and theology of women's oppression perpetuated by patriarchal biblical texts and clerical patriarchy must be understood for what it is. This history and theology must not be allowed to cancel out the memory of the struggle, life, and leadership of biblical women who spoke and acted in the power of the Spirit.

Fourth: Such historical reconstructions of women's biblical history need to be supplemented by a *hermeneutics of creative actualization* that expresses the active engagement of women in the ongoing biblical story of liberation. While a feminist hermeneutics of remembrance is interested in historical-critical reconstruction, a feminist hermeneutics of creative actualization allows women to enter the biblical story with the help of historical imagination, artistic recreation, and liturgical ritualization. A feminist biblical interpretation, therefore, must not only be critical but also constructive, not only be oriented toward the past but also toward the future of women-church.

Such a hermeneutics of creative actualization seeks to retell biblical stories from a feminist perspective, to reformulate biblical visions and injunctions in the perspective of the discipleship of equals, and to create midrashic amplifications of the feminist remnants that have survived in patriarchal texts. In this process of creative re-vision it utilizes all available means of artistic imagination, literary creativity, music, and dance. The Bible as formative prototype has inspired artistic creativity and legendary embellishments throughout the centuries. In midrash and apocryphal writings, in liturgy and sacred hymns, the patriarchal church has ritualized certain aspects of the biblical story and celebrated the "founding fathers" of biblical religion.

A feminist hermeneutics of creative actualization reclaims for the church of women the same imaginative freedom, popular creativity, and ritual powers. Women today not only rewrite biblical stories about women, but also reformulate patriarchal prayers and create feminist rituals celebrating our ancestors. We rediscover in story and poetry, in drama and liturgy, in song and dance, our biblical foresisters' sufferings and victories. In feminist liturgy and haggada, women retell the story of the Passover or that of the "last supper." We re-vision the liturgy of Advent or the baptismal ritual. In ever new images and symbols we seek to rename the God of the Bible and the significance of Jesus. We not only spin tales about the voyages of Prisca, the missionary, or about Junia, the apostle, but also dance Sarah's circle and experience prophetic enthusiasm. We sing litanies of praise to our foresisters and pray laments of mourning for the lost stories of our foremothers. Only by reclaiming our religious imagination and our sacred powers of naming can women-church "dream new dreams and see new visions."

We do so, however, in the full awareness that such creative participation in the biblical story must be won in and through a feminist critical process of interpretation that repents of the structural sin and internalized values of patriarchal sexism. The religious creativity and feminist power of re-creation actualized in the church of women seem to me the feminist "leaven" of the bakerwoman God that will transform patriarchal biblical religion so that the biblical story will become truly a resource for all who seek for a sustaining vision in their struggle for liberation from patriarchal oppression.

Notes

[1] Although I use here still the designation "patriarchal," I clearly understand it in terms of kyriarchy, that is, the domination of the emperor, lord, father, husband, elite propertied man, a term I first introduced in my book *But She Said: Feminist Practices of Biblical Interpretation* (Boston: Beacon, 1992). However, it is clear that I understood wo/men's oppression already in the mid 80s not just in terms of sexism and patriarchy but in terms of intersecting multiple structures of domination.

[2] See my "Discipleship and Patriarchy: Early Christian Ethos and Christian Ethics in a Feminist Theological Perspective," in L. Rasmussen, ed., *The Annual of the Society of Christian Ethics* (Waterloo: Wilfried Laurier University, 1982), 131–72. For further development and documentation of the material discussed in this chapter, see my book *In Memory of Her: A Feminist Theological Reconstruction of Christian Origins* (New York: Crossroad, 1983).

[3] Redstockings, *New York Manifesto*, 1975.

[4] As quoted in bell hooks, *Ain't I a Woman: Black Women and Feminism* (Boston: South End, 1981), 193.

[5] E. Cady Stanton, *The Original Feminist Attack on the Bible. The Woman's Bible*, intr. B. Welter, reprint of 1895 ed. (New York: Arno, 1974), 7.

[6] Rosemary Radford Ruether, "Feminism and Patriarchal Religion: Principles of Ideological Critique of the Bible," *JSOT* 22 (1982): 54–66.

[7] "Feminist Critique: Opportunity for Cooperation," 68.

[8] See my "'For the Sake of Our Salvation': Biblical Interpretation as The*logical Task," in D. Durken, ed., *Sin, Salvation, and the Spirit* (Collegeville: Liturgical, 1979), 21–39.

[9] Bernadette J. Brooten, "Women Leaders in the Ancient Synagogue," *Brown Judaic Studies* 36 (Chico: Scholars, 1982).

[10] See R. S. Kraemer, "Women in the Religions of the Greco-Roman World," in *Religious Studies Review* 9 (1983), for an extensive discussion of historical-critical studies.

[11] See J. B. Metz, *Faith in History and Society: Toward a Practical Fundamental Theology*, trans. D. Smith (New York: Crossroad, 1980).

5

The Will to Choose or to Reject

Continuing Our Critical Work

I'm ceded—I've stopped being Theirs—
The name They dropped upon my face
With water, in the country church
Is finished using, now,
And They can put it with my Dolls,
My childhood, and the string of spools,
I've finished threading—too—
    Baptized before, without the choice,
But this time, consciously, of Grace—
Unto supremest name—
Called to my Full—The Crescent dropped—
Existence's whole Arc, filled up,
With one small Diadem.
    My second Rank—too small the first—
Crowned—Crowing—on my Father's breast—
A half unconscious Queen—
But this time—Adequate—Erect,
With Will to choose, or to reject,
And I choose, just a Crown.
    —*Emily Dickinson*

Adrienne Rich has pointed out that this poem of Emily Dickinson's is a poem of great pride and self-confirmation, of transcending the patriarchal condition, of movement from unconsciousness to consciousness. She cautions us, however, not to give it a theological reading, because Emily Dickinson "used the Christian metaphor far more than she let it use her."[1]

I have quoted both Dickinson and Rich because they articulate at different levels the central challenge of a feminist biblical hermeneutics. Feminist consciousness radically throws into question all traditional religious names, texts, rituals, laws, and interpretative metaphors because they all bear "our

Father's names." With Carol Christ[2] I would insist that the central spiritual and religious feminist quest is the quest for women's self-affirmation, survival, power, and self-determination.

Some of us have therefore argued that as self-identified women we cannot but leave behind patriarchal biblical religion and communities and create a new feminist religion on the boundaries of patriarchal religion and theology. Others claim biblical religion as an integral part of their own historical identity and religious experience. The Jewish feminist Alice Bloch articulates this claim well: "I take pride in my Jewish heritage, and I am tired of hearing women dismiss Jewish identity as 'oppressive' and 'patriarchal'. . . . Jewish identity is important to me, because being Jewish is an integral part of myself; it's my inheritance, my roots. Christian women sometimes have a hard time understanding this, because Christian identity is so much tied up with religious beliefs. It is possible to be an ex-Roman Catholic or an ex-Baptist, but it is really not possible to be an ex-Jew."[3]

While agreeing with her insight that women's personal and religious self-identity is intertwined, I would maintain that Christian self-identity is not just tied up with religious beliefs but is also a communal-historical identity. Christian (and in my case Catholic) feminists also do not relinquish their biblical roots and heritage. As the *ekklesia* of women, we claim the center of Christian faith and community in a feminist process of transformation.

THE HERMENEUTICAL CENTER: WOMEN-CHURCH

The hermeneutical center of feminist biblical interpretation is women-church (*ekklesia gynaikon*), the movement of justice-seeking women and feminist men in biblical religion. The *ekklesia* of women is part of the wider women's movement in society and in religion that conceives itself not just as a civil rights movement but as a women's liberation movement. Its goal is not simply the "full humanity" of women, since humanity as we know it is male defined, but women's religious self-affirmation, power, and liberation from all patriarchal alienation, marginalization, and oppression. The Greek term *ekklesia* means the public gathering of free citizens who assemble in order to determine their own and their children's communal well-being. It can be translated as the assembly, the synagogue, or the church of women. When as a Christian I use the expression *ekklesia* of women, I do not use it as an exclusionary[4] but as a political-oppositional term to patriarchy. Since in its original meaning *ekklesia* does not mean church but connotes the assembly of full citizens, I also seek with it to make the connections between the women's movements in religion and in society that struggle for full citizenship in patriarchal societies and religions.

It thus becomes necessary to clarify here the way in which I use patriarchy as an explanatory political concept. I do not define it in a general sense as a societal system in which men have power over women[5] but in the classical sense as it was defined in Aristotelian philosophy. Just as feminism is not just a worldview or perspective but a women's movement for change, so patriarchy is in my understanding not just ideological dualism or androcentric world construction in language but a social, economic, and political system of gradated subjugations and oppressions. Therefore I do not speak simply about male oppressors and female oppressed, or see all men over and against all women. Patriarchy as a male pyramid specifies women's oppression in terms of the class, race, country, or religion of the men to whom they "belong." [6]

Patriarchy as the basic heuristic model for feminist analysis allows us to conceptualize not only sexism but also racism and property-class relationships as basic structures of women's oppression. In a patriarchal society or religion, all women are bound into a system of male privilege and domination, but impoverished third world women constitute the bottom of the oppressive patriarchal pyramid. Patriarchy cannot be toppled except when the women who form the bottom of the patriarchal pyramid—triply oppressed women— become liberated. All women's oppression and liberation is bound up with that of the colonialized and economically most exploited women. This was already recognized by one of the earliest statements of the radical women's liberation movement: "Until every woman is free, no woman is free."[7] "Equal- ity from below" must become the liberative goal of the *ekklesia* of women. In other words, as long as societal and religious patriarchy exists, women are not "liberated" and must struggle for survival and self-determination. Conversely, there is no one feminist theory, religion, or group that can claim to be fully liberated.

Since a critical analysis of patriarchy allows us to conceptualize the interaction of sexism, racism, classism, and militarist colonialism, such a feminist interpretation of liberation is not in its conception and goals white middle-class. All of us who are sufficiently educated to participate in a hermeneutical or theological discussion do not live our lives on the bottom of the patriarchal pyramid. Our experiences of oppression and marginalization are very different, but as women we all live in a society and culture that still denies us our sexual self-determination.

My life and experience is quite different, for example, from that of my mother. In 1944, during street fighting, she had to leave her home with two small children and literally walk from Romania to a bombed-out Germany, surviving from day to day, begging for food, shelter, and clothing for her children. Nevertheless, my own struggles for survival as a woman in a clerical male profession have enabled me to understand more than my mother ever did what it means to be a woman in a patriarchal society. A feminist analysis of my own experience helps me realize that the baby given up for adoption could have been mine, the peasant girl in Guatemala without a childhood could have been my daughter, the medieval woman burnt by the church as a witch could have been me, the senile woman left for days without food could be my future.

I have therefore argued that feminist theology must articulate its advocacy position not as an option for the oppressed but as the self-identification as women in patriarchal society and religion, since all women are socialized to identify with men.[8] The more we identify as women and thereby overcome our patriarchal self-alienation, the more we will realize that the separation between white and black women, middle-class and poor women, native American and European women, Jewish and Christian women, Protestant and Catholic women, lesbian and heterosexual women, nun-women and lay-women is, in the words of Adrienne Rich, "a separation from ourselves."[9] Conversely, option for the most oppressed woman is an option for our women selves. Such an option allows us "to find God in ourselves" and to "love Her fiercely."[10]

The locus or place of divine revelation and grace is therefore not the Bible or the tradition of a patriarchal church but the *ekklesia* of women and the lives of women who live the "option for our women selves." It is not simply "the experience" of women but the experience of women (and all those oppressed) struggling for liberation from patriarchal oppression. "The dream of freedom for oneself in a world in which all women are free emerges from one's own life experience in which one is not free, precisely because one is a woman. The liberation of women is thus not an abstract goal . . . but is the motive for that process. Individual freedom and the freedom of all women are linked when one has reached the critical consciousness that we are united first in our unfreedom."[11]

The patriarchal dehumanization and victimization of multiple oppressed women exhibits the full death-dealing powers of patriarchy, while their struggles for liberation and courage to survive is the fullest experience of God's grace in our midst. A feminist critical theology of liberation needs therefore to be particular and concrete. It theologically explores women's particular experiences of marginalization, victimization, and oppression. At the same time it has to articulate our individual and historical experiences of liberation. The God of Judith as well as the God of Jesus is Emmanuel, God with us, in our struggles for liberation, freedom, and wholeness. The spiritual authority of the *ekklesia* of women rests on this experience of grace in our midst.

Feminist biblical interpretation therefore challenges the scriptural authority of patriarchal texts and explores how the Bible is used as a weapon against women in our struggles for liberation. It also investigates as to whether and how the Bible can become a resource in these struggles. A feminist biblical interpretation is thus first of all a political task. It remains obligatory because the Bible and its authority has been and again today is used as a weapon against women struggling for liberation.

From its inception, feminist interpretation and concern with scripture has been generated by the fact that the Bible was used to halt the emancipation of women and slaves. Not only in the last century but also today, the political right laces its attacks against the feminist struggle for women's rights and freedoms in the political, economic, reproductive, intellectual, and religious spheres with biblical quotations and appeals to scriptural authority.[12] From countless pulpits and Sunday school classes, such patriarchal attacks are proclaimed as the "word of God." Anti-ERA groups, the cultural Total Woman movement, and the Moral Majority appeal to the teachings of the Bible on the American family and on creational differences between the sexes supposedly resulting in a different societal and ecclesial calling. At the same time, the political right does not hesitate to quote the Bible against shelters for battered women, for physical punishment of children, against abortion even in cases of rape or child pregnancy, against lesbians, or against women's studies programs at state universities.[13]

At the same time the Bible has not served only to legitimate the oppression of disenfranchised white women, slaves, native Americans, Jews, and the poor. It has also provided authorization for women who rejected slavery, colonial exploitation, anti-Semitism, and misogynism as unbiblical and against God's will. It has inspired countless women to speak out against injustice, exploitation, and stereotyping and energized them to struggle against poverty, unfreedom, and vilification. The Guatemalan Indian and Christian revolutionary Rigoberta Menchu testifies to this: "In the community we began to reflect together on what the Bible told us. The story of Judith, for example, impressed me very much: she beheaded the king to save her people. We too understood that faced with the violence of the rich, we have to respond with another kind of violence. The violence of justice."[14]

A FEMINIST INTERPRETIVE MODEL OF CRITICAL EVALUATION

I propose elsewhere[15] that a feminist critical theology of liberation should develop a multidimensional model of biblical interpretation in order to assist women in their struggle for liberation. Such a model must be a feminist-critical and a historical-concrete model. It must not only show how individual biblical texts and writings functioned in their historical-political settings but also pay increased attention to the intersection and interplay of biblical texts with contemporary politics and socialization. It should not search for a feminist formalized principle, a universal perspective, or a historical liberating dynamics but should carefully analyze how the Bible functions concretely in women's struggle for survival. Key elements in such a model, as far as I can see, are the following: (1) suspicion rather than acceptance of biblical authority, (2) critical evaluation rather than correlation, (3) interpretation through proclamation, (4) remembrance and historical reconstruction, and (5) interpretation through celebration and ritual.

First: A feminist Christian apologetics presumes that we can trust our lives to the "word of God" in the Bible and that we should submit to its authority and liberating power. It therefore insists that a hermeneutics of suspicion should only be applied to the history of exegesis and contemporary interpretations. While a liberation-theological interpretation affirms the liberating dynamics of the biblical texts, a feminist critical hermeneutics of suspicion places a warning label on all biblical texts: *Caution! Could be dangerous to your health and survival.* Not only is scripture interpreted by a long line of men and proclaimed in patriarchal churches, it is also authored by men, written in androcentric language, reflective of religious male experience, and selected and transmitted by male religious leadership. Without question, the Bible is a male book. If Mary Daly is right that here also "the medium is the message," self-identified women struggling for survival should avoid it like the plague. The first and never-ending task of a hermeneutics of suspicion, therefore, is to elaborate as much as possible the patriarchal, destructive aspects and oppressive elements in the Bible. Such an interpretation must uncover not only sexist biblical language but also the oppressive language of racism, anti-Judaism, exploitation, colonialism, and militarism. An interpretation of suspicion must name the language of hate by its true name and not mystify it or explain it away.

Yet women in all walks of life testify to a different, inspiring, challenging, and liberating experience with the Bible. If we cannot write off all women who find meaning in scripture as unliberated and not feminist, we have to use a hermeneutics of suspicion to detect the anti-patriarchal elements and functions of biblical texts, which are obscured and made invisible by androcentric language and concepts. Moreover, we have to acknowledge that not all biblical stories, traditions, and texts reflect the experience of men in power or were written in order to legitimate the patriarchal status quo.

Second: If the *ekklesia* of women has the authority "to choose and to reject" biblical texts, we have to develop a theological interpretive principle for feminist critical evaluation rather than an interpretive principle and method of correlation. Such an interpretation must sort through particular biblical texts and test out in a process of critical analysis and evaluation how much their content and function perpetrates and legitimates patriarchal structures, not only in their original historical contexts but also in our contemporary situation. Conversely, all biblical texts must be tested as to their feminist liberating content and function in their historical and contemporary contexts. Such a feminist hermeneutics of critical evaluation has to articulate criteria and principles for evaluating particular texts, biblical books, traditions, or interpretations. Such criteria or principles must be derived from a systematic exploration of women's experience of oppression and liberation.

Because of the importance of specific feminist analyses and critical evaluations, I have argued that a feminist interpretation ought not to reduce the richness of biblical texts and traditions to one particular text or tradition, as the neoorthodox "canon within the canon" model does. It also should not separate form and content and then formalize and universalize them to a principle or dynamic, as the method of critical correlation (Schillebeeckx, Tracy) or confrontation (Küng) does.[16] Although Tillich had criticized Barth's dialectical method, his "neo-dialectical method of correlation" is still motivated by the apologetic intent that engages in a critical dialogue of "yes and no" between contemporary culture and biblical religion in order to end with an affirmative "yes" to religion. Such a method of correlation, however, rests on "the distinction between the unchanging content of the Christian message and the changing forms of cultural expression."[17]

A feminist method of correlation adopts the same distinction insofar as it separates the sociocritical prophetic-messianic principle or dynamics from its concrete historical articulations and deformations on the one hand and formalizes feminist experience and analysis on the other, in such a way that it becomes a critical principle of "affirmation and promotion of the full humanity of women." It does so in order to correlate both the prophetic-biblical and the feminist critical principles with each other. As Rosemary Ruether has argued: "The Bible can be appropriated as a source of liberating paradigms only if it can be seen that there is a correlation between the feminist critical principle and that critical principle by which biblical thought critiques itself and renews its vision as the authentic Word of God over against corrupting and sinful deformations. It is my contention here that there is such a correlation between biblical and feminist critical principles."[18]

As alternative option I have proposed that biblical feminists need not presume such a correlation or configuration, but nevertheless in a process of critical evaluation we are able to find some liberating paradigms and resources in biblical texts. This is the case not because a correlation between feminist and biblical critical principles can be presupposed but because the historical experience of women-church with the Bible allows us to do so. Yet in order to find feminist biblical resources, we have first to bring to bear the full force of the feminist critique upon biblical texts and religion.

Third: Since today, as in the past, the political right fights its "holy war" against feminism under the banner of the doctrinal paradigm of biblical interpretation, our defense must directly address the question of the word of God as proclaimed in scripture.[19] We have therefore to develop a hermeneutics of proclamation that undercuts the authority claims of patriarchal scriptural texts. As I have already suggested in my contribution to *The Liberating Word*, feminist theology must first of all denounce all texts and traditions that perpetrate and legitimate oppressive patriarchal structures and ideologies. We no longer should proclaim them as the "word of God" for contemporary communities and people if we do not want to turn God into a God of oppression.

A careful feminist assessment of the selection and reception of biblical texts for proclamation in the liturgy must therefore precede an inclusive translation of them. Patriarchal texts should not be allowed to remain in the lectionary but should be replaced by texts affirming the discipleship of equals. An "inclusive translation" can only be made of those lectionary texts that, in a critical feminist process of evaluation, are identified as articulating a liberating vision for women struggling for self-affirmation and wholeness, lest we are in danger of covering up the patriarchal character of the Bible.

Such a hermeneutics of proclamation also needs to assess the contemporary political context and psychological function of biblical interpretations and texts. It must explore how even feminist-neutral or feminist-positive biblical texts can have an oppressive impact on the lives of contemporary women, if they are used in order to inculcate misogynist attitudes and patriarchal behavior. For instance, in our culture, in which women, primarily, are socialized into sacrificing love and self-abnegation, the biblical commandment of love and the proclamation of the cross can be culturally misused to sustain voluntary service and the acceptance of sexual violence. In exploring the interaction between biblical texts and societal feminine values and behavior, we also have to pay attention to its religious contexts. As Susan Thistlethwaite has pointed out, biblical texts have a different meaning and authority for battered women rooted in different ecclesial communities.[20] Much more work needs to be done on the intersection of the Bible with contemporary culture, politics, and society.

Fourth: A hermeneutics of proclamation must be balanced by a hermeneutics of remembrance, which recovers *all* biblical traditions and texts through a feminist historical reconstruction. Feminist meaning is not only derived from the egalitarian-feminist surplus of androcentric texts but is also to be found in and through androcentric texts and patriarchal history. Rather than abandon the memory of our foresisters' sufferings, visions, and hopes in our patriarchal biblical past, such a hermeneutics reclaims their sufferings, struggles, and victories through the subversive power of the "remembered" past. Rather than relinquish patriarchal biblical traditions, a hermeneutics of remembrance seeks to develop a feminist critical method and historical model for moving beyond the androcentric text to the history of women in biblical religion.

Such an interpretation recognizes methodologically that androcentric language as generic conventional language makes women invisible by subsuming us under linguistic masculine terms. It mentions women only when we are exceptional or cause problems. To take androcentric biblical texts as reflecting reality does not recognize the ideological, obfuscating character of androcentric language. To reconstruct women's participation in biblical history, we therefore have to read the "women passages" as indicators and clues that women were at the center of biblical life. In other words, if we take the conventional ideological character of androcentric language seriously, we can claim that women were leaders and full members in biblical religion until proven otherwise. The burden of historical proof is shifted when we read texts that speak about the leadership and presence of women, or those that are injunctions to proper "feminine" behavior, not as descriptive and comprehensive information but as the visible tip of an iceberg that, for the most part, is submerged.

An interpretation through remembrance articulates theoretical models that can place women not on the periphery but at the center of biblical community and history. In my book *In Memory of Her*, I have proposed patriarchy as such a sociohistorical model for reconstructing early Christian origins in a feminist perspective. While feminist theology usually utilizes androcentric dualism as its basic exploratory concept for feminist analysis and reconstruction, I propose that we use patriarchy as articulated in Aristotelian philosophy as a basic explanatory concept for the reconstruction of women's history in Western society in general and in Christian history in particular.

Androcentric dualism is then best understood as ideological justification of patriarchal structures. It is articulated whenever non-patriarchal, egalitarian societal or religious possibilities exist or are at least thinkable. This was the case in Athenian democracy, where it became necessary to claim "different natures" for freeborn women and slave women as well as men because of the democratic notion of citizenship. Similarly, in early Christianity, misogynist texts and patriarchal injunctions were generated because the discipleship of equals stood in tension with Greco-Roman patriarchal structures. The gradual patriarchalization of the church in the second and third centuries not only engendered the exclusion of all women from ecclesial leadership but also eliminated the freedoms that slave women had gained by joining the Christian movement.

Insofar as androcentric biblical texts are generated by the tension between patriarchal societal and ecclesial structures and the vision and praxis of the discipleship of equals, they allow us still a glimpse of women's engagement and leadership in the early Christian movement. Although the scriptural canon preserves only remnants of the non-patriarchal early Christian ethos, these remnants allow us still to recognize that patriarchal structures are not inherent to Christian community, although they have become historically dominant. Therefore a feminist hermeneutics of remembrance can reclaim early Christian history as our own history and religious vision. Women-church has a long history and tradition, which can claim the discipleship of equals as its scriptural roots. In sum, a feminist hermeneutics of remembrance has to keep alive the memory of patriarchal biblical oppression as well as the memory of the struggles and victories of biblical women who acted in the power of the Spirit.

Fifth: Interpretation through remembrance and historical reconstruction needs to be supplemented by a hermeneutics of creative ritualization. Such an interpretation allows women-church to enter the biblical story with the help of historical imagination, artistic recreation, and liturgical celebration. A method of creative actualization seeks to retell biblical stories from a feminist perspective, to reformulate biblical visions and injunctions in the perspective of the discipleship of equals, and to create narrative amplifications of the feminist remnants that have survived in biblical texts. In such a process of creative re-visioning, women-church can utilize all available means of artistic imagination, literary creativity, music, and dance.

In legend and apocryphal writings, in liturgy and sacred hymns, in feast days and liturgical cycles, the patriarchal church has ritualized certain aspects and texts of the Bible as well as celebrated the "founding fathers" of biblical religion. A feminist interpretation of creative ritualization reclaims for women-church the same imaginative freedoms, popular creativity, and liturgical powers. Women not only rewrite biblical stories but also reformulate patriarchal prayers and create feminist rituals for celebrating our foremothers. We rediscover in story and poetry, in drama and dance, in song and liturgy our biblical foresisters' sufferings and victories. In ever-new images and symbols, feminist liturgies seek to rename the God of the Bible and the biblical vision. We sing litanies of praise to our foresisters and pray laments of mourning for the wasted lives of our foremothers. Only by reclaiming our religious imagination and our ritual powers of naming can women-church dream new dreams and see new visions. We do so, however, in the full awareness that such creative feminist participation in the biblical story and history must be won in and through a critical process of evaluation.

In conclusion, what leads us to perceive biblical texts as providing resources in the struggle for liberation from patriarchal oppression, as well as models for the transformation of the patriarchal church, is not some special canon of texts that can claim divine authority. Rather, it is the experience of women themselves in their struggles for liberation. I have therefore suggested that we understand the Bible as a structuring prototype of women-church rather than as a definite archetype; as an open-ended paradigm that sets experiences in motion and invites transformations. Rather than reduce its pluriformity and richness to abstract principle or ontological immutable archetype to be applied to and repeated in ever-new situations, I suggest the notion of historical prototype open to its own transformation.

Such an understanding of the Bible as formative prototype allows us to explore models and traditions of liberating praxis as well as of patriarchal repression. It allows us to reclaim the whole Bible not as normative but as an experiential enabling authority, as the legacy and heritage of women-church.

Such a notion of the Bible not as a mythic archetype but as a historical prototype provides women-church with a sense of its own ongoing history as well as Christian identity. It is able to acknowledge the dynamic process of biblical resources, challenges, and new visions under the changing conditions of the church's cultural-historical situations.

In and through structural and creative transformation, the Bible can become holy scripture for women-church. Insofar as the interpretive model proposed here does not identify biblical revelation with androcentric texts and patriarchal structures, it maintains that such revelation and inspiration is found among the discipleship community of equals in the past and the present. Insofar as the model proposed here locates revelation not in biblical texts but in the experience of women struggling for liberation from patriarchy, it requires that a feminist critical hermeneutics of liberation read and actualize the Bible in the context of believing communities of women, in the context of women-church.

Notes

[1] Adrienne Rich, "Vesuvius at Home: The Power of Emily Dickinson (1975)," in *On Lies, Secrets, and Silence: Selected Prose 1966–1978* (Norton, 1979), 172. The poem appeared in *The Complete Poems of Emily Dickinson* (Boston: Little, Brown, and Company, 1924).

[2] Carol Christ, "Why Women Need the Goddess: Phenomenological, Psychological, and Political Reflections," in Carol Christ and Judith Plaskow, eds., *Womanspirit Rising: A Feminist Reader in Religion* (Harper and Row, 1979), 273–87.

[3] Alice Bloch, "Scenes from the Life of a Jewish Lesbian," in Susannah Heschel, ed., *On Being a Jewish Feminist: A Reader* (Schocken, 1983), 174.

[4] In speaking about a feminist biblical interpretation, I also do not want to imply that feminist Jewish and Christian biblical interpretations are the same or must develop along the same lines. As Drorah Setel has rightly pointed out, references to the "Judeo-Christian" tradition or heritage ignore the significant inequalities in that relationship. However, insofar as the Old Testament or Hebrew Bible is part of the Christian Bible, a feminist Christian hermeneutics must deal with the Jewish Bible while a Jewish feminist hermeneutics does not need to pay attention to the New Testament.

[5] For definition and discussion of patriarchy, see, for example, Heidi Hartmann, "Capitalism, Patriarchy, and Job Segregation by Sex," in Elizabeth and Emily K. Abel, eds., *The Signs Reader: Women, Gender, and Scholarship* (Chicago: University of Chicago Press, 1983): 193–225.

[6] Although I still use here the term *patriarchy*, I already attempt to define it in terms of intersectional structures of oppression, what I would later call kyriarchy.

[7] "Redstockings: April 1969"; reprinted in *Feminist Revolution* (New York: Random, 1975), 205.

[8] See my "Toward a Feminist Biblical Hermeneutics," in *The Challenge of Liberation The*logy*, 91–112, which was presented in 1979 at a conference sponsored by Chicago Divinity School.

[9] Adrienne Rich, "Disloyal to Civilization: Feminism, Fascism, Gynephobia (1978)," in *On Lies*, 307.

[10] Ntozake Shange's ending chorus is often quoted by religious feminists. However, it must not be overlooked that such an affirmation is only achieved in and through the experience and naming of racist-heterosexist patriarchal oppressions. *For Colored Girls Who Have Considered Suicide/When the Rainbow Is Enuf: A Choreopoem* (New York: Macmillan, 1977).

[11] Marcia Westkott, "Women's Studies as a Strategy for Change: Between Criticism and Vision," in Gloria Bowles and Renate Duelli-Klein, eds., *Theories of Women's Studies* (London: Routledge, 1983), 213.

[12] For example, Shirley Rogers Radl, *The Invisible Woman: Target of the Religious New Right* (Delta, 1983).

[13] Betty Willis Brooks and Sharon L. Sievers, "The New Right Challenges Women's Studies: The Long Beach Women's Studies Program," in Charlotte Bunch and Sandra Pollack, eds., *Learning Our Way: Essays in Feminist Education* (Crossing, 1983), 78–88.

[14] *We Continue Forever: Sorrow and Strength of Guatemalan Women* (International Resource Exchange, 1983), 18.

[15] See my book *Bread Not Stone: Introduction to a Feminist Interpretation of Scripture* (Boston: Beacon, 1984).

[16] See the overview and discussion of David Tracy, "Particular Questions within General Consensus," in Leonard Swidler, ed., *Consensus in Theology?* (Westminster, 1980), 33–39.

[17] See John Clayton, "Was ist falsch in der Korrelationstheorie?," *Neue Zeitschrift für Systematische Theologie* 16:93–111 (1974), and Francis Schüssler Fiorenza, *Foundational Theology: Jesus and the Church* (Crossroad, 1984), to whom I am indebted for this reference.

[18] Letty M. Russell, ed., *Feminist Interpretation of the Bible*, 117.

[19] Charlene Spretnack, "The Christian Right's 'Holy War' against Feminism," in *The Politics of Women's Spirituality* (New York: Doubleday, 1982), 470–96.

[20] Letty M. Russell, ed., *Feminist Interpretation of the Bible*, 99.

6

Feminist Hermeneutics

Writing a dictionary article on feminist hermeneutics may encourage several misconceptions. It gives the impression that feminist hermeneutics is a finished research product rather than an ongoing process within the context of women's societal and ecclesial struggles for justice and liberation. It also highlights proposed solutions rather than the experiences and questions that have engendered them. Insofar as this article is qualified by "feminist" and other entries are not marked, for instance, as "masculinist" or "white," readers may assume that an objective discipline and unqualified approach to hermeneutics exists. As long as other contributions do not explicitly articulate the fact that knowledge and scholarship is perspectival, such a misapprehension seems unavoidable. Yet feminist inquiry is not more, but less, ideological because it deliberately articulates its theoretical perspective without pretending to be value-free, positivistic, universal knowledge.

Delineation of Terms

Since the expression "feminist" evokes reactions, emotions, and prejudices, it becomes necessary to delineate the ways in which the term is here used in conjunction with hermeneutics.

1. Feminist/Womanist

The term "feminist" is commonly used today for describing those who seek to eliminate women's subordination and marginalization. Although women have resisted their subordinate position of exploitation throughout the centuries, the roots of feminism as a social and intellectual movement are found in the European Enlightenment.

a. Although there are diverse articulations of feminism, feminists generally agree in their critique of masculine supremacy and hold that gender roles are socially constructed rather than innate. The "root experience" of feminism is women's realization that cultural "common sense," dominant perspectives, scientific theories, and historical knowledge are androcentric, that is, male-biased, and therefore not objective but ideological. This breakthrough experience causes not only disillusionment and anger but also a sense of possibility and power.

Feminist analyses often utilize categories such as *patriarchy, androcentrism,* or *gender-dualism* as synonymous or overlapping concepts. Patriarchy is generally defined as gender dualism or as the domination and control of man over woman. Androcentrism refers to a linguistic structure and theoretical perspective in which man or male represents the human. Western languages such as Hebrew, Greek, German, or English—grammatically masculine languages that function as so-called generic languages—use the terms "male" or "human" as inclusive of "woman" and the pronoun "he" as inclusive of "she." Man is the paradigmatic human, woman is the other.

Masculine and feminine are the two opposite or complementary poles in a binary gender system, which is asymmetric insofar as masculine is the primary and positive pole. Dualistic oppositions such as subject/object, culture/nature, law/chaos, orthodoxy/heresy, and man/woman, legitimate masculine supremacy and feminine inferiority. Franco-feminist criticism therefore has termed this structuring of man as the central reference point "phallocentrism," understanding the phallus as a signifier of sociocultural authority.

The philosophical construction of reason positions elite Western man as the transcendent, universal subject with privileged access to truth and knowledge. The Western construction of reason and rationality has been conceived within the binary structure of male dominance as transcendence of the feminine. Femininity is constituted as an exclusion. In analogy to "woman" and the "feminine" the nature of subordinated and colonized peoples is projected as the devalued other or the deficit opposite of elite Western man, rationalizing the exclusion of the "others" from the institutions of knowledge and culture.

b. In protest of this ideological construction, feminist liberation movements around the globe unmask the universalist essentializing discourse on "woman" and the colonized "other" as the totalizing discourses of the Western "man of reason." Instead they insist on the specific historical-cultural contexts and subjectivity, as well as on the plurality, of "women."

Women of color consistently maintain that an analysis of women's exploitation and oppression only in terms of gender does not suffice, for it does not comprehend the complex systemic interstructuring of gender, race, class, and culture that determines women's lives. Therefore, feminist hermeneutics must reconceptualize its categories of analysis. It has to distinguish between the categories of *androcentrism* or gender dualism as ideological obfuscations and legitimizations of elite male power on the one hand, and *patriarchy* in the strict sense of the word—defined as a complex social system of male domination structured by racism, sexism, classism, and colonialism—on the other hand. The system of Western patriarchal ideology was articulated centuries ago by Aristotle and Plato in their attempt to define the democratic *polis*, which restricted full citizenship to Greek, freeborn, propertied, male heads of household. Although cultural and religious patriarchy as a "master-centered" political and cultural system has been modified throughout the centuries, its basic structures of domination and ideological legitimization are still operative today.

African American feminists in religious studies, therefore, have introduced Alice Walker's term "womanist" (that is, feminist of color) to signal the fact that feminism is more than a political movement and theoretical perspective of white women. When we speak of Africans, Europeans, the poor, minorities, *and* women, we speak as if women do not belong to all the other groups mentioned. Yet the expression "women" includes not just white, elite, Western, middle- or upper-class women as conventional language suggests, but all women. Whereas feminist scholarship has become skilled in detecting the androcentric language and patriarchal contextualizations of malestream theory and biblical interpretation, it does not always pay attention to its own inoculation with gender stereotypes, white supremacy, class prejudice, and theological confessionalism.

Jewish feminists in turn have pointed out that Christian feminists perpetuate the antisemitic discourse of otherness ingrained in Christian identity formation when they uncritically reproduce the anti-Jewish tendencies inscribed in Christian Scriptures and perpetrated by malestream biblical scholarship. This is the case, for example, when Judaism is blamed for the "death of the Goddess" or when Jesus, the feminist, is set over and against patriarchal Judaism. It also would be the case if this article on "feminist hermeneutics" would be read as giving a descriptive and comprehensive account of feminist biblical hermeneutics as such, although it is written from a Christian but not from a Jewish or Islamic hermeneutical perspective. If feminist interpretation does not wish to continually reproduce its own internalized structures of oppression, it must bring into critical reflection the oppressive patriarchal contextualizations of contemporary discourses and those of the biblical writings themselves.

2. FEMINIST/WOMANIST HERMENEUTICS

While women have read the Scriptures throughout the centuries, a feminist/womanist hermeneutics as the theoretical exploration of biblical interpretation in the interest of women is of very recent vintage.

a. When one remembers Miriam, Hulda, Hannah, Mary, Prisca, Felicitas, Proba, Macrina, Melania, Hildegard of Bingen, Margaret Fell, Antoinette

Brown, Elizabeth Cady Stanton, Jarena Lee, Katherine Bushnell, Margaret Brackenbury Crook, Georgia Harkness, or Else Kähler, it becomes apparent that women have always interpreted the Bible. Moreover, books about women in the Bible—mostly written by men—as well as studies of prescriptive biblical male texts about women's role and place have been numerous throughout the centuries.

Biblical scholarship *about women* engages diverse historical, social, anthropological, psychological, or literary models of interpretation without analyzing their androcentric frameworks. In addition, it tends to adopt the scientific posture of "detached" inquiry that eschews feminist politics. Although such scholarship focuses on "women," it reproduces and reinscribes the androcentric-patriarchal dynamics of the text as long as it does not question the androcentric character of biblical texts and reconstructive models.

Only in the context of the women's movement in the last century, and especially in the past twenty years, have feminists begun to explore the implications and possibilities of a biblical interpretation that takes the androcentric or patriarchal character of Scripture into account. This exploration is situated within the context of both the academy and the church. Insofar as feminist analysis seeks to transform academic as well as ecclesial biblical interpretation, it has a theoretical and practical goal. This praxis-orientation locates feminist hermeneutics in the context of philosophical/theological hermeneutics as well as critical theory and liberation theology.

b. The technical term *hermeneutics* comes from the Greek words *hermeneuein/hermeneia* and means the practice and theory of interpretation. The expression was first used as a technical term for exegetical handbooks that dealt with philology, grammar, syntax, and style. Today the term *exegesis* is generally used to describe the rules and principles for establishing not only the philological, but also the historical sense, of biblical texts.

Hermeneutics, by contrast, explores the dialogical interaction between the text and the contemporary interpreter in which the subject matter of the text or the reference of discourse itself "comes-into-language." It is not simply conveyed by, but manifested in and through, the language of the text. Understanding the meaning of texts emerges from a dialogical process between interpreter and text. This dialogical process presupposes a common preunderstanding of the subject matter of the text, since we cannot comprehend what is totally alien to our own experience and perception.

Biblical interpretation seeks to understand the text and its world as a rhetorical expression in a certain historical situation. Insofar as the interpreter always approaches biblical texts with certain preunderstandings, and from within a definite linguistic-historical tradition, the act of interpretation has to overcome the distance between the world of the text and that of the interpreter in a "fusion of horizons." Interpretation has as its goal to establish agreement with and acceptance of the subject matter of the text. Understanding is achieved when the interpreter appropriates the ways of being human projected by the text. According to Gadamer the authority of the text has nothing to do with blind obedience, but rests on recognition (*Anerkennung*), because the subject matter of the text can be accepted in principle.

c. However, insofar as patriarchal ideology and systemic domination have been passed down through the medium of Christian Scriptures, feminist biblical interpretation seeks not only to understand but also to assess critically the meaning of androcentric texts and their sociopolitical functions. Although I have introduced the nomenclature "feminist hermeneutics" into the theological discussions, I have at the same time maintained that a critical feminist interpretation has to move beyond dialogical hermeneutics. It does not just aim at understanding biblical texts but also engages in thelogical critique, evaluation, and transformation of biblical traditions and interpretations from the vantage point of its particular sociopolitical religious location. Not to defend biblical authority but to articulate the religious authority of women is the main task of a critical feminist hermeneutics.

Insofar as hermeneutical theory insists on the linguisticality of all reality and on the sociohistorical conditioning of the act of interpretation, it is useful for womanist/feminist biblical interpretation. However, dialogical hermeneutics does not consider that classic texts and traditions are also a systematically distorted expression of communication under unacknowledged conditions of repression and violence. It therefore is not able to critique the androcentric, male-centered character of Western classics and texts, nor to problematize the patriarchal character of the "world of the text" and of our own. Even Ricoeur's insistence on the restoration of the link between exegesis and hermeneutics as the dialectic between alienating distanciation and appropriating recognition cannot encompass the transformative aims of a critical feminist hermeneutics for liberation, because such a dialectic does not get hold of the "doubled vision" of feminist hermeneutics.

3. A CRITICAL FEMINIST HERMENEUTICS OF LIBERATION

Feminists/womanists have become conscious of women's conflicting position within two contradictory discourses offered by society. Unconsciously, women participate at one and the same time in the specifically "feminine" discourse of submission, inadequacy, inferiority, dependency, and irrational intuition on the one hand and in the "masculine" discourse of subjectivity, self-determination, freedom, justice, and equality on the other hand. If this participation becomes conscious, it allows the feminist/womanist interpreter to become a reader resisting the reifying power of the androcentric text.

a. The theoretical exploration of this contradictory position of women from the vantage point of an emancipatory standpoint makes it possible to "imagine" a *different* interpretation and historical reconstruction. For change to take place, women and other nonpersons must concretely and explicitly claim as their very own those values and visions that Western Man has reserved for himself. Yet they can do so only to the extent that these values and visions foster the liberation of women who suffer from multiple oppressions.

This "doubled vision" of feminism leads to the realization that gender relations are neither natural nor divinely ordained but linguistically and socially constructed in the interest of patriarchal power relations. Androcentric language and texts, literary classics and visual art, works of science, anthropology, sociology, or theology do not describe and comprehend reality. Rather they are ideological constructs that produce the invisibility and marginality of women. Therefore a critical feminist interpretation insists on a *hermeneutics of suspicion* that can unmask the ideological functions of androcentric text and commentary. It does not do so because it assumes a patriarchal conspiracy of the biblical writers and their contemporary interpreters but because when reading grammatically masculine supposedly generic texts women do not, in fact, know whether they are meant or not.

b. The realization that women are socialized into the "feminine discourse" of their culture and thus are ideologically "scripted" and implicated in power relations engenders the recognition that women suffer also from "a false consciousness." As long as they live in a patriarchal world of oppression, women are never fully "liberated." However, this does not lead feminists to argue that historical agency and knowledge of the world are not possible. Western science, philosophy, and theology have not known the world as it is. Rather they have created it in their own interest and likeness as they wished it to be. Therefore, feminists/womanists insist that it is possible for liberatory discourses to articulate a different historical knowledge and vision of the world.

In order to do so feminist/womanist scholars utilize women's experience of reality and practical activity as a scientific resource and a significant indicator of the reality against which hypotheses are to be tested. A critical feminist version of objectivity recognizes the provisionality and multiplicity of particular knowledge as situated and "embodied" knowledge. Knowledge is not totally relative, however. It is possible from the perspective of the excluded and dominated to give a more adequate account of the "world." In short, womanists/feminists insist that women are "scripted" and at the same time are historical subjects and agents.

Therefore, a critical feminist/womanist hermeneutics seeks to articulate biblical interpretation as a complex process of reading for a cultural-theological praxis of resistance and transformation. To that end it utilizes not only historical and literary-critical methods that focus on the rhetoric of the text in its historical contexts, but also storytelling, bibliodrama, and ritual for creating a "different" feminist imagination.

APPROACHES AND METHODS

In conjunction with feminist literary criticism, critical theory, and historiography, four major hermeneutical strategies have been developed for such a critical process of interpretation.

1. TEXTS ABOUT WOMEN

a. In pondering the absence of women's experience and voice from biblical texts and history, a first strategy seeks to recover information *about women* and to examine what biblical texts teach about women. This analysis usually focuses on "key" women's passages such as Genesis 1–3; the biblical laws with regard to women; or on the Pauline and post-Pauline statements on women's place and role. This selective approach was adopted by Elizabeth Cady Stanton in *The Woman's Bible* and has strongly influenced subsequent interpretations. Its "cutting up and cutting out" method isolates passages about women from their literary and historical contexts and interprets them "out of context."

After having gathered the texts about women, scholars then catalog and systematize these texts and traditions in a dualistic fashion. They isolate positive and negative statements in order to point to the positive biblical tradition about woman. They isolate positive texts about women and the feminine from "texts of terror" that are stories of women's victimization. All statements about woman and feminine imagery about God are cataloged as positive, ambivalent, or negative strands in Hebrew-Jewish and early Christian tradition. Negative elements are found in the Hebrew Bible as well as in the intertestamental and postbiblical writings of Judaism, whereas in the Christian tradition they are seen as limited to the writings of the Church Fathers. Such a biased classification favoring Christian over and against Jewish tradition engenders anti-Jewish attitudes and interpretations.

b. A second approach focuses on the *women characters* in the Bible. From its inception, feminist/womanist interpretation has sought to actualize these stories in role-playing, storytelling, and song. Whereas the retelling of biblical stories in midrash or legend is quite familiar to Jewish and Catholic women, it is often a new avenue of interpretation for Protestant women. Interpretations that focus on the women characters in the androcentric text invite readers to identify positively with the biblical women as the text presents them.

Since popular books on "the women of the Bible" often utilize biblical stories about women for inculcating the values of conservative womanhood, a feminist/womanist interpretation approaches these stories with a *hermeneutics of suspicion*. It critically analyzes not only their history of interpretation but also their function in the overall rhetoric of the biblical text. Such a critical interpretation questions the emotions they evoke and the values and roles they project before it can reimagine and retell them in feminist/womanist key.

Within the African American tradition of storytelling, for example, Renita Weems creatively reconstructs the "possible emotions and issues that motivated biblical women in their relation with each other" in order to draw "attention to the parallels between the plight of biblical women and women today." Weems informs her readers that the only way she could "let the women speak for themselves" was to wrestle their stories from the presumably male narrators. Although it is important to retell the biblical women's stories, it is also necessary to reimagine biblical stories without women characters. In order to break the marginalizing tendencies of the androcentric text, feminists/womanists have also to retell in a female voice and womanist perspective those stories that do not explicitly mention women.

c. A third approach seeks to recover *works written by women* in order to restore critical attention to female voices in the tradition. This work has restored many forgotten or obscured women writers. In early Christian studies scholars have, for example, argued that the gospels of Mark and John were written by a woman evangelist or that Hebrews was authored by Prisca. Others have pointed out that at least half of the Lukan material on women must be ascribed to a special pre-Lukan source that may have owed its existence to a woman evangelist. While such a suggestion expands our historical-theological imagination, it does not critically explore whether the androcentric text communicates patriarchal values and visions, and if so to what degree. It fails to consider that women also have internalized androcentric stereotypes and therefore can reproduce the patriarchal politics of otherness in their speaking and writing.

d. Historical studies of women in the Bible or that of Jewish, Greek, or Roman women are generally *topological* studies that utilize androcentric texts and archaeological artifacts *about women* as source texts. They understand these sources as descriptive data about women in the biblical worlds and as "windows" to and "mirrors" of women's reality in antiquity. Sourcebooks on women in the Greco-Roman world assemble in English translation literary documents as well as inscriptions and papyri about women's religious activities in Greco-Roman antiquity. However, such source collections are in a certain sense precritical insofar as they obscure that androcentric texts are ideological constructions. They must be utilized with a *hermeneutics of suspicion* and placed within a feminist model of reconstruction.

Recognizing the absence or marginality of women in the androcentric text, feminist historians have sought to articulate the problem of how to write women back into history, of how to capture the memory of women's historical experience and contribution. The historian Joan Kelly has succinctly stated the dual goal of women's history as both to restore women to history and to restore our history to women.

Feminist/womanist historical interpretation conceptualizes women's history not simply as the history of women's oppression by men but as the story of women's historical agency, resistance, and struggles. Women have made sociocultural contributions and challenged dominant institutions and values as well as wielded destructive power and collaborated in patriarchal structure.

Feminist/womanist scholars in religion have begun to open up many new areas of research by asking different historical questions that seek to understand the socioreligious life-world of women in antiquity. What do we know about the everyday life of women in Israel, Syria, Greece, Egypt, Asia Minor, or Rome? How did freeborn women, slave women, wealthy women, or businesswomen live? Could women read and write, what rights did they have, how did they dress, or which powers and influence did they gain through patronage? Or what did it mean for a woman of Corinth to join the Isis cult, the synagogue, or the Christian group? What did imprisonment mean for Junia, or how did Philippian women receive Luke-Acts?

Although many of these questions still need to be addressed and might never be answered, asking these questions has made it possible for instance to rediscover Sarah, the priestess, or to unearth the leadership of women in Judaism as well as in early Christianity, or to locate the household-code texts in Aristotelian political philosophy. However, insofar as such sociohistorical studies do not problematize the descriptive character of the androcentric source text as reflecting sociohistorical reality, they cannot break through the marginalizing ideological tendencies of the androcentric text.

2. IDEOLOGICAL INSCRIPTION AND RECEPTION

Whereas feminist historical interpretation tends to be caught up in the factual, objectivist, and antiquarian paradigm of biblical studies, literary-critical studies insist that we are not able to move beyond the androcentric text to the historical reality of women. They reject a positivist understanding of the biblical text as a transparent medium as reflecting historical reality or as providing historical data and facts.

a. Their first hermeneutical strategy attends to the ideological inscriptions of androcentric dualisms or the politics of gender in cultural and religious texts. The relationship between androcentric text and historical reality cannot be construed as a mirror image but must be decoded as a complex ideological construction. The silences, contradictions, arguments, prescriptions, and projections of the androcentric text as well as its discourses on gender, race, class, or culture must be unraveled as the ideological inscription of the patriarchal politics of otherness.

Feminist literary studies—be they formalist, structuralist, or narratological—carefully show how the androcentric text constructs the politics of gender and feminine representation. By tracing out the binary structures of a text or by focusing on the "feminine" character constructs (for example, mother, daughter, bride) of biblical narratives, structuralist and deconstructionist readings run the risk of reinscribing rather than dislodging the dualistic gender politics of the text.

By laying out the androcentric bias of the text, feminist literary criticism seeks to foster a hermeneutics of resistance to the androcentric politics of the canonical text. Such a feminist literary hermeneutics aims to deconstruct, debunk, and reject the biblical text. However, by refusing any possibility of a positive retrieval they reinscribe the totalizing dynamics of the androcentric texts that marginalize women and other nonpersons or eliminate them altogether from the historical record. Such a hermeneutics relinquishes the heritage of women, be it cultural or religious, since not only the Bible but all cultural classics written in androcentric language contain such an androcentric politics. A critical feminist reading can only break the mold of the sacred androcentric text and its authority over us when it resists the androcentric directives and hierarchically arranged binary oppositions of the text, when it reads texts against "their androcentric grain."

b. A second strategy of feminist reading shifts the attention from the androcentric text to the reading subject. Feminist reader-response criticism makes conscious the complex process of reading androcentric texts as a cultural practice. By showing how our gender affects the way we read, it underlines the importance of the reader's particular sociocultural location. Reading and thinking in an androcentric symbol system forces readers to identify with what is culturally "male." This intensifies women's internalization of a cultural patriarchal system whose misogynist values alienate women from themselves.

The androcentric biblical text derives its seductive "power" from its generic aspirations. For instance, women can read stories about Jesus without giving any significance to the maleness of Jesus. However, thelogical emphasis on the maleness of Jesus reinforces women's male identification and establishes Christian identity as a male identity in a cultural masculine/feminine contextualization. Focusing on the figure of Jesus, the Son of the Father, when reading the Bible "doubles" women's oppression; women not only suffer in the act of reading from the alienating division of self against self but also from the realization that to be female is not to be "divine" or "a son of God." Recognizing these internalizing functions of androcentric scriptural texts that in the liturgy are proclaimed as "word of God," feminist/womanist theologians have insisted on an inclusive translation of the lectionary.

Women's reading of generic androcentric biblical texts, however, does not always lead with necessity to the reader's masculine identification. Women's reading can deactivate masculine/feminine gender contextualization in favor of an abstract degenderized reading. Empirical studies have documented that so-called generic masculine language ("man," pronoun "he") is read differently by men and by women. Whereas men connect male images with such language, women do not connect images with the androcentric text but read it in an abstract fashion. This is possible because of the ambiguity of generic masculine language. In the absence of any clear contextual markers a statement such as "all men are created equal" can be understood as generic-inclusive or as masculine-exclusive.

When women recognize their contradictory ideological position in a generic androcentric language system they can become readers resisting the *master-identification* of the androcentric, racist, classist, or colonialist text. However, if this contradiction is not brought into consciousness, it cannot be exploited for change but leads to further self-alienation. For change to take place, women and other nonpersons must concretely and explicitly claim as our very own the human values and visions that the androcentric text ascribes to "generic" man. Yet once readers have become conscious of the oppressive rhetorical functions of androcentric language, they no longer are able to read "generically" but must insist on a feminist/womanist contextualization of interpretation as a liberating practice in the struggle to end patriarchal relations of exploitation that generate "the languages of oppression" and are legitimated by it.

3. A Critical Rhetorical Paradigm of Historical Reconstruction

A third approach seeks to overcome the methodological split between historical studies that understand their sources as windows to historical reality and literary critical studies that tend to reinscribe the binary structures and dualistic constructions of the androcentric text. It does so by analyzing the rhetorical functions of the text as well as by articulating models for historical reconstruction that can displace the dualistic model of the androcentric text. It does not deny but recognizes that androcentric texts are produced in and by particular historical debates and struggles. It seeks to exploit the contradictions inscribed in the text for reconstructing not only the narrative "world of the biblical text" but also the sociohistorical worlds that have made possible the particular world construction of the text.

a. Such a critical feminist reconstruction, therefore, does not heighten the opposition of masculine/feminine inscribed in the androcentric text but seeks to dislodge it by focusing on the text as a rhetorical-historical practice. Androcentric texts produce the marginality and absence of women from historical records by subsuming women under masculine terms. How we read the silences of such unmarked grammatically masculine generic texts and how we fill in their blank spaces depends on their contextualization in historical and present experience.

Grammatically, masculine language mentions women specifically only as a special case, as the exception from the rule or as a problem. Whereas grammatically masculine language means both women and men, this is not the case for language referring to women. Moreover, the texts about women are not descriptive of women's historical reality and agency but only indicators of it. They signify the presence of women that is marginalized by the androcentric text. A historically adequate reading of such generic androcentric texts therefore would have to read grammatically masculine biblical texts as inclusive of women and men, unless a case can be made for an exclusive reading.

By tracing the defensive strategies of the androcentric text, one can make visible not only what the text marginalizes or excludes but also show how the text shapes what it includes. Androcentric biblical texts tell stories and construct social worlds and symbolic universes that mythologize, reverse, absolutize, and idealize patriarchal differences and in doing so obliterate or marginalize the historical presence of the devalued "others" of their communities.

Androcentric biblical texts and interpretations are not descriptive of objective reality, but they are persuasive and prescriptive texts that construct historical reality and its sources. Scholars have selected original manuscript readings, established the original text, translated it into English, and commented on biblical writings in terms of their own androcentric-patriarchal knowledge of the world. Androcentric tendencies that marginalize women can also be detected in the biblical writers' selection and redaction of traditional materials as well as in the selective canonization of texts. It is also evident in the use of the Bible in liturgy and theological discourse. As androcentric rhetorical texts, biblical texts and their interpretations construct a world in which those whose arguments they oppose become the "deviant others" or are no longer present at all. The categories of orthodoxy and heresy reinscribe such a patriarchal rhetoric.

Biblical texts about women are like the tip of an iceberg indicating what is submerged in historical silence. They have to be read as touchstones of the reality that they repress and construct at the same time. Just as other texts, so also are biblical texts sites of competing discourses and rhetorical constructions of the world. We are able to disclose and unravel "the politics of otherness" constructed by the androcentric text, because it is produced by a historical reality in which "the absent others" are present and active.

A feminist/womanist interpretation is able to unmask the politics of the text, because women participate not only in the androcentric discourse of marginalization and subordination but also in the democratic discourse of freedom, self-determination, justice, and equality. Insofar as this "humanistic" discourse has been constituted as elite "male" discourse, the reality to which it points is at the same time already realized and still utopian. It has to be imagined *differently*. Such "imagination" is, however, not pure fantasy but historical imagination because it refers to a reality that has been accomplished not only in discourse but also in the practices and struggles of "the subjugated others."

b. The second strategy elaborates models of historical reconstruction that can subvert the androcentric dynamics of the biblical text and its interpretations by focusing on the "reality" that the androcentric text marginalizes and silences. One has to take the texts about women out of their androcentric historical source contexts and reassemble them like mosaic stones in a feminist/womanist model of historical reconstruction that does not recuperate the marginalizing tendencies of the text.

A critical feminist reconstructive model, therefore, aims not only to reconstruct women's history in early Christianity but seeks also a feminist reconstruction of early Christian origins. To that end it cannot limit itself to the canonical texts but must utilize *all* available texts and materials.

Another strategy questions androcentric models of interpretation that interpret early Christian origins, for example, in terms of the split between the public and private spheres. This model renders women's witness to the resurrection and their leadership in the early Christian movements "unofficial" or distorts it to fit "feminine" cultural roles. Another strategy looks at economic and social status, at domestic and political structures, at legal prescriptions, cultic prohibitions, and religious organizations. However, reconstructions of the social world often uncritically adopt sociological or anthropological models of interpretation without testing them for their androcentric ideological implications.

The strategy of a "negative" mirror image that constructs early Christian women's history in contrast to that of Jewish women or Greco-Roman and Asian women in the first century is not only biased but also methodologically inadequate. Instead, a feminist reconstruction must elaborate emancipatory tendencies in Greco-Roman antiquity that made it possible for the early Christian movements to stand in critical tension to their dominant patriarchal society. It must identify institutional formations that have enabled the active participation of women and other nonpersons.

Finally, a critical feminist/womanist reconstruction does not take the texts indicating the gradual adaptation of the early Christian movement to its dominant patriarchal culture as descriptive of historical reality. Rather it understands them as rhetorical arguments about the patriarchal "politics of submission." They do not reflect "what really happened," but construct prescriptive arguments for what the authors wished would happen. This applies not only to biblical texts but also to those "parallel" texts that are cited for the "depraved status" of Jewish or Greco-Roman women.

In short, in a critical model early Christian history is reconstructed not from the perspective of the "historical winners" but from that of the "silenced" in order to achieve a historically adequate description of the social worlds of early Christian women and men. The objectivity and reliability of scientific historical reconstructions must therefore be assessed in terms of whether and how much they can make present the historical losers and their arguments, how much they can make visible those who have been made "doubly invisible" in androcentric sources.

Feminist/womanist historiography, therefore, understands itself not as antiquarian science but as engaged inquiry since it seeks to retrieve women's history as memory and heritage for the present and the future. Insofar as reconstructions of the past are always done in the interest of the present and the future, a critical reconstruction of early Christian history as the history of those who have struggled against hegemonic patriarchal structures seeks to empower those who today engage in the struggle to end patriarchy.

Theological Hermeneutics

Both sides in the often bitter struggles for ecclesial leadership and full citizenship of freeborn women, for emancipation of slave women and men, and for the survival of poor women and their children have invoked biblical authority to legitimate their claims. Consequently, a feminist theological hermeneutics has centered around the question of scriptural authority.

Several hermeneutical positions have crystallized in confrontation with biblical authority claims. The first rejects the Bible because of its patriarchal character. The Bible is not the word of God but that of elite men justifying their patriarchal interests. The opposite argument insists that the Bible must be "depatriarchalized" because, correctly understood, it fosters the liberation of women. A middle position concedes that the Bible is written by men and rooted in a patriarchal culture but nevertheless maintains that some biblical texts, traditions, or at least the basic core, essence, or central principle of the Bible are liberating and stand in critique of patriarchy.

1. *Biblical Apologetics*

Historically and today the Bible has functioned as a weapon against women in their struggles for access to public speaking, to theological education, or to ordained ministry. In response, a Christian feminist apologetics asserts that the Bible, correctly understood, does not prohibit but rather authorizes the equal rights and liberation of women. A feminist hermeneutics therefore has the task to elaborate this correct understanding of the Bible so that its authority can be claimed.

However, insofar as historical-critical scholarship has elaborated the rich diversity and often-contradictory character of biblical texts, it has shown that taken as a whole the canon cannot constitute an effective theological norm. Therefore it becomes difficult to sustain the traditional understanding that the canon forms a doctrinal unity that in all its parts possesses equal authority and which in principle rules out theological inconsistencies.

Feminists who feel bound by this understanding of canonical authority propose three different hermeneutical strategies. A *loyalist* hermeneutics argues that biblical texts about women can be explained in terms of a hierarchy of truth. Whereas traditionalists argue that the household code texts require the submission and subordination of women or that Gal. 3:28 must be understood in light of them, evangelical feminists hold that Ephesians 5 requires mutual submission and that the injunctions to submission must be judged in light of the canonical authority of Gal. 3:28.

A second strategy is *revisionist.* It makes a distinction between historically conditioned texts that speak only to their own time and those texts with authority for all times. For instance, the injunction of 1 Cor. 11:2-16 to wear head covering or a certain hairstyle is seen as time-conditioned whereas Gal. 3:28 pronounces the equality of women and men for all times.

A third approach is *compensatory.* It challenges the overwhelmingly androcentric language and images of the Bible by pointing to the feminine images of God found throughout the sacred writings of Judaism and Christianity, uncritically embraces the divine female figure of Wisdom or the feminine character of the Holy Spirit in order to legitimate the use of feminine language for God and the Holy Spirit today.

2. *A Feminist Canon*

Recognizing the pervasive androcentric character of biblical texts, other feminists isolate an authoritative essence or central principle that biblically authorizes equal rights and liberation struggles. Such a liberation hermeneutics does not aim to dislodge the authority of the Bible but to reclaim the empowering authority of Scripture over and against conservative, right-wing, biblical antifeminism.

A first strategy seeks to identify an authoritative *canon within the canon,* a central principle or *the* "gospel message." Since it is generally recognized that the Bible is written in androcentric language and rooted in patriarchal cultures, such a normative center of Scripture allows one to claim biblical authority while rejecting the accusation that the Bible is an instrument of oppression. Feminist biblical and liberation theological scholarship has not invented but inherited this search for an authoritative "canon within the canon" from historical-theological exegesis that recognizes the historical contingency and contradictory pluriformity of Scripture but nevertheless maintains the normative unity of the Bible.

Just as male liberation theologians stress God's liberating acts in history or single out the Exodus or Jesus' salvific deeds as "canon within the canon," so feminist liberation theologians have sought to identify God's intention for a mended creation, with the prophetic tradition or the prophetic critical principle as the authoritative biblical norm. However, such a strategy reduces the historical particularity and pluriformity of biblical texts to a feminist "canon within the canon" or a liberating formalized principle.

The debate continues in feminist hermeneutics as to whether such a feminist normative criterion must be derived from or at least correlated with the Bible so that Scripture remains the normative foundation of feminist biblical faith and community.

Some would argue that the Bible becomes authoritative in the hermeneutical dialogue between the ancient world that produced the text, the literary world of the text, and the world of the modern reader. Yet such a position rejects any criteria extrinisic to the biblical text for evaluating the diverse, often contradictory biblical voices. Instead it maintains that the Bible contains its own critique. It points, for instance, to the vision of a transformed creation in Isa. 11:6-9 as a criterion intrinsic to Scripture. The principle of "no harm"— "they shall not hurt or destroy in all my holy mountain"—is the normative criterion for assessing biblical texts. However, this approach does not critically reflect that it is the interpreter who selects this criterion and thereby gives it normative canonical status.

A second strategy recognizes that a feminist critical norm is not articulated by the biblical text. However, it insists that a *correlation* can be established between the feminist critical norm and that by which the Bible critiques itself and renews its liberating vision over and against corrupting deformations. Such a feminist hermeneutics correlates, for instance, the feminist critical principle of the full humanity of women with the prophetic-messianic critical principle or dynamics by which the Bible critiques itself. However, such a hermeneutics of correlation reduces the particularity and diversity not only of biblical texts but also of feminist articulations to abstract formalized principle and norm. It neglects biblical interpretation as the site of competing discursive practices and struggles.

A third hermeneutical strategy argues that feminists must create as a new textual base a feminist *Third Testament* that canonizes women's experiences of God's presence. Out of their revelatory experiences of agony and victimization, survival, empowerment, and new life, women write new canonical stories. Such a proposal recognizes women's experiences of struggle and survival as places of divine presence. Just as the androcentric texts of the First and Second Testaments reflecting male experience deserve canonical status, so also do the stories rooted in women's experience deserve canonical status. However, such a canonization of women's stories rescribes cultural-theological male-female dualism as canonical dualism. Just like canonized male texts, so also are women's texts embedded and structured by patriarchal culture and religion. Consequently both must be subjected to a process of critical evaluation.

3. CRITICAL PROCESS OF INTERPRETATION

A critical feminist hermeneutics of liberation therefore abandons the quest for a liberating canonical text and shifts its focus to a discussion of the *process of biblical interpretation* that can grapple with the oppressive as well as the liberating functions of particular biblical texts in women's lives and struggles.

Such a critical process of feminist/womanist interpretation for liberation presupposes feminist conscientization and systemic analysis. Its interpretive process has four key moments. It begins with a *hermeneutics of suspicion* scrutinizing the presuppositions and interests of interpreters, and those of biblical commentators as well as the androcentric strategies of the biblical text itself. A *hermeneutics of historical interpretation and reconstruction* works not only in the interest of historical distanciation but also for an increase in historical imagination. It displaces the androcentric dynamic of the text and its contexts by recontextualizing the text in a sociopolitical model of reconstruction that can make the subordinated and marginalized "others" visible.

A *hermeneutics of ethical and theological evaluation* assesses the oppressive or liberatory tendencies inscribed in the text as well as the functions of the text in historical and contemporary situations. It insists for theological reasons that Christians stop preaching patriarchal texts as the "word of God," and cease to proclaim the Christian God as legitimating patriarchal oppression. Finally, a *hermeneutics of creative imagination and ritualization* retells biblical stories and celebrates our biblical foresisters in a feminist/womanist key.

Since such a critical process of interpretation aims not just to understand biblical texts but to change biblical religion, it requires a theological reconception of the Bible as a formative root model rather than as a normative archetype of Christian faith and community. As a root model, the Bible informs but does not provide the articulation of criteria for a critical feminist/womanist evaluation of particular interests of liberation. Christian identity that is grounded in the Bible as its formative prototype must in ever-new readings be deconstructed and reconstructed in terms of a global praxis for the liberation not only of women but of all other nonpersons.

Such a proposal does not abandon the canon as some critics have charged. It also cannot be characterized as extrinsic to the text, insofar as it works with the notion of inspiration. Inspiration is a much broader concept than canonical authority insofar as it is not restricted to the canon but holds that throughout the centuries the whole church has been inspired and empowered by the Spirit. The New Testament writings did not become canonical because they were believed to be uniquely inspired; rather they were judged to be inspired because the church gave them canonical status. Inspiration—the life-giving breath and power of Sophia-Spirit—has not ceased with canonization but is still at work today in the critical discernment of the spirits. It empowers women and others excluded from ecclesial authority to reclaim *as church* their theological authority of biblical interpretation and spiritual validation.

The "canon within the canon" or the hermeneutics of correlation locates authority formally if not always materially in the Bible, thereby obscuring its own process of finding and selecting theological norms and visions either from the Bible, tradition, doctrine, or contemporary life. In contrast, a critical evaluative hermeneutics makes explicit that it takes its theological authority from the experience of God's liberating presence in today's struggles to end patriarchal relationships of domination. Such divine Presence manifests itself when people acknowledge the oppressive and dehumanizing power of the patriarchal interstructuring of sexism, racism, economic exploitation, and militarist colonialism and when Christians name these destructive systems theologically as structural "sin" and "heresy." For this process of naming we will find many resources in the Bible but also in many other religious, cultural, and intellectual traditions.

Understanding the act of critical reading as a moment in the global praxis for liberation compels a critical feminist hermeneutics to decenter the authority of the androcentric text and to take control of its own readings. It deconstructs the politics of otherness inscribed in the text and our own readings in order to retrieve biblical visions of salvation and well-being in the interest of the present and the future.

7

Theology as Rhetoric, Ethics, and Critique of Ideology

A critical feminist theology of liberation, I have argued, demands a reformulation of biblical scholarship as critique of ideology,[1] rhetoric, and ethics. It poses a fundamental scholarly theoretical question to the self-concept of biblical scholarship, theological scholarship, and ethics, and insists on the theo-ethical principle that wo/men are theological subjects. It brings the traditional relationship between ethics, theological scholarship, and biblical scholarship critically into view by pointing to the rhetorical and ideological character not only of biblical scholarship but also of ethics and theological scholarship. Kyriarchal practices of power in theology and church lead to a situation in which theology and ethics continue to be produced as kyriocentric forms of knowledge.

On the one hand, academic scholarship and theology as we have known them treat humanity as identical with manhood, subsume "woman" under "man," and regard "woman" as either an inferior or a glorified form of humanity. On the other hand, Christian tradition, church hierarchy, and university scholarship have for centuries excluded wo/men from university, theology, and church not only by law, but also by custom.

This still happens today to the extent that moral theological and systematic doctrines are formulated and defined as normative while wo/men remain excluded. While research on wo/men and gender make "woman" or gender the object of scholarly research, a critical-feminist scholarship and theology seeks to place liberation movements of rights-deprived and oppressed people in which wo/men are acting subjects at the center of theological research and to articulate its key categories, central perspectives on interpretation, and practices of transformation theoretically with a view to them.

Feminist scholarship thus has the goal of transforming andro-kyriocentric scholarship and everyday knowledge in such a way that they become truly inclusive and able to regard all people as subjects for research and theology. Feminist scholarship and theology thus seek to introduce a scholarly paradigm shift that makes it possible for wo/men to articulate theology in the interest of wo/men, who struggle for survival at the bottom of the kyriarchal pyramid.[2] Only such a paradigm shift can prevent theological scholarship, biblical scholarship, and ethics from continuing to reinscribe kyriarchal conditions and relationships. It affects all fields of theology and scholarship, but here I want to explicate it particularly in terms of biblical scholarship.

Paradigms of Biblical Scholarship

Thomas Kuhn's concept of paradigm[3] can help us to understand this shift in thinking. Kuhn, a physicist, introduced the concept of scientific paradigm or heuristic model into discussions in the natural sciences. He takes a stance in opposition to the common idea according to which science develops through a cumulative process of accretion of individual research findings. To the contrary, he argues that science makes progress through new discoveries and new scientific approaches that do not occur as the result of cumulative research.

He thus opposes science's unquestioning faith in progress. Contrary to the assumption of a continuous, goal-directed development of science, Kuhn emphasizes that changes in science take place on the basis of "scientific revolutions," which he sees as "tradition-subversive" interruptions in the tradition-bound actions of normal science. Feminist research and theology is undoubtedly such a "tradition-subversive" interruption.

Kuhn defines a scientific paradigm as a consensus in research that for a particular period of time shapes the investigations and analyses of a community of professionals. A paradigm shift always occurs

- when aporiae, anomalies, and crises arise within the dominant paradigm,
- when the rebuilding of the research field is accomplished on different bases and a competing paradigm arises, and finally
- when views of the research field, its methods and goals, have so fundamentally changed that the old paradigm is dissolved and replaced by a new direction in research, new research discourses arise, and a new scholarly community is created.

According to Kuhn, then, a new paradigm has three levels or interrogative directions:

- the scientific matrix or disciplinary system, its values, thought initiatives, approaches, and thought frameworks,
- the model examples, that is, concrete solutions to problems, explicit rules and materials of research and methods of investigation that can be summarized under the concept of a model and are to be distinguished from the paradigm, as a more inclusive concept, and finally

- the scholarly community and institutions that support the paradigm.

Thus a scientific paradigm determines all aspects of scholarly research: observations, theories, models of explanation, scholarly traditions, philosophical-theoretical assumptions about the world, the overall worldview, and especially the scholarly institutions such as universities, periodicals, books, and so on. All these factors shape scholarly thought and ideas about framework that, like reading glasses, function to determine how things are seen and whether they are seen at all. All data and observations are theory-laden. Naked and uninterpreted data and sources do not exist. The Bible can thus never be an unambiguous authoritative source for theological scholarship and ethics. To the extent that it has always already been interpreted it requires an ideological-critical analysis and evaluation. It is just as true that there are no criteria and frameworks for research that are independent of the scholarly paradigm in which they were developed. Hence biblical scholarship that works with ideological criticism must learn to see itself as an ethics of interpretation.

I introduced Kuhn's concept of paradigm into the discussion of feminist theological and biblical hermeneutics more than thirty years ago[4] in order to argue that the shift from androcentric or, better, kyriocentric interpretation to a feminist interpretation of the world and the Bible resulted in a revolutionary shift of the scholarly paradigm. Since paradigms determine how scholars understand the world or the Bible, the shift from a kyriocentric to a feminist-critical basic paradigm implies a radical transformation of both ordinary and scholarly self-understanding and power of imagination. It presumes an intellectual conversion that cannot simply be derived logically from within the discipline but is rooted in a transformation of kyriarchal social, ecclesial, or scholarly relationships of dominance.

Such an intellectual conversion effects a change in interests and obligations that makes it possible for the community of researchers to see old knowledge in a completely new perspective. The confrontation between kyriocentric and critical feminist scholarship is an indicator of the struggle between rival paradigms, which at least in the transitional phase can continue to exist alongside each other if their institutional basis also endures but from the perspective of their frameworks of research are mutually exclusive.

The hierarchical structures of academic institutions secure the continuation of the kyriocentric paradigm of scholarship. While this kyriocentric scholarly paradigm is rooted in male-controlled academic institutions, the critical feminist paradigm has its bases in the new emancipatory directions of study and movements for liberation.[5] Its interest lies not only in a new view and renaming of the world, but in the fundamental transformation of institutionalized scholarship and theology—that is, it is about social-ecclesial transformation.

A scholarly typology of interpretative paradigms[6] allows us to locate feminist interpretation, intellectually and hermeneutically, within an overarching emancipatory paradigm of liberation. While the goal of the dogmatic-ecclesial paradigm is believing obedience and that of the historical-critical paradigm is factual knowledge, the hermeneutical-cultural paradigm strives to convey meaning[7] and inquires about the meaning of sacred scripture for people today.

The emancipatory-political paradigm of liberation, within which feminist hermeneutics works, is interested not only in finding meaning but still more in liberation and transformation. While the dogmatic-normative paradigm adduces philosophy and metaphysics in particular as its supporting sciences, while the positivistic-scholarly paradigm rests on philology and historical research and the hermeneutical-cultural paradigm uses mainly literary and cultural studies, the emancipatory-political paradigm works with a critical sociopolitical theory and critique of ideology.

The hermeneutical-scientific model of interpretation has sought to mediate among the three paradigms of interpretation by insisting on a division of labor between scientific exegesis and the practical theological application of a text. In this dichotomous model of interpretation, scholarly exegesis has the task of working out the clear meaning of a text, while the work of ethics and practical theology is to relate this historical meaning of a biblical text as worked out by scholarship—for example, 1 Corinthians 14, "let women keep silent in the *ekklēsia*"—to the present and to give it meaning for today.

At the basis of each of these three paradigms of interpretation lies also a different understanding of language. While the theological-normative paradigm in its full fundamentalist form regards biblical language magically and mystically as the direct word of G*d and the positivistic-scholarly paradigm sees language as a transparent window on reality that permits us to determine the facts or the definitive sense of a text, the hermeneutical-cultural paradigm works with a dialogical understanding of interpretation in which the text is personified as a partner in interpretation. Such a hermeneutical interpretation of the Bible, however, fails to recognize that it is using the text as a mirror that always projects back the face of those who are looking into it.

The fourth paradigm of interpretation, political-emancipatory, is not primarily directed to faith, knowledge, or the understanding of meaning, but to emancipation and liberation.[8] Such a paradigm is not skeptical of faith, knowledge, and understanding, let alone hostile to them; rather, it seeks to integrate faith, knowledge, and understanding into a praxis of liberation. Thus it does not articulate itself in contrast to the preceding paradigms but in opposition to an apolitical, positivistic understanding of faith, knowledge, and understanding as expressed in the fundamentalist understanding of the word of G*d and in the modern concept of scholarship. To such a positivistic understanding of language and scholarship, a critical feminist hermeneutics opposes a rhetorical view of both. This rhetorical paradigm applies to the language, the method of interpretation, the rhetorical situation, and the interests that are at work in the interpretation.

With this distinction between positivistic-scholarly and rhetorical-scientific interpretation I am joining the revival of ancient rhetoric that has taken place in biblical scholarship in the last twenty years or so, but I seek to avoid its positivistic tendencies. A rhetorical analysis emphasizes that in the process of interpretation texts and symbols cannot be understood directly or their true sense determined (hermeneutics). Rather, language is always already an exercise of power and an action that either continues kyriarchy or seeks to interrupt it. Interpretation is not simply a one-way street leading to the discovery of a single meaning of the text, but rather is a multivocal discourse that seeks to persuade and convince.

Biblical scholars are flesh-and-blood human beings with specific personal experiences and cultural horizons. They not only pursue particular interests and goals, but also bring with them unconscious assumptions and unreflected presuppositions when they seek to understand the text. Interpretation is best understood as a rhetorical creative action, since the reading of a text is always already an imaginative re-creation. An objective, clear reproduction of an original sense of the text or of the author's intention, independent of the person of the interpreter and her sociopolitical situation, is impossible and has long since been left behind by scholarly theory.

In a critical-emancipatory paradigm of interpretation, the perception of one's own social location, theoretical perspective, and rhetorical situation are integral components of the process of interpretation. This does not mean, however, that any and all interpretations of the text are acceptable. The text does contain multiple possible meanings, but it is best understood as a multifocal spectrum of meanings, each limited by a particular context. This many-faceted spectrum is activated differently each time in the active process of interpretation, depending on the theo-ethical and sociopolitical standpoint not only of the interpreter, but also of her audience.

Nevertheless, academic and popular biblical interpretation still works largely with a concept of knowledge that is long out of date. Many interpreters still make the claim that with controlled scholarly methods they can work out objectively a single correct meaning and objective significance of a biblical text and thus its kernel of truth.[9] But such unchanging, objectively attainable truth cannot be filtered out of the text once and for all. Instead, the text must be understood as a speech act motivated by particular interests in specific sociopolitical and historical contexts. What is true of the textual level is true also of the level of interpretation. Only in this way can the multiplicity of meanings of the textual signs and linguistic symbols be held within limits and the possible or probable field of play of meanings in the text be marked.

SCHOLARLY TURNS AND TRANSFORMATIONS

Such a non-positivistic, scholarly-rhetorical understanding of text and interpretation, which is the basis of the fourth emancipatory-political paradigm of
interpretation, has been made possible through four crucial epistemological
turns and changes in our understanding of scholarship.

The Rhetorical Turn[10]: As distinct from a historical analysis that is intended to establish historical facts, and a literary-critical interpretation that
concentrates on the literary form and deep structures of a text and seeks
to translate this analysis into universal categories, a rhetorical analysis of
discourse emphasizes the significance of the context, the power relationships
inscribed in and the sociohistorical situation of the text, in order not only to
understand the persuasive power of its argumentation but also to be able to
evaluate it. It analyzes the persuasive power of a rhetorical discourse not only
with respect to the linguistic convention, literary style, or overall composition,
but also and especially with respect to the interaction between author and
addressees or interpreter and reading public, as well as to the social-religious
location and interests of the process of persuasion inscribed in a text.[11] Such a
critical-rhetorical interpretation of the Bible therefore demands a the*-ethical
evaluation.

Rhetoric analyzes, for example, the Gospel of John as a moment of
cultural-religious communication and as a scene for theological argumentation between "John" and his hearers, as well as between interpreters of the
Fourth Gospel and their readers. Between the two—John and his historical
hearers as well as the interpreters of the Fourth Gospel and their readers—
such an argumentative communication seeking to persuade is only possible
because each pair lives historically in the same cultural-religious, sociopolitical, and linguistic-symbolic world. The rhetorical situation is thus of crucial
importance for the success of persuasive communication, and yet it also makes
it difficult insofar as the historical-cultural-religious situation of the first
readers and that of today's interpreters is very, very different.

If scholarship were to turn away from its centuries-old prejudice that views
rhetoric as "mere" rhetoric, as a technical means, style, and polished speech,
and turn to an understanding of rhetoric as "the power to persuade and
convince through argumentation," it would be capable of a renewed analysis
of the process of communication as a power-determined, action-oriented
process.[12] Such an analysis would draw attention to how arguments are
constructed, who speaks and who is silenced, to whom and when something
is said, who is addressed and why, in what power relationships a text seeks
to intervene, and in what way the discourse of interpretation itself attempts
to influence the social conditions of which it is a part. Rhetorical analysis
seeks not only to uncover the means with which authors and interpreters try

to convince and motivate their readers, but also to seek out and consider the kyriarchal structures inscribed in the text and their function in a particular rhetorical situation and a particular sociohistorical location.

Thus I distinguish, as does reader response criticism, between the implied author inscribed in the text, the implied audience inscribed in the text, the implied rhetorical-historical situation inscribed in the text, and the implied symbolic world inscribed in the text on the one hand, and the real historical author, addressee, situation, and symbolic world on the other. None of the four text-immanent factors—author, addressee, situation, and symbolic world—is identical with the actual, really existing historical author, audience, situation, and the symbolic world of a text; these are linguistic constructs that allude to their historical situatedness.[13]

For example, Paul represents himself in his letters as an apostle with singular authority over his communities. But we know that this was not historically the case; instead, Paul was an outsider for many in his time, one who did not know Jesus himself or follow him and whose theology remained controversial well into the second century. The same can be said of the addressees, situations, and symbolic worlds of his letters, which we can only see through Pauline textual lenses. But the author, addressee, situation, and symbolic world inscribed in the text are not to be seen as purely fictional; they must have some relationship to reality if communication is to succeed and people are to be persuaded.

When someone engages in rhetorical discourse, according to classical rhetoric she must not only decide what questions and themes she wants to address and what position she will take; she must also establish the tenor and goal of her rhetorical intervention. This often requires a mixture of speech genres. In classical rhetoric the persuasive power of an argument was determined by *ethos*, *pathos*, and *pistis*. *Ethos* and *pathos* were supposed to be effective throughout the entire speech, but *ethos* is particularly effective at the beginning of the speech, and *pathos* at the end.

Topics with which rhetoric concerns itself refer to social and political problems worthy of discussion. Decisive for the formulation of arguments that, for example, would appeal to conservative readers are traditional points of view, cultural conventions, commonplaces, and established customs—in short, the ways in which the mind generally views the world. Such "common sense" arguments are supported by appeals to universally valid points of view and convictions, called *pisteis* or "proofs." Important in the discussion of such proofs are the strategies for forming an argument and the material to be chosen. Three kinds of examples or *paradigmata* were generally regarded as necessary: a familiar example from history, an analogy from the world of everyday behavior, and finally the *mythos* that creates an imaginary world. All three are applied as proofs and not simply as illustrations.

However, these rules and categories of ancient rhetoric must not be misunderstood as templates or preexisting forms into which meaning and texts had to be pressed, as is often the case in the reception of classical rhetoric in positivistic-scholarly exegesis. Rather, they are analytic means for discovering the argumentative and persuasive power of a text. They are not technical guides, but seek to throw light on substantive questions of inscribed power relationships. Rhetoric as discourse is inseparable from the sociopolitical conditions of its production.

Debates in public democratic assemblies, contests before judicial instances, and hymnic compositions that celebrate heroes and gods: these are the originating places of classical rhetoric, each determined by its pragmatic situation of origin.[14] A critical rhetorical analysis therefore seeks to discover not only the rhetorical stylistic means, but especially also the ideological practices, social location, and persuasive strategies of a text. In short, a rhetorical interpretive analysis understands the text as a discursive interactive conversation between its sociopolitical-religious locations, authors, hearers, and rhetorical situations. A rhetorical praxis of liberating interpretation, therefor, has to have its social location in communities of interpretation that critically examine power relationships and seek to change them.

The Socio-Political Turn[15]: Since the sociohistorical location of ancient rhetoric was the public space of the Greek city-state, the *polis*, and the *ekklēsia*,[16] a rhetorical analysis requires a revolutionary change in scholarly ethos; it demands a turning away from a value-neutral understanding of scholarship to a reformulation that can give voice to the political interests of texts and their interpretation as well as critically examine them.[17]

Thus public character and political responsibility become integral components of textual interpretation and historical reconstruction. If biblical scholarship is understood as a rhetorical and communicative praxis, its task is to analyze and demonstrate how biblical texts and their contemporary interpretation are part of political and religious discourses that are always already involved in power structures and thus are political.

This understanding of rhetoric as a political, communicative praxis[18] that articulates interests, values, and visions is not simply another form of literary analysis. Rather, rhetorical analysis is a means for showing how biblical texts and their interpretations take part either in creating and legitimating structures of oppression and kyriarchal relations of domination, or else in setting free theo-ethical values, liberative visions, and sociopolitical acts creating well-being.

In distinction to a formalized and positivistic scholarly interpretation of the Bible, a critical-emancipatory rhetoric insists, in concert with theologies of liberation, that context is as important as text. What we see depends on where we stand. The social location and context of both the author and of the interpreter determine how they see the world, perceive and articulate reality, or read biblical texts. A critical-feminist biblical interpretation that understands itself as a rhetorical-discursive praxis thus seeks to replace the objectivistic, positivistic, and supposedly apolitical interpretive methods of established biblical scholarship with rhetorical inquiry. It is interested in the formation of a critical, historical-cultural, and religio-political consciousness and works toward that end.

The feminist reshaping of biblical research as a critical-rhetorical praxis of interpretation and not simply a positivistic or hermeneutical one, I argue, makes available a framework for research in which not only historical, archaeological, sociological, literary, and theological methods of reading and questions of interpretation are admitted and cultivated, but where sociopolitical and the*-ethical questions may be understood as constitutive of the process of interpretation. Rhetorical interpretation sees the text not as a window on reality or a two-way mirror of self-reflection, but as a perspectival, context-bound political discourse that has ideological functions. Therefore the turn from hermeneutics to ideology critique is of central importance for an emancipatory-rhetorical paradigm.

THE TURN FROM HERMENEUTICS TO CRITIQUE OF IDEOLOGY

However, it must not be forgotten that the political discourses of *ekklēsia* and *politeia* in antiquity and modernity were articulated under conditions of kyriarchal relations.[19] Rhetoric lays open the fact that the relationship between language and power in particular historical moments is inscribed in texts. Acknowledging the rhetorical kyriarchal character of democratic discourses or the kyriocentric definition of politico-religious concepts such as equality, democracy, and justice does not mean rejecting these political discourses altogether as unusable by or dangerous to feminism. It only means that they must be critically analyzed and newly formulated to serve emancipatory interests. The same is true for biblical texts whose language is kyriocentrically shaped.

Hence the ideology-critical turn[20] goes hand in hand with a political turn. According to Jürgen Habermas, the ideological-critical turn, in contrast to the positivistic-scholarly and hermeneutical program, consists in making the power question central to the understanding of language, tradition, and canon.[21] As is well known, Habermas distinguishes three fundamental forms of knowledge: the *empirical-analytical*, the *hermeneutical-historical*, and the *critical-emancipatory* forms of knowledge of the world. We seek knowledge in order to control social conditions and natural circumstances (*empirical-analytical*), to understand these realities by evaluating and interpreting them (*hermeneutical-historical*), and to transform our individual and collective consciousness of reality (*critical-emancipatory*) so that the human potential and possibilities for liberty and equality may be enlarged and maximized.[22]

While the scholarly interpretation of the Bible devotes itself to the analysis of the text and the description of its contexts, and hermeneutics is interested in discovering both the meaning and the surplus of meaning, a critical-emancipatory analysis concentrates on the absence and deforming of contexts of meaning and scholarly methods that are shaped by conditions of power and kyriarchal relationships. Cultural, religious, and social speech acts and traditions are constituted in circumstances of unequal power and must be critically examined to uncover those circumstances.

Like critical theory, a feminist critical analysis concentrates especially on the corruption and ideological alienation of speech acts. Its fundamental methodological insight consists in having recognized the androcentric and kyriocentric functions of language.[23] It emphasizes that grammatically androcentric language does not describe and reflect reality, but regulates and constructs it. Andro-kyriocentric language is not only descriptive-reflective, but also active-performative. It both creates and shapes the symbolic worlds it pretends only to describe.

Language therefore, as an active-performative action, is always already political. Kyriocentric language shapes and is shaped by existing conditions of reality and kyriarchal relationships. Andro-kyriocentric language serves kyriarchal interests and, in turn, kyriarchal interests determine the content of andro-kyriocentric language. Therefore an intra- and intertextual analysis of language and text is insufficient. It must be strengthened by a critical systemic analysis of religio-political kyriarchal structures that exercise violence and exclusion.

Andro-kyriocentric language and knowledge about the patri-kyriarchal world are thus rhetorical; that is, they are articulated by particular people for a particular circle of readers, and they work with particular expressed or unexpressed interests and goals. Since all the texts of sacred scripture and all knowledge about the world are both rhetorical and political, it is possible to analyze and change the cultural and religious frames of thought and constructs that are continually newly inscribed by such texts.

Rhetorical analysis is thus best understood as critique of ideology. It is kyriarchal and power relationships that produce twisted forms of communication and result in the self-deception of scholars and their audiences who are not conscious of their interests, needs, and distorted perceptions of the social and religious world. Critique of ideology thus understands language as a means and a way to inscribe forms of power in contexts of meaning and significance. Researching ideologies thus means not only analyzing a particular type of discourse, but also investigating types of interpretation and bestowals of meaning that serve either to maintain kyriarchal relations of domination or to undermine them.

According to John B. Thompson, ideology works by means of three types of operations or strategies.[24] The *first strategy* founds the legitimacy of kyriarchy on traditional bases (for example, the Vatican's argument that Jesus and the apostles did not ordain any wo/men, although it is known that Jesus did not ordain anyone), while the *second strategy* conceals kyriarchal relationships and their existence (for example, models of womanhood are used to impress on wo/men that selfless service corresponds to their natural and essential aptitude for heterosexual relationships and maternity). These strategies prevent the critical analysis and calling into question of the bases for society, religion, or scholarship. The *third strategy* in turn reifies and naturalizes processes and attitudes that have become common in society. For example, it impresses the idea that motherhood is determined by nature and corresponds to the essence of "woman." It presents temporal, cultural, social, and historical situations as if they were given by nature, permanent, timeless, or revealed.

Ideology thus creates the distorted self-concept of oppressed people and inculcates it further into them. It shapes the consciousness of people who thereby internalize their subordinate status either as natural and inborn or as willed by G*d. A rhetorical emancipatory analysis of kyriocentric biblical texts therefore requires not only a new awareness and critique of ideology, but also a critical ethics of interpretation.

The Turn to a Political-Theological Ethics

Biblical[25] scholarship that continues to subscribe to a value-neutral theory of scholarship[26] not only represents an apolitical conservative interpretation of texts that kyriocentrically further and deeper inscribe kyriarchal relationships. It is also unable to accept responsibility for the structures of prejudice that are further and more deeply inscribed by biblical texts and their interpretations. Only when biblical scholarship begins to acknowledge its own social location and religious-political interests shaped by race, gender, nationality, and socioreligious class identity will scholars be able to give an account of their standpoints to their hearers/readers. Therefore ethics assumes a central place in an emancipatory-political and liberation-theological paradigm of interpretation.[27]

Debates about the relationship between rhetoric and morality have continued throughout the whole history of rhetoric. However, in the modern era scholars have tended to adopt individualistic and privatized models of ethics instead of establishing a rhetorical public site that articulates, applies, and enriches ethics and morality through generally accessible arguments. Such an emancipatory public site has, however, been created by social movements for liberation.

To give one example: only someone who has understood and taken seriously the post-colonial struggle of wo/men for their rights can fully comprehend the problem of racism and its ghastly consequences inscribed in texts. Participants in such moral-rhetorical discourses of liberation are agents who actively create such a moral public site by coming together, encouraging each other, justifying and contending with one another about how well-being and the good life for all can look and be made a reality. Such an intersubjective, political, and public conceptualization of ethics has rhetoric at its heart.

Rhetoric as intersubjective democratic process[28] is ethical in a twofold sense: on the one hand it opens up the author's choice of reality and the methods she has selected for portraying reality, and on the other hand it permits readers to have a free choice instead of requiring total and necessary acceptance. Truth that is rhetorically established presumes freedom of choice and perception of alternative realities. It must therefore seek to avoid the Scylla of idealism and the Charybdis of semantics.

While an idealistic ethics seeks, in Platonic fashion, to discover the truth behind reality, a semantic ethics regards language as a map and assumes that a good map does not show mountains and rivers where there are none. While in semantic ethics language reflects a given reality, in idealistic ethics rhetoric has the task of discovering truth rather than creating it. After she has "discovered" the truth the idealist can no longer be made responsible for it, since this truth is something already given.[29]

In the case of both idealistic and semantic ethics it is supposed that "the truth, the world, or reality" not only exist objectively outside language but can also be grasped as such. In contrast, an intersubjective democratic-emancipatory ethics understands "the world, the truth, and reality" as rhetorically and linguistically created and stresses the responsibility of those. Since the turn to ethics has made it clear that morality and truth, vision and knowledge of a good life are rhetorically and linguistically produced and transmitted, biblical scholarship, using an emancipatory-political paradigm, must develop both an emancipatory ethics of reading and an ethics of interpretation.

Such an ethics of interpretation, which regards texts as rhetorical constructions, cannot restrict itself to the exegesis of the text, but must also be critically responsible ethically, politically, and theologically for its own interpretive methods, goals, and interests. Such an ethical-rhetorical paradigm of interpretation sees objectivity and methods differently. While in a positivistic-scholarly paradigm methods are understood as rules and directions or recipes, in an ethical-rhetorical paradigm of liberation they are seen as questions to be posed or perspectives to be clarified.

Since biblical scholarship is at home in the kyriarchal institutions of university and church, a feminist biblical interpretation cannot simply assume that biblical research produces knowledge that liberates and transforms. Instead, it must critically inquire of and evaluate all interpretations of the text and claims to knowledge to discover whether they interrupt kyriarchal interests or inscribe them further. Therefore it insists that all scholarly methods, approaches to thought, and results must be subjected to an ethical-rhetorical analysis and asked how and whether they reinscribe oppression or whether they open possibilities for liberation. In short, an emancipatory-rhetorical hermeneutics is no less scholarly than established exegesis. On the contrary, the emancipatory-political paradigm of interpretation opens up the possibility and points the way to a greater kind of scholarship that can accept responsibility for the well-being of all in the global cosmopolis.

For a theological hermeneutic this means that both the Protestant "canon within the canon" and the Catholic "Scripture, Tradition, and Magisterium" hermeneutics must be critically examined. If texts always already serve ideologically shaped kyriarchal interests, they must be critically examined regarding their kyriarchal functions. If biblical texts are always G*d's word in human words, they must be subjected to an ideology-critical reflection and theo-ethical evaluation directed toward liberation. A critical, political, feminist theology therefore seeks critically and creatively to rethink the traditional theological discipline of "discernment of spirits" and to put it into practice.

NOTES

[1] Michèle Barrett, *The Politics of Truth: From Marx to Foucault* (Palo Alto: Stanford University Press, 1991).

[2] For an analysis of kyriarchy, see the chapters above and my books *But She Said. Feminist Practices of Biblical Interpretation* (Boston: Beacon, 1992); and *Jesus: Miriam's Child, Sophia's Prophet: Critical Issues in Feminist Christology* (New York: Continuum, 1994).

[3] Thomas Kuhn, *The Structure of Scientific Revolutions* (Chicago: University of Chicago Press, 1970).

[4] Elisabeth Schüssler Fiorenza, "Women in Early Christianity. Methodological Considerations," in Thomas J. Ryan, ed., *Critical History and Biblical Faith in New Testament Perspective*, CTS Annual Publication (Villanova: Villanova University Press, 1979), 30–58; and "For the Sake of Our Salvation: Biblical Interpretation as The*logical Task," in Daniel Durken, ed., *Sin, Salvation, and the Spirit* (Collegeville: Liturgical, 1979), 21–39.

[5] See Jill M. Bystydzienski and Joti Sekhon, eds., *Democratization and Women's Grassroots Movements* (Bloomington: Indiana University Press, 1999); Christa Wichterich, *The Globalized Woman: Reports from a Future of Inequality*, trans. Patrick Camiller (North Sydney: Spinifex, 2000).

[6] See my book *Rhetoric and Ethic. The Politics of Biblical Interpretation* (Minneapolis: Fortress Press, 1999); and Fernando F. Segovia, "Introduction: 'And They Began to Speak in Other Tongues.' Competing Modes of Discourse in Contemporary Biblical Criticism," in Segovia and Tolbert, eds., *Reading from This Place: Social Location and Biblical Interpretation in the United States* (Minneapolis: Fortress Press, 1995), 1–32; see also his article, "Pedagogical Discourse and Practices in Cultural Studies," in Segovia and Tolbert, eds., *Teaching the Bible: The Discourses and Politics of Biblical Pedagogy* (Maryknoll: Orbis, 1998), 137–67.

[7] Klaus Berger, *Hermeneutik des Neuen Testaments* (Gütersloh: Gütersloher, 1988); Paul Ricoeur, *Hermeneutics and the Human Sciences*, ed. and trans. John B. Thompson (Cambridge: Cambridge University Press, 1981).

[8] Rasiah S. Sugirtharajah, "The Margin as a Site of Creative Revisioning," in Sugirtharajah, ed., *Voices from the Margin: Interpreting the Bible in the Third World* (Maryknoll: Orbis, 1995), 1–8.

[9] For example, Gerd Theissen, "Methodenkonkurrenz und hermeneutischer Konflikt: Pluralismus in Exegese und Lektüre der Bibel," in Joachim Mehlhausen, ed., *Pluralismus und Identität* (Gütersloh: Kaiser, 1995), 127–40.

[10] See Amos N. Wilder, "Scholars, Theologians, and Ancient Rhetoric," *JBL* 75 (1956): 1–11; and his book *Early Christian Rhetoric: The Language of the Gospel* (Cambridge: Harvard University Press, 1971); Dale Patrick and Allen Scult, *Rhetoric and Biblical Interpretation* (Sheffield: Almond, 1990).

[11] Susan Shapiro, "Rhetoric as Ideology Critique: The Gadamer-Habermas Debate Reinvented," *JAAR* 62, no. 1 (1994): 123–50; Lorraine Code, *Rhetorical Spaces: Essays on Gendered Locations* (New York: Routledge, 1995); John Bender and David E. Wellbery, "Rhetoricality: On the Modernist Return of Rhetoric," in John Bender and David E. Wellbery, eds., *The Ends of Rhetoric: History, Theory, Practice* (Palo Alto: Stanford University Press, 1990); Cheryl Glenn, *Rhetoric Retold: Regendering the Tradition from Antiquity through the Renaissance* (Carbondale: Southern Illinois University Press, 1997).

[12] John Louis Lucaites, Celeste Michelle Condit, and Sally Caudill, eds., *Contemporary Rhetorical Theory: A Reader* (New York: Guilford, 1999).

[13] Schüssler Fiorenza, *Rhetoric and Ethic*, 105–28.

[14] See Susan C. Jarratt, *Rereading the Sophists: Classical Rhetoric Refigured* (Carbondale: Southern Illinois University Press, 1991).

[15] Johannes Thiele, "Bibelauslegung im gesellschaftlich-politischen Kontext," in Wolfgang Langer, ed., *Handbuch der Bibelarbeit* (Munich: Kösel, 1987), 106–14.

[16] Jennifer Tolbert Roberts, *Athens on Trial: The Antidemocratic Tradition in Western Thought* (Princeton: Princeton University Press, 1994); Jane Sutton, "The Death of Rhetoric and Its Rebirth in Philosophy," *Rhetorica* 4 (1986): 203–26; "The Taming of Polos/Polis: Rhetoric as an Achievement without Women," in John Louis Lucaites, et al., eds., *Contemporary Rhetorical Theory. A Reader* (New York: Guilford, 1999), 101–27.

[17] Lawrence J. Prelli, "The Rhetorical Construction of Scientific Ethos," in Herbert W. Simons, ed., *Rhetoric in the Human Sciences* (Newbury Park: Sage, 1989), 48; see also the contribution by Robert K. Merton in Norman W. Storer, ed., *The Sociology of Science: Theoretical and Empirical Investigations* (Chicago: University of Chicago Press, 1973), 267–78; Michael Mulkay, *Science and Sociology of Knowledge* (London and Boston: Allen and Unwin, 1979); Rayme McKerrow, "Critical Rhetoric. Theory and Practice," in Lucaites et al., eds., *Contemporary Rhetorical Theory*, 441–63.

[18] Richard Harvey Brown, *Society as Text: Essays on Rhetoric, Reason, and Reality* (Chicago: University of Chicago Press, 1987), 85. See also John S. Nelson, Allan Megill, and Donald McCloskey, eds., *The Rhetoric of the Human Sciences: Language and Argument in Scholarship and Public Affairs* (Madison: University of Wisconsin Press, 1987); Hayden White, *Tropics of Discourse: Essays in Cultural Criticism* (Baltimore: Johns Hopkins University Press, 1978); John S. Nelson, "Political Theory as Political Rhetoric," in Nelson, ed., *What Should Political Theory Be Now?* (Albany: SUNY Press, 1983), 169–240.

[19] Richard Bernstein, "What Is the Difference that Makes a Difference? Gadamer, Habermas, and Rorty," in Brice R. Wachterhauser, ed., *Hermeneutics and Modern Philosophy* (Albany: SUNY Press, 1986), 343–76; Victoria E. Bonnell and Lynn Hunt, eds., *Beyond the Cultural Turn: New Directions in the Study of Society and Culture* (Berkeley: University of California Press, 1999).

[20] David Jobling and Tina Pippin, eds., *Ideological Criticism of Biblical Texts*, Semeia 59 (Atlanta: Scholars, 1992); Fernando F. Segovia, "Cultural Studies and Contemporary Biblical Criticism: Ideological Criticism as a Mode of Discourse," in Segovia and Tolbert, eds., *Reading from This Place*, vol. 2, *Social Location and Biblical Interpretation in Global Perspective* (Minneapolis: Fortress Press, 1995), 1–17.

[21] Jürgen Habermas, "Ideology," in Tom Bottomore, ed., *Modern Interpretations of Marx* (Oxford: Oxford University Press, 1981), 166.

[22] Raymond A. Morrow with David D. Baron, *Critical Theory and Methodology* (Thousand Oaks: Sage, 1994).

[23] See, for example, my book *In Memory of Her: A Feminist Reconstruction of Christian Origins* (New York: Crossroad, 1983); Dennis Baron, *Grammar and Gender* (New Haven: Yale University Press, 1986); Robert H. Robins, *A Short History of Linguistics* (London and New York: Longman, 1979); Casey Miller and Kate Swift, *Words and Women: New Language in New Times* (New York: Doubleday, 1977); Gloria A. Marshall, "Racial Classifications: Popular and Scientific," in Sandra Harding, ed., *The "Racial" Economy of Science* (Bloomington: Indiana University Press, 1990), 116–27. For a comparison of sexist and racist language see the essays in Mary Vetterling-Braggin, ed., *Sexist Language: A Modern Philosophical Analysis* (Totowa: Rowman and Littlefield, 1981).

[24] John B. Thompson, *Studies in the Theory of Ideology* (Cambridge: Polity, 1984), 254.

[25] For example, Danna Nolan Fewell and Gary A. Phillips, eds., *Bible and Ethics of Reading, Semeia 77* (Atlanta: Scholars, 1997).

[26] For a defense of social-science objectivistic interpretation see Bruce J. Malina, "Rhetorical Criticism and Social-Scientific Criticism: Why Won't Romanticism Leave Us Alone?" in Stanley E. Porter and Thomas H. Olbricht, eds., *Rhetoric, Scripture and Theology: Essays from the 1994 Pretoria Conference* (Sheffield: Sheffield Academic, 1996), 72–96.

[27] Rey Chow, *Ethics after Idealism: Theory–Culture–Ethnicity–Reading* (Bloomington: Indiana University Press, 1998).

[28] Celeste Michelle Condit, "Democracy and Civil Rights: The Universalizing Influence of Public Argumentation," *Communication Monographs* 54 (1987): 1–20; Frank Lentricchia, *Criticism and Social Change* (Chicago: University of Chicago Press, 1983).

[29] Jane Adamson, Richard Freedman, and David Parke, eds., *Renegotiating Ethics in Literature, Philosophy, and Theory* (Cambridge: Cambridge University Press, 1998); Peter Baker, *Deconstruction and the Ethical Turn* (Gainesville: University Press of Florida, 1995); Peter Singer, ed., *Ethics* (Oxford: Oxford University Press, 1994), 1–15; Annemarie Pieper, *Ethik und Moral: Eine Einführung in die praktische Philosophie* (Munich: Beck, 1985), 10–43; Gunhild Buse, *Macht, Moral, Weiblichkeit: Eine feministisch-theologische Auseinandersetzung mit Carol Gilligan und Frigga Haug* (Mainz: Grünewald, 1993).

8

Disciplinary Matters

A Critical Rhetoric and Ethic of Inquiry

In the past decade or so rhetorical criticism has developed not only as a textual-exegetical practice but also as an interdisciplinary rhetoric of inquiry that serves as a epistemological meta-reflection on the theoretical and methodological practices of the discipline.[1] Thomas Olbricht has pointed to the broad interdisciplinary character of rhetorical criticism since the academic study of rhetoric encompasses divergent fields of inquiry.[2] However, such an interdisciplinary rhetoric of inquiry has not yet been fully developed in biblical rhetorical criticism.[3]

For that reason my own work has advocated a paradigm shift from an ethos of positivist scientism and cultural hermeneutics to rhetorical criticism as an interdisciplinary critical inquiry in biblical studies. Paradigm criticism[4] explores theoretically the struggle between different epistemological approaches, the theological, the historical, the hermeneutic,[5] and the rhetorical paradigms—a struggle that has been underway for quite some time in biblical studies. I have initiated such a discussion of disciplinary paradigms[6] in order to bring about a change in the ethos and ethics of biblical studies. Only if we bring about a critical rhetorical-emancipatory[7] paradigm shift will the theoretical contributions of the margins—such as feminism, postcolonialism, critical race, and ethnic-cultural studies—be able to be heard.

The emerging paradigm shift from a positivist-scientific to a critical emancipatory ethos, from rhetoric as a purely technical exegetical analysis that focuses on the text to rhetoric as critical meta-level inquiry into the practices of biblical criticism, a process that has been underway in the past decade or so in biblical studies and which has far-reaching consequences for the self-understanding and ethos of the discipline.[8] Rhetorical criticism has been enthralled for far too long by the "scientific" method, historical positivism, and the use of classical categories. It has tended to remain on the literary level of text and exegesis rather than become engaged in an interdisciplinary rhetoric of inquiry.

A Rhetoric of Inquiry

My book *Rhetoric and Ethic*[9] outlined the methodological and theoretical conceptualization of rhetorical criticism as a critical emancipatory rhetoric and ethic of inquiry. In this chapter I seek to deepen this approach by focusing on the disciplinary discourses of biblical studies. Since the conference at which this paper was originally presented had the theme of "rhetorics, ethics and moral persuasion in biblical discourse," I will explore the discipline's self-understanding and professional discourses in terms of "ethos and ethics." Hence, I will look at both the pedagogical professionalizing practices and disciplinary discourses of biblical studies.[10]

Because of space limitations I can only indicate here the importance of a reconsideration of the professional educational and rhetorical practices shaping the discipline. The articulation of the critical pedagogy that Fernando Segovia and Mary Ann Tolbert pioneered with *Teaching the Bible*,[11] is an important next step in the rhetorical rearticulation of the discipline, particularly because of the growing recognition that biblical studies are unable to intervene critically in the discourses and uses of the Bible in either public societal discourses and global interreligious contexts or religious communities, churches, mosques, and synagogues.

I will conclude my argument by looking at two concrete examples of hegemonic scholarly discourse and their "othering rhetoric" in order to see how they consciously or not marginalize and exclude those intellectual voices that have been silenced for centuries from disciplinary authority and power. I will end my exploration by showing that it is impossible for minority speakers to be heard if the disciplinary ethos of biblical studies continues to be defined as a "rhetorical space" in which critical challenges to the hegemonic ethos of the discipline are construed either as romanticized or as oppositional discourse.

Such a rhetoric of inquiry pays special attention to the argumentative discourses of scholarship and their theoretical presuppositions, social locations, investigative methods, and sociopolitical functions. Since the space of rhetorical discourse is the public and political realm, a rhetoric of inquiry does not need to suppress but is able to investigate the sociopolitical frameworks, cultural perspectives, modes of argumentation, and symbolic universes of religious texts and biblical interpretations.[12] It is keenly interested in exploring the notion of ethos and ethic in epistemological rhetorical terms.

A critical rhetorical conceptualization of the discipline seeks to foster a discussion of the disciplinary practices of the field and to propose theoretical-methodological steps for reconstructing biblical studies in ethical-emancipatory and feminist-rhetorical terms. I thereby understand rhetorical criticism not only as a form of textual-hermeneutical analysis but also, as Susan Jarratt explains, as a "meta-discipline through which a whole spectrum of language uses and their outcome as social action can be refracted for analysis."[13]

I would suggest that a rhetoric and ethic of inquiry as a critical meta-discipline and the redefinition of biblical studies as ethical-rhetorical inquiry into the religious, cultural, social, and political functions of past and present biblical discourses would at the very least include the following areas of analysis:

- The rhetoric and ethic of reading pertains to the text and the methods used to interpret it. Such exegetical and interpretive practices are usually the focus of rhetorical criticism, which is focused on text and texture as object of analysis rather than on the agents of such an analysis.
- The rhetoric and ethic of interpretive practices or scientific production has the task to critically analyze the research methods used and to investigate the process of how interpretation is produced, authorized, communicated, and used and in what kind of power relations it is embedded.
- The rhetoric and ethic of the discipline inquires into the ethos, social location, and positionality of biblical studies: how the field is structured, what kind of assumptions are governing its practices, how professional authority is exercised, how academic excellence is adjudicated, or what kind of discourses are excluded.
- The rhetoric and ethic of communicative practices analyzes biblical and contemporary rhetoric as an ideological/theological communicative undertaking that promotes either violence or well-being for all. Hence, biblical rhetoric must be assessed in terms of an ethics and politics of interpretation.

In short, rhetoric is best understood as epistemic because it reveals an ethical dimension of knowledge production as political practice. Rhetorics, politics, and ethics are epistemologically as well as historically intertwined. Since its goal is persuasion, the ethical knowledge rhetoric strives to achieve is that of commitment and accountability.[14] A reconceptualization of the discipline, moreover, would require that disciplinary excellence be judged not only in terms of competence in historical-literary critical and hermeneutical-cultural methods but also in terms of a critical rhetorical meta-reflection on the ethical, communicative, and educational practices of the discipline.

By an ethic of inquiry I mean a new evaluative form of cultural practice and critical investigation that is no longer circumscribed by the positivist objectivism, subjectivism, liberalism, and nationalism of modernity or the masculine rationalism and European colonialism that have tended to relegate rhetoric to mere talk and to the dustbins of history. Thus my project understands rhetoric not so much as *technê* that limits itself to a literary analysis in terms of classical or modern rhetoric. Instead rhetoric as a field of study insists on bringing together textuality, society, religion, and politics and is concerned with how "knowledge" is constructed, the ways individuals and groups wield power, and the values and visions biblical discourses engender. Such a rhetoric of inquiry necessitates a critical assessment of the ethics and ethos of the discipline.

ETHICS AND ETHOS

Disputes about the relationship between rhetoric and ethic[15] have been alive in rhetorical theory throughout its history. As Celeste Michelle Condit has pointed out, however, recently theorists have tended to use privatized and individualistic models of morality, such as the conversational model of discourse, rather than engage in public rhetoric "viewed as a process in which basic human desires are transformed into shared moral codes."[16] A rhetoric of morality is constructed, implemented, and enhanced through public argument. It "utilizes the capacity of discourse simultaneously to create, extend, and apply moral concepts," a process that is "bounded by an inductive historical objectivity."[17] It is both intersubjective and political, made and unmade by rhetorical practices, which are not to be seen as mirrors that reflect the world back to us.

Participants in such moral discourse are active moral agents who deliberate, urge, validate, and argue meanings and actions with each other. Such a critical democratic conceptualization of ethic has rhetoric at its center. Rhetoric as an intersubjective-democratic process "is doubly ethical: it is the result of a choice on the part of the rhetor as to the reality advocated and the method of doing so, and it urges choice rather than complete and necessary acceptance on the part of the audience. Truth that is rhetorically made encourages choice and awareness of alternative realities."[18]

The meaning of *ethos*, just like that of rhetoric,[19] changes over time and its definition is different in different cultures. According to Baumlin, in antiquity *ethos* articulates the "problematic relation between human character and discourse. More specifically it raises questions concerning the inclusion of the speaker's character as an aspect of discourse, the representation of that character in discourse, and the role of that character in persuasion."[20] In modernity Peter Ramus greatly influenced the ethos of the discipline[21] insofar as he held sway among Protestant interpreters of the sixteenth century. Since he sought to sever logic from rhetoric and then to retain logic as the only valid component that generates a mode of "pure reasoning," he introduced the split of rhetoric from logic that demoted rhetoric to mere style, decoration, manipulation, and eloquence in oral performance.

Etymologically the meaning of *ethos* can be derived either from the Greek *ethos*, meaning custom, habit, usage, folkways, or from the Greek *ēthos*, meaning character formation as the totality of all characteristic traits rather than mere custom or morally approved habits. A third etymological root suggested by Susan Jarratt and Nedra Reynolds is *ēthea*, a plural noun that is the original root of both terms and means "haunts" or "hang outs." This etymology understands *ethos* as a space where customs and character are formed, "where one is accustomed to being."[22] Ethos as a disciplinary space determines the professional character of individuals and expresses the way one lives. *Ethos* in this spatial sense theorizes the "positionality" inherent in rhetoric. This notion of ethos is, for instance, typical for Hannah Arendt's political philosophy, as John McGowan has pointed out: "By extension, ethics can thus be understood not simply to encompass the formation and judgment of character, but also to include the production of a place that character can inhabit. To put it in even more strongly Arendtian terms, ethics must build on the intimate connection between character to place. Only where we create a certain kind of place can a certain kind of person emerge."[23]

Habit and customs always form character in a social space and locate the speaker in the practices and experiences of the group to which s/he belongs or speaks. *Ethos*, like experience, then can be understood in terms of "positionality" as the "place from which values are interpreted and constructed rather than as a locus of an already determined set of values."[24] *Ethos* understood as positioning is "the awareness that one always speaks from a particular place in a social structure."[25] The willingness of the audience to step into the space occupied (temporarily) by the speaker is crucial in establishing the ethics of ethos while acknowledging the differences rather than the sameness between speaker and audience.

Read through a feminist optic, *ethos* can be understood "as an ethical and political tool, as a way of claiming and taking responsibility for our positions in the world, for the ways we see, the places from where we speak."[26] To understand *ethos* in terms of "rhetorical space" elucidates why voice and position are central to rhetorical inquiry and scholarly authority. According to Lorraine Code, rhetorical spaces "are fictive but not fanciful or fixed locations whose tacit (rarely spoken) territorial imperatives structure and limit the kind of utterances that can be voiced within them with a reasonable expectation of uptake and choral support, an expectation of being heard, understood, taken seriously. They are the sites where the very possibility of an utterance counting as 'true-or-false' or of a discussion yielding insight is made manifest."[27]

To understand feminist rhetorical biblical criticism as an hermeneutic of epistemological[28] space would mean first of all to examine the conditions for the possibility of constructing and using biblical knowledge that does not reinforce the structural violence of the status quo in society, church, and academy. It would mean the investigation of the kyriarchal (gendered, raced, classed, and colonized) structures and circumstances in which wo/men and subaltern men "occupy positions of minimal epistemic authority and where questions of differential power and privilege figure centrally."[29]

Such a feminist rhetorical reconceptualization of the disciplinary *ethos* of biblical studies is necessary for overcoming the false dichotomy between engaged, socially located scholarship (for example, feminist, postcolonial, African American, queer, and other sub-disciplines) and value neutral "scientific" (malestream) biblical interpretation. Whereas the former allegedly utilizes ethical criteria, the latter is said to live up to a scientific *ethos* by making use of cognitive criteria. Instead, I would argue that a scientific ethos demands both ethical and cognitive criteria, which must be reasoned out in terms of intersubjectively understandable and communicable knowledge.

In short, if *ethos* is a habit or a pattern of social practices that are inseparable from social location and are always shaped by relations of power, it becomes important to explore the concept not just in terms of the *ethos* of the individual biblical scholar but also in terms of the professional *ethos* of the discipline that determines the social self-identity, positioning, and socialization of the emerging biblical scholar.

PROFESSIONAL ETHOS

Traditionally, rhetorical theories have been linked to the goal of education as a means of transforming society. For instance, while Plato constructs a perfect *polis* in order to educate its citizens in accordance with it, Isocrates wants to educate citizens to eliminate strife and enmity by teaching them how to achieve *homonoia* (like-mindedness), and Aristotle teaches rhetoric as a faculty for using the means of persuasion in any given situation. For Cicero, in turn, the point of education is its application to the practical ends of daily lives, and in the Pan-Hellenic program of Alexander the Great the goal is *enkyklios paidaia, the "rounded education,"* which consists in instruction in the trivium grammar, rhetoric, logic, and in the quadrivium arithmetic, geometry, music and astronomy. Thus explorations of the role of ethos have been crucial not only for rhetorical theories but also for rhetorical pedagogy.[30]

In the nineteenth and beginning of the twentieth century, the scientific *ethos* of value-free scholarship that was presumed to be untainted by social relations and political interest has been institutionalized in professions that assure the continuation of the dominant disciplinary ethos. Among others, Nancy Leys Stepan and Sander Gilman have pointed out that the professional institutionalization of scholarship as value-neutral, apolitical, universal, empirical and methodologically objective science and an "unbiased arena of knowledge" was not a "natural" outcome of unbiased study but "a social outcome of a process whereby science was historically and materially constituted to have certain meanings, functions and interests. In a complex series of innovations, science's epistemological claims were given definition and institutional representation in the form of new scientific societies and organizations sharply delimited from other institutions. These innovations were tied not only to industrialization, but to the politics of class and the closing of ranks of bourgeois society. . . . Race and gender were also crucial in the construction of modern science, in that science was defined as 'masculine' in its abstraction, detachment and objectivity."[31]

This professionalization of the academic disciplines engendered theoretical dichotomies such as pure and impure, theoretical or applied science. Dualistic opposites such as rational and irrational, objective and subjective, hard and soft, male and female, Europeans and colonials, secular and religious were given material form not only in professional disciplines but also in their discursive practices. For instance, the methodologically dense, scientific, depersonalized, empirical-factual text of the research paper emerged as a new standardized academic genre. This genre replaced the more metaphorically porous, literary varied, understandable forms of writing that were accessible also to the non-scientific "popular" reader.

The development of biblical studies as a scientific discipline adopted a similar scientific professional elite male ethos.[32] The SBL was founded in 1880,[33] around the same time that the American Philological Association (1869), the American Social Science Association (1869), the Archeological Institute of America (1879), the Modern Language Association (1883), and the American Historical Society (1884) were initiated. The feminist historian Bonnie G. Smith has argued that, for instance, the ethos of the American Historical Association cultivated a value-detached, "gender-neutral" community of scholars and developed an "objective" narrative in the course of professionalization as "a modern scientific profession." Its practices were not only unconcerned with considerations of gender, class, politics, culture, or society at large but they openly required "a commitment to objectivity" over and above such categories as class and gender; they demanded "the strict use of evidence, the taming of historical narrative to a less rhetorical style, the development of archives and professional libraries, the organization of university training in seminars and tutorials, and in the case of the United States, a commitment to democratic access to the profession based on ability." In addition, professionalizing historians attempted to "eliminate all personal or subjective meaning from their work. Thus historians created a space inhabited by an invisible 'I,' one without politics, without an ego or persona, and certainly ungendered."[34]

Like its brother-profession the American Historical Society, the SBL was founded by Protestant "gentlemen,"[35] who were for the most part "European trained in such universities as Berlin, Heidelberg, Halle, and Tübingen."[36] Even though the overall theoretical position of the SBL was apparently "impartial," seeking to make available "a forum for the expression and critique of diverse positions on the study of the scriptures," the position of the so-called higher criticism won increasing influence.[37] The professional scientific stance was complicated in biblical studies by the struggle of the discipline not only to prove its scientific "value-neutral" character within the Enlightenment university, which had only very recently more or less successfully thrown off the shackles of religion. It also was marked by the struggle to free itself from the dogmatic fetters of the Protestant and Roman Catholic[38] churches. This conflict emerged between the advocates of scientific "higher criticism" and those interested in safeguarding the theological "purity" of the Bible in the "heresy trials" at the turn of the twentieth century.

The same rhetorical tension remains inscribed in biblical studies as a profession still today. Emblazoned in the professional *ethos* of biblical criticism is the conflict of how to study the Bible. Should it be viewed either as a collection of ancient texts or as a normative document of biblical religions? Is the critical study of the theological meaning and normativity of traditions and scriptures part of the research program of biblical studies or must it be left to confessional theology? Is it part of the professional program of "higher criticism" to study the communities of discourse that have produced and sustained scriptural texts and readings in the past and still do so in the present? Finally, does competence in biblical criticism entail the ability to engage in a critical-theoretical interdisciplinary meta-reflection on the work of biblical studies? Would this require that students of the Bible be trained not only in textual-historical analysis but also in the ideological analysis of the social and political discursive positionings and social religious-political relations of the discipline and its practitioners?

The scientific, academic ethos of the discipline also governs its pedagogical and credentializing practices. It reproduces the professional "club culture" that has engendered modern detached and value-free science. As Saunders puts it:

> We have noted occasional concerns to define the public audiences to which the work of the learned society is addressed. Obviously the primary concern is with the academic community. Truth for truth's sake and the scholarly enterprise answerable to itself has been the customs of the confraternity of experts. But the ivory tower and mentality have been under heavy attack in recent times. [If results are not shared with church, synagogue and a wider public] the Society becomes (some would say has become) an antiquarian association more closely resembling an English gentleman's club than a laboratory. Do the Cabots speak only to the Lodges and the Lodges speak only to God? Some think so.[39]

If professionalization seeks to "discipline" its practitioners, since it has the "making of professionals" as its goal, doctoral education becomes central to maintaining such a positivist elite masculine ethos. Hence, one must problematize the discipline not only in theoretical terms but also with respect to its educational practices.[40] A *Rhetoric and Ethic of Inquiry* therefore must also critically investigate the pedagogical practices of the discipline. Not only doctoral but also ministerial students need to be educated in this new interdisciplinary rhetorical paradigm of inquiry, of critical reflexivity, and research that studies the pervasive and often only partly conscious set of value-laden dispositions, inclinations, attitudes, and habits of biblical studies as an academic discipline. Rather than reproducing, for example, in dissertation after dissertation on Paul or John, the scientist-positivist approach that restricts biblical studies to ascertaining the single true meaning of the text, research could focus both on the rhetorical function of biblical and other ancient texts in their past and present historical and literary contexts and on the ideological justifications presented by their ever more technically refined interpretations.

In the last section of this chapter I therefore will analyze two examples of argumentative discourse in order to show how professional ethos determines disciplinary discourses by establishing what can be said and what is a priori ruled out of court. I have chosen these rhetorical examples not because I want to enter into a personal quarrel with these scholars but because their work enjoys wide recognition within the discipline of rhetorical biblical criticism. In short, I have chosen these disciplinary discourses as examples for showing how their argumentative moves establish disciplinary power and "rhetorical space" or ethos that marginalizes oppositional discourses.

Oppositional Discourse Labeled As Romantic Rhetoric

In his Pretoria Conference paper Bruce Malina also refers to the statement of Wilhelm Wüllner, which I have quoted in the introduction, but reads it in terms of the methodological split between historical social scientific and romantic or aesthetic literary biblical criticism rather than in terms of disciplinary ethos and rhetorical theory.[41] Malina intellectually locates himself as a "socio-rational empiricist" who has developed a social-scientific method that reads early Christian texts with the "awareness of the cultural perspective that generated those meanings."[42] Hence, the interpreter must use a social system to understand social texts.

Malina concedes that the articulation and choice of a social system such as honor and shame in Mediterranean culture must begin with the contemporary articulation of this social system in anthropology or sociology. Malina does not engage in a critical epistemological reflection on the scientific articulation of social systems or of how persons reading the Bible today communicate with and influence each other. However, he insists that with the method of retrodiction it is possible to "strip off" from such a system all "post-first century accretions."[43]

Rather than engaging in a critical epistemological reflection, Malina constructs a dichotomy between historical and social-scientific rhetorical criticism on the one hand and aesthetic or Romantic rhetorical criticism on the other. This dualistic typology seems to lump all (postmodern) critical intellectual approaches together under the rubric of Romanticism, which Malina defines as "Storybookism,"[44] because as he says, "Life in the new post-rationalist world is like a story in a novel."[45] He sees "little use, if any, for literary–aesthetic rhetoric in biblical studies since concern for texts, texture, and intertexture and the like has no impact on what an author said and meant to say to an original audience."[46]

Still, Malina's concern is really not with literary and aesthetic rhetoricism but lies elsewhere, as the following blanket statement indicates: "For it seems to me that the recent offshoots of the Romantic approach to the Bible include feminism, deconstructionism, fundamentalism, and hermeneutics. What all of these have in common is that they all dismiss the concrete, physical situation-conditioned, culturally based orientation of the first telling of the Christian story, much like Gnosticism in antiquity. . . . Thus like Romantics and their transcending self, feminism, deconstructionism, fundamentalism and hermeneutics are essential anti-incarnational. They are not interested in taking the *literal* [emphasis added], historical meaning of the New Testament seriously."[47]

While Malina's rhetoric theologically warms up the old chestnut of heretical Gnosticism as "anti-incarnational," his ire is really directed against all those who do not share his own reading of the Enlightenment and "its emphasis on objective universals." This is because the "Enlightenment's credo of freedom, equality and brotherhood remained accessible only to elites."[48] It is the reality of elite men and the truncated historical knowledge they have produced and still produce as social-scientific fact that Malina defends. Rather than arguing, for instance, why he does not recognize patriarchy—or as I would prefer, kyriarchy—as the overarching social system of the Mediterranean with which to interface biblical and other ancient texts in a critical reading, Malina categorically states: "The hell of the feminists is patriarchy. . . . Yet the presence of untrustworthy patriarchy ironically underscores the fact that there really would be no patriarchs and patriarchy without enculturation of males into their patriarchal roles, a task performed almost exclusively by their mothers."[49]

Historical social-scientific criticism here conveniently forgets that male education in antiquity was not performed "almost exclusively by their mothers" but was in the hand of male rhetoricians and tutors. Such historical forgetfulness is fueled by a polemical apologetics that seeks not only to forget its own rhetoricity and sociohistorical location but also to avoid critical theoretical engagement with the issues raised by "feminism, hermeneutics, fundamentalism and post-structuralism."

A rhetoric of value-neutrality, cultural impartiality, and scientific method understood as rules and procedures policed by juries of peers maintains the separateness and immunity of science from all kinds of social-political influences: The meanings scientific statements carry are irrelevant to their actual content. For instance, research on the social abuses of science in the interest of racism, heterosexism, and colonialism are, according to such a social-scientific discourse, irrelevant to the validity of scientific concepts, theories, and methods. Although the enthusiasm for modern science is fundamentally motivated by democratic social values, and science is constituted by certain social values, its *ethos* is such that at its best it neither defends nor recommends any particular social values. As Sandra Harding observes: "What the defenders of the fundamental value-neutrality, the purity, of science really mean, they say, is that science's logic and methodology, and the empirical core of scientific facts these produce, are totally immune from social influences; that logic and scientific method will in the long run winnow out the factual from the social in the results of scientific research."[50]

Then again these defenders do not acknowledge that if scientific "fact" is a product of a particular social group and society, it is always already affected by the sociocultural framework of the scientist producing such knowledge. The social-scientific rhetoric of Malina does not acknowledge that scientific "fact" and "objective data" are the results and a reflection of the power relations of the disciplinary culture in which they were developed. Hence, a critical rhetoric and ethic of inquiry must insist that biblical scholars analyze the ways in which both institutional power and disciplinary discourses help to construct the body of hegemonic biblical knowledge about gender, race, class, nation, or disability and the ways it is communicated.

OPPOSITIONAL DISCOURSE LABELED AS ADVERSARIAL RHETORIC

Since Malina's polemics are theoretically rooted in a positivist or socio-rational empiricist stance, he feels free to explicitly attack feminism and patriarchy. In contrast, Vernon Robbins's Florence Conference paper[51] seems to look at feminism favorably but resorts to an antifeminist pathos by claiming that feminist biblical interpretation has achieved the power and authority of hegemonic discourse. Because of this misjudgment of power relations, Robbins misconstrues oppositional discourse as "adversarial rhetoric," a strategic move that allows him to portray oppositional rather than hegemonic discourse in a negative light. Robbins plays on the title of my Pretoria paper "Challenging the Rhetorical Half-Turn: Feminist and Rhetorical Biblical Criticism,"[52] but blames feminist biblical interpretation for not having made a rhetorical full-turn.[53] Instead of acknowledging that we work with two different theoretical frameworks[54]—he with that of relationalism and I with that of kyriarchal domination—Robbins thwarts my critical challenge to the discipline by stigmatizing my argument as "oppositional rhetoric," which he defines as adversarial.

In my Pretoria paper, I argued that biblical rhetorical criticism has not sufficiently developed a critical "rhetoric of inquiry" because it has not yet fully engaged the contributions of feminist and liberationist scholarship for the rearticulation of the discipline. It has not done so, I suggested, because of its unreflected disciplinary anxiety about becoming tainted with the centuries-old negative reputation of "mere rhetoric," which is traditionally figured as "feminine." I had used one of Robbins's articles to illustrate my argument that even a liberal rhetorical critic sympathetic to feminist concerns tends to resort to positivist and empiricist scientific arguments without critically assessing their ideological implications. I deliberately did not engage his argument on an exegetical-textual level but insisted on discussing the matter on a theoretical level. Insofar as he does not distinguish these two levels of inquiry, Robbins is able to claim that I acted against my own radical democratic ethos when I engaged in oppositional rhetoric, which he defines as closing off issues rather than moving them "into a context of free exchange among equal partners in dialogue. This kind of political discourse, then, is a rhetorical half-turn rather than a full-turn. Turning away from serious scholarly deliberation, it attacks *typical rather than specific actions* to establish a frame for instructing disciples rather than engaging seriously with colleagues in scholarly investigation, exchange and debate."[55]

Emotionally loaded formulations such as "turning away from serious scholarly deliberation" or "to establish a frame instructing disciples rather than seriously engaging with colleagues" appeal to academic *pathos* in order to rhetorically undermine the *ethos* of oppositional discourse. Moreover, Robbins stereotypes such "oppositional rhetoric" as having as its goal "to dominate" and to make "generalized accusations."[56]

He then goes on to characterize such "oppositional rhetoric" with reference to the anti-Jewish rhetoric of John 8:43-47 and Matthew 23, suggesting that my "adoption of oppositional rhetoric as a central mode of discourse . . . has a strong precedence in the New Testament literature itself." In addition, he links my argument to the conservative writings of Luke Timothy Johnson whose rhetoric in Robbins's view is guilty of "accusing people in categorical terms rather than picking up specific pieces of evidence" and "engaging in invective against groups of people who are 'misguided.'"[57]

By lumping my argument together with the anti-Jewish rhetoric of the Christian Testament and the anti-historical and anti-diversity rhetoric of Luke Timothy Johnson, Robbins subtly discredits critical feminist oppositional rhetoric before a scholarly audience of mostly male biblical critics by privatizing and caricaturing it. Through the politics of citation he at the same time indirectly seeks to undermine my feminist ethos by positively quoting to wo/men scholars who agree with him. Robbins ends by advocating a liberal political rhetoric of an "equal playing field" by promoting a liberal pluralism of debate without recognizing that the "we" who engages in this debate is still the "we" of elite male scholars: "we must do it not only by joining voices and actions with women's voices and marginalized peoples in wide regions of our global village. We must engage in dialogical interpretation that includes disenfranchised voices, marginalized voices, recently liberated voices and powerfully located voices."[58]

What then is the concrete issue that has caused the ire of my colleague? The bone of contention appears to be our different readings of the story of the wo/man who anointed Jesus in Mark. Whereas in *In Memory of Her*[59] I read the anointing story in terms of the biblical story of Samuel's anointing of Saul, Robbins read it in terms of Malina's social-scientific reconstruction of Mediterranean culture. Far from refusing to engage his interpretation, I pointed out that a critical rhetoric of inquiry would need to analyze carefully the historical, ideological, and theological interests of the twentieth century ethnological construct of the Mediterranean when using it to interpret the text.

In no way did this imply, as Robbins alleges, that my "construction of a Jewish scriptural context is not equally a scholarly construct." Rather, I suggested that what he has termed a "Bible-class" construct was as historically possible and plausible (and therefore as scientific) as his Mediterranean culture construct. However, I also pointed out that both constructs had different implications for the reading of the text and for our knowledge of wo/men's historical agency in early Christianity. What I objected to was Robbins's uncritical acceptance of the intertext of Mediterranean hegemonic culture as social-scientific while rejecting the Jewish-scriptural intertext of 1 Samuel as "Bible-land" story, without reflecting on the ideological function of the constructed social scientific cultural intertext that reduces the wo/man's prophetic sign-action to hegemonic cultural femininity.

My main point was not to claim "correct" exegesis of the text but rather an epistemological one: without critically exploring the ideological functions of the social-scientific construct of hegemonic Mediterranean culture, rhetorical interpretation imports hegemonic gender stereotypes that make wo/men's historical agency invisible again. Liberal scholarship is thereby in danger of serving antifeminist ends by trivializing or erasing the new insights of feminist scholarship, although it does not intend to do so.

My main concern with Robbins's Florence paper is not with his miscon-strual of my argument but with his labeling of "oppositional" rhetoric as adversarial. I believe it is necessary to analyze this rhetorical move because more is at stake than simply a quarrel between good colleagues. Robbins's construal of my argument as "oppositional rhetoric," which according to him "attacks typical rather than specific actions" and "has as its goal to dominate," allows him *not* to engage my critical proposal for a rhetoric of inquiry.

At the same time this move permits him to indict as "the will to dominate" all "oppositional discourse," which in my case speaks from a critical feminist political positionality. It allows him to use liberal *pathos* to appeal to the audience while at the same time constructing a politically explicit voice and proposal for a different disciplinary ethos as an "adversarial" discourse with scriptural anti-Jewish precedent. These rhetorical strategies make it possible to avoid a direct engagement with my feminist arguments, which would require recognition of my theoretical proposal as an alternative methodological discourse on rhetorical criticism. It would have meant granting equal authority to both a critical feminist epistemological proposal and to a liberal one.

Can a Critical Feminist Rhetoric Be Heard?

The postcolonial feminist critic Gyatri Chakravorty Spivak asks in a famous essay: "Can the subaltern speak?" After analyzing Malina's and Robbins's scholarly polemics one is tempted to ask: "Can the subaltern be heard and understood?" The definition and indictment of oppositional discourse as either romanticized or as adversarial discourse not only overlooks the power differential between oppositional and hegemonic disciplinary discourse but also the different implications of romanticized and adversarial rhetoric.

Whereas romanticized discourse overlooks the violence of oppressive power, adversarial rhetoric turns one's conversation partners into enemies to be obliterated in argument. In contrast, oppositional discourse as a critical ethical discourse opposes power relations that are perceived as wrong, dangerous, oppressive, or mistaken in order to correct such violent relations. It concerns domination and pertains to persons only insofar as they engage in practices of oppressive power. Whereas in a positivist methodological approach adversarial debate is the preferred method for ascertaining truth (the arguments that can withstand the greatest assault survive intact, and become the strongest truth),[60] oppositional rhetoric seeks to make the point of view of the subaltern heard.[61]

In response, those in the center of power tend to turn oppositional arguments into idealizing or adversarial rhetoric in order to avoid hearing the points being made, becoming accountable, and changing. Rather than reconsidering their theoretical proposals and exercise of disciplinary power, scholars use carefully crafted persuasive rhetorical strategies that work via identification for legitimating hegemonic arguments intellectually and ethically. When people identify with a speaker, they can be maneuvered into accepting the speaker's ideas, visions, and values. Key to persuasion "is not the response to logical and factual reasoning but the prior gesture of identification. Character [ethos] is not something behind an argument but the force of an argument."[62]

Minoritized speakers and oppositional discourses, however, find themselves in a different persuasive situation. As Gayatri Chakravorty Spivak has argued: "The woman in the West and its sphere of influences exemplifies the 'subaltern' in that she never defines the position of the masterful subject, the one always benefiting from the exercise of power. On the periphery of culture and political relations, 'she' is not completely separated from power and a particular woman could even occupy that position, but 'she' will always be positioned against a colonial and hegemonic 'center' of values so that speech is never in her own voice. The *ethos* of the subaltern I is self-limiting and self-negating in that the women who speak on their own behalf will be 'subjects' only in the sense of being subject to domination, like a feudal subject under an absolute monarch."[63]

Hence, the subaltern can only speak either through ventriloquism, that is, "her" speech is always already defined and related to the master voice and discourse of those in power, or if s/he speaks in her own voice she is not heard at all. For that reason, the situation of the intellectual inhabiting a hegemonic subject position is always already implicated.[64]

Since elite academic men still control language and knowledge production, it is difficult for the subaltern to find an acceptable "scientific" discourse and code for critiquing privileged men in power. As Chris Kamarae and Dale Spender observe: "The absence of such a code allows individual males to respond personally and emotionally to critiques of the structure and dynamic of dominance. And while [elite] male is the norm , and as such is assumed to be unproblematic, it is those who are critical of this state who can be seen to constitute the problem. By locating the problem in the [subaltern] who protests rather than in their own privilege, [elite] men can deny their own agency."[65]

At stake in the "othering" rhetoric of malestream scholarship is the scientific ethos and academic authority of oppositional speakers. The malestream response to such scholars is often negative, undermining their academic ethos and standing. Since hegemonic scholarship is not able to identify with the scientific arguments and ideological/theological interests of subaltern biblical critics, it tends to categorizes their work as cultural-ideological rather than "exegetical" and text-focused discourse. Alternatively, such hegemonic rhetoric trivializes subaltern scholarship as "nothing new" or as "merely repeating old readings in a new epistemological guise."

Despite all attempts of subaltern scholars to articulate the scientific and innovative character of their work, it is often not possible to convince dissertation teams, hiring committees, promotion boards, academic publishers, or grant-giving institutions that such work is of high interdisciplinary quality.

When interpreted through glasses colored by the very biases a work would challenge, the innovative quality of the work becomes invisible and inaudible. If scholarly authority lies in the dominant cultural voice, how can a minority speaker impersonate such a voice if s/he is conscious of the problematics of her marginal status and refuses to revert to ventriloquism?

How can doctoral education and biblical pedagogy avoid reinscribing the rhetorics and politics of power that reproduce and inculcate the elite male positivist scientific ethos of the discipline? These are not mere "rhetorical questions" important only for the subaltern scholar. They are relevant to all of us concerned with changing both the ethos of biblical studies in general and the ethos of rhetorical criticism in particular. Indeed, interdisciplinary ethos, moral persuasion, and public accountability—in short, a rhetoric and ethic of inquiry—must become central to the disciplinary professional discourses of biblical rhetorical criticism.

NOTES

[1] I want to thank first of all professor Thomas Olbricht for inviting me to the tenth anniversary Conference on Rhetoric in Heidelberg, even though such an invitation entailed a certain risk. In the past two decades professor Olbricht has not only done much to revive rhetorical biblical criticism but also insisted on the need for a critical historiography of biblical studies. I am particularly grateful that he graciously has allowed me to peruse his unpublished manuscript on the history of biblical studies in the United States. I am also grateful to Laura Beth Bugg for cleaning up my text and notes and to Francis Schüssler Fiorenza for reading several drafts of this paper and especially for saving me from the pitfalls of computer illiteracy.

[2] Thomas H. Olbricht, "The Flowering of Rhetorical Criticism in America," in *The Rhetorical Analysis of Scripture: Essays from the 1995 Conference*, ed. Stanley E. Porter and Thomas H. Olbricht (Sheffield: Sheffield Academic, 1997), 79–102. See also J. D. H. Amador, "The Word Made Flesh: Epistemology, Ontology, and Postmodern Rhetoric," 53–65.

[3] The dissertation of David Hester Amador has carefully analyzed the academic discourses of rhetoric in Christian Testament studies. However, his argument for a rhetoric of power has not received the attention and recognition it deserves. See J. David Hester Amador, *Academic Constraints in Rhetorical Criticism of the New Testament: An Introduction to a Rhetoric of Power* (Sheffield: Sheffield Academic, 1999).

[4] For a different paradigm construction see the various publications of Fernando Segovia, especially his contributions in Fernando Segovia and Mary Ann Tolbert, eds., *Teaching the Bible: The Discourses and Politics of Biblical Pedagogy* (Maryknoll: Orbis, 1998), 1–30; 137–67.

[5] In his contribution to the Pretoria Conference Peter F. Craffert argued for a historical hermeneutics and ethics of interpretation that would respect the integrity of the text in its past Otherness. He mentions three paradigms—the the*logical, the historical, and the rhetorical—as operative in the practices of an ethics of interpretation in South Africa, but he himself opts for a hermeneutical-rhetorical approach that insists on personifying the text and respecting its past Otherness. However, Craffert overlooks the fact that the hermeneutical and the rhetorical paradigm are based on two different methodological assumptions. Whereas the hermeneutical paradigm construes a spiraling dialogue between the interpreter and the text, us and the past, the rhetorical paradigm presupposes the interaction between "rhetor-audience-situation-world" on the one hand, and the distinction between the inscribed textual and reconstructed historical rhetoric on the "other." It thereby avoids both the dualistic "othering rhetoric" engendered by the hermeneutical-cultural paradigm and the positivist reification of the rhetorical process. Peter F.

Craffert, "Reading and Divine Sanction: The Ethics of Interpreting the New Testament in South Africa," in *Rhetoric, Scripture, and Theology: Essays from the 1994 Pretoria Conference* (ed. S. E. Porter and T. H. Olbricht: Sheffield: Sheffield Academic, 1996), 54–71.

[6]Elisabeth Schüssler Fiorenza, "For the Sake of Our Salvation: Biblical Interpretation as The*logical Task," in *Sin, Salvation and the Spirit*, ed. D. Durken (Collegeville: Liturgical, 1979), 21–39. See also Elisabeth Schüssler Fiorenza, *Bread Not Stone* (Boston: Beacon, 1984).

[7]For the concept of emancipation see Jan Nederveen Pieterse, ed., *Emancipations: Modern and Postmodern* (London: Sage, 1992).

[8]Elisabeth Schüssler Fiorenza, "Challenging the Rhetorical Half-Turn: Feminist and Rhetorical Biblical Criticism," in *Rhetoric, Scripture and Theology: Essays from the 1994 Pretoria Conference*, ed. S. E. Porter and T. H. Olbricht: Sheffield: Sheffield Academic, 1996).

[9]Elisabeth Schüssler Fiorenza, *Rhetoric and Ethic: The Politics of Biblical Studies* (Minneapolis: Fortress, 2000).

[10]For the exploration of the relation between discourse and rhetoric see Stephen R. Yarbrough, *After Rhetoric: The Study of Discourse Beyond Language and Culture* (Carbondale: Southern Illinois University Press, 1999); Diane MacDonell, *Theories of Discourse: An Introduction* (Cambridge: Blackwell, 1986). For an exploration of rhetoric as argumentation see Anders Eriksson, Thomas H. Olbricht, and Walter Übelacker, eds., *Rhetorical Argumentation in Biblical Texts* (Harrisburg: Trinity International, 2002).

[11]See the contributions in Fernando Segovia and Mary Ann Tolbert, eds., *Teaching the Bible*.

[12]For an exploration of rhetoric as argumentation see Eriksson, Olbricht, and Übelacker, eds., *Rhetorical Argumentation in Biblical Texts*.

[13]Susan C. Jarratt, *Rereading the Sophists: Classical Rhetoric Reconfigured* (Carbondale: Southern Illinois University Press, 1991), 14. See also Franco Crespi, *Social Action and Power* (Cambridge: Blackwell, 1992), 52. He argues, "When knowledge is being oriented towards descriptive and value-neutrality, as the only basis for rationality and science, then the concept of action becomes a nuisance . . . since action, as opposed to the concept of behaviour, has always to be referred to subjectivity, it appears to be fatally opposed to the aforementioned idea of science, for it stresses precisely those dimensions of affective and evaluative *un-neutrality* and unpredictability which undermine the model of natural science."

[14]Robert L. Scott, "On Viewing Rhetoric as Epistemic: Ten Years Later," in *Methods of Rhetorical Criticism: A Twentieth Century Perspective*, 3rd ed., edited by B. L. Brock, R. L. Scott, and J. W. Chesebro (Detroit: Wayne State University Press, 1989), 140–41.

[15]For a critical discussion of ethics, see among others Marjorie Garber, Beatrice Hanssen, and Rebecca L. Walkowitz, eds., *The Turn to Ethics* (New York: Routledge, 2000); Annemarie Pieper, *Ethik und Moral: Eine Einführung in die praktische Philosophie* (München: Kösel, 1985), 10–43; Gunhild Buse, *Macht-Moral-Weiblichkeit: Eine feministisch-theologische Auseinandersetzung mit Carol Gilligan und Frigga Haug* (Mainz: Grünewald, 1993); and Rey Chow, *Ethics after Idealism: Theory-Culture-Ethnicity-Reading* (Bloomington: Indiana University Press, 1998).

[16]Celeste Michelle Condit, "Crafting Virtue: The Rhetorical Construction of Public Morality," in Contemporary *Rhetorical Theory*, ed. Lucaites et al., 311.

[17]Ibid., 320.

[18]Barry Brummett, "Some Implications of 'Process' or 'Intersubjectivity' in Postmodern Rhetoric," in *Contemporary Rhetorical Theory*, ed. Lucaites et al., 166. However, a purely intersubjective conceptualization is still too privatized and individualist. Hence, I have qualified it with "democratic."

[19]For a history of rhetoric see, for example, Thomas M. Conley, *Rhetoric in the European Tradition* (Chicago: The University of Chicago Press, 1990). For a feminist history of rhetoric see Cheryl Glenn, *Rhetoric Retold: Regendering the Tradition from Antiquity through the Renaissance* (Carbondale: Southern Illinois University Press, 1997).

[20]James S. Baumlin, "Positioning Ethos in Historical and Contemporary Theory," in *Ethos*, xiii. See also William W. Fortenbaugh, "Aristotle's Accounts of Persuasion through Character," in *Theory, Text, Context: Issues in Greek Rhetoric and Oratory*, edited by Christopher Lyle Johnstone

(Albany: SUNY Press, 1996), 147–68. George A. Kennedy, "Reworking Aristotle's Rhetoric," 169–84, and especially Nan Johnson, "Ethos and The Aims of Rhetoric," in *Essays on Classical Rhetoric and Modern Discourse*, edited by R. J. Connors, L. S. Ede, and A. A. Lunsford (Carbondale: Southern Illinois University Press, 1984), 98–114. See also the contributions of Kraus, Eriksson, Olbricht, Vander Stichele, Penner, and Hester Amador.

21 See Thomas Olbricht, "Rhetorical Criticism in America," 80: "Studies in rhetoric were not unfamiliar to our Puritan forefathers. Puritan scholars embraced particularly the grammar, rhetoric and logic of Peter Ramus (1515–1572) and Omer Talon . . . . The biblical scholars of the era borrowed from these insights, structuring commentaries according to dictates of the Ramian logical divisions and subdivisions."

22 Susan C. Jarratt and Nedra Reynolds, "The Splitting Image: Contemporary Feminisms and the Ethics of Ethos," in *Ethos: New Essays in Rhetorical and Critical Theory*, edited by James S. Baumlin and Tita French Baumlin (Dallas: Southern Methodist University Press, 1994), 48. See also Tobin Siebers, *Morals and Stories* (New York: Columbia University Press, 1992), 63.

23 John McGowan, *Hannah Arendt: An Introduction* (Minneapolis: University of Minnesota Press, 1998), 167.

24 Linda Alcoff, "Cultural Feminism versus Post-Structuralism: The Identity Crisis in Feminist Theory," *Signs* 13 (1988): 434.

25 Susan C. Jarratt and Nedra Reynolds, "The Splitting Image," 47.

26 Ibid., 52.

27 Lorraine Code, *Rhetorical Spaces: Essays on Gendered Locations* (New York: Routledge, 1995), ix–x. For the discussion of feminist epistemology see also Nancy Tuana and Sandra Morgan, eds., *Engendering Rationalities* (Albany: SUNY Press, 2001), and Liz Stanley, ed., *Knowing Feminisms: On Academic Borders, Territories, and Tribes* (Thousand Oaks: Sage 1997).

28 See the essays in Part II, "Rhetoric and Epistemology," in John Lois Lucaites, Celeste Michelle Condit, Sally Caudill, eds., *Contemporary Rhetorical Theory: A Reader* (New York: Guilford, 1999), 137–247; Richard A. Cherwitz and James W. Hikins, *Communication and Knowledge: An Investigation in Rhetorical Epistemology* (Columbia: University of South Carolina Press, 1986); see also Richard Harvey Brown, *Society as Text: Essays on Rhetoric, Reason, and Reality* (Chicago: University of Chicago Press, 1987).

29 Lorraine Code, *Rhetorical Spaces*, viii.

30 For this section, see not only Conley and Baumlin but especially also Nan Johnson, "Ethos and the Aims of Rhetoric," in *Essays on Classical Rhetoric and Modern Discourse*, edited by Robert J. Connors, Lisa S. Ede, and Andrea A. Lunsford (Carbondale: Southern Illinois University Press, 1984), 98–114.

31 Nancy Leys Stepan and Sander L. Gilman, "Appropriating the Idioms of Science: The Rejection of Scientific Racism," in *The "Racial" Economy of Science: Toward a Democratic Future*, ed. Sandra Harding (Bloomington: Indiana University Press, 1993), 173. See also Londa Schiebinger, *The Mind Has No Sex? Wo/men in the Origins of Modern Science* (Oxford: Oxford University Press, 1981).

32 For the medical profession, see Anne Witz, *Professions and Patriarchy* (New York: Routledge, 1992). For the notion of professional authority, see the sociological study by Terrence J. Johnson, *Professions and Power* (London: MacMillan, 1972).

33 For the history of biblical studies, see the book of Thomas Olbricht and his various published contributions, for example, Thomas Olbricht, "Alexander Campbell in the Context of American Biblical Studies," *Restoration Quarterly* 33 (1991): 13–28; "Biblical Interpretation in North America in the Twentieth Century," in *Historical Handbook of Major Biblical Interpreters*, edited by Donald K. McKim (Downers Grove: InterVarsity, 1998), 541–57; and "Histories of North American Biblical Scholarship," *Current Research in Biblical Studies* 7 (1999): 237–56.

34 Bonnie G. Smith, "Gender, Objectivity, and the Rise of Scientific History," in *Objectivity and Its Other*, edited by W. Natter, Th. R. Schatzki, and J. Jones (New York: Guilford, 1995), 52.

35 *JBL* 9 (1890): vi.

36 See J. W. Brown, *The Rise of Biblical Criticism in America 1858–1870: The New England Scholars* (Middleton: Wesleyan University Press, 1988), the above references to Thomas Olbricht's work, and Ernest W. Saunders, *Searching the Scriptures: A History of the Society of Biblical Literature 1880–1980* (Chico: Scholars, 1982), 6.

37 E. Saunders, *Searching the Scriptures*, 11.

38 For the history of Roman Catholic scholarship see Gerald Fogarty, *American Catholic Biblical Scholarship: A History from the Early Republic to Vatican II* (San Francisco: Harper and Row, 1989); for Jewish scholarship see S. D. Sperling, ed., *Students of the Covenant: A History of Jewish Biblical Scholarship in North America* (Atlanta: Scholars, 1992).

39 E. Saunders, *Searching the Scriptures*, 101.

40 For a feminist educational introduction to biblical studies see my *Wisdom Ways: Introducing Feminist Biblical Interpretation* (Maryknoll: Orbis, 2001). For a critical discussion of pedagogy, see chapter 6 of my *But She Said* (Boston: Beacon, 1992).

41 Bruce J. Malina, "Rhetorical Criticism and Social-Scientific Criticism: Why Won't Romanticism Leave Us Alone?" in *Rhetoric, Scripture, and Theology: Essays from the 1994 Pretoria Conference*, ed. Stanley E. Porter and Thomas H. Olbricht (Sheffield: Sheffield Academic, 1996), 72–101.

42 Ibid., 73.

43 Ibid., 97.

44 Ibid., 86.

45 Ibid., 85.

46 Ibid., 85.

47 Ibid., 96.

48 Ibid., 87.

49 Ibid., 97.

50 Sandra Harding, *The Science Question in Feminism* (Ithaca: Cornell University Press, 1986), 40.

51 Vernon K. Robbins, "The Rhetorical Full-Turn in Biblical Interpretation. Reconfiguring Rhetorical-Political Analysis," in *Rhetorical Criticism and the Bible*, edited by Stanley E. Porter and Dennis L. Stamps: Sheffield: Sheffield Academic, 2002), 48–60. See also his books *Exploring the Texture of Texts: A Guide to Socio-Rhetorical Interpretation* (Valley Forge: Trinity International, 1996), and *The Tapestry of Early Christian Discourse: Rhetoric, Society and Ideology* (New York: Routledge, 1996).

52 Elisabeth Schüssler Fiorenza, "Challenging the Rhetorical Half-Turn: Feminist and Rhetorical Biblical Criticism," in *Rhetoric, Scripture, and Theology*, edited by S. E. Porter and T. H. Olbricht, 28–53 (London: T & T Clark).

53 This was made powerfully clear in his presentation of his Florence paper at the 2002 International SBL meeting in Berlin.

54 See also Robbins's London Conference contribution "The Present and Future of Rhetorical Analysis," in *The Rhetorical Analysis of Scripture*, edited by S. Porter and T. Olbricht, 24–52.

55 Vernon K. Robbins, "The Rhetorical Full-Turn in Biblical Interpretation," 56.

56 Ibid., 58.

57 Ibid., 56.

58 Ibid., 58.

59 Elisabeth Schüssler Fiorenza, *In Memory of Her: A Feminist Reconstruction of Christian Origins*, Tenth Anniversary Edition (New York: Crossroad, 1984).

60 Patricia Hill Collins, *Black Feminist Thought: Knowledge, Consciousness and the Politics of Empowerment* (Boston: Unwin Hyman, 1990), 205. See also Patricia Hill Collins, *Fighting Words: Black Women and the Search for Justice* (Minneapolis: University of Minnesota Press, 1998).

61 See my response to Heikki Räisänen, "Defending the Center, Trivializing the Margins," in *Reading the Bible in the Global Village*, edited by Heiki Räisänen et al. (Atlanta: SBL, 2000), 29–48.

62 Marshall W. Alcorn Jr., "Self-Structure as a Political Device: Modern Ethos and the Division of the Self," in *Ethos: New Essays in Rhetorical and Critical Theory*, ed. James S. Baumlin and Tita French Baumlin (Dallas: Southern Methodist University Press, 1994), 4.

[63] Robert Con Davis and David S. Gross, "Gayatri Spivak and the Ethos of the Subaltern," in Baumlin and Baumlin, *Ethos*, 72. See Gayatri Chakravorty Spivak, "Can the Subaltern Speak?" in *Marxism and the Interpretation of Culture*, edited by Cary Nelson and Lawrence Grossberg (Urbana: University of Illinois Press, 1988), 271–313.

[64] Davis and Gross, "Gayatri Spivak and the Ethos of the Subaltern," 67.

[65] Chris Kamarae and Dale Spender, eds., *The Knowledge Explosion: Generations of Feminist Scholarship*, Athene Series (New York: Teachers College, 1992), 10.

9

The Power of Empire and the Rhetoric of Scripture

In the past several years scholars have focused on empire[1]—the Roman and the American—and assessed its impact on the rhetorical power of Scripture,[2] which is claimed by Christians to be the authoritative revealed, sacred word of G*d.[3] Scholars concerned about the function of the Bible in people's lives and seek to read the signs of the times, endeavor to critically evaluate the Bible's function in inculcating the ethos of domination and submission. We also seek to enable readers to question biblical authority, which has been understood throughout the centuries in analogy to imperial power. Such power of empire is wielded by a few and demands the obedience and submission of the many, either in the name of G*d or in the name of patriotism.

Hence, biblical scholars have to explore not only how the power of empire has historically shaped and affected Christian Scriptures but also how it continues to shape cultural and religious self-understandings today. Christian Scriptures and interpretations, I argue, could and can rightly be used in the service of empire, colonialist expansion, and heterosexist discrimination because they have been formulated in the context of Roman imperial power.[4] Therefore biblical language is determined by this rhetorical political imperial context. If people do not become aware of the language of empire at work today, they internalize the ethos of empire: violence exclusion and submission to G*d, the almighty King and Christ the Lord, in and through the process of reading Scripture.

In order to avoid such internalizations of the ethos of empire, scholars need to develop an understanding of Scripture that will allow people to deal critically with the scriptural language of empire rather than compel them to repeat and reinscribe it today. Historically, the language of democracy has provided an alternative discourse to imperialism and domination. Although democracy has different shades of meaning that are not always liberating, democracy through the times, has been and still is the discourse that sets the terms for critique of imperial power and institutions and creates the basis for their change.[5] Radical democracy, which I have called the *ekklēsia of wo/men*, offers the language and space for the imagination to develop a public religious discourse wherein, according to Adriana Hernández, "justice, participation, difference, freedom, equality and solidarity set the ethical conditions."[6]

The challenge for biblical and theological scholars then today is to develop modes of interpretation that not only can recognize imperial biblical language. We also have to trace languages and imaginations of radical democratic equality equally inscribed in Scripture as well as those scriptural discourses that are different from those of empire. Since Christian fundamentalism draws on the language of empire inscribed in Christian Scriptures, progressive biblical scholarship needs not only to critically make conscious such inscriptions, but also to articulate elements of a radical democratic egalitarian vision that is also inscribed in Christian Scriptures. This is not just a theological problem within Christianity but is a challenge to all those who seek to change the cultural-political ethos of empire today. It becomes more and more pressing at a time when in the name of G*d and the Bible antidemocratic tendencies are on the rise.

To explore this problem more fully, I will first discuss the contemporary context of our reading of Scripture. In a second step, I will reflect on the rhetorical power ascribed to Scripture and finally indicate an approach to Scripture that is able to recognize the inscriptions of empire and free us from their internalizations of subordination.

EMPIRE AS THE CONTEXT OF SCRIPTURE TODAY

In recent years, New Testament—or as I would prefer, Christian Testament[7]— scholarship has rediscovered or reemphasized the Roman Empire and its impact on early Christian life and literature as an important field of study. Such studies of the Roman Empire have emerged in the biblical academy at one and the same time as publications on contemporary forms of empire and its exploitations have been discussed widely.

While the study of the Roman Empire has always been part and parcel of historical Christian Testament scholarship, such studies have often tended to either celebrate Rome's accomplishments as a great civilizing power in the Mediterranean world of the first century CE, or they have narrowly focused on the persecution of Christians by the Roman authorities. For instance, in the 1980s a debate had ensued in scholarship on the book of Revelation between liberationist scholars from Latin America, who interpreted the book's symbolic language as anti-Roman, and other scholars from North America or Europe, who denied that harassment and persecutions of Christians were at work at the time at all.[8] These scholars praised the benevolent cultural impact of imperial Rome for the citizens of Asia Minor reading the anti-Roman symbolic language of this book as expressing the "resentment" of the author.

In contrast, the new scholarship on empire and Scripture tends to read such language as language critical of the Roman Empire. But often they do not pay attention as to how the Bible inscribes the language of empire into public discourse and religious ethos.

This renewed focus of Early Christian scholarship on the Roman Empire and its exercise of power has been invigorated by new approaches in the field of classics such as the Study of Roman Imperialism and in cultural studies. It also has benefited from inspirations from postcolonial biblical studies and its forerunner, liberationist biblical studies. However, like all malestream studies, it has not much engaged with or learned from critical feminist studies. This new approach has left its footprints in diverse areas of early Christian Studies, but it has especially sought to change Pauline Studies, which has focused on Paul, the great individual and his religious opponents, rather than on Paul's sociopolitical context, the imperial power of Rome.

Nevertheless, such studies often still tend to proceed in an apologetic fashion. Studies of the Gospels, the Pauline literature, or other Christian Testament writings and their attitude toward the Roman Empire have tended to argue that these writings were critical of Roman imperial power and resisted its structures of domination. Yet, such an argument overlooks that even resistance literature will reinscribe the structures of domination that it seeks to overcome. For instance, writings like the Book of Revelation transfer the titles of the Roman emperor to G*d and Christ when they describe G*d as a Great Monarch and Christ as King of Kings and Lord of Lords. Although Revelation uses imperial language as anti-language, it still reinscribes the ethos of empire so that Bible readers are convinced that G*d sits on a throne or Christ is Lord and King.

The Gospels also function as apologetics of empire insofar as they displace the responsibility for the execution of Jesus from the Roman imperial representatives to the Jews and thereby continue to engender anti-Judaism in and through their proclamation. The Pauline literature in turn fosters imperial subordination, insofar as it interprets the execution of Jesus as dying for our sins, which according to 1 Timothy were brought into the world by a wo/man. The stress of the post-Pauline literature on the subordination and obedience of slave and freeborn wo/men as well as of the whole community to kyriarchal (that is, emperor, lord, slave-master, father, husband, propertied free male) authority fuels the Christian right's rhetoric on family values and same-sex marriage.

In short, if one does not consciously question the language of imperial domination in which early Christian texts remain caught up, one cannot but internalize it either in cultural or religious terms. For instance, words such as "gospel" or "parousia" are derived from the ideology and propaganda of the Roman Empire. "Gospel" meant first the "good news" about the emperor and in an analogous way also the "good news" of G*d. It announces the glad tidings brought about by Roman imperial power and in an analogous way the glad tidings brought about by G*d. King and Lord are first titles of the emperor celebrating his power of domination and in an analogous way construe the power of G*d in imperial terms.

In attempting to rescue early Christian Scriptures as anti-imperial literature, scriptural apologetics tends to overlook that the language of empire and its violence that is encoded in Christian Scriptures has shaped Christian religious and Western cultural self-understanding and ethos throughout the centuries and still does so today. Hence, today this language is understood as legitimating a culture of domination even if in its original setting it was used as anti-language. Such language of domination, subordination, obedience and control is not just historical language. Rather as sacred Scripture it is performative language that determines Christian identity and praxis. It does not need just to be understood, but must be made conscious and critically evaluated.

However, academic biblical scholars are for the most part not trained to investigate and study the interplay of biblical imperial language and ethos with contemporary public discourses. The historical-philological bent of the field and the defense of biblical writers such as Paul as anti-imperial has prevented critical exploration of the workings of Scripture texts and language in public discourses today.

True, this new interest of biblical scholars in the study of the Roman Empire has been engendered by public discussions of the United States or of globalization as an imperial political and cultural power, but for the most part it has not focused on how the discipline needs to change if it should equip biblical readers to read "the signs of the times." The intellectual context of such studies, moreover, has not just been the renewed popular and academic interest in empire but also the arrival of postcolonial criticism[9] in religious, theological, and biblical studies—albeit these studies see themselves often as the more sophisticated replacement of liberation theologies and hence are ill equipped to move out of the academy into the public square.[10] Finally, the growing political influence of biblical and other religious fundamentalisms around the world has sparked renewed interest in religion. Violence and religion has become a topic of intense discussion in the universities but less so in biblical studies.

In the past few years a stream of books has appeared indicting the United States as empire or conceptualizing globalization in terms of empire. Some of these books discuss the rise and fall of the American empire. Others argue that China will be the next empire in the global market. Again others elaborate the moral and economic price to be paid for being an empire. While the American people fervently believe that the United States is a democracy, some historians argue that it has always been an empire.

As in earlier instances so also the present expansion of the capitalist glob-alization of empire is secured by the American military-industrial complex. In his book *American Empire*, Andrew Bacevich, a former military officer, quotes Theodore Roosevelt who, in December 1899, stated, "Of course, our whole national history has been one of expansion," and Madeleine Albright who remarked in February 1998: "If we have to use force, it is because we are America. We are the indispensable nation." To quote Bacevich: "Bill Clinton interpreted the end of the Cold War as signifying the 'fullness of time'—a scriptural allusion to the moment when G*d chose to transform history. . . . As the bloody twentieth century drew to a close, God's promise of peace on earth remained unfulfilled; it was now incumbent upon the United States, having ascended to the status of sole superpower, to complete God's work—or as members of a largely secularized elite, preferred it, to guide history toward its intended destination."[11]

The present expansion of capitalist globalization is secured by the military-industrial complex and justified also in Christian religious terms. As Kim Yong-Bok observes: "The emergence of the Global Empire provides the new global context of theology. This context is ecumenical and universal. No theological reflection can avoid this context. All faiths and religions are bound to deal with this context. There may be different starting points, depending on the locus of the faith community. Whether one is at the seat and center of the empire or at its periphery, one is not outside of the empire."[12]

Economic globalization[13] has been created with the specific goal of giving primacy to corporate profits installing and codifying such market values globally. It was designed to amalgamate and merge all economic activities around the world within a single model of global monoculture. Neocapitalist globalization of the economy, which keeps profits high by outsourcing and reducing labor costs, has engendered a redistribution of wealth from the middle and working classes into the hands of the top 10 percent of the population. Such capitalist and militarist globalization conceived in terms of empire threatens democracy and human rights.

Yet, globalization also presents possibilities for a more radical democrat-ization worldwide. It narrows geographical distances between people, fosters their growing interdependence, makes experientially available the intercon-nectedness of all beings, and engenders the possibility of communication and solidaric organization across national boarders on the basis of human rights and justice for all.

Consequently, religious communities and biblical studies face a theo-ethical choice today: we can strengthen global capitalist dehumanization or we can support the growing interdependence of people; we can spiritually sustain the exploitation of capitalist globalization or we can engage the possibilities of radical democratization for greater freedom, justice, and solidarity. Religion can either foster fundamentalism, exclusivism, and the exploitation of a totalitarian global monoculture or it can advocate radical democratic spiritual values and visions that celebrate diversity, multiplicity, tolerance, equality, justice, and well-being for all. Such an ethical either-or choice does not re-inscribe the dualisms created by structures of domination but struggles to overcome and abolish them.

Yet, in the public square the religious right and the emergence of global cultural and religious fundamentalisms claim the power to define the true nature and essence of religion. Right-wing religious movements around the globe have insisted in the past decades on the figuration of emancipated wo/men either as signifiers of Western decadence or of modern atheistic secularism, and at the same time they have presented masculine power as the expression of divine power. The interconnection between religious antidemocratic arguments and the debate with regard to wo/men's place and role is not accidental or of merely intrareligious significance.

Christian religion and Scriptures have been used consistently for legitim-ating Western expansionism and military rule as well as for inculcating the mentality of obedience and submission to the powers of empire. The Bible and biblical studies are clearly implicated in empire since they are associated with Western colonialism. This is aptly expressed in the pithy saying ascribed to Bishop Tutu: "When the missionaries arrived they had the Bible and we had the land. Now we have the Bible and they have the land."

The form of biblical and religious legitimization most closely associated with colonialism has been monarchical Catholicism and biblicist Protest-antism, both of which are oriented toward the salvation of the soul and profess an individualistic theology that preaches personal submission to the authority of Scripture or to the pope. In contrast, critical biblical studies at first glance seem not to be aligned explicitly with Western imperialism because they allegedly are driven by scientific rationality and objectivity. Yet, anyone studying the history of biblical scholarship will recognize that it has been articulated for the most part not only by elite, Western educated clergymen but also in the interest of imperial, cultural, and political power. In recent years critical feminist and postcolonial biblical studies have amply documented this function of positivist biblical scholarship in the interest of empire, whereas feminist studies have shown that the majority of those dehumanized by global imperialism are wo/men and children dependent on wo/men.

In many respects wo/men are suffering not only from the globalization of market capitalism but also from the sexual exploitation instigated by it. However, the scriptural roots of systemic inequality, abuse, violence, discrim-ination, starvation, poverty, neglect, and denial of wo/men's rights that afflict the lives of wo/men around the globe are still not taken seriously by biblical scholars but are seen as an unacademic special interest issue of middle class white wo/men. However, a glance at statistical data on wo/men's situations around the world will easily show that wo/men as a group are disadvantaged worldwide in and through the processes of globalization. In most parts of the world, wo/men still earn only two-thirds of what men in similar situations earn; the majority of people living in poverty are wo/men; violence against wo/men and gynecide—that is, the killing of wo/men—is on the increase; sexual trafficking, various forms of forced labor, illiteracy, migration, and refugee camps spell out wo/men's increasing exploitation globally. Rose Wu sums up this situation: "The borderless societies that the global economy promotes continue to exploit women by selling them as 'wives,' forcing them into prostitution or engaging them in other kinds of exploitative work, such as working in sweatshops or working as domestic labor. . . . Women displaced from farms and collapsed domestic industries because of trade liberalisation have been forced to seek survival by migrating to foreign lands where they often suffer abuse and harsh treatment at the hands of their recruiters and/or employers. Many become victims of sex trafficking."[14]

Wo/men's struggles for survival and well-being must therefore remain at the heart of all discussions of global empire and its death-dealing violence. The question of feminism and Scripture, I argue, must become central to any discussion of empire, globalization, and religion since according to fundamentalist voices, feminism equals godless humanism and Western decadence. Because the authority of the Bible as the "word of G*d" has been and still is used to justify the violence of empire against wo/men, it is necessary to investigate more closely what kind of power Scripture develops in the public square.

POWER AND SCRIPTURE

To bring notions of Scripture and empire together has an irritating, upsetting, and disturbing effect on people's minds; it jars religious imagination and sensibilities. Whereas Scripture is believed by many to be the authoritative sacred word of G*d, empire evokes the notion of domination, conquest, and subjugation. If Scripture is understood as demanding unquestioned obedience and submission, it is conceived in terms of empire. At the same time, it is claimed that Scripture is the liberating word of a just and loving G*d. This understanding of Scripture is contradictory to and clashes with the rhetoric of empire that advocates domination and submission. Hence, it is necessary to learn how to distinguish the sacred power of Scripture from the power of empire if biblical readers should be able to resist the global exploitation of empire.

Such an adjudication is possible because power can be seen and exercised not only as "power over"—as power of domination and rule, as control and command, as the power of empire—but power also can be understood as

"power for" or as "power to," as capacity, energy, and potential,[15] as energizing, enabling and transformative power, as creative activity and strength.[16]
The power of Scripture can be wielded only by a few to dominate the many
or it can be seen as energizing everyone—as enriching, creative possibility for
community and justice.[17]

If power always has this dual connotation, then biblical readers must learn
to adjudicate in a process of critical evaluation what kind of power each
scriptural text espouses and authorizes, since Christian Scriptures share in the
rhetoric of "power over" and in the "power to." In light of these two definitions
of power, Scripture can be understood as "power over" in terms of the imperial
"command-obedience, superordination, and submission" structure inscribed
in Scripture or it can be seen as enabling and energizing power.

The power of the Word to exclude and to legitimate wo/men's second class
citizenship and thereby to re-inscribe the "power over" of empire is explicit,
for instance, in the following Pauline injunction:

> As in all the *ekklesiai* (= assemblies of the saints),
> the women should keep silence in the *ekklesiai* (= assemblies).
> For they are not permitted to speak,
> but should be subordinate, as even the law says. (1 Cor. 14:33)

Not all scriptural texts are so obvious in promoting imperial power
relations, but all of them must be carefully analyzed and critically assessed as
to what kind of power they advocate. Insofar as the power of the word and the
authority of Scripture as "power over" are understood as divinely sanctioned,
the authority of Scripture has been understood in analogy to imperial power
that is exercised by a few and demands submission and obedience from the
many. Biblical interpretation therefore cannot but reinscribe the rhetoric of
empire as divine rhetoric if it understands Scripture as the direct word of G*d.

Scriptural language symbolization and rhetoric call for critical feminist
assessment and theo-ethical evaluation in contemporary rhetorical situations
of empire. Such a critical ideological evaluation is necessary because the
symbolic world of Scripture is not only a theo-ethical model *of* its own
sociopolitical-religious world but also serves as a theo-ethical model *for*
sociopolitical-religious life today. The scriptural language and metaphors
we use shape our perception of the world in which we live. The uncritical
fundamentalist or positivist reinscriptions of the rhetoric of empire as the
word of G*d do not simply misunderstand or misconstrue Scripture. Rather
they are correct because the Roman and other Near Eastern empires are as the
context of Scripture historically constitutive of it.

Nevertheless, inscribed in Scripture is not only the rhetoric of empire
as "power over" and its demand for submission, suffering, obedience, and
control. We also still can find traces of an alternative rhetoric of power that
understands power as "power to," as creative liberating power for. Hence,

all language of power inscribed in Scripture must be carefully explored and critically assessed in terms of what it does to those who submit to its sacred power of imagination: whether it advocates imperial "power over" or radical democratic "power to." What the Spirit says today to our own particular sociopolitical situations must be assessed in an ethical practice of rhetorical analysis and ideology critique that can trace G*d's power for justice and well-being both in the Bible and in today's political struggles against the domination of global empire.

SACRED SCRIPTURE AND ITS INTERPRETATION

Biblical readers are not taught to engage in such a critical reading of Scripture, however. Biblical readers early on learn to develop strategies of textual valorization and validation rather than hermeneutical skills to critically interrogate and assess scriptural interpretations and texts along with their visions, values, and prescriptions. In order to foster the ability of spiritual discernment, cultural and religious education needs to enable readers to take a critical stance toward all human words, especially to those that claim the unmediated power and authority of G*d. Whereas historical and literary biblical scholarship has flourished, biblical studies has generally neglected its critical theological or ideology critical task. Hence, neither biblical scholarship nor biblical readers are able to understand the authority of Scripture as inviting them in a critical process of discernment to liberate the words of Scripture from their inscriptions of empire.

Instead of giving the power of interpretation to so-called popular audiences or common readers, biblical scholarship and preaching generally do not give people the tools for investigating the ideologies, discourses, and knowledge that shape their religious self-identity and determine their lives. Instead of empowering Bible readers as critical thinkers, education in general and biblical education in particular often contributes to their self-alienation and adaptation to the values and mores of imperial society and religion.

An objectivist scientific academic ethos neglects the spiritual desire for the Sacred that has brought many students to the university and the study of the Bible.[18] bell hooks reflects on this experience, saying that she knew when she went to Stanford University from her small town that there would be no "discussion of divine spirit." Her years of teaching at elite universities confirmed the knowledge "that it was only the mind that mattered, that any care of our souls—our spirits—had to take place in private." However, as a student and later as a faculty person she continued to "reclaim the sacred at the heart of knowing, teaching and learning." Hence she asserts: "It is essential that we build into our teaching vision a place where spirit matters, a place where our spirits can be renewed and our souls be restored."[19]

A feminist emancipatory, radical democratic model of biblical reading seeks to inhabit this visionary space "where spirit matters," a space that I have called the "open house of Wisdom."[20] In this space biblical studies no longer serve to internalize kyriarchal biblical teachings and malestream scientific knowledge, but they seek to foster critical thinking, ethical accountability, and intellectual self-esteem. The basic assumption is that knowledge is publicly available to all and that everyone has something to contribute to religious knowledge. Such an ethos seeks to engender radical democratic thinking that requires a particular quality of vision and civic imagination.

Feminist postcolonial biblical studies are thus best understood in a radical democratic Wisdom key insisting that all wo/men are competent biblical interpreters. They seek to facilitate wo/men's critical readings by fostering examination of our own presuppositions and social locations. Radical demo-cratic Bible study searches for freedom from cultural bias and religious prejudice and seeks to replace them with critical arguments that appeal to both reason *and* the emotions. It wants to foster the ability to ask what it would be like to be in the shoes of someone different from oneself and to see the world from the point of view of an other who is not like oneself, but still much like oneself.

Instead of looking to "great books" and "great men," a radical democratic model of biblical reading/learning in the open house of Wisdom engages in critical questioning, exploration, and debate in order to be able to arrive at a deliberative judgment about the Bible's contributions to the "good life," to democratic self-determination and self-esteem. It is about choice, deliberation, and the power to take charge of our own life and thought, rather than about control, dependence, obedience, and passive reception. Its style of reasoning is not combative-competitive but deliberative, engaging in conversations about values and beliefs that are most important to us rather than retreating into positivism, dogmatism, or relativism that avoids engagement with differences.

In this Wisdom model of learning, thought and study are problem oriented rather than positivistic or dogmatic; perspectival rather than relativistic; they are contextual-collaborative, recognizing that our own perspective and knowledge are limited by our social-religious location and that differences enrich our thought and life. Truth and meaning are not a given fact or hidden revelation but are achieved in critical practices of deliberation.

To be able to achieve a constructive engagement with religious difference and diversity inscribed in the Bible and in contemporary reading contexts, biblical readers need to become aware of the pitfalls of one-dimensional thinking that strives to find in the Bible definite answers and final solutions. As the Jewish feminist Alicia Suskin Ostriker so succinctly puts it:

> Human civilization has a stake in plural readings. We've seen this
> at least since the eighteenth century when the notion of religious

tolerance was invented to keep the Christian sects from killing each other. The notion of racial tolerance came later. . . . Most people need "right" answers, just as they need "superior" races . . . At this particular moment it happens to be feminists and other socially marginal types who are battling for cultural pluralism. Still, this is an activity we're undertaking on behalf of humanity, all of whom would be the happier, I believe, were they to give up their addiction to final solutions.[21]

Because of the all-too-human need to use the Bible in an imperialistic way for bolstering our identity over and against that of others, because of our need for using the Bible as a security-blanket, as an avenue for controlling the divine, or as a means for possessing revelatory knowledge as an exclusive privilege, we are ever tempted to use Scripture as a weapon to keep others in line: the homosexuals, the feminists, or the terrorists.

To understand the Bible in the paradigm of the open cosmopolitan house of Divine Wisdom allows one to conceptualize Scripture as an open-ended prototype rather than as an archetype that has to be repeated in every generation. It enables one to understand the Bible as a site of struggle over meaning and biblical interpretation as debate and argument rather than as transcript of the unchanging, inerrant Word of G*d. It requires that we rethink the notion of struggle, debate, and argument that is usually understood in terms of battle, combat, and competition. Within the radical democratic space of Wisdom-Spirit, struggle can be recognized as turning conflict into opportunity and debate and argument as fostering difference and respect for a multiplicity of voices.

Wisdom teaching holds out as a promise the fullness and possibility of the "good life" and encourages a search for justice and order in the world that can be discerned by experience. Wisdom teaching does not keep faith and knowledge apart, it does not divide the world into religious and secular, but provides a model for living a "mysticism of everyday things." In short, the educational space of Wisdom are debate and discussion, public places and open borders, nourishment and celebration. Divine Wisdom provides sustenance in the struggles for justice and cultivates creation and life in fullness.

The open cosmic house of Divine Wisdom needs no exclusive walls or boundaries, no fortifications and barricades to separate and shut up the insiders from the outsiders, the Bible from its surrounding world. Wisdom imagination engenders a different understanding of the Bible. To approach the Bible as Wisdom's dwelling of cosmic dimensions means to acknowledge its multivalence and its openness to change. It means to give up using it as a "security blanket" or as an instrument of violence; it means to recognize that the free spaces between its seven pillars invite the Spirit to blow where it wills. Biblical authority and biblical studies renewed in the paradigm of Divine Wisdom will be able to foster such creativity, strength, self-affirmation, and freedom of the sacred in the public square.

NOTES

[1] See Richard A. Horsley's works on *Religion and Empire, Jesus and Empire,* and *Paul and Empire.*

[2] See my book *Rhetoric and Ethic: The Politics of Biblical Studies* (Minneapolis: Fortress Press, 1999).

[3] In order to indicate the brokeness and inadequacy of human language to name the divine, I have switched in my book *Jesus: Miriam's Child, Sophia's Prophet—Critical Issues in Feminist Christology* (New York: Continuum, 1994) from the orthodox Jewish writing of G-d which I had adopted in *But She Said* and *Discipleship of Equals,* to this spelling of G*d, which seeks to avoid the conservative malestream association that the writing of G-d has for Jewish feminists.

[4] For a more developed argument, see my book *The Power of the Word: Scripture and the Rhetoric of Empire* (Minneapolis: Fortress Press, 2007).

[5] Adriana Hernández, *Pedagogy, Democracy, and Feminism: Rethinking the Public Sphere* (New York: SUNY Press, 1997), 31.

[6] Adriana Hernández, *Pedagogy, Democracy, and Feminism,* 32.

[7] I use Christian Testament instead of New Testament in order to avoid the supersessionist anti-Jewish implications of the designations Old and New Testament.

[8] See my book *The Book of Revelation: Justice and Judgment,* (Philadelphia: Fortress, 1985).

[9] See, for example, Wes Avram, ed., *Anxious about Empire: Theological Essays about the New Global Realities* (Grand Rapids: Brazon, 2004); David Ray Griffin, John B. Cobb, Richard A. Falk, Catherine Keller, *The American Empire and the Commonwealth of God* (Louisville: Westminster John Knox, 2006); Richard A. Horsley, *Religion and Empire: People, Power, and the Life of the Spirit* (Minneapolis: Fortress Press, 2003).

[10] See R. S. Sugirtharajah, ed., *Voices from the Margins: Interpreting the Bible in the Third World* (Maryknoll: Orbis, 2006) 3–6.

[11] Andrew J. Bacevich, *American Empire: The Realities and Consequences of American Diplomacy* (Cambridge: Harvard University Press, 2002), 1–7.

[12] Kim Yong-Bok, "Asian Quest for Jesus in the Global Empire," *Madang* 1, no. 2 (2004), 2.

[13] See Jan Nederveen Pieterse, ed., *Christianity and Hegemony,* 11–31. See also Paul E. Sigmund, "Christian Democracy, Liberation Theology, the Catholic Right and Democracy in Latin America," in John Witte Jr., ed., *Christianity and Democracy in Global Context* (Boulder: Westview, 1993), 187–207.

[14] Rose Wu, "Poverty, AIDS, and the Struggle of Women to Live," in *G*d's Image* 24, no. 3 (2005): 11.

[15] Nancy Hartsock, *Money, Sex, and Power: Toward a Feminist Historical Materialism* (New York: Longman, 1983), 12.

[16] For this distinction, see Hardt and Negri who ascribe it to Spinoza.

[17] Thomas E. Wartenberg, *The Forms of Power: From Domination to Transformation* (Philadelphia: Temple University Press, 1990), 5. See also Steven Lukes, ed., *Power: Readings in Social and Political Theory* (New York: New York University Press, 1986); Franco Crespi, *Social Action and Power* (Cambridge: Blackwell, 1992); Michael Kelly, ed., *Critique and Power: Recasting the Foucault/Habermas Debate* (Cambridge: MIT Press, 1995).

[18] For the development of biblical scholarship in the United States, see my articles "Rethinking the Educational Practices of Biblical Doctoral Studies," *Teaching The*logy and Religion* 6 (April 2003): 65–75; "Disciplinary Matters: A Critical Rhetoric and Ethic of Inquiry," in Tom H. Olbricht and Anders Eriksson, eds., *Rhetoric, Ethic, and Moral Persuasion in Biblical Discourse: Essays from the 2002 Heidelberg Papers* (New York: T and T Clark, 2005), 9–32; "The Power of the Word: Charting Critical Global Feminist Biblical Studies," in Kathleen O'Brien Wicker, Althea Spencer Miller,

and Musa W. Dube, eds., *Feminist New Testament Studies: Global and Future Perspectives* (New York: Palgrave MacMillan, 2005), 43–62.

[19]bell hooks, *Teaching Community: A Pedagogy of Hope* (New York: Routledge, 2003), 183.

[20]See my book *WisdomWays: Introducing Feminist Biblical Interpretation* (Maryknoll: Orbis, 2001).

[21]Alicia Suskin Ostriker, *Feminist Revision and the Bible* (Cambridge: Blackwell, 1993), 122–23.

PART II

Practicing Feminist Biblical Interpretation

10

To Set the Record Straight

Biblical Women's Studies

In the early 1970s, women's studies emerged as an independent discipline. In all areas of scientific knowledge, courses and research projects were developed to expand our knowledge of women's cultural-scientific contributions as well as to challenge androcentric texts, scholarly frameworks, and scientific reconstructions that overlooked or marginalized wo/men. Women's studies in religion participate in these intellectual and educational goals of the Women's Studies movement, while feminist theology and feminist studies in religion share in the liberative goals of the feminist movement in society and church.

In the context of this two-pronged movement, feminist biblical studies have moved from the concentration on what men have said *about women* in the Bible and from the apologetic-thematic focus on *women in the Bible* to a new *critical reading* of biblical texts in a feminist perspective. In this process we have moved from discussing statements about wo/men by Paul or the "Fathers" and Rabbis to the rediscovery of biblical wo/men's leadership and oppression as crucial for the revelatory process of God's liberation reflected in the Jewish and Christian Scriptures.

In the past decade or so, I have regularly taught an undergraduate course on "wo/men in the Bible" at Notre Dame that seeks to integrate historical-critical biblical scholarship, the intellectual Women's Studies approach, and feminist-theological concerns. Over the years, this course has evolved into three basic sections that could easily be taught as separate courses or be integrated as a whole or in part into other biblical studies, religious studies, or women's studies courses. The course presupposes that students have had an introductory course in the*logy and that both wo/men and men are enrolled in the class. Although the title announces that the course will discuss the whole Bible, I have come to realize that this is an impossible undertaking within the context of a single course, especially if students have no skills in historical-critical analysis and lack basic historical knowledge about biblical times and situations.

Since my own area of specialization is New Testament studies, I tend to discuss Old Testament/Hebrew Bible and "patristic" texts only selectively and to concentrate on New Testament texts. However, I suggest that my methodological approach can be employed equally well in the discussion of Old Testament/Hebrew Bible texts and early church writings.

It is obviously impossible to give even a detailed course syllabus and description in such a limited space. What I will try to do, therefore, is sketch the main sections of the course, make some suggestions for student learning processes and assignments, and mention some books that I have found helpful in teaching the course. Since I cannot develop here fully the theological rationale and exegetical content of each section, I refer those interested in a fuller theoretical development to my book *In Memory of Her: A Feminist Theological Reconstruction of Christian Origins* (New York: Crossroad, 1983). Helpful general introductions are also Letty Russell, editor, *The Liberating World* (Philadelphia: Westminster, 1976) and the papers of the 1980 Society of Biblical Literature panel on *The Effects of Women's Studies on Biblical Studies*, which were edited by Phyllis Trible and appeared in the *Journal for the Study of the Old Testament* 22 (1982): 3–71.

The bibliography suggested is neither comprehensive nor paradigmatic. I simply mention the books and collections of essays that I have found helpful in preparing and teaching the course. The past decade has produced numerous articles and popular books on "Woman in the Bible," but the available literature is very uneven in its scholarly quality and feminist the*logical outlook. For a comprehensive bibliographical review essay, see Ross Kraemer, "Women in the Religions of the Greco-Roman World," which appeared in *Religious Studies Review* in 1983.

ISSUES IN BIBLICAL INTERPRETATION

Despite having taken introductory level courses, students often have not acquired sufficient skills to read the Bible historically, nor have they learned to articulate feminist the*logical-critical questions with respect to biblical texts. They usually approach Scripture with a literalist understanding of inspiration and with very little knowledge of the historical world of the Bible or the literary forms and traditions found in it. It is necessary, therefore, to discuss general introductory questions of biblical interpretation as well as to explore general feminist the*logical perspectives before it is possible to introduce specific historical and the*logical issues.

This section of the course, therefore, addresses the following:

1. the problems of androcentric language, worldview, texts, and translations;
2. the question of who wrote biblical books and why they were written;

3. problems of contemporary interpretation, androcentric presuppositions, models, and prejudices; and
4. questions of biblical resources and historical reconstructions.

This whole introductory section or parts of it can also be taught as segments of general introductory Bible courses, as elements in general courses on religion/the*logy, and as sections in "wo/men in religion or Christianity" courses. Naturally these segments should also have a place in such specialized Scripture courses or seminars as the Pentateuch, the Prophets, the Pauline letters, the Gospels, or church history.

Androcentric Language: Since biblical studies are concerned with the revelatory "word," it is necessary to look carefully at the functions and distortions of androcentric language and male-biased translations. While some students might have been alerted to gender-inclusive language either in high school or earlier college classes, in my experience most students are not conscious of the problem.

The use of "reverse language" is helpful here in raising consciousness. Throughout a whole class period, for example, I will use wo/man (instead of man) in a generic/inclusive way, use the pronoun she instead of he, and speak about the "boys" on the faculty or in the administration. Since such an exercise will stir a lot of emotions, it is necessary to spend the last part of the class in articulating and discussing such emotions. Another helpful exercise is to read first an androcentric translation of a biblical text such as a psalm, and then to read the same text in an inclusive form of translation using wo/men and men, she and he, sisters and brothers, God and Godself. Another class period will be spent in a discussion of male-biased translation and the reasons for it. It is very helpful to compare four or five different translations of passages such as Gen. 1:27; Jer. 31:15-22; 1 Cor. 11:3; or Rom. 16:1. A further question to be explored here is the textual critical question of how our original text was established. Examples are Rom. 16:7 and the identification of "Junia" as a male or female name, or Col. 4:15 and its variant readings of "Nympha and the church in her house."

The discussion of these texts can show how androcentric mind-sets and traditions influence the determination and definition of the original text. Do grammatically masculine words such as brothers, saints, elect, apostles, deacons, or elders refer only to men or also to wo/men? What inferences are made in the process of translation? Check the translations of the pronouns for the Holy Spirit in the Bible: Do scholars refer to *her* in the Old Testament and to *it* in the New Testament? How do they translate the term and on the basis of which language? I realize that such exercises require at least some rudimentary knowledge of the biblical languages on the part of the instructor. However, I have found that students can become passionately involved in such questions, and their exploration of these androcentric language issues in a "scientific" manner helps them to question their "literalist" Bible understanding that every word is dictated or inspired by God.

Female authorship: Most helpful in challenging our historical-the*logical frameworks and assumptions is the question of female authorship of biblical writings. Traditionally, all biblical books are believed to be written by male authors, although most of the biblical writings are anonymous or pseudonymous. Such an assumption of female authorship is supported by the suggestions of scholars that a wo/man could have written, for example, the "Song of Songs" (Trible), Mark (Achtemeier), Proto-Luke (Swidler), John (Schneiders), or Hebrews (Harnack). However, such suggestions often presuppose a "feminine" style, experience, or sensibility that is difficult to establish. Nevertheless such suggestions of female authorship bring to consciousness our unreflected bias that only males could formulate holy Scripture and could claim the authority to do so.

Moreover, the assumption of female authorship also has great value in engendering a different historical imagination. For instance, I find very helpful the creative exercise of writing "apostolic" letters to be attributed to Old Testament or early Christian wo/men leaders. Students can write, for example, an announcement of Deborah to the people of Israel, a letter of Phoebe to the community at Cenchreae, a sermon of the apostle Junia addressed to the church of Jerusalem, or a letter of the missionary Prisca to the church of Ephesus. Such letter writing requires students to discuss the form of the letter in antiquity, the situation of the recipients, the motives of the author, and the social-religious context of the time.

Feminist Hermeneutics: This discussion will lead the class into explorations of contemporary interpretations and their presuppositions and prejudices. One can compare different scholarly interpretations of biblical texts on wo/men and their presuppositions or implications. Another valuable exercise is role-playing. For example, choose Exod. 1:12—2:10: The birth of Moses and his adoption by Pharaoh's daughter. Read the text aloud and have the whole class identify the main characters of the text; then break into smaller groups, each choosing one character to be discussed and impersonated. The smaller groups discuss the event, clarify historical questions, and imagine the scene by speaking in the first person: "I [the midwife or the daughter of the Pharaoh] thought, feared, hoped," and so on. When the whole class comes together again, the small groups stay together and engage as "group-persons" in a dialogue raising questions, expressing their feelings in the situation, and acting out the story. At the end, take fifteen minutes to evaluate the role play and its assumptions with the whole class: Discuss the issues that remain open, elaborate historical aspects, and reflect on the attitudes, emotions, and insights generated by the role play. What kind of assumptions were made about the midwife, the mother of Moses, the daughter of Pharaoh, or God?

Among other texts that lend themselves to such role play and the exploration of presuppositions, attitudes, and feelings are Hosea 1–4 (Hosea and Gomer); Genesis 29–31 (Leah, Rachel, and Bilhah); Mark 7:34-40 (the Syrophoenician Woman); and Acts 12:12-17. It is important, however, to alert students not only to anti-wo/man biases but also to class, race, or anti-Jewish assumptions that may also color their role interaction and come to the fore in the roleplay. Another suggestion: watch "Jesus Christ Superstar" and see how Mary Magdalene is portrayed, or discuss the liturgical readings for her feast day in different lectionaries.

Androcetric Sources: Not only contemporary interpretations but also scriptural writings themselves reflect an androcentric worldview and patriarchal structures. It becomes necessary, therefore, to speak about tradition and redaction as well as about literary form and purposes of biblical writings. It is important to elaborate, for example, that Genesis 2–3 is an etiological story that seeks to understand the origin of the world and the evil in it. Students must relinquish their preconception that this story is a historical record and accurate description of what happened. Similarly, they have to abandon their assumption that Acts gives us a comprehensive and accurate historical description of developments in the beginnings of the church. It is thus helpful to compare the references to wo/men in the Pauline letters with those of Acts, or to compare the understandings of apostleship in Paul and Luke-Acts.

Equally helpful is a comparison of the Gospel stories on wo/men to see which writer has more stories or how the different Gospels picture the leading wo/men and the leading men in the discipleship of Jesus. A careful comparison of one Gospel story found in all four accounts—the wo/man who anointed Jesus, for example—is also fruitful. Walter Wink has suggested a "socratic" method for dialoguing with the Gospel texts. However, rather than bringing the wo/man into a direct dialogue with Jesus or oneself, it is better to let students write a dialogue between the wo/man and the writer of Luke's Gospel, asking him why he portrayed her as he did, why he made her a public sinner, and so on. This approach avoids a simplistic historicizing of the text and makes redactional deliberations conscious.

Another possibility is to rewrite the story of Miriam or Jezebel, the prophetess, from the point of view of one of her followers, or to let the wo/men who experienced Jesus' miraculous feeding or the mother of Jairus's daughter tell these stories from their own perspectives. How would one tell the story of the prodigal son from his mother's perspective? What the*logical implications come to the fore in doing so? Another way to raise questions of tradition and redaction is to divide students into small groups, giving each group the same materials (stories, sayings, songs, prayers, commands, folk sayings, reports, advertisements), and asking them to use these materials to compose a letter, a children's-hour, a the*logical lecture, a commencement speech, or a sermon.

At the end, discuss why the group selected certain texts and not others, why they established a certain sequence, what their major goals were, whom they addressed and how this determined their choice of materials. Another suggestion: let students collect pictures of the annunciation and discuss the different representations found in different centuries and cultures in order to highlight how every generation or group understands and interprets the same tradition differently.[1]

Wo/men in the Bible

This section seeks to analyze and reinterpret the information on wo/men that we find in biblical writings. It is important to distinguish clearly between two types of texts. On the one hand, we have those texts that inform us about the actual situation and role of Greco-Roman, Jewish, and early Christian wo/men, reminding us that Christian wo/men remained Jews, Asians, Romans, Greeks, or Syrians, although they were all defined politically by the Roman empire and culturally by Hellenism. On the other hand, we have those texts that express men's opinions, judgments, or injunctions about wo/men. Such a distinction is preferable over the widespread differentiation between positive and negative texts or traditions, which does not sufficiently reflect on the interaction of these texts and the social-ecclesial struggles reflected in them.

Students must first become conscious of how little they know about the subject matter and of how greatly this knowledge may be tainted by prejudice. When asked to list ten biblical wo/men, many students, despite extensive religious schooling, are able to mention only Eve and Mary, the Mother of Jesus, and perhaps Mary Magdalene, the so-called prostitute. Assigned interviews with their friends and other students usually produce similar results. More importantly, many students are ignorant either about Greco-Roman antiquity or about Judaism in antiquity. Yet almost all have picked up the apologetic argument that Christianity has very much improved the status of wo/men, who in Judaism or the Greco-Roman world were supposedly considered to be minors, "chattel," or "immoral."

It is therefore important to make students aware that the first followers of Jesus and the earliest Christian missionaries were Jewish and Greco-Roman wo/men who were free to convert and to define their own religious-social commitments. A discussion of the patriarchal structures of the ancient world therefore needs to point out that within the Greco-Roman world of the first century, wo/men—especially rich wo/men—had achieved a relative emancipation that often gave them more autonomy and freedom than that of wo/men of the nineteenth century or even today.

An example of an independent Jewish wo/man is found in the book of Judith, while the excavations of Pompeii, for instance, have documented the economic wealth of some wo/men and the participation even of working wo/men in the public life of the city. The androcentric character of statements made by male authors about wo/men must be analyzed not only in early Christian but also in Jewish and Greco-Roman writings. For example, the satires of Juvenal give us information about the high level of wo/men's education, but at the same time they distort this information because of their misogynist slant. Similarly, Rabbinic statements are not descriptions of wo/men's situation in the first century but rather projections and injunctions that reflect the male centered mind-set of their authors.

The ministry of Jesus and the movement initiated by him must therefore not be reconstructed over and against Judaism but in the awareness that Jesus' vision is nurtured by the emancipatory traditions of Judaism and that his first followers were Jewish wo/men and men. The religion and heritage of Judaism are the inspiration and matrix of the Jesus movement. The same holds true for the early Christian missionary movement, which at first was carried on by Jewish wo/men but then moved beyond the boundaries of Judaism. This movement too was possible only because there were groups and associations in the Greco-Roman world that were not patterned after the patriarchal structures of the dominant culture.

Reconstruction of the early Christian movements must therefore take into account the relative emancipation of wo/men in the Greco-Roman world as well as chart the relationship of the early Christian movement to its dominant patriarchal culture. The transition from the pre-Pauline to the post-Pauline churches must be carefully analyzed, and the role of Paul in this transition must be pinpointed. Most of the post-Pauline writings are addressed to or located in Asia Minor. The so-called household-code-texts that reintroduce patriarchal values and structures into the Christian movement are all addressed to communities in this area. This is significant, since we know that the status of Asian wo/men was exceptionally high. It needs to be kept in mind when discussing the role of wo/men in Revelation, 1 Peter, the Pastoral Epistles, the Johannine Epistles, or Ignatius that slave wo/men were most negatively affected by the patriarchalization of the church.

In order to place the New Testament writings in their early Christian contexts, it is important to discuss what information we have about wo/men of the first Christian centuries and to familiarize students with the Apocryphal Acts, Gnostic writings, Montanist oracles, church orders, or "patristic" writers. I have found tests and short papers most helpful in achieving the goal of this section, which is to broaden students' biblical-historical and the*logical knowledge. I usually assign certain readings, hand out study questions, ask them to look up words, to draw maps, or to analyze certain texts. Since many of my students do not come from Arts and Letters, but from Business Administration, Architecture, or the Sciences, they usually are better equipped to handle informational questions and "true or false" tests than to write research papers. Some of the more advanced students, however, have written papers on topics such as male and female disciples in the Gospel of Mark; interpretations of Gal. 3:28; Wo/men in the Fourth Gospel; comparison between Paul's references to wo/men and those in Acts; the "widow" in the Pastoral epistles; Ephesians 5 in the wedding liturgy; the matriarchs in the Old Testament; wo/men prophets in the Old Testament and New Testament; Ruth and Naomi; wo/men in the Acts of Thecla and Paul; "Should we proclaim patriarchal texts as the 'word of G*d'?"; marriage legislation in Jewish and Roman law; Isis and her worship; and comparison of different creation stories. However, most students who are not the*logy majors find that such papers are often too complex and discouraging.[2]

Biblical The*logical Issues Today

This section of the course explores the significance and importance of biblical texts for today. It does so by confronting students with questions directed to the Bible by women's studies in religion or by the feminist movement in church and society. Some students will be aware of such questions as masculine god-language or the ordination of women, others will encounter them for the first time, while a few students might have enrolled in the course because they are wrestling with these the*logical questions. I usually do not teach this segment of the course as a separate section, but rather integrate the topics into the lectures of the first two sections or assign group projects. Generally, I leave it up to the group as to how they want to explore the topic, to formulate their questions, and to present their insights to the whole class. Naturally this section could be taught as an independent course or could be integrated into other courses of the*logy or women's studies in religion.

Topics of such group projects include: Are wo/men the image of G*d? (see Gen. 1:3; 1 Cor. 11:3; and 1 Tim. 2); Christian Discipleship and Patriarchal Marriage; the "independent" wo/man today and in antiquity; G*d the Father or How do you pray?; Is "maleness" constitutive in the New Testament for understanding Jesus Christ?; nonsexist prayers and Bible stories for children; a celebration of Mary Magdalene and other biblical wo/men; Is the church patriarchal?; biblical arguments against the ordination of wo/men; wo/men's ordination in other Christian churches; women in Judaism; biblical arguments of the Moral Majority for the patriarchal family; contemporary and biblical attitudes toward menstruation and sexual "purity"; the function of the Bible against slaves' and women's suffrage in the nineteenth century; Mary the Mother of G*d and the Goddesses of antiquity.

Students have developed creative ways of presenting and exploring these problems and topics. One group that discussed the "image of God" question staged a retrial of Eve in order to adjudicate whether her punishment fit her crime. Since most of the group members intended to go to law school, they carefully followed court protocol. At the end, the class voted narrowly that Eve's punishment by far exceeded her crime. Another group followed the model of Judith Plaskow's story "The Coming of Lilith," but retold the Genesis story from an African or Asian perspective. Another group prepared a Passover meal and haggadah, while others celebrated a feminist baptismal liturgy. A multimedia show on the Goddess was worked out in cooperation with a professor from the art department. Other groups polled their fellow students on questions such as menstruation or inclusive G*d-language, interviewed parents about nonsexist religious education or interviewed priests and nuns on campus about "religious life." Others visited ministers from other churches for an interview or visited a Catholic Pentecostal household.

Other projects included television shows, for example, on divorce and the church; a counseling session with a couple disagreeing on child-rearing; a role-play on the house-church of Nympha; a radio interview with the pope, Sister Theresa Kane, Hans Küng, and Phyllis Schlafly on wo/men's ordination. These group projects are usually more interesting when some members are older, married, or members of religious orders. Usually they are the most exciting part of the course since they not only foster the*logical research skills but also allow students to display their imagination or professional skills. Moreover they bring students together in "teamwork" and often result in friendship groups. Although it is difficult to evaluate these group-events, I would not want to miss them. They allow for a biblical-historical and feminist-the*logical integration that cannot be accomplished by the instructor alone.[3]

NOTES

[1] For a general discussion of the interaction between culture, society, and the definition of gender roles, see Ann Oakley, *Sex, Gender, and Society* (San Francisco: Harper and Row, 1972). See especially Casey Miller and Kate Swift, *Words and Women* (Garden City: Doubleday Anchor, 1977) for the discussion of inclusive language. Suggestions for female biblical language metaphors are found in Phyllis Trible, *God and the Rhetoric of Sexuality* (Philadelphia: Fortress Press, 1978). See also her interpretation of Genesis 1–3 and the book of Ruth. Interpretations of Gospel stories from a woman's point of view are found in Rachel Conrad Wahlberg, *Jesus According to a Woman* (New York: Paulist, 1975) and *Jesus and the Freed Woman* (New York: Paulist, 1978), whereas Leonard Swidler, *Biblical Affirmations of Woman* (Philadelphia: Westminster, 1979) provides a good overview of all the biblical texts on women. Elisabeth Moltmann Wendel's *The Women around Jesus* (New York: Crossroad, 1982) is not only helpful for interpreting the Gospel stories about wo/men but also for tracing the tradition of interpretation. A helpful general introduction to feminist the*logical questions is Carol Christ and Judith Plaskow, eds., *Womanspirit Rising* (San Francisco: Harper and Row, 1979), especially the editors' introduction.

[2] J. H. Otwell, *And Sarah Laughed: The Status of Women in the Old Testament* (Philadelphia: Westminster, 1977) and Evelyn and Frank Stagg, *Woman in the World of Jesus* (Philadelphia: Westminster, 1978) discuss a wealth of information, although their tone is sometimes apologetic-defensive. More critical and feminist in outlook are the first six chapters in Rosemary Radford Ruether, ed., *Religion and Sexism* (New York: Simon and Schuster, 1974), while the first two

chapters in Rosemary Ruether and Eleanor Mclaughlin, eds., *Women of Spirit* (New York: Simon and Schuster, 1979), seek to highlight women's contributions to early Christianity. A concise and useful discussion of women's ministry in early Christianity is Elizabeth M. Tetlow's *Women and Ministry in the New Testament* (New York: Paulist, 1980), although it sometimes simplifies difficult exegetical problems. Information on women in the Greco-Roman world is found in Sarah B. Pomeroy, *Goddesses, Whores, Wives, and Slaves* (New York: Schocken, 1975) and Mary R. Lefkowitz and Maureen B. Fant, eds., *Women in Greece and Rome* (Toronto: Samuel-Stevens, 1977). Bernadette Brooten, *Women Leaders in the Ancient Synagogue* (Chico: Scholars, 1983) corrects the anti-Jewish assumptions found in much of Christian literature on "Women in the Bible." The following are helpful for study of women in various groups of the early church: P. Wilson-Kastner, et al., *A Lost Tradition: Women Writers of the Early Church* (Washington, DC: University Press of America, 1981) discuss the writings of Perpetua, Proba, Egeria, and Eudokia, whereas Jean LaPorte, *The Role of Women in Early Christianity* (New York: Mellen, 1982) has edited texts of the "Fathers" on women. S. L. Davies, *The Revolt of the Widows* (Carbondale: Southern Illinois University Press, 1980) proposes that the apocryphal Acts are written by and for women, whereas Elaine Pagels, *The Gnostic Gospels* (New York: Random, 1979) discusses women and the divine in Gnosticism.

[3]Walter Burkhardt, ed., *Woman: New Dimensions* (New York: Paulist, 1975); Rosemary Radford Ruether, *Sexism and God-Talk* (Boston: Beacon, 1983); Mary Daly, *Beyond God the Father* (Boston: Beacon, 1973); Carol P. Christ, *Diving Deep and Surfacing* (Boston: Beacon, 1980); Judith Plaskow, *Sex, Sin and Grace* (Washington, DC: University Press of America, 1980); J. Chamberlain Engelsman, *The Feminine Dimension of the Divine* (Philadelphia: Westminster, 1979) "fits" the texts into a Jungian interpretational pattern; Robert Hamerton Kelly, *God the Father* (Philadelphia: Fortress Press, 1979) is somewhat apologetic; Rosemary Radford Ruether, *Mary, the Feminine Face of the Church* (Philadelphia: Westminster, 1977); Raymond E. Brown et al., eds., *Mary in the New Testament* (Philadelphia: Fortress Press, 1978); Marina Warner, *Alone of All Her Sex* (New York: Knopf, 1976); N. Shange, *For Colored Girls Who Have Considered Suicide: When the Rainbow Is Enuf* (New York: Macmillan, 1975); Arlene Swidler, *Sistercelebrations* (Philadelphia: Fortress Press, 1974); Leonard and Arlene Swidler, eds., *Women Priests* (New York: Paulist, 1977); E. Koltun, *The Jewish Woman* (New York: Schocken, 1976); C. F. Parvey, *Ordination of Women in Ecumenical Perspective*, Faith and Order Paper, 105 (Geneva: WCC, 1980).

11

Biblical Interpretation and Critical Commitment

The Gospel of John

> It is told that at a synod in Ephesus, "the robber synod," a sharp dispute arose among the the*logians, about whether or not God had a body.[1] And when the majority of the learned decided that God did not have a body, there was an old Egyptian hermit who left the assembly crying, with the words: "They have taken my God from me and I do not know where I shall go and search for him." I am in sympathy with the old monk.[2]

Sigmund Mowinckel told this story in a debate about the church as a "spiritual community." Both the old hermit and the Norwegian professor could not conceive of a conceptualization of religion, the divine, and the church that did not take historical, particular, embodied reality into account. Unlike the hermit and the professor I am concerned here not so much with the concrete embodiment of the divine and of religion but with that of biblical scholarship. Is it possible for biblical scholarship to be value-neutral, objective, detached, and unbiased or should it be? How does the commitment to a particular community, theoretical perspective, and historical struggle impinge on or foster critical inquiry and biblical scholarship? To approach this question it is appropriate to identify my own social location. I speak here today as a wo/man who because of her gender traditionally has been excluded from the articulation of the*logy and church leadership by church law and academic convention. I was invited as a biblical scholar whose academic home is the United States, where the political right utilizes biblical language and authority for sustaining a reactionary and antidemocratic "politics of subordination." And I speak in a German accent as a Christian the*logian at the fiftieth anniversary of the *Kristallnacht* on November 9, 1938, the year I was born.

This particular social location raises important epistemological and hermeneutical questions and concerns. As a wo/man privileged by education and race, I ask how scholarship in general and biblical scholarship in particular can be changed in such a way that the voices and contributions of the previously excluded "others" can become central to our understanding of the biblical world, religion, and the divine. As a member of the American academy, I am concerned with how biblical scholarship can transform its ivory tower mentality in such a way that it can contribute to the public-political articulation of a religious vision for a more humane future of the world. Finally, as a Christian the*logian I must take responsibility for the violence perpetrated by religion in general and Christian the*logy in particular whenever the divine is "embodied" in exclusive, elite terms of privilege fostering oppression and vilification of the subordinated "others."

As a feminist biblical scholar and the*logian I do not raise these questions for individualistic and confessional reasons. Rather I have delineated my own rhetorical situation in the interest of changing the discipline that marginalizes such "embodied" scholarly engagement. Therefore, the following three arguments engendered by my particular social location will structure this paper. I argue in the *first* place that biblical scholarship must recognize its scientistic posture of universalist objectivity as masking its "masculine embodiment."[3] *Secondly,* biblical studies needs to reconceptualize its task and self-understanding as engaged rhetoric rooted in a particular historical situation. *Finally,* I will indicate how such a reconceptualization of biblical discourse and interpretation in terms of rhetoric can open up the problem of anti-Judaism in the Fourth Gospel for critical reflection and the*logical evaluation.

THE EMPIRICIST PARADIGM OF BIBLICAL STUDIES

The value-free rhetoric of historical-critical studies was shaped in the political context of heresy trials and the struggle of biblical scholarship to free itself from dogmatic authority and ecclesiastical controls.[4] It corresponded with the professionalization of academic life and the rise of the university. Just as history as an academic discipline sought in the nineteenth century to prove itself as an objective science in analogy to the natural sciences, so also did biblical studies. The mandate to eliminate value considerations and normative concepts in the immediate encounter with the text is to assure that the resulting historical accounts would be free of ideology and dogmatic imposition.

While biblical scholarship asserts its scientific character by rejecting all overt the*logical and religious institutional bias, at the same time it inhabits a name and space marked by the traditional biblical canon. To the extent that biblical studies and history-of-religions scholarship continues to mask their hermeneutical character, advocacy position, and rootedness in historical-religious power-struggles, they are not able to cultivate a critical self-reflexivity on how their sociopolitical location shapes their research practices and self-understandings.

This scholarly rhetoric of objective detached inquiry insists that biblical critics need to stand somehow outside their own time, have no positive or negative attitude toward the object of their research, and conceptualize biblical time and world as totally "Other." Kurt Rudolph, for instance, insists on the scientific character of the history of religions over and against the*logy normatively understood: "Historians of religion will to be sure, have a certain prior knowledge of the object of their research, but to the extent that they have neither a positive nor a negative attitude toward the object of their study, they will be without prejudice. It is in this sense that historians of religion must be objective, that they must be as neutral as possible."[5]

What makes biblical interpretation scientific is radical detachment—emotional, intellectual, and political distancing. Disinterested and dispassionate scholarship enables biblical critics to enter the minds and world of historical people and to study history on its own terms, unencumbered by contemporary questions, values, and interests.

Although scholars of religion often hold that the*logical commitments compromise critical rationality and scientific objectivity and confessional the*logians in turn show a disdain for the rationalistic criticism of their colleagues, they nevertheless both unite in denying any concrete political-religious commitments and in claiming scientific objectivity and positivist empiricism for biblical studies. Therefore both tend to reject the work of liberation the*logians and feminist scholars in religion as ideologically biased and unscientific. Positivist objectivism is blind to the fact that the world of historical data can never be perceived independently from the linguistic con-ceptualizations of the investigating interpreter. It also denies the relationships of power inscribed in its own discourses.

Such a positivist objectivism is a truncation of the historical impulse of the Enlightenment tradition. The ideal of the Euro-American Enlightenment was critically accomplished knowledge in the interest of human freedom, equality, and justice. Its principle of unqualified critical inquiry and assessment does not exempt any given reality, authority, tradition, or institution. Knowledge is not a given but a culturally and historically embodied language and therefore always open to probing inquiry and relentless critique.[6] The critical principle of the Enlightenment was institutionalized in the modern university as the rationalist paradigm of knowledge that gives primacy to experienced data and empirical inquiry. Its "logic of facts" relies on abstraction for the sake of rigor, evidence, and precision. Objectivism, literalism, methodology, and formalism are the hallmarks of the institutionalization of the critical principle in its rationalist form.

The critical principle of the Enlightenment has also engendered three historical correctives of its institutionalized form of objectivist literalism that underline the figurality, complexity, particularity, and corruption of reality. The aesthetic or romantic corrective stresses intuitive imagination over selective abstraction,[7] the religious-cultural corrective insists on tradition as wisdom and heritage, and the political-practical corrective asserts that there is no pure reason as an instrument of knowledge that could lead to a just society. In the beginning was not pure reason but power. The institutions of so-called pure reason—such as the sciences, scholarly organizations, and the university—hide from themselves their own complicity in societal agendas of power. These three corrective paradigms introduce the hermeneutical principle as a second principle of critical inquiry.[8]

To be sure, the argument of these correctives is not with empirical research, analytical scholarship, or critical abstraction itself but with an uncritical conception of reason, knowledge, and scholarship. The atrophy and anorexia of the critical principle in the modern university has engendered an ethos of allegedly disinterested impartial research, a proliferation of techniques and specializations and ever-narrower fields of professionalization—practices that are reinforced by the university's reward system. However, insofar as this institutionalized ethos fails to apply the critical principle of the Enlightenment to its own self-understanding and its institutions of knowledge, it cannot recognize its own dogmatic scientistic character but has to marginalize its correctives as "ideological." Yet by doing so, the modern research-university fails to advance the Enlightenment goal of a just and democratic society.

This is especially underlined by the fourth corrective that, I would suggest, is in the process of being articulated. In interaction with postmodernism and critical theory, so-called "minoritized" discourses question the Enlightenment's notion of the universal transcendental subject as the disembodied voice of reason. These discourses assert that the political-social and intellectual-ideological creation of the devalued "Others" goes hand in hand with the creation of the Western Man of Reason,[9] who as the rational subject positions himself outside of time and space. By positioning himself as the abstract knower and disembodied speaker of Enlightenment science, he claims to produce objective accounts of the world independent of the investigating subject.

Minoritized discourses such as feminist or third world theories have shown that the Western "logic of identity" and conceptualization of reason lives from the marginalization, silence, repression, and exploitation of the "Others" of Western elite men. But in distinction to postmodernism, minority discourses insist that the colonialized "Others" cannot afford to abandon the notion of the subject and the possibility of defining the world. Rather, the subordinated "Others" must engage in a political and theoretical process of becoming the subjects of knowledge and history. We who have previously been excluded from the*logical scholarship have to use what we know about the world and our lives for critiquing the dominant disembodied ethos of scholarship and for fostering appreciation of pluriform difference and particular articulation.[10]

But in order not to become co-opted as the "same," feminist and minority discourses have to consciously undo the rhetoric of unitary otherness. Women are not just the excluded Others, but the majority of women are doubly invisible and doubly silenced. Whereas elite women and men of subordinated races, classes, and cultures are the Others of elite men, women oppressed by racism, classism, religious discrimination, and colonialism are the "Others of the Others." As Jewish feminists[11] have pointed out, as long as feminist the*logy and biblical interpretation do not explicitly address anti-Semitism as a *feminist* the*logical issue, it will reproduce the anti-Jewish rhetorics of otherness inscribed in early Christian texts and their subsequent interpretations.

A RHETORICAL PARADIGM OF BIBLICAL STUDIES

The "inclusion" of the previously excluded "Others" as critical historical and the*logical subjects particularizes the universalist claims of abstract scientific inquiry as elite men's rhetorical constructions of reality. It requires, I argue, a paradigm shift in the conceptualization of biblical studies from a scientistic to a rhetorical genre, from an objectivist-detached to a participatory ethos of engagement.[12]

Since rhetorical practices display not only a referential moment about something and a moment of self-implication by a speaker or actor but also a persuasive moment of directedness to involve the other, they elicit not only reason but also emotions, interests, judgments, and commitments directed toward common values and visions. Biblical texts and interpretations as cultural-religious practices are rhetorical practices. As an institutional and intellectual discursive practice biblical scholarship is "positioned" within a historical web of power relationships. Intellectual neutrality is not possible in a world of exploitation and oppression. *Bildungswissen*—knowledge for its own sake—functions either as *Herrschaftswissen*, knowledge for the sake of domination, or as *Befreiungswissen*, knowledge for the sake of liberation.[13]

By rhetorical I mean a communicative praxis that links knowledge with action and passion and discloses that biblical scholarship as a socioreligious rhetorical practice calls for public discussion and ethical judgment. Biblical interpretation understood as communicative praxis unmasks the value detached posture of biblical scholarship as well as the doctrinal certainty of the*logy narrowly conceived as authoritarian rhetorics.

Such a rhetorical self-understanding would reconstitute biblical studies as religious ethical practices of critical inquiry and particular commitments. "The turn to rhetoric" that has engendered critical theory in literary, historical, political, and social studies, I suggest, fashions also a theoretical context for such a paradigm shift in biblical studies.[14] The sociology of knowledge, critical theory, postmodernism, minority discourses, reader response criticism, and the "new historicism" represent the contemporary revival of the rhetorical tradition.[15]

The analytical and practical tradition of rhetoric utilizes both theories of rhetoric and the rhetoric of theories to display how—as historical, cultural, political, and religious discursive practices—biblical texts and their contemporary interpretations involve both authorial aims and strategies, and audience perceptions and constructions. It rejects the misconstrual of rhetoric as stylistic ornament, technical skill, cynical deception, or linguistic manipulation, and maintains not only "that rhetoric is epistemic but also that epistemology and ontology are themselves rhetorical."[16] Biblical scholarship is a communicative practice that involves interests, values, commitments, and visions.

A rhetorical paradigm shift situates biblical scholarship in such a way that its public character and political responsibility become an integral part of its literary readings and historical reconstructions of the biblical world. In distinction to formalist literary criticism, a critical theory of rhetoric insists that context is as important as text. What we see depends on where we stand. One's social location or rhetorical context is decisive of how one sees the world, constructs reality, or interprets biblical texts. Therefore, competing interpretations of texts are not simply either right or wrong.[17] They constitute different ways of reading and constructing historical, religious, and ethical meaning. Not detached value-neutrality but an explicit interrogation of one's commitments, theoretical perspectives, ethical criteria, interpretative strategies, and sociopolitical location is appropriate in such a rhetorical paradigm of biblical studies.

The reconceptualization of biblical studies in rhetorical rather than objectivistic terms, I suggest, provides a research framework not only for integrating historical, archeological, sociological, literary, and the*logical approaches as perspectival readings of texts but also for raising ethical, religious, and the*logical questions of contemporary meaning as constitutive to the interpretive process. A rhetorical hermeneutic does not assume that the text is a window to historical reality nor operate with a correspondence theory of truth. It does not understand historical sources as given data and empirical evidence but sees them as perspectival discourses constructing their worlds and symbolic universes.[18] Since alternative symbolic universes engender competing definitions of the world, they cannot be reduced to one and the same meaning.

The rhetorical understanding of discourse as creating a world of pluriform meanings and a pluralism of symbolic universes raises the question of power. How meaning is constructed, whose interests are served, what kind of worlds are envisioned, what roles, duties, and values are advocated, which sociopolitical practices are legitimated, or which communities of discourse take responsibility—such and similar questions become central to scholarly discussion.

Questions raised by feminist scholars in religion, liberation the*logians, the*logians of the so-called third world, and by others traditionally absent from the exegetical enterprise would no longer remain peripheral or nonexistent in such a self-critical scholarly discourse. Rather their insights and challenges could become central to the scholarly discourse of the discipline.

However, once biblical scholarship begins to explicitly recognize the social interests of the investigating subject, whether defined by race, gender, culture, or class, and once it begins to recognize the need for a sophisticated and pluralistic reading of texts that questions the fixity of meaning constituted by the silencing and exclusion of the "Others," then a *double ethics* is called for.

An *ethics of historical reading* changes the task of interpretation from establishing historical facts and finding out "what the text meant" to the question of what kind of readings can do justice to the text and can elaborate the rhetorical strategies of the text in its historical and our own contemporary contexts. It investigates how the text constructs what it includes or "silences." Such a focus on the ideological scripts of a biblical text and its interpretations does not replace historical text-oriented readings but presupposes them. As literary and historical critical exegesis attends to the text in its historical contexts, so rhetorical criticism seeks to make conscious how the text "works" in its complex historical as well as contemporary cultural, social, religious, or the*logical contexts.[19]

Needless to say that I do not want to be misunderstood as abandoning a careful analysis of biblical sources, as eschewing the reconstruction of their historical-religious contexts, or as advocating a return to the precritical readings and facile the*logical imposition of dogmastic frameworks on biblical texts. Rather I am interested in decentering the dominant value-detached ethos of biblical scholarship by recentering it in a critical interpretive praxis for liberation. Although such an *ethics of historical reading* is aware of the pluralism of historical- and literary-critical methods as well as the pluralism of interpretations appropriate to the text, it nevertheless insists that the number of interpretations that can legitimately be given to a text are limited. The boundaries set by our sources separate historical reconstruction from historical fiction.

The rhetorical character of biblical interpretations and historical reconstructions requires secondly an *ethics of accountability* that stands responsible for the choice of its theoretical interpretive models and for the ethical-political implications of its interpretations of a different praxis. If scriptural texts and interpretations have been used for legitimating war, nurturing anti-Judaism and misogynism, justifying the institution of slavery, and for promoting colonial dehumanization, then biblical scholarship must not only trace the rhetorical strategies and identity formations inscribed in biblical texts but also evaluate the discursive construction of their historical worlds and symbolic universes. If the Bible has become a classic of Western culture because of its normativity, then the responsibility of the biblical scholar[20] must include the elucidation of the ethical implications and political functions of the biblical texts themselves and the violence they have legitimated in Western history and culture.[21]

If critical scholarship should not continue to reproduce the "rhetorics of otherness" inscribed in biblical texts, it has to open up its own strategies and contextualizations as well as those of biblical discourses for critical discussion and the*logical assessment. Hence, in the last section of this paper I seek to sketch how such a rhetorical approach would interrogate the strategies of biblical interpretations for their operative commitments. I will discuss as a case study the scholarly interpretation of the anti-Jewish polemics inscribed in the Fourth Gospel.

The Johannine "Politics of Otherness" in Discussion

The anti-Jewish polemics of the Fourth Gospel lends itself for such an exploration of the rhetorical character of biblical scholarship for several reasons. No one seriously debates the fact of such anti-Jewish language. Exegetes only disagree about its social-literary function and its the*logical evaluation. Moreover the sociopolitical location of the debate[22] on whether the language of the Gospel is anti-Jewish or antisemitic is apparent and not masked. It is the experience of the Holocaust and the subsequent Jewish-Christian dialogue that has spawned the inquiry as to whether Christian Scriptures in general and the Gospel of John in particular have fostered anti-Jewish prejudice not only in Christian churches but also in Western cultures. Scholars have therefore called for an explicit the*logical critique[23] and even change of such anti-Jewish discursive practices, although apologetic appropriation of such anti-Jewish texts is still prevalent.

Since the inquiry into Johannine anti-Judaism addresses the "Others" of Christians, it is treated as a "special" topic and therefore marginalized.[24] Many commentaries and monographs on the Fourth Gospel's the*logy still do not explicitly raise the problem of anti-Judaism. If they do so, they compartmentalize the problem of the Gospel's "language of hate" in an *excursus* but do not systematically develop its impact on the the*logy, christology, and identity-construction of the writer and audience.

In the last twenty years or so, New Testament scholarship has highlighted the sectarianism and anti-Jewish polemics of the Gospel and elaborated its social world and symbolic universe. Although the language and "world" of the Fourth Gospel is Jewish, the term "the Jews" is used predominantly as a negative term. It does not include Jesus and his followers as Jews but distances them from "the Jews." However, according to the Gospel, not all Jews have rejected Jesus but many have believed in him. The expression "the Jews" occurs as a positive the*logical affirmation in the dialogue with the Samaritan woman: "Salvation comes from the Jews" (4:22). However, in the overall context this positive statement reinforces the anti-Jewish polemics of the Gospel. Although salvation originates with the Jews, it is not the Jews but the non-Jews who recognize and accept it.[25] The Gospel's polemics bespeak not just fear of expulsion but aggressive sectarian affirmation.

This anti-Jewish polemic is situated in a cosmological dualism of light and darkness, spirit and flesh, life and death, above and below, "the world" and the believer, God and Satan. One could say that the whole narrative of the Gospel is woven within a framework of dualism. This dualistic framework engenders not only anti-Judaism but also christological absolutism that breeds religious exclusivism and sectarian isolation.

Although it is still debated whether the controversy with gnostic interpreters of the Jesus traditions has engendered the dualistic language and christological myth of the Gospel,[26] the majority of scholars tend to argue that the conflict of the Johannine community with its community of origin and the expulsion of its members from the synagogue has generated the social-religious alienation of the Johannine community and its anti-Jewish polemic. Relying on the work of J. Louis Martyn and R. E. Brown,[27] scholars construct the expulsion from Judaism as the specific historical situation for the vituperative anti-Jewish rhetoric of the Gospel. This traumatic event is retrojected back unto the life and ministry of Jesus. To quote the influential Johannine scholar D. M. Smith: "Because of the trauma of the rupture, the Johannine community defined and understood itself as the obverse of the synagogue and saw in the latter the enemy par excellence. But the hostility of the Synagogue was matched by the rejection of the world generally, and the community came to regard the Jewish opposition as archetypal of this rejection."[28]

Although Jewish scholars have disputed that such an official synagogue ban existed at the time of the Gospel's redaction and that the rabbis would have had the power to enforce it,[29] Christian scholars persist in collapsing the rhetorical situation of the Gospel with its historical situation.[30] Reviewing the counterarguments, David Rensberger, for example, insists: "Nevertheless, whatever the means employed and whatever the role, if any, of rabbinic degrees emanating from Jamnia, it seems incontrovertible from the thrice repeated reference in John 9:22; 12:42; and 16:2 that the Johannine community experienced such an expulsion. . . . We may know less than we would like about the details, but it is surely correct to give this experience a central role in understanding the background of the Fourth Gospel."[31]

This rhetoric "of fact" masks the the*logical implications resulting from such a scholarly construction of the historical "substory" to the Johannine text. It does not ask why other New Testament writers did not develop such vituperative anti-Jewish language although they knew of harassment and expulsion from the synagogue.[32] Such a reconstruction of the Gospel's historical subtext in terms of its vituperative anti-Jewish rhetorics reinforces Christian anti-Jewish identity formation today, especially if it is connected with a liberation the*logical posture.[33] It implies that Christians persecuted Jews when they came to power, just as Jews had persecuted Christians when they were in power.

As a reader-response critic, Alan Culpepper does not shirk the question as to the function and impact of the Gospel's rhetoric today. He points out that the reading experience of the original reader was quite different from that of the contemporary reader, since the world of the text is quite different from our own. Insofar as modern readers distinguish between empirical and fictional narratives, between history and literature, they assume that they must read the Gospels as "literally true."

Culpepper thus shares the concern of modern "progressive" the*logy when he insists that the real question and issue for contemporary readers is whether John's story can be true if it is not history. In response he argues, if contemporary readers no longer will read the text as a window to the life of Jesus but with openness to the ways it calls "readers to interact with it, with life, and with their own world," they will again be able to read the Gospel as the original audience read it. The rhetorical effect of the Gospel is then profound: "The incentive the narrative offers for accepting its world as the true understanding of the "real" world is enormous. It places the reader's world under the providence of God, gives the reader an identity with a past and secure future, and promises the presence of God's Spirit with the believer, forgiveness for sin and an experience of salvation which includes assurance of life beyond the grave. The gospel offers contemporary readers a refuge from all the unreliable narrators of modern life and literature."[34]

Culpepper's summary appropriately underlines how the Fourth Gospel narrative engenders Christian identity formation today, but does not attend to the fact that such Christian identity is articulated in terms of androcentric dualism, christological exclusivism, and anti-Judaism.[35] Moreover, he does not raise the problem as to the political effects of the Gospel's narrative that according to him offers "a refuge from all unreliable narrators" of contemporary society and life.

Assuming that this characterization of "what the narrative offers" is adequate, the whole narrative of the Fourth Gospel and not only elements in it must be interrogated and assessed if we want to unravel its anti-Jewish

Christian identity formation rather than repress it as something long past. This identity-formation is shot through with racism. Although in classical and New Testament times "darkness" was generally not associated with race, and therefore the original readers would not have interpreted the dualistic matrix of the Gospel in racist terms, a long history of racist interpretation provides the contextualization for racist readings today. Such racist readings draw out the "antisemitic potential" inscribed in the Fourth Gospel.

In conclusion: I have argued that biblical scholarship has the responsibility not only to elaborate the historical-religious meanings of biblical texts but also to critically reflect on the Christian identity formations they produce. It has to do so because the biblical icon has shaped and still shapes not only Christian community but also Western culture. After the Holocaust biblical scholarship can no longer treat the anti-Jewish rhetoric of the Fourth Gospel as an issue of the past divorced from our present that the scholar can approach "without bias and with utmost neutrality." Instead it has to interrogate its own strategies and models of interpretation as to how much they contribute to the proliferation of anti-Jewish prejudice. Just as hegemonic biblical scholarship must abandon its apologetic the*logical gesture, so also must feminist and liberation the*logical biblical scholarship if it should not continue to collaborate in the "rhetorics and politics of otherness" that make Jewish women the doubly excluded and vilified "others of the others."

Sigmund Mowinckel's work shared the interests of the history-of-religions movement, which sought to break out of the confines of canon and ecclesiastical dogma, out of a systematizing the*logical restatement of biblical texts and the philological confines of source-critical operations (Literarkritik). Instead the history-of-religion approach sought to understand biblical texts as generated by a historical web of religious experiences. Searching for the Sitz im Leben of biblical texts, it sought to retrace the traditions and transformations in the life of biblical religion intertwined with its sociopolitical and cultural-religious contexts.

My own argument for a paradigm-shift in the self-understanding of biblical studies is structurally similar. Just as we have learned from the history-of-religions approach that biblical texts must be understood as embedded in the religious-cultural-political life-world of their authors and communities, so we must cultivate a theoretical self-reflexivity that can explore the experiences and interests that generate and determine biblical interpretation and its rhetorical-historical situation today. For as Eichhorn, the father of the history-of-religions school, recognized more than hundred years ago: "A historian is only the one who understands the present,"[36] and, I would add, therefore takes responsibility for the past and the future.

Notes

[1] This article is a revised and annotated version of the Sigmund Mowinckel lecture delivered at the faculty of the University of Oslo on November 11, 1988. I want to thank the Mowinckel lectureship committee and especially my colleagues Halvor Moxnes, Turid Karlsen Seim, and Inger Marie Lindboe for their efforts in preparing this event. Thanks are also due to Professor Lone Fatum who invited me to lecture at the University of Copenhagen.

[2] As quoted by Nils Dahl, "Sigmund Mowinckel Historian of Religion," *Scandinavian Journal of the Old Testament* 2 (1988): 17. Dahl derived this quote from an article entitled "The Spirit without Body," which appeared 1954 but is not listed in the extensive bibliography of Kvale and Rian, 95–168.

[3] For the interconnection of the exclusion of women from philosophy and the articulation of "objective" knowledge and "pure" reason, see R. May Schott, *Cognition and Eros: A Critique of the Kantian Paradigm* (Boston: Beacon, 1988).

[4] D. La Capra, *History and Criticism* (Ithaca: Cornell University Press, 1985), elaborates this self-understanding of historiography as "the documentary model of knowledge."

[5] K. Rudolph, *Historical Fundamentals and the Study of Religion* (New York: Macmillan, 1985), 38.

[6] For this characterization of the Enlightenment and its interventions see E. Farley, *The Fragility of Knowledge: Theological Education in the Church and the University* (Philadelphia: Fortress Press, 1988). See also the discussion of literature on the Enlightenment and biblical scholarship in E. Krentz, *The Historical-Critical Method* (Philadelphia: Fortress Press, 1975).

[7] For this emphasis in Mowinckel's work, see M. Ravndal Hauge, "Sigmund Mowinckel and the Psalms: A Query Into His Concerns," *Scandinavian Journal of the Old Testament* 2 (1988): 56–71.

[8] For the presence of these correctives in the discussion of the history-of-religions method, see K. Muller, "Die religionsgeschichtliche Methode: Erwagungen zu ihrem Verstandnis und zur Praxis ihrer Vollzüge an neutestamentlichen Texten," *Biblische Zeitschrift* 29 (1985): 161–92.

[9] For this expression, see the book of G. Lloyd, *The Man of Reason: Male and Female in Western Philosophy* (Minneapolis: University of Minnesota Press, 1984).

[10] See, for example, N. Hartsock, "Rethinking Modernism: Minority vs. Majority Theories," *Cultural Critique* 7 (1987): 187–206, and my contribution "Text and Reality: Reality as Text," in this volume.

[11] See especially J. Plaskow, "Blaming the Jews for the Birth of Patriarchy," *Cross Currents* 28 (1978), 306–9, and S. Heschel, "Jüdisch-feministische Theologie und Antijudaismus in christlich-feministischer Theologie," in L. Siegele-Wenschkewitz, ed., *Verdringte Vergangenheit, die uns bedriingt* (Munchen: Kaiser, 1988), 54–103.

[12] See C. O. Schrag, *Communicative Praxis and the Space of Subjectivity* (Bloomington: University of Indiana Press, 1986), 179–214.

[13] I have changed here Scheler's use of *Heilswissen* to *Befreiungswissen*.

[14] See my article "Rhetorical Situation and Historical Reconstruction in 1 Corinthians," *NTS* 33 (1987): 386–403, and Wilhelm Wuellner, "Where is Rhetorical Criticism Taking Us?" *CBQ* 49 (1987): 448–63, for further literature.

[15] For bringing together the insights of this paper I have found especially helpful the works of feminist literary and cultural criticism. See, for example, S. Benhabib and D. Cornell, eds., *Feminism as Critique* (Minneapolis: University of Minnesota Press, 1987); Gayatri Chakravorty Spivak, *In Other Worlds: Essays in Cultural Politics* (New York: Methuen, 1987); Teresa de Lauretis, ed., *Feminist Studies/Critical Studies* (Bloomington: University of Indiana Press, 1986); E. A. Flynn and P. Schweickart, eds., *Gender and Reading: Essays on Reader, Texts, and Contexts* (Baltimore: John Hopkins University Press, 1986); G. Greene and C. Kaplan, eds., *Making a Difference: Feminist Literary Criticism* (New York: Methuen, 1983); Elizabeth A. Meese, *Crossing the Double Cross: The Practice of Feminist Criticism* (Chapel Hill: University of North Carolina Press, 1986); J. Newton and D. Rosenfelt, eds., *Feminist Criticism and Social Change* (New York: Methuen, 1985); M. Pryse and Hortense J. Spillers, eds., *Conjuring Black Women: Fiction and Literary Tradition* (Bloomington:

University of Indiana Press, 1985); Chris Weedon, *Feminist Practice and Poststructuralist Theory* (London: Blackwell, 1987).

[16]Richard Harvey Brown, *Society as Text: Essays on Rhetoric, Reason and Reality* (Chicago: University of Chicago Press, 1987), 85. See also J. Nelson, A. Megills, D. McCloskey, eds., *The Rhetoric of the Human Sciences: Language and Argument in Scholarship and Public Affairs* (Madison: University of Wisconsin Press, 1987); Hayden White, *Tropics of Discourse: Essays in Cultural Criticism* (Baltimore: John Hopkins, 1978); Ricca Edmondsen, *Rhetoric in Sociology* (New York: Cambridge University Press, 1985); John S. Nelson, "Political Theory as Political Rhetoric," in *What Should Political Theory Be Now?* (Albany: SUNY Press, 1983), 169–240.

[17]Maurice Mandelbaum, *The Anatomy of Historical Knowledge* (Baltimore: John Hopkins University Press, 1977), 150.

[18]See the discussion of scientific theory-choice by Linda Alcoff, "Justifying Feminist Social Science," *Hypatia* 2 (1987), 107–27.

[19]D. La Capra, 36–44, elaborates eight ways of how rhetoric bears on historiography.

[20]Krister Stendahl, "The Bible as a Classic and the Bible as Holy Scripture," *JBL* 103 (1984): 10.

[21]See also my article "The Ethics of Biblical Interpretation: Decentering Biblical Scholarship," *JBL* 107 (1988), 3–17.

[22]See the review of the discussion by John G. Gager, *The Origins of Anti-Semitism* (New York: Oxford University Press, 1985).

[23]See, for example, Eldon J. Epp, "Anti-Semitism and the Popularity of the Fourth Gospel in Christianity," *Central Conference of American Rabbis Journal* 22 (1975), 35–57, who, however, does not seek to change the language of the Gospel but points to its time-bound expression. See, however, the much more extensive hermeneutical and practical suggestions of the Jewish scholar Michael J. Cook, "The Gospel of John and the Jews," *Review and Expositor* 84 (1987): 259–71, for dealing with the problem.

[24]See, for example, R. Leistner, *Antijudaismus im Johannesevangelium* (Bern: Lang, 1974); W. A. Meeks, "Am I A Jew? Johannine Christianity and Judaism," in *Christianity, Judaism, and Other Greco-Roman Cults*, vol. 1, edited by J. Neusner, 163–68 (Leiden: Brill, 1975); V. C. von Wahlde, "The Johannine 'Jews': A Critical Survey," *NTS* 28 (1982): 33–60; J. Ashton, "The Identity and Function of the *Ioudaioi* in the Fourth Gospel," *Novum Testamentum* 27 (1985): 40–75.

[25]See the reader-response analysis of chapter 4 by Gail R. O'Day, *Revelation in the Fourth Gospel* (Philadelphia: Fortress Press, 1986), 70, who does not, however, sufficiently interrogate the anti-Jewish articulation of revelation by the Fourth Gospel.

[26]See for instance Helmut Koester, "The History-of-Religions School, Gnosis, and the Gospel of John," *Studia Theologica* 40 (1986): 115–36.

[27]L. J. Martyn, *History and Theology in the Fourth Gospel*, 2nd rev. ed. (Nashville: Abingdon, 1979); R. E. Brown, *The Community of the Beloved Disciple* (New York: Paulist, 1979).

[28]D. Moody Smith, *John: Proclamation Commentaries* (Philadelphia: Fortress Press, 1976), 70; see also 45, 65, 94.

[29]See the balanced judgment of St. S. Katz, "Issues in the Separation of Judaism and Christianity after 70 C.E.: A Reconsideration," *JBL* 103 (1984): 45–76.

[30]For two distinct but different approaches, see W. A. Meeks, "Breaking Away: Three New Testament Pictures of Christianity's Separation from the Jewish Communities," *"To See Ourselves as Others See Us": Christians, Jews, 'Others' in Late Antiquity*, edited by Neusner/Frerichs (Atlanta: Scholars, 1985), 93–116, and S. Freyne, "Vilifying the Other and Defining the Self: Matthew's and John's Anti-Jewish Polemic in Focus," 117–44.

[31]D. Rensberger, *Johannine Faith and Liberating Community* (Philadelphia: Westminster, 1988), 26. Therefore, he understands the Johannine community as an oppressed community.

[32]See, for example, Luke 6:22/Matt. 5:11 (Q) and Mark 13:9; see Gal. 1:13.

[33]Rensberger does not claim to be a liberation theologian but only to provide "an offering from the realm of critical biblical scholarship of raw material only partially shaped" (ibid., 108).

[34]Ibid., 235.

35In a later article, R. Alan Culpepper, "The Gospel of John and the Jews," *Review and Expositor* 84 (1987), 273–87, addresses the hermeneutical problem raised by the vilification of 'the Jews' in the Fourth Gospel but weakens his proposals by stating: "No one's hands are clean. Dialogue between Jews and Christians requires that we each confess the guilt of our own contributions and those of our respective religious traditions to the sharpening of theological differences into the outrage of anti-Semitism in all its subtle and violent forms." [185]. He thereby draws out the the*logical implications of a scholarly interpretation that makes "the victims" accountable for their own vilification.

36These 13: "Historiker ist nur, wer die Gegenwart versteht." See H.-J. Kraus, *Geschichte der historisch-kritischen Erforschung des Alten Testaments* (Neukirchen: Erziehungsverein, 1956), 297.

12

The Politics of Otherness

Biblical Interpretation as a Critical Praxis for Liberation

Gustavo Gutiérrez has placed in the center of the*logical reflection the poor, the "others," the nonpersons who are absent from history. He has insisted over and against Euro-American "progressive" the*logy that the point of departure for Latin American liberation the*logy is not the question of the modern *nonbeliever* but the struggle of the *nonperson*[1] for justice and freedom. However, Latin American liberation the*logy has not sufficiently attended to the fact that the majority of the poor in the world are wo/men and children dependent on wo/men. This realization requires not just an incorporation of "wo/men's questions" into the framework of liberation the*logy[2] but calls for a different analysis and theoretical framework.

Since Simone de Beauvoir, feminist theory also has focused on the "other." Therefore feminist theory and the*logy for the most part has understood patriarchy as the domination of men over wo/men.[3] Yet, feminist theory in my view has not sufficiently attended to the fact that most wo/men in the world are not just the "others" of white Euro-American men but are the "others" of "the others." This insight asks for a transformation in the self-understanding of feminist analysis and struggle that must address not only sexism but also racism, classism, and colonialism as structures constituting wo/men's oppression.[4] I have therefore proposed that we understand patriarchy as a differentiated political system of graduated domination and subordination that found its classic Western legitimization in the philosophy of otherness and is best understood as kyriarchy—the domination of the emperor, lord, father, slavemaster, husband, and propertied elite man.

The Canadian writer Margaret Atwood has given us a political novel that displays the discursive practices constituting the politics of otherness. Atwood's narrative articulates the interstructuring of sexism, racism, class differences, and colonialism on the one hand and the availability of the Bible as language and legitimization for totalitarian ends on the other. *The Handmaid's Tale* decodes the history of a future totalitarian society whose structures and language are modeled after the Bible.

The speaking subject of the novel is a wo/man whose real name and identity is not known. She is a handmaid called Offred who lives in the Republic of Gilead. Gilead has replaced the United States of America and is ruled by a group espousing an ideology similar to that of the Moral Majority in the late twentieth century. After the president and congress of the United States have been massacred, the regime of this modern biblical republic is established. Wo/men lose their right to property and employment; the black population, the children of Ham, are resettled in segregated national homelands; and Jews are repatriated through the Jewish boat-plans. In this biblical republic, reading and writing are outlawed, the news media censured and controlled, and everyone is required to spy on everyone.

The stratifications of Gileadean society are marked by dress and color developed by the secret think tank of the Sons of Jacob. White wo/men, for example, are classified according to their functions: the wives of the Commanders of the Faithful are blue-clad and their daughters white-veiled. Those who do household work are called Marthas and have to wear a dull green. The wives of poor men, the Econowives, wear red-, blue-, or green-striped dresses, because they have to fulfill all functions divided among different wo/men in the elite households. Unwo/men are those wo/men who have been shipped to the Colonies, because they are childless, infertile, older wo/men, nuns, lesbians, or other insurrectionary elements.

Handmaids are chosen because of their reproductive capabilities. Their attire is a red dress paired with a white headdress. The Handmaid's role in the *Ceremony* and her whole rationale of being is patterned after that of Bilhah, the maid of Rachel in Genesis 30:1-3. Handmaids and Wives are under the control of Aunts, who as female overseers are to control wo/men in the most cost-effective way.

I have chosen Atwood's narrative to indicate the political context of American scholarly discourse on the Bible as well as of the discourses of liberation the*logies. For the*logical discourses that remain unconscious of their rhetorical functions and abstracted from their political contexts are in danger of "squandering the word." Atwood's futuristic projection of a totalitarian state re-creating classic-biblical patriarchy in modern technocratic terms underlines that liberation the*logies cannot afford to engage in a purely apologetic reading of the Bible or to relegate a critical biblical interpretation to "bourgeois" scholarship addressing the question of the nonbeliever. Rather, a biblical interpretation for liberation has to engage in a critical analysis that can lay open the "politics of otherness" inscribed in Christian scriptures. By making feminist theoretical discourse central to my hermeneutical explorations, I invite not only biblical scholarship but also malestream[5] liberation the*logies to attend to the conversation of the "others" on the patriarchal politics of "otherness."

Issues in Feminist Biblical Interpretation

Because the Bible is the foundational document for the Republic of Gilead, it is reserved for the elite and only to be read by men in power: "The Bible is kept locked up, the way people once kept tea locked up, so the servants wouldn't steal it. It is an incendiary device: who knows what we'd make of it, if we ever got our hands on it? We can be read to from it, by him, but we cannot read. Our heads turn toward him, we are expectant, here comes our bedtime story. . . . He has something we don't have, he has the word. How we squandered it, once."[6]

Atwood's narrator not only discloses the dehumanizing horrors of the totalitarian kyriarchal state but also alludes to the potentially "incendiary" character of the Bible if it were given into the hands of "the subordinate others," the nonpersons of Gilead. In the awareness that reading can be subversive, elite men have kept the key to biblical interpretation in their own hands. It is mostly elite men who still read their Revised Standard Versions to us in liturgical celebrations and academic lectures. In the past forty years wo/men have entered the*logical schools in significant numbers and have begun to produce biblical scholarship. Yet replacing men with wo/men and other nonpersons in pulpits, universities, the Supreme Court, or Buckingham Palace does not guarantee that the word read to us will no longer be a bedtime story legitimating situations of oppression.

Although still a marginalized minority in academy, church, and synagogue, contemporary feminist the*logical scholarship and studies in religion have begun to claim the the*logical word and religious symbol-systems of biblical religions in the interest of women. However, the more feminist articulations are in circulation, the more it becomes pressing to ask how we can prevent that our readings function like the Aunts of Atwood's Gileadean Republic who manipulate and adjust women's intellectual and spiritual needs in order to survive by serving the patriarchal system. For women's readings of androcentric texts and patriarchal traditions are always in danger of recuperating the "Commander's readings to us," of using the "biblical bedtime-story" for quieting women's and other nonpersons' anger and rebellion. Finally to own "the word" could mean in the end to own a word that legitimates the totalitarian regime of Gilead.

How, then, can a feminist biblical hermeneutics situate its readings of the Bible in such a way that they do not support the totalizing discourses of Gilead but empower women and other nonpersons in struggles for justice and freedom? In order to minimize the possibility of such a co-optation in the interests of Western patriarchy, I suggest that feminist biblical interpretation must reconceptualize its act of critical interpretation as a moment in the global praxis for liberation. In order to do so, we need to decenter the authority of the androcentric biblical text, to take control of our own readings, and to deconstruct the politics of otherness inscribed in the text before we can positively retrieve biblical language and visions of liberation.7

Insofar as feminist biblical interpretation has been motivated by an apologetic retrieval of biblical authority, it has focused on biblical texts about women, on male injunctions for woman, on the biblical teaching on womanhood, on the great women of the Bible, or on feminine biblical language and symbols. By using "woman" or "the feminine" as a hermeneutical key, such gynecentric biblical interpretations, however, are in danger of recuperating the totalizing discourse of Western gender dualism.

Moreover, in its academic forms feminist scholarship has not only adopted diverse historical, social, anthropological, psychological, or literary critical methods of interpretation, but also the academic posture of "detached" inquiry. For the sake of scientific objectivity, such biblical scholarship often masks its own location and forecloses the*logical or ethical evaluation. Speaking uncritically of "woman" or the "feminine," it cannot but reproduce the whitemale[8] androcentric discourse.

Finally, feminist biblical interpretation seems to remain caught up in the same "logic of identity." Feminist critics have elucidated the indebtedness of modern political theories to the classic kyriarchal discourses of Plato and Aristotle, and especially criticized the theories of Rousseau and Hegel, which understand the civic public expressing the "impartial and universal point of view of normative reason," on the one hand, in opposition to the private realm, which encompasses the family as the domain of wo/men, on the other. *Ratio* as the "logic of identity" "consists in an unrelenting urge to think things together, in a unity," to formulate "an essence that brings concrete particulars into unity."9

To achieve the*logical unity, feminist hermeneutics has attempted to reduce the historical particularity and pluriform character of biblical writings to a feminist "canon within the canon" or a liberating "organizing principle" as the normative center of Scripture. Feminist biblical and liberation the*logical scholarship has inherited this search for an interpretative key or authoritative "canon within the canon" from historical-the*logical exegesis that has recognized the contradictory multiform character of Scripture.

Although liberationist biblical discourses have rejected the value-neutral, objective, apolitical rhetoric of academic biblical scholarship, they have not avoided its "drive to unity and essence." Just as male liberation the*logians stress God's liberating act in history, single out the Exodus as "canon within the canon," and focus on a "new reading of the Bible," or stress the liberating "biblical recollection and regathering of God's salvific deeds," so also feminist liberation the*logians have sought to identify a liberating theme, tradition, text, or principle as the hermeneutical key to the Bible as an androcentric-patriarchal book in order to reclaim the authority of Scripture. In this search for a "canon within the canon" or the "unity" of Scripture, biblical the*logical interpretation engages in the universalist "logic of identity," which eliminates the irreducible particularity of historical texts and the the*logical differences among biblical writers and contemporary interpreters.

A debated question in feminist liberation hermeneutics remains: Must such a feminist critical hermeneutical key be derived from or at least be correlated with the Bible so that Scripture remains the normative foundation of feminist biblical faith and community? Or—as I have argued—should it be continually rearticulated and called into question in the contemporary liberation struggles?[10] The Bible is to be understood as formative root-model, I have argued, rather than to be obeyed as a normative archetype of Christian faith and community. Whereas a feminist apologetics locates authority formally if not always materially in the Bible, a critical feminist reading derives its the*logical authority from women's experience of G*d's liberating presence in today's struggles to end patriarchal relationships of domination. Such divine presence, for instance, is at work today in the emerging Christian recognition that the systemic oppressive patriarchal contextualizations of our readings— sexism, racism, economic exploitation, military colonialism, and many more— are structural sin.

My own work, therefore, has sought to shift the focus of a feminist liberation discourse on the Bible away from not only the discourse on "woman in the Bible" to the feminist reconstruction of Christian origins,[11] but also away from the drive to construct a unifying biblical canon and universalist principle to a discussion of the process of biblical interpretation and evaluation that could display and assess the oppressive as well as the liberating functions of particular biblical texts in actual situations of wo/men's lives and struggles. Concern with biblical positivity, normativity, and authority is in danger of too quickly foreclosing such a critical analysis and feminist evaluation of particular biblical texts and traditions. It neglects the Bible and its interpretation as a site of competing discursive practices.

A critical feminist the*logical hermeneutics of liberation thus needs to position itself at the intersection of three the*logical discursive practices— historical and literary biblical criticism, liberation the*logies, and feminist critical theory—practices that question the Western totalizing "logic of identity." However, this positioning can only be appreciated when the interrelation of all three critical discourses is seen not as correlative but as mutually corrective interacting in the matrix of a feminist commitment and struggle for overcoming the kyriarchal politics of otherness.

THE POLITICS OF OTHERNESS

The Euro-American "classic" form of the politics of otherness is rooted in the practices of the andro-social Greek *polis*, its politico-philosophical subtext is democracy, and its social formation is patriarchy, best called kyriarchy, the governing dominance of elite propertied male heads of households. Free-born propertied wo/men, poor wo/men, slave-wo/men, as well as barbarian wo/men, were excluded from the democratic government of the city-state. This exclusion required ideological justifications as to why only freeborn propertied Greek male heads of households could be full citizens if, as the Sophists maintained, all are equal by nature.

The articulation of human-animal/male-female dualism, of andro-kyriocentrism fostering the marginalization of Greek wo/men and the exclusion of barbarian wo/men, as well as the articulation of the "natural" inferiority of freeborn wo/men and of slavewo/men, of nonpersons, are ideological constructs of difference formulated by Plato and Aristotle. They continue to define relations of dominance and submission in Western culture and philosophical discourse today.[12] They were reproduced not only in early Christian writings and malestream the*logies but also in the modern democratic discourses of political philosophy, in the Enlightenment construction of the *Man of Reason*,[13] as well as in colonialist articulations of racism.[14] This political and philosophical rhetoric of otherness masks the oppressive relations of domination and exclusion in systemic patriarchy. However, it must be recognized that it does not simply elaborate the *generic person* but the Sovereign-Father, the kyrios, or in black idiom, the Boss-Man, as the universal subject. Its totalizing discourse of male/female dualism masks the complex interstructuring of kyriarchal domination in Western societies and religions.

Insofar as feminist theory has focused on "woman" as the "other" of man, it has tended to identify patriarchy with sexism or gender-dualism. It has not focused on the complex interstructuring of kyriarchal domination in wo/men's lives. Although one of the earliest manifestos of the wo/men's liberation movement in the United States categorically states that "no woman is free until and unless every woman is free," feminist analyses and strategies generally have not taken their political measure, standpoint, and strategy for change with the wo/men on the totem pole of kyriarchal oppressions, with the "others of the others." Instead Euro-American feminist discourses have tended to take their measure from an idealized version of the Man of Reason, the sovereign subject of history, culture, and religion. This oppositional discourse has been in danger of reproducing the cultural-symbolic construction of masculine-feminine polarity and heterosexual antagonism that is constitutive of the "politics of otherness."

Wo/men's studies in all academic disciplines have greatly enriched our knowledge *about women* but have not been able to undo the marginalizing dynamics of the andro-kyriocentric text and its institutions. In order to dislodge the andro-kyriocentrism of Western metaphysical discourse, feminist theories (or the*logies of femininity)—whether they have as godfathers Tillich,

Lacan, or Derrida—have valorized woman, body, sexuality, maternity, nature-as-feminine archetype, essence, or divinity. Yet in this attempt to construct an oppositional discourse on woman or on gender differences, feminist theory has kept in circulation the discourse of classic Western philosophy and the*logy on gender-dualism or gender-polarity that understands man as the subject of history, culture, and religion, and woman as the other.

This universalist Euro-American feminist discourse on "woman as the other of man" is more and more interrupted by the diverse resistant discourses of an emerging global feminist movement coming in to consciousness. In an anthology of the international wo/men's movement entitled *Sisterhood Is Global*, Robin Morgan has compiled statistics and collected reports on the worldwide struggle of wo/men for liberation.[15] The global character of this movement is displayed in its very particular and concrete political situations that are not to be universalized, because the configurations of kyriarchy are different in different historico-cultural formations.

The voices of this movement insist that feminism requires a political commitment not only to the struggle against sexism but also to the struggles against racism, classism, colonialism, and militarism as structures of wo/men's exploitation and oppression. Feminism's self-understanding and analysis must therefore shift from a preoccupation with gender-dualism in order to attend to the interstructuring of sex, race, class, culture, and religion in systems of domination.[16] This insistence of black, Hispanic, Jewish, Asian, African, or Palestinian women asks for a new analysis of the kyriarchal "politics of otherness." For only when patriarchy is understood not as a universal transcultural binary structure but as a historical political system of dominations can it be changed.

The rhetoric of the feminist movement that is emerging around the globe, therefore, is directed not only against male supremacy but also against the totalizing discourse of Western universalist feminism. Insofar as this rhetoric elaborates racial, political, cultural, national, ideological, sexual, religious, age, class, and other systemic differences and discriminations among wo/men, it challenges the essentialist definition of *woman* and female culture as "the other" of man and male culture. However, because of its commitment to the political liberation struggle, its insistence on the perspectival character and historical particularity of knowledge does not degenerate into an endless play of deconstruction and negative reaction nor lead to a determinism and nihilism that denies wo/men's subjectivity and historical agency.

Unraveling the unitary otherness of *woman* from *man* in Western philosophic-political discourse, the emerging discourses of global feminism insist on the specific historical cultural context and subjectivity as well as the plurality of wo/men. By deconstructing the ideological construct *woman*, such global feminist discourses also elucidate how the identity of women of subordinated races, classes, cultures, or religions is constructed as "other" of the "other," as negative foil for the feminine identity of the White Lady. For instance, with her analysis of lynching, Ida B. Wells has elucidated the patriarchal manipulation of race and gender in the interest of terrorism, economic oppression, and sexual exploitation.[17] The variety of feminist discourses emerging around the globe thus enjoins middle-class feminists in the First World not to reduplicate the whitemale universalistic discourse of gender dualism and at the same time cautions third world middle-class feminists not to reproduce the colonial discourse on woman and femininity.

The differences and often-irreconcilable contradictions among wo/men and within wo/men are always concretely embedded in power relationships. To collapse them into a unitary identity, homogeneous image, or totalizing discourse of universalist feminism—be it Euro-American or Afro-American, lesbian or straight, activist or academic, or any other feminism—would mean to reproduce the androcentric discourses of universalist abstract humanism on *woman* or to reinscribe differences and contradictions among women as kyriarchal divisions and oppositions.[18]

However, if—just as race, nationality, or social status—gender is a social-cultural-historical construct and not a feminine substance or universal female essence, then the question arises: How can wo/men transcend our being socially constructed as *women* and at the same time become historical subjects as *women* against kyriarchal domination? If subjectivity is seen as totally determined by gender, one ends up with feminine essentialism; if it is understood as genderless, then one reverts to the generic human subject of liberalism for whom gender, class, or race are irrelevant.

This theoretical either-or posed by cultural and poststructuralist feminism[19] can be negotiated—I would suggest—if we attend to the kyriarchal politics of otherness in Western culture. The totalizing ideologies of sexism, racism, classism, or colonialism that make kyriarchal oppression and exploitation of "the others" of elite white men appear to be "natural" and "common sense," produce at the same time contradictions and fissures in the social psychological identity construction of the nonperson. Far from being irrelevant to human subjectivity, the experience and articulation of gender, race, class, cultural, or religious alienation and exploitation motivate the nonperson to struggle for human rights, dignity, freedom, and equality:

"What is emerging in feminist writings is, instead [of the posthumanist Lacanian white male subject], the concept of a multiple, shifting, and often self contradictory identity, a subject that is not divided in, but rather at odds with, language; an identity made up of heterogeneous and heteronomous representations of gender, race, and class, and often indeed across languages and cultures. An identity that one decides to reclaim from a history of multiple assimilations, and that one insists on as a strategy: 'I think,' writes

Bulkin, 'of all the women [of mixed heritage] who were told to choose between or among identities, insist on selecting all.'"[20]

In short, in order to sustain a global feminist movement for ending kyriarchal oppressions, all feminist discourses need to engage at one and at the same time in a continuing critical deconstruction of the politics of otherness, in reclaiming and reconstructing our particular experiences, histories, and identities, as well as in sustaining a permanent reflection on our common differences. The subordinated others need to reject the rhetoric of selflessness and articulate the "option for the oppressed" as an *option for ourselves.* Self-identity *as wo/men* cannot be assumed but must be chosen in the commitment to the struggle for ending patriarchal structures of oppression. Moreover, the "politics of otherness" can be displaced only when identity is no longer articulated as unitary universal identity and established either by exclusion and domination of the others or by the others' self-negation and subordination.

The hermeneutical insights and the*logical challenges of the heterogeneous voices emerging from the global movements of liberation must, therefore, become central to a differentiated the*logical discourse on biblical interpretation and evaluation. A historical and global contextualization of biblical interpretation has to deconstruct the totalizing biblical rhetoric of Gilead and to generate new possibilities for the communicative construction of self and world. Christian identity grounded by the reading of the Bible must in ever-new readings be deconstructed and reconstructed in terms of a global praxis for liberation. Insofar as the Bible still is used in Western public discourse for reinforcing a Euro-American identity formation based on the exclusion and subordination or vilification of "the others," it becomes important to deconstruct the "politics of otherness" inscribed in its pages.

THE POLITICS OF OTHERNESS INSCRIBED IN THE FOURTH GOSPEL

If feminist biblical interpretation should not continue to reproduce the kyriarchal politics of otherness, it has to reconceive its task as critical consciousness-raising or conscientization that can explore the functions and kyriarchal contextualizations of biblical discourses, and replace them with a diversified public biblical rhetoric[21] and feminist frameworks of reference.

In the following cursory discussion of the Fourth Gospel[22] I will indicate the complex process of such a critical feminist reading understood as a strategy and process of conscientization. Such a focus on the contemporary reading process does not replace historical text-oriented readings but presupposes an evaluative analysis of their textual interpretations and of their reconstructions of particular historical contexts. My focus on certain Johannine problems and my the*logical emphases indicate my subject position as a white German Christian feminist biblical scholar and the*logian living in the United States. Such a particular reading invites other readings that begin from a different subject position in the liberation struggle.

Whereas historical critical exegesis attends to the text in its historical contexts, but not to its ideological formation and textual "politics of otherness," rhetorical analyses and reader response criticism seek to make conscious how the text "works" in the complex process of reading as a cultural or the*logical praxis. By elucidating how gender determines the reading process, feminist reader-response criticism underlines the importance of the reader's particular sociocultural location.

Every reader brings cultural (grammatical principles, social customs, cultural attitudes, historical experiences) and personal contexts (personal experience, social location, education, beliefs, and commitments) to the act of reading. "Contextualization" is often assumed but not articulated; it is often masked in order to produce an "unbiased" objective reading. Such contextual knowledge operates as "a kind of grid that obscures certain meanings and brings others to the foreground."[23] However, whereas feminist biblical scholarship has become skilled in detecting the androcentric contextualizations in malestream biblical interpretation, it has not paid sufficient attention to its own inoculation with gender stereotypes, racism, sexism, or the*logical confessionalism.

In recent years, New Testament scholarship has elaborated the social world and symbolic universe of the Fourth Gospel. It has highlighted the leadership role of wo/men in the Johannine community, its sectarianism and anti-Jewish polemics, as well as its dualistic worldview and religious exclusivism. In all three instances of inscribed Otherness, a certain tension or contradiction in the text has been elaborated.

First, the Fourth Gospel presents the Christian community as a circle of friends, an egalitarian community of the children of G*d, which does not exclude the leadership of wo/men, but appeals to the apostolic wo/men disciples of Jesus for its legitimization of this practice. Nevertheless, its symbolic language and universe is not only androcentric but kyriarchal because it stresses that the Father is revealed only through the Son and at the same time co-opts the language of sophia-the*logy and masculinizes it.

Second, although the language of the Fourth Gospel is very "Jewish," the term "the Jews" is predominantly a negative term. It does not include Jesus and his followers as Jews but distances them from "*the Jews*." The expression can also be used in a neutral sense, in order to mark that not all Jews have rejected Jesus but many have believed, or even as a positive the*logical affirmation in the dialogue with the Samaritan wo/man: "Salvation comes from the Jews" (4:22). However, anti-Jewish language is predominant in the Gospel. It bespeaks not just fear of expulsion but aggressive sectarian an affirmation.

Third, this anti-Jewish polemic is generated by a cosmological dualism of light and darkness, spirit and flesh, life and death, above and below, "the world" and the believer, G*d and Satan. One could say that the whole narrative of the Gospel is woven within a framework of dualism. However, the cosmological dualism of the Fourth Gospel is not absolute: G*d has sent the Son not for the condemnation but for the salvation of the "world."

This dualistic framework engenders not only anti-Judaism but also christological absolutism that breeds religious exclusivism, although the Gospel's intent is universal—namely, to present Jesus in an idiom that reflects the profound interests of the Greco-Roman world in religious syncretism and with religious symbols that have the widest appeal. In light of the Gospel's dualistic framework and its religious exclusivism, it is remarkable that its dualism does not include the pair male and female. Nevertheless, the Gospel exhibits a kyriarchal identity formation characterized by the politics of otherness.

In the last twenty years historical critical scholarship has moved away from a Gnostic or anti-Gnostic interpretation of the Fourth Gospel's *Sitz im Leben* toward an understanding of its anti-Jewish polemic as an expression of the socioreligious alienation of the Johannine community because of synagogue expulsion.[24] Although Jewish scholars have disputed that such an official synagogue ban had existed at the time of the Gospel's redaction, Christian scholars maintain that explicit references to the expulsion from the synagogue of those who believe in Christ testify to the strained relationship between the Jewish leadership and the emergent Jewish-Christian movement. However, scholars do not reflect critically that such a reconstruction of the historical subtext of the Gospel reinforces anti-Jewish Christian identity formation today.

Like historical-critical exegesis, so also have liberation the*logical interpretations have explained away the Johannine "politics of Otherness," if they have addressed it as a the*logical problem at all. Jose Miranda, for instance, seeks to "undo" the traditional spiritualistic interpretation of the Gospel by stressing that belief in Jesus Christ (John 20:31) means that the kingdom has arrived in Jesus of Nazareth, the messianic kingdom that "consists in justice being done to all the poor of the earth."[25] Luise Schottroff in turn rejects the term "anti-Judaism" for the interpretation of the Fourth Gospel by pointing to the oppression under which both Jews and the emerging Christian community lived. "To accuse the Jewish leadership as it is portrayed in John's Gospel of opportunism vis-a-vis the Romans, or to accuse the Christians . . . of anti-Judaism, is to apply labels which are inappropriate to the historical situation."[26]

Stress on the prophetic principle or the prophetic activity of Jesus also makes it possible to explain the anti-Jewish statements of the Gospel historically as a remembrance of Jesus' "prophetic renunciation of a corrupt religious establishment" or as prophetic call to conversion and renewal. A feminist apologetic reading in turn has proposed to dissolve the tensions in the text by claiming that the Gospel contains its own critical principle, when it says that salvation comes from the Jews, that believers are children [not sons] of God, and that "God loves the world." Such liberation the*logical attempts of characterizing the Johannine text positively as a liberating text, however, are not able to unravel and critically reject the patriarchal Christian identity formation inscribed in it.

Literary critical studies on the other hand have shown that the Gospel narrative integrates these apparent tensions and contradictions of the Gospel into a realistic unitary story. Since the masculine figure of the Son as the revealer from above is the narrative axis of the Gospel, the stories about wo/men, for example, function to harness the affection of the historical wo/men readers for the masculine revealer of the Father. Further, the "Jewish" language of the Gospel in its positive or neutral use serves to reinforce the conflict of the revealer Son with "the Jews" whose Father is the devil, a conflict that climaxes in the passion narrative. Finally, the Gospel's relative cosmological dualism aims at a radical the*logical-ethical dualism. Those who do not believe—the world, the Jews, and their leaders—will continue in darkness (15:18-16:4).

According to Culpepper, the Gospel's characterization, plot, comments, misunderstanding, irony, and symbolism "all work together in leading the reader to accept the evangelist's understanding of Jesus as the divine re-vealer."[27] As a reader-response critic, Culpepper does not shirk the question as to the function and impact of the Gospel's rhetoric today when he points out that the reading experience of the original reader was quite different from that of the contemporary reader, for the world of the text is quite different from our own. Insofar as modern readers distinguish between empirical and fictional narratives, between history and literature, they assume that they must read the Gospels as "literally true."

Culpepper thus shares the concern of modern "progressive" the*logy when he insists that the real question and issue for contemporary readers is whether John's story can be true if it is not history. In response he suggests that if contemporary readers no longer would read the text as a window to the life of Jesus but with openness to the ways it calls "readers to interact with it, with life, and with their own world," they will be able to read the Gospel as the original audience read it. The rhetorical impact of the Gospel is then profound: "The incentive the narrative offers for accepting its world as the true understanding of the 'real' world is enormous. It places the reader's world under the providence of God, gives the reader an identity with a past and secure future, and promises the presence of God's Spirit with the believer, forgiveness for sin, and an experience of salvation which includes assurance of life beyond the grave. The gospel offers contemporary readers a refuge from all unreliable narrators of modern life and literature."[28]

Culpepper's summary appropriately underlines that the Fourth Gospel narrative engenders Christian identity formation today, but he does not attend to the fact that such Christian identity is articulated in terms of androcentric dualism, religious exclusivism, and anti-Judaism. Moreover, he does not problematize the political effects of the Gospel's narrative, which, according to him, offers "a refuge from all unreliable narrators" of contemporary society and life. Assuming that this characterization of "what the narrative offers" is adequate, the whole narrative of the Fourth Gospel—and not only elements in it—must be problematized and assessed if we want to unravel its anti-Jewish Christian identity formation, which is shot through with racism. Although in classical and New Testament times "darkness" was not associated with race, and therefore the original readers would not have interpreted the dualistic matrix of the Gospel in racist terms, a long history of racist interpretation provides the contextualization for racist readings today.

Whereas historical and literary criticism focus attention on the text and its historical context but do not explore and critically assess the textual inscription of the kyriarchal "politics of otherness," a critical feminist hermeneutic for liberation seeks to make conscious the complex process of reading as a cultural and the*logical praxis. Feminist reader-response criticism has shown that reading and thinking in an andro-kyriocentric symbol system produces reader *emasculation*. It requires identification with men and therefore intensifies wo/men's feminine socialization and internalization of cultural values that are self-alienating and often misogynist.

The andro-kyriocentric text of the Fourth Gospel derives its seductive "power" that plays on wo/men's authentic desires and liberative aspirations in order to harness them for the process of *emasculation*. The Gospel's christological focus and attention to "the love of the Father for the Son" reinforces the*logically the linguistic and cultural process of *emasculation* and establishes Christian identity as male identity in a cultural masculine-feminine contextualization. Focusing on the figure of Jesus, the Son of the Father, when reading the Fourth Gospel, "doubles" wo/men's self-alienation. Not only is our experience not articulated, but we also suffer "the powerlessness which results from the endless division of self against self, the consequence of the invocation to identify as male while being reminded that to be male—to be universal—is to be *not female*."[29] Conversely, the andro-kyriocentric scriptural text communicates that to be female is to be *not* divine.

However, such a conceptualization of the first moment of reading in feminist reader response criticism is in danger of recuperating the totalizing discourse of gender dualism when it insists that one read "as a man" or "as a woman." Reading *as a woman* does not necessarily mean to activate solely the ideological context of gender and femininity. Wo/men readers can read from a lesbian, black, Asian, or any number of "contexts." The identity of the reader is not a fixed gender position maintained by the exclusion of other contexts.

The reading subject is not unitary but as the agent of her reading can activate different subject locations and positions. In the process of reading, identity is always assumed and then discarded, decentered and reassumed.

This means that we have to learn in a series of readings from different contextualizations to unravel the full dynamics of the Christian identity formation produced by the Johannine text and elaborated in its subsequent interpretations. A feminist biblical interpretation for liberation that under-stands its task as ongoing conscientization engages in an ongoing process of reading that deconstructs the politics of otherness inscribed in the biblical text without getting lost in the endless play of textual deconstruction and undecidability. Different starting points in the reading process will result in competing readings of the Gospel. Nevertheless, all such feminist readings must be assessed in terms of the liberation of the wo/men on the bottom of the kyriarchal pyramid of domination.

A feminist analysis of the politics of otherness and commitment to the liberation struggle of all nonpersons also will avoid the liberal pitfall that declares race, gender, class, or cultural differences insignificant for the reading process, because in essence we are all human and the same. Empirical studies have documented that so-called generic masculine language ["man"; pronoun "he") is read differently by men and by wo/men. This is possible because of the ambiguity of generic masculine language. In the absence of any clear contextual markers, a statement such as "all men are created equal" can be understood as generic-inclusive or as masculine exclusive.

Insofar as a feminist analysis elucidates the function of andro-kyriocentric language in different contexts, it challenges the presumption that such lan-guage functions as "generic" language in kyriarchal contexts. Inasmuch as wo/men's reading tends to deactivate masculine/feminine gender contextu-alization in favor of an abstract degenderized reading, such an analysis makes a conscious discrimination between kyriarchal and generic-inclusive language contexts possible. Moreover, reading experiments have provided evidence that men report a higher incidence of male imagery when completing neutral sentences with generic pronouns. Wo/men, in turn, "associate virtually no images with generic masculine pronouns in such cases probably because we are required to suppress the literal meaning in order to be able to understand ourselves as included in the values of freedom, self-determination, and human rights."[30]

Therefore, Christian wo/men have read and still read biblical texts without attending to the fact of Jesus' maleness or the masculine images of Father-Son. As Virginia Fabella insists: "In the Asian Women's Consultation in Manila, the fact that Jesus was male was not an issue, for he was never seen as having used his maleness to oppress or dominate wo/men."[31]

Catherine Belsey elaborates this contradictory ideological position of wo/men reading unmarked generic male texts: "We (wo/men readers) participate both in the liberal-humanist discourse of freedom, self-determination, and rationality, and at the same time in the specifically feminine discourse offered by society of submission, relative inadequacy, and irrational intuition."[32] However, I submit, only if this ideological position becomes conscious in a process of feminist conscientization are wo/men readers able to become readers resisting the *emasculation* of the androcentric, racist, classist, or colonialist text. If this contradiction is not brought into consciousness, it cannot be exploited for change but leads to further self-alienation.

For change to take place, wo/men and other nonpersons must concretely and explicitly reject an abstract reading. For instance, in reading the Fourth Gospel we should not too quickly resort to abstract G*d language such as G*d is love or G*d is light, without deconstructing the structural dynamics of the Gospel's Father-Son language and replacing it with images of G*d gleaned from the concrete contextualizations of wo/men's life. Or if as liberation the*logians we insist that G*d is on the side of the poor, we need to spell out the*logically what it actually means that G*d is on the side of poor wo/men and children dependent on wo/men.

Hence, we can appropriate as our very own only those "human" values and "Christian" utopias that can be reasoned out in a feminist process of conscientization as liberating not only for Euro-American white elite wo/men but also for those wo/men who suffer from multiple oppressions. Only after having deconstructed the politics of otherness, which constitutes the dualistic frame and the*logical identity formation of the Fourth Gospel, will we be able to reclaim its vision of life and love in the context of the global movements for liberation. Christian identity that is grounded by the reading of the Fourth Gospel's inscribed kyriarchal politics of otherness must in ever-new readings be deconstructed and reconstructed in terms of a global praxis for the liberation not only of wo/men but of all other nonpersons.

NOTES

[1] For this expression, see for instance Gustavo Gutiérrez, *The Power of the Poor in History* (Maryknoll: Orbis, 1983), 93. See also C. Cadorette, *From the Heart of the People: The Theology of Gustavo Gutierrez* (Oak Park: Meyer-Stone, 1988).

[2] See the interviews of leading male Latin American liberation theologians by Elsa Tamez, *Against Machismo* (Oak Park: Meyer-Stone, 1987). See also Schüssler Fiorenza and Carr, eds., *Women, Work, and Poverty* (Edinburgh: Clark, 1987).

[3] See the overview and discussion by Sylvia Walby, *Patriarchy at Work: Patriarchal and Capitalist Relations in Employment* (Minneapolis: University of Minnesota Press, 1986), and the definition of the term by G. Lerner, *The Creation of Patriarchy* (New York: Oxford University Press, 1986).

[4] See especially bell hooks, *Feminist Theory: From Margin to Center* (Boston: South End, 1984).

[5] I owe this expression to the feminist sociologist Dorothy Smith.

[6] Margaret Atwood, *The Handmaid's Tale* (New York: Ballantine, 1987), 112–13.

[7]For the fuller development of a model for a critical feminist interpretation for liberation, see my book *Bread Not Stone: The Challenge of Feminist Biblical Interpretation* (Boston: Beacon, 1984).

[8]For this expression, see Katie G. Cannon, *Black Womanist Ethics*, AAR Academy Series 60 (Atlanta: Scholars, 1988).

[9]I. Young, "Impartiality and the Civic Public: Some Implications of Feminist Critiques of Moral and Political Theory," in Benhabib and Cornell, eds., *Feminism as Critique* (Minneapolis: University of Minnesota Press, 1987), 61.

[10]For this discussion, see the essays in L. Russell, ed., *Feminist Interpretation of the Bible* (Philadelphia: Westminster, 1985).

[11]See especially the methodological chapters in *In Memory of Her: A Feminist Theological Reconstruction of Early Christian Origins* (New York: Crossroad, 1983).

[12]See also Page duBois, *Centaurs and Amazons: Women and the Pre-History of the Great Chain of Being* (Ann Arbor: University of Michigan Press, 1979).

[13]See G. Lloyd, *The Man of Reason: "Male" and "Female" in Western Philosophy* (Minneapolis: University of Minnesota Press, 1984).

[14]See, for example, the essays in Jan Mohamed and Lloyd, eds., *The Nature and Context of Minority Discourse*, which have appeared as special issues of *Cultural Critique* 6 (1987) and 7 (1987).

[15]R. Morgan, *Sisterhood Is Global: The International Women's Movement Anthology* (Garden City: Anchor, 1984). See also V. Fabella and M. Arnba Oduyoye, eds., *With Passion and Compassion: Third World Women Doing Theology* (Maryknoll: Orbis, 1988).

[16]See, for example, the dialogue between G. J. Joseph and J. Lewis, *Common Differences: Conflicts in Black and White Feminist Perspectives* (Boston: South End, 1981).

[17]This is pointed out by H. V. Carby, "'On the Threshold of Woman's Era': Lynching, Empire and Sexuality," in H. L. Gates Jr., ed., *"Race," Writing, and Difference* (Chicago: University of Chicago Press, 1986), 301–28.

[18]See E. W. Said, "An Ideology of Difference," in Gates, *"Race," Writing, and Difference*, 38–58.

[19]See also N. Hartsock, "Rethinking Modernism: Minority vs. Majority Theories," *Cultural Critique* 7 (1987), 187–206; L. Alcoff, "Cultural Feminism versus Post-Structuralism: The Identity Crisis in Feminist Theory," *Signs* 13 (1988): 405–36.

[20]T. de Lauretis, ed., *Feminist Studies/Critical Studies* (Bloomington: University of Indiana Press, 1986), 9.

[21]See my "The Ethics of Biblical Interpretation: Decentering Biblical Scholarship," *JBL* 107 (1988) 3–17.

[22]For an overview, see R. Kysar, "The Gospel of John in Recent Research," *RSR* 9 (1983): 314–23. See also D. Moody Smith, *John*, 2nd ed. (Philadelphia: Fortress Press, 1986) and the commentary by R. Schnackenburg, *The Gospel according to John*, 3 vols. (New York: Crossroad, 1968–82).

[23]S. S. Lanser, "(Feminist) Criticism in the Garden: Inferring Genesis 2-3," *Semeia* 41 (1988), 77.

[24]See the very influential work of L. J. Martyn, *History and Theology in the Fourth Gospel*, 2nd ed. (Nashville: Abingdon, 1979).

[25]Jose Miranda, *Being and the Messiah: The Message of St. John* (Maryknoll: Orbis, 1977), 88.

[26]L. Schottroff, "Antijudaism in the New Testament," in Elisabeth Schüssler Fiorenza and David Tracy, eds., *The Holocaust as Interruption*, Concilium 175 (Edinburgh: Clark, 1984), 59.

[27]R. A. Culpepper, *Anatomy of the Fourth Gospel: A Study in Literary Design* (Philadelphia: Fortress Press, 1983), 226.

[28]Ibid., 235.

[29]Schweikart, "Reading Ourselves: Toward a Feminist Theory of Reading," in Flynn and Schweikart, eds., *Gender and Reading: Essays on Readers, Texts, and Contexts* (Baltimore: Johns Hopkins University Press, 1986), 42.

[30]M. Crawford and R. Chaffin, "The Reader's Construction of Meaning: Cognitive Research on Gender and Comprehension," in *Gender and Reading*, 14–16.

[31]Virginia Fabella, "A Common Methodology for Diverse Christologies," in *With Passion and Compassion*, 116.

32 C. Belsey, "Constructing the Subject: Deconstructing the Text," in *Feminist Criticism and Social Change: Sex, Class, and Race in Literature and Culture*, edited by Newton and Rosenfelt (New York: Methuen, 1985), 50.

13

"Waiting at Table"

A Critical Feminist The*logical Reflection on Diakonia

The Greek term *diakonia* means literally "waiting at tables" but is usually translated as "service" or "ministry."[1] We can distinguish two different meanings in the New Testament usage of the word-cluster *diakonia/diakonos/diakonein* that have become paradigmatic for later the*logy. In a religious-spiritualized sense the word-cluster signifies an honorary activity, a person standing in the service of G*d/s, in the service of a city or commonwealth, or in the service of great ideas or ideals. When used in the New Testament in this sense the word-cluster characterizes Christian preachers and missionaries like Paul or Phoebe as representatives and messengers of G*d.

However, in its original sense the term means actual material service, waiting at table and other menial tasks. As today so also in antiquity the "servant" had a low social position, was dependent on her or his master/mistress, and could not command respect. However, despite the debasing negative social connotations of its social and ancient meaning, "service" has become the key-symbol for the revival of a "servant ecclesiology" with progressive intentions. Feminist the*logical attempts to salvage this biblical symbol in the face of the stringent feminist critique of its cultural-political function in the oppression of women share the assumption of such a "servant ecclesiology," that self-sacrificing "service" is central to Christian identity and community.

SERVANT ECCLESIOLOGY AND WO/MEN'S MINISTRY

Since the early 1960s the image of the servant-church has come to dominate progressive Roman Catholic and Protestant ecclesiologies and ministerial self-understandings. This revival of a the*logy of *diakonia* went hand in hand with a change in the church's attitude to the "world." For instance, the Pastoral Constitution on the Church in the Modem World of Vatican II teaches in Article 3 that just as Jesus Christ became human not to be served but to serve so also the church seeks to serve, the world by fostering the "brotherhood of all men."

In his book *Models of the Church*, Avery Dulles points out that a similar servant ecclesiology motivates official statements of other churches: "Remarkable in this respect are the Presbyterian Confession of 1967, the Uppsala Report of the World Council of Churches in 1968, the Conclusion of the Second General Conference of Latin American Bishops at Medellin in 1968, and the document on Justice in the World issued by the Roman Catholic Synod of Bishops at its fall meeting in 1971."[2]

Such a servant ecclesiology insists with Bonhoeffer "that the church is the church only when it exists for others."[3] Insofar as this the*logy does not critically analyze the social underpinnings of servant-language, it is not able to recognize it as ideology or "the*logical double-speak" since the the*logy of service has different implications for men and women, ordained and non-ordained, powerful and powerless.

This servant ecclesiology legitimates a diversification of "ministry" in the Roman Catholic context. Its the*logians argue that ministries are functional, that they are a specific gift and service to the community. They exist for the building up of the community and do not consist in special status, lifestyle, or sacred office. Since the servant church as the ministerial community is prior to its ministers,[4] the church can officially sanction new ministries that complement the traditional hierarchical ministries of bishop, priest, and deacon.[5] Thus this the*logy does not seriously challenge the church's structures of patriarchal-kyriarchal hierarchy and the ontological "class" division between ordained and non-ordained ministries but exhorts those who have kyriarchal clerical status and ecclesiastical powers to serve the laity and those in need.

In Roman Catholicism this ecclesiology was developed in response to the shortage of priests in many parts of the world. It has engendered an explosion of specialized ministries that seek to serve not only the needs of the church but also those of the world. It has allowed wo/men to exercise ministerial functions, even though the official stance against the inclusion of wo/men in the ordained ministry has increasingly hardened. In short, the "progressive" the*logy of ministry as service as well as of the church as the servant of the world has supported not only a variety of ministries but also the participation of wo/men in the ministry of the church.[6]

However, because of their gender wo/men are relegated by church law to subservient tasks, auxiliary roles, and secondary status in ministry, since according to Canon Law only those in orders can receive jurisdiction (the power of decision-making) and are entitled to officially exercise sacramental powers. While the Vatican has acknowledged that the majority of people in evangelization are wo/men,[7] an American study on wo/men in ministry has documented that most wo/men in ministry do unpaid volunteer work—or are minimally paid if they are remunerated at all. Wo/men engaged in such volunteer ministry are mostly middle-aged, middle-class, married wo/men whose children have left the home, who have no professional career, and whose husbands are able to support them. At the price of their continuing economic dependence they can "afford" ministry, whereas poor wo/men are not able to do so. The "double-speak of ministry" is illustrated by this study, insofar as men exercise ministry by virtue of ordination—that is, incorporation into the sacred kyriarchal pyramid—whereas wo/men render ministry only when they do not receive financial, social, or professional remuneration.[8]

At the same time this servant ecclesiology has motivated wo/men to acquiesce to their "second class" ministerial status and prevented us from insisting on our rights as church-workers. Several years ago I met with a group of pastoral assistants in Germany who complained that as wo/men they are not allowed to preach, whereas permanent male deacons were able to do so despite having had much less the*logical education and pastoral experience. When it was suggested that all the pastoral assistants in the city should "go on strike" in protest against such blatant discrimination, the wo/men were horrified because—as one of them put it—they had dedicated their life to the "service" of the church.

Such subservient and secondary ministerial status of wo/men is also found in other Christian churches that ordain wo/men.[9] Governing boards and decision-making positions are often restricted to male clergy. Wo/men clergy are frequently relegated to small rural parishes, are paid less than men with comparable qualifications, and remain at the level of assistant ministers. At the same time clergywo/men are, as ordained professionals, better off than other female church workers and volunteer-staff. In the churches as in society at large the majority of social-charitable volunteer workers are wo/men.[10] The servanthood of the church thus seems to be represented by wo/men.

In a ministerial situation of institutional inequality, the the*logy of ministry as service and its underlying servant ecclesiology serve to internalize and legitimate the kyriarchal-hierarchical status quo in the*logical-spiritual terms. Despite its progressive intentions, a servant-ecclesiology reproduces the asymmetric dualism between church and world, clergy and laity, religious and secular, men and wo/men that is generated by patriarchal-hierarchical church structures.

Insofar as ecclesial relationships are structured and conceptualized in such a way that the church, clergy, religious, and men remain still the defining subjects, a servant ecclesiology rhetorically claims service and servanthood for those who have patriarchal-hierarchical status and exercise spiritual power and control. For instance, the "Pope (Holy Father)" has supreme authority and power in the Roman Catholic church but is at the same time called *servus servorum dei*, the "servant of G*d's servants." As long as actual power relationships and status privileges are not changed, such a servant rhetoric must remain a mere moralistic sentiment and appeal that mystifies structures of domination.

CULTURAL CONTEXT AND FUNCTION

Such a the*logy of servanthood becomes even more questionable when its cultural-social contexts come into view. In Western cultures wo/men are socialized to selfless love in order to perform unpaid services in the family as well as volunteer services in the public domain. The myth of "true wo/manhood," romantic love, and domesticity defines wo/men's nature as "being for others," and wo/men's identity as derived from husband and children. Wo/men are expected to give up their names, their careers, and their possessions for the well-being of their families and for the sake of "personal relationships." Especially mothers are to sacrifice their life in the service of their children and all those in need.

Whereas men are socialized into masculine roles of self-assertion, independence, and control, wo/men are socialized to self-denial, self-abnegation, and self-sacrifice in the service of others. Our sin is the failure to become a self.[11] This cultural socialization of wo/men to selfless femininity and altruistic behavior is reinforced and perpetuated by the Christian preaching of self-sacrificing love and self-denying service. Since Jesus Christ humbled himself and sacrificed his life for the salvation of others, the notion of self-sacrificing love and humble service is at the heart of Christian ethics. Not only Christ, the perfect servant and sacrifice of G*d, but also Mary, the obedient handmaid of G*d, are the models of true Christian womanhood.

However, this Christian the*logy of service must be scrutinized, not only for its cultural androcentric presuppositions and implications. It must also be analyzed with respect to its classist, racist, and colonialist underpinnings. Beginning with Plato and Aristotle, Western political philosophy has argued that the freeborn, propertied, educated man is the highest of mortal beings and that all other members of the human race are defined by their functions in his service. Wo/men as well as slaves and barbarians are by "nature" inferior to him and therefore destined to be the instruments of his well-being.[12] Modern political and philosophical anthropology continues to assume that propertied, educated "White Western Man" is defined by reason, self-determination, and full citizenship whereas wo/men and other subordinated peoples are characterized by emotion, service, and dependence.[13] They are seen not as rational and responsible but as emotional and childlike.

In short, kyriarchal society and culture is not only characterized by its sexual and economic exploitation of all wo/men, which is sustained and legitimized by the cult of true womanhood, the myth of femininity, romantic love, and education to domesticity.[14] It also needs for its functioning a "servant class," a "servant race," or a "servant people," be they slaves, serfs, house servants, "coolies," or "mammies." The existence of such a "servant class" is maintained through law, education, socialization, and brute violence. It is sustained by the belief that members of a "servant class" of people are by nature or by divine decree inferior to those whom they are destined to serve.[15]

Moreover, the cultural "hierarchy of service" implicates wo/men in the exploitation of other wo/men. True, even the noble lady of the castle or the white lady of the plantation was to be subservient to her father or husband as the "lord and master of the house." Yet she was able to delegate her labors to a "servant group" of people, especially to impoverished, uneducated, and colonialized wo/men.[16] The cultural assumption of all wo/men's sexual and domestic subservience to the "Man" thus pits wo/men against wo/men in a patriarchal society insofar as wo/men have to control and supervise the low-paid domestic service and work of other wo/men. The more the economic power of working- and middle-class male salaries erodes, wo/men of these economic strata also have increasingly to shoulder the triple burden of unpaid housework, care of children as well as of the elderly and infirm, and work outside the home.[17] Lower class, Black and Hispanic wo/men workers always had to do so.

Finally, the increase of virulent right-wing ideologies in the past decade—such as racism, anti-Semitism, "work-fare" programs for the poor, biblicist fundamentalism, militarist colonialism, and "the new cult of femininity and the family"—seek to maintain the servanthood of exploited people by insisting that by the will of G*d or by "nature" some groups of people are superior and others subservient. The renewed ecclesiastical insistence that wo/men must live their true womanhood in complementarity with men as well as that the ordained differ "in essence" from the laity, must be seen in this context. As Letty Russell so succinctly states: "Regardless of what we say about ministry as a function, we [the clergy] are still placed in a position of permanent superiority in the life of the church. In this sense ordination becomes an indelible mark of caste rather than the recognition of spiritual gifts for a particular ministry in the church."[18] Thus the*logical language of ordained ministry as servant leadership does not abolish the ecclesial "class" division between clergy and laity but mystifies and perpetrates it.

SERVANTHOOD ECCLESIOLOGY IN FEMINIST THE*LOGY

However, in spite of the feminist critique of the cultural and religious socialization of wo/men and other subordinated peoples to self-sacrificing love and selfless service for others, the notion of ministry as service is still a powerful symbol for Christian feminists. Some have argued that "as Christians we cannot avoid the word, despite of its oppressive overtones," since *diakonia* is central to the understanding of the mission and ministry of Christ as well as to that of the church.[19] Such a feminist the*logical retrieval of a servanthood-ecclesiology basically follows two strategies of interpretation.

The *first strategy* elaborates the New Testament distinction between *diakonein* and *douleuein* in order to stress that freely chosen service means liberation. *Diakonia*-service is to be differentiated from servility. Servanthood without choice is not *diakonia* but becomes slavery (*douleia*). However, "servanthood through choice is an act of the total self. The powerlessness of servanthood can be redemptive only when it results from free and conscious choice." Such freely chosen servanthood is not self-denial, self-elimination, self-ignorance, or self-immolation. Rather it is the "capacity to look beyond ourselves to see the needs of others." It is the "empathy to want to help and the skill to know how to help."

Jesus is the model of such freely chosen service because he has made choices of self-giving and self-sacrifice rather than allowing society to dictate his behavior. *Diakonia* is realized in the life of Jesus who came "not to be served but to serve and to give his life as ransom for many" (Mark 10:45). If "servanthood is being in love with the world as G*d is in love with it," then servanthood means, in the last analysis, liberation. "We find ourselves liberated into servanthood."[20] However this feminist proposal for the the*logical recuperation of servanthood does not take into account that people who in a patriarchal culture and church are powerless, singled out and socialized into subservience and a life of servanthood, are not able "to choose freely" servanthood.

By revalorizing service and servanthood the*logically this strategy extends the the*logical "double-speak" about service to the the*logical concept of liberation. For those who are destined by patriarchal culture and sociopolitical structures to become "servants" to those who have power over them, the the*logical or ecclesiological retrieval of "service/servant/slave/waiter" language cannot have a liberating function as long as kyriarchal structures in society and religion continue to divide people into those who serve and those who are served. Rather than elaborate the the*logical symbols of service/servitude/and self-sacrifice, a critical feminist the*logy of liberation needs instead to seek for New Testament concepts such as *dynamis/ exousia/ soteria* (power/authority/and well-being) that can critically challenge the religious reproduction of a cultural servant mentality.

A *second feminist the*logical strategy* for retrieving the the*logy of service does not so much focus on the freely chosen integration of wo/men's cultural and Christian socialization for selfless service and love but concentrates on a redefinition of ministry. By combining the the*logy of "freely chosen" service with an understanding of ministry not as "power over" but as "power for," it seeks to recover the early Christian understanding of ministry as service of G*d and as the building up of the community. It also takes Jesus Christ and his incarnation as "suffering servant" as the model of Christian ministry: Diakonia, it is argued, "is kenotic or self-emptying of power as domination. Ministry transforms power from power over others to empowerment of others. The abdication of power as domination has nothing to do with servility. . . . Rather ministry means exercising power in a new way, as a means of liberation of one another."[21]

Although this reconceptualization of ministry seeks to retrieve the New Testament model of *diakonia* equaling service, for a feminist ecclesial self-understanding in and through a redefinition of power, it nevertheless valorizes the kyriarchal concept and institution of service/servanthood the*logically. The the*logical language of ministry as service, that is, as "power for" rather than as "power over" the church and the world obfuscates the fact that the kyriarchal church continues to exercise its ministry as "power over." It remains structured into a hierarchy of power dualisms: ordained/nonordained, clergy/laity, religious/secular, church/world.

Continuing to use the the*logical notion of service as a central feminist category for ministry, this the*logy of service reduplicates the cultural pattern of self-sacrificing service for wo/men and other subordinate peoples, while at the same time continuing to serve as a moralistic appeal to those who have positions of power and control in church leadership. Dependence, obedience, second-class citizenship, and powerlessness remain intrinsic to the notion of "service/servanthood" as long as society and church structurally reproduce a "servant" class of people. Therefore, in seeking to define wo/men's ministry a feminist ecclesiology of liberation must reject the categories of service and servanthood as disempowering to wo/men. New Testament categories for ecclesial leadership functions—such as, apostles, prophets, facilitators, missionary coworkers, and co-laborers dedicated to the *oikodome*, that is, "the building up of the community"—would be more appropriate to express a feminist understanding of ministry as empowerment.

One must therefore be asked whether the New Testament notion of diakonia as service should be completely discarded by feminists. I would suggest that the notion of diakonia can be reclaimed by feminist the*logy solely as a critical category challenging those who have actual power and privilege in kyriarchal churches and societies. Since oppressions are interstructured, hierarchized, and multifaceted, wo/men who do not live on the bottom of the kyriarchal pyramid are not only exploited by but they also benefit from the structures of domination and service. Those of us who are marginalized and subordinated but at the same time privileged either by virtue of ordination, education, wealth, nationality, race, health, or age have to use our privileges for bringing about change. Feminist ministers do not seek to be incorporated into the lowest ranks of the clergy and kyriarchal hierarchy as altar-servers, lectors, deaconesses, or even priests but seek to engage in ministry in order to subvert clerical-hierarchal structures and to transform the kyriarchal church into a discipleship community of equals.

Such a retrieval of diakonia for a critical challenge to the structures of domination corresponds to its meaning in the Gospel traditions. The core saying of Mark 10:42-44, which in some form is assumed to go back to the historical Jesus, juxtaposes "great/servant" and "first/slave." The subject under discussion is the contrast between societal structures of domination and the "discipleship of equals."[22] It clearly presupposes a society in which those who "rule and have authority over" are the kings and great ones, whereas those who are servants and slaves are required to take orders, to render obeisance, and provide services. It challenges those in positions of dominance and power to become "equal" with those who are powerless. Masters should relinquish domination over their slaves and servants and step into their shoes.

The importance of this saying is indicated by its inclusion in the synoptic tradition in a sevenfold combination (Mark 10:42-45 par. Matt. 20:25-27; 23:11; Luke 22:26; Mark 9:33-37 par. Matt. 18:1-4; Luke 9:48). Its meaning is also central to the Fourth Gospel (John 12:25-26 and 13:4-5, 12-17). This Jesus-tradition does not exhort all Christians to become servants and slaves, but only those who have status and power in the kyriarchal pyramid. It seeks to create "equality from below" not by incorporating those on the bottom of the kyriarchal pyramid into its lower ranks. Rather it rejects the patriarchal-hierarchical pyramid as such. It seeks to level it by calling those on the top of the pyramid to join the work and labor of those on the bottom, thereby making a "servant class" of people superfluous. By denying the validity of master and lord positions and by ironically calling the "would-be" great and leaders to live on the bottom of the kyriarchal pyramid of domination, this Jesus-tradition paradoxically rejects all kyriarchal-hierarchical structures and positions.

In the process of interpretation the Gospel writers applied a saying originally addressed to the whole people of Israel to their own community structures and relationships. Structures of domination and servanthood should not be tolerated in the community of equals. True leadership in this community must be rooted in solidarity with each other. This ecclesial process of interpretation takes place at the same time as the post-Pauline traditions in the interest of "good citizenship" advocate the adaptation of the Christian community as "the household of G*d" to its kyriarchal societal structures. This patriarchalizing tendency also had impact on the interpretation of *diakonia* in the Gospels.

Whereas Mark and Matthew acknowledge no "great" and "first" in the community at all, Luke does so. His only requirement is that their style of leadership orient itself on the example of Jesus. Like Luke and the post-Pauline tradition, later the*logians have no longer understood the radical paradox of the discipleship of equals when they called those in positions of wealth and power to "charitable service." This the*logy of service did not question but confirmed kyriarchal status and privileges. Since it has defined mainline Christian self-understanding and community and has condoned structures of "domination and authority over," a feminist the*logy of ministry must deconstruct such patri-kyriarchal Christian self-understandings and ecclesial structures and not perpetuate it by valorizing the notion of service and servanthood. Ministry is no longer to be construed as "service" or as "waiting on someone," but should be understood as "equality from below" in solidarity with all those who struggle for survival, self-love, and justice.

NOTES

[1] See H. W. Beyer, "*Diakoneō*," *Theological Dictionary of the New Testament*, vol. 2, 81–93; K. H. Rengstorf, "*Doulos*," 261–80; K. H. Hess, "Serve," *New International Dictionary of New Testament Theology*, vol. 3, 544–49; R. Tuente, "slave," 592–98.

[2] Avery Dulles, *Models of the Church* (Garden City: 1974), 87. See also J. E. Booty, *The Servant Church* (Wilton: 1984).

[3] D. Bonhoeffer, *Letters and Papers from Prison* (rev. ed. New York, 1967), 203.

[4] See, for example, E. Schillebeeckx, *Ministry: Leadership in the Community of Jesus Christ* (New York, 1982), 147; D. Power, *Gifts that Differ: Lay Ministries Established and Unestablished* (New York, 1980), 106.

[5] See J. A. Coleman, "A Theology of Ministry," *The Way* 25 (1985), 15–17, with reference to Chirico "Pastoral Ministry in a Time of Priest Shortage," *Clergy Review* 69 (1984), 81–84.

[6] The first list of proposals made by the 1987 Synod on the Laity contained the following recommendation, which reflected the mind of the Synod: "Because of the fundamental equal dignity of the disciples of Christ, all offices and tasks in the church except the ministries which require the power of orders should be open to women as well as men, with due regard to local sensibilities." However, this and the recommendations to study the admission of women to the ministry of deaconesses as well as to that of "altar-servers" disappeared without any convincing explanation from the subsequent drafts. See Hebblethwaite, "Reports Reveal Curia Derailed Lay Synod," *National Catholic Reporter* 24 (5 February 1988): 28.

[7] "The Role of Women in Evangelization," issued by the Pastoral Commission of the Vatican Congregation for the Evangelization of Peoples. The text can be found in *Origins* 5 (April 1976): 702–7.

[8] *Women and Ministry: A Survey of the Experience of Roman Catholic Women in the United States* (Washington, DC: 1980). See my analysis of this study: "'We Are Still Invisible': The*logical Analysis of Women and Ministry," in *Women and Ministry: Present Experience and Future Hope*, edited by D. Gottemoeller and R. Hofbauer (Washington, DC: 1981), 29–43.

[9] See J. W. Carroll, B. Hargrove, and A. Lummis, *Women of the Cloth* (San Francisco: 1983); J. L. Weidman, ed., *Women Ministers* (San Francisco: 1981); A. Schilthuis-Stokvis, "Women as Workers in the Church Seen from the Ecumenical Point of View," *Concilium* 194 (1987), 85–90.

[10] See, for example, G. Notz, "Frauenarbeit zum Nulltarif: Zur ehrenamtlichen Tätigkeit von Frauen," in Arbeitsgemeinschaft Frauenforschung der Universität Bonn, *Studium Feminale* (Bonn 1986), 134–51.

[11] See Judith Plaskow, *Sex, Sin, and Grace* (Washington, DC: 1980).

[12] Susan Moller Okin, *Women in Western Political Thought* (Princeton: 1979): 73–96.

[13] See Elisabeth List, "Homo Politicus-Femina Privata: Thesen zur Kritik der politischen Anthropologie," in J. Conrad and U. Konnertz, *Weiblichkeit in der Moderne: Ansätze feministischer Vernunftkritik* (Tübingen 1986), 75–95.

[14] See Brigitte Weisshaupt, "Selbstlosigkeit und Wissen," in *Weiblichkeit in der Moderne*, 21–38.

[15]See, for example, the biographical reflection and analysis of apartheid as an ideology and institution for maintaining a "servant people" by Mark Mathabene, *Kaffir Boy: The True Story of a Black Youth's Coming of Age in Apartheid South Africa* (New York: 1986).

[16]See, for example, Martha Mamozai, *Herrenmenschen: Frauen im deutschen Kolonialismus* (Rheinbeck: 1982).

[17]See the contributions in E. Schüssler Fiorenza and A. Carr, ed., *Women, Work, and Poverty*, Concilium 194 (Edinburgh: 1987).

[18]Letty M. Russell, "Women and Ministry: Problem or Possibility?" in J. L. Weidman, ed., *Christian Feminism—Visions of a New Humanity* (San Francisco 1984), 89.

[19]Letty M. Russell, "Women and Ministry," in *Sexist Religion and Women in the Church*, A. L. Hageman (New York, 1974), 55.

[20]All quotations are taken from R. Richardson Smith, "Liberating the Servant," *Christian Century* 98 (1981): 13–14. See also R. Propst, "Servanthood Redefined: Coping Mechanism for Women within Protestant Christianity," *Journal of Pastoral Counseling* 17 (1982): 14–18.

[21]Rosemary Radford Ruether, *Sexism and God-Talk: Toward a Feminist Theology* (Boston: 1983), 207. See also the various contributions of Letty M. Russell.

[22]For the following, see my book *In Memory of Her: A Feminist The*logical Reconstruction of Christian Origins* (New York, 1983), 148–51.

14

The Twelve and the Discipleship of Equals

THE PROBLEM

Against the understanding of the early Christian movement as a discipleship of equals[1] it is often argued that Jesus chose and commissioned twelve men to be the apostolic leaders of the early church.[2] The institution of the twelve apostles—so the argument goes—proves that the hierarchically ordered apostolic ministry stood above the equality of all believers[3] in the very beginnings of the church. Since the twelve apostles were, according to the Gospels, without exception men, it is concluded that wo/men could not have had equal access to leadership functions either in the Jesus movement or in the early Christian missionary movement. Therefore, the notion of a "discipleship of equals" is declared to be a feminist projection back into the first century, which has no support in our source texts.

Such an argument rests, however, on several faulty assumptions. It overlooks the understandings of the early Christian movement that I have conceptualized as a "discipleship community of equals," as "equality in the Spirit," as "equality from below," or as *ekklēsia*, that is, the democratic decision-making assembly of equals as counter-term to the structures of domination and exclusion that are institutionalized in Graeco-Roman kyriarchy.[4]

Moreover, the argument against the reconstruction of early Christianity as a "discipleship of equals" seems to imply that social equality expressed in decentralized, horizontal social structures does not admit of leadership functions. However, studies of Hellenistic and Jewish—as well as early Christian—missionary propaganda have shown that although the vast majority of religions in the Graeco-Roman world "did not develop centralized hierarchical structures," they were not without missionary leadership.[5]

In addition, this objection presupposes not only that the maleness of the Twelve is constitutive for their early Christian function but also that this function was that of apostolic leadership in the early Christian churches. Thus this objection seems to assume that the circle of the Twelve was identical with the wider circle of apostles, as well as with the wider circle of disciples.

Finally, this objection to the understanding of the early Christian movements as a "discipleship of equals" reads the Gospels in a positivist fashion as an accurate description of the events and agents in early Christian beginnings. However, on methodological grounds, such an assumption must be judged as outdated and ideological.[6] It overlooks the rhetorical character of the Gospels as the*logical responses to particular historical ecclesial situations.

THE TWELVE AND THE APOSTLES

Popular and ecclesiastical understandings[7] generally assume that the terms "apostles" and the "Twelve" are coextensive categories as if both terms connote the very same historical circle and the same disciple functions. Yet this assumption goes against the scholarly consensus that the apostles and the Twelve were different circles in early Christianity, which only in the course of time were identified with each other.[8] Originally the word "apostle" describes the function of a commissioned messenger. In the Pauline correspondence it designates a missionary sent by the Resurrected One. Clearly, the title is not restricted to the group of the Twelve, since Paul would not then qualify as an apostle. Insofar as not every apostle was a member of the Twelve, the term *apostle* seems to connote originally an independent and more comprehensive circle of leadership in the early church.

Only at a later stage of the tradition are the Twelve identified with the apostles (see Mark 6:30; Matt. 10:2; Rev. 21:14), an identification that is especially characteristic of the Lukan work. However, it remains debated at what point of the tradition the Twelve were also understood as apostles. Paul and Barnabas, for instance, are known as apostles in early Christianity (see Acts 14:4,14), but they definitely did not belong to the circle of the Twelve.

Moreover, our sources indicate that the circle of the Twelve as a circle independent of the apostles is firmly rooted in the tradition. They are already traditional figures of the past toward the end of the first century (see Rev. 21:14).[9] The terms used are "the Twelve," "The twelve disciples," the "twelve apostles," and "the Eleven." It is astonishing that direct references to the Twelve are rare in the Pauline writings (one in a traditional formula) and the Johannine literature (four) and completely absent in the Catholic and Pastoral Epistles. In the Pastorals it is Paul who has become the apostle par excellence.

Finally, although the four Gospel accounts about the Twelve (Mark 3:16-19; Matt. 10:2-4; Luke 6:12-16; Acts 1:13) differ,[10] they agree in listing only male names. Therefore, popular understanding assumes that the maleness of the Twelve is essential for their function and mission. One must ask whether it is essential for the Twelve's mission and historical significance that they are males and whether masculinity is integral to their function.

Do the early traditions about the Twelve elaborate the male gender of the Twelve and do they reflect on it? Moreover, is the function and mission of the Twelve, according to our sources, continued in the structure and leadership of the early church? Did the Twelve have successors, and if so did they have to be male? In other words, do we find any evidence in early Christian sources for the assumption that biological maleness and masculine gender were intrinsic to the function and mission of the Twelve and therefore must remain intrinsic to the apostolic office of the church?

THE EARLIEST TRADITIONS ABOUT THE TWELVE

First Corinthians 15:5 and the Jesus saying in Matt. 19:28 (see Luke 22:30) are the two oldest source-texts that refer to the Twelve. In 1 Cor. 15:3-5, Paul quotes a tradition has already received.[11] This pre-Pauline tradition maintains that the Resurrected One appeared first to Cephas and then to the Twelve. The text refers to the Twelve as a fixed and well-known group. Since it does not speak of Peter and the Eleven, the text does not reflect the defection of Judas as the resurrection narratives of the Gospels do when they consistently refer to the Eleven. Furthermore, the traditional formula in 1 Cor. 15:3-5 does not indicate whether the group of the Twelve existed already before Easter as a definite circle of disciples in the ministry of Jesus, or whether it was constituted by the resurrection appearances and commission of the Risen One.

Paul's account parallels the statement in 1 Cor. 15:5 with the statement in 15:7, which refers to the appearance of the Risen One to James and then to "all the apostles." It is not clear whether it was Paul who articulated the parallel statements of 1 Corinthians 15:5 and 15:7 or whether he had already found this parallel in his tradition.[12]

In any case, the present text appears to combine two different traditions and to speak of two different groups, namely, the Twelve and the apostles. As Peter stands out among the Twelve, so does James among the apostles. However, neither the pre-Pauline tradition nor the Pauline text reflect upon the gender of the Twelve nor on that of the apostles.

The very old saying, Matt. 19:28 (parallel text, Luke 22:30), has a quite different form and setting in Matthew and Luke. Even though the Matthean and Lukan form of the saying are redactional,[13] the contrast between present sufferings and future glory is common to both. In its original form the saying is an eschatological promise to the disciples who have followed Jesus. This Q-logion,[14] in its Matthean form, explicitly interprets the number twelve. When in the new world the Human One *(huios tou anthrōpou)* will be revealed in all splendor and glory, the followers of Jesus also will sit "on twelve thrones to judge [or rule] the twelve tribes of Israel" (Matt. 19:28).

The text clearly does not underline the historical existence of a group of twelve men but emphasizes the function the disciples of Jesus would have for Israel in the eschatological future. The faithful disciples will share with Jesus in the exercise of authority and power when the *basileia* is established. Since at the time of Jesus only two and a half tribes still existed, the number twelve is clearly symbolic. The circle of the Twelve thus has an eschatological-symbolic function.

The number twelve refers back to the ancient constitution of Israel consisting of twelve tribes, as well as forward to the eschatological restitution of Israel. The "maleness" of the twelve disciples is not explicitly mentioned by this Q-logion. It could be inferred that the Twelve must be male since the text seems to refer to and to symbolize the ancient tribal constitution of Israel, which in its religious and political leadership was patriarchal.[15] Yet the Q-logion does not refer to the historical constitution of Israel but rather points to Israel's eschatological future. It does not refer to the church in the interim time but to the eschatological restitution of the people of Israel. This Q-saying does not postulate a historical continuum between Jesus, the Twelve, and the church, but establishes a symbolic coherence between Jesus, the Twelve, and the eschatological reconstitution of the twelve tribes of Israel.

Revelation 21:14 also indicates that the signifying function of the Twelve is eschatological-symbolic rather than historical-masculine. According to this text the eschatological city, the New Jerusalem, is patterned after the twelve tribes of Israel: "The city walls stood on twelve foundation stones, each one of which bore the name of one of the twelve apostles of the Lamb." Here the twelve apostles are not said to be the foundation of the church but of the New Jerusalem, which clearly is an eschatological reality.[16]

Finally, one cannot argue that this Q-saying was formulated only late in the ministry of Jesus and therefore did not have a great impact on the mission and the function of the Twelve. Since the present position of the saying in Matthew and Luke is editorial, we no longer know when this saying was formulated. From a tradition-historical point of view, it could have been spoken by the historical Jesus since it reflects the heart of his preaching to and concern for the renewal of his own people (Matt. 10:5-6). Thus it seems justified to conclude: "The Twelve exemplified the awakening of Israel and its gathering in the eschatological salvific community, something beginning then through Jesus. They exemplified this gathering simply through the fact that they were created as twelve but they also exemplified it through being sent out to all of Israel."[17]

The Markan Understanding of the Twelve

According to the Gospel of Mark the Twelve are likewise sent to the messianic people of G*d, Israel, in order to carry on Jesus' ministry and work. The two main passages cited for the historical mission of the Twelve are Mark 3:13-19 and 6:6b-13. Most scholars suggest that these texts were formulated by the Markan redaction.[18] They therefore do not reflect the earliest tradition but spell out Mark's the*logical understanding of the Twelve. These Markan texts stress that the specific power and authority given to the Twelve is that of exorcism.[19] Mark 3:14 mentions their mission to preach but underlines that power is given to them to cast out demons. According to the commissioning scene in Mark 6:6b-13, they are neither explicitly authorized (v. 7b) nor commissioned (vv. 8-10) to preach. Their preaching is not mentioned in the concluding statement of verse 12. But the following verse (13) stresses again the power of the Twelve to heal and to cast out demons. A careful reading of the text indicates that in Mark's view the Twelve are primarily sent, having received the power of exorcism and healing, while Jesus is the one who proclaims the gospel of the *basileia* (1:14f).[20]

It should be noted that Mark's the*logical emphasis on the empowerment of the Twelve to cast out demons and to heal is completely neglected by the the*logical articulation of "apostolic succession." Moreover, according to Mark, not only the twelve apostles preach (*keryssein*), but also John the Baptist (1:4,7) and those who are healed (1:45; 5:20) or who are witnesses of healing (7:36), as well as the post-Easter community as a whole (13:10; 14:9). Further, the preaching activity of the Twelve addresses Israel. Since, in distinction to Matthew (28:16-20), Mark does not know of a post-Easter commissioning of the Twelve to universal mission, it could be inferred that Mark intends to limit the preaching of the Twelve to Galilee.

Finally, Mark 3:13-19 and 6:6b-13 do not stress that the Twelve have *to be* like Jesus but demand that, as the disciples of Jesus, the Twelve have *to do* what Jesus did. In Mark's view, Jesus is the teacher par excellence who has great authority over demons and the power to heal. Jesus' power is demonstrated by exorcisms and healing miracles. If Mark understands the Twelve and all the other disciples to be the functional successors of Jesus, then it is not their maleness but their preaching, exorcising, and healing power that continues Jesus' mission.

Important too is the fact that Mark does not differentiate between but rather identifies the Twelve and the disciples.[21] A comparison of Mark 11:11 with 11:14, and Mark 14:12, 14 with 14:17 speaks for the overlapping of both groups. Mark 4:10 does not provide a sufficient textual basis for a clear-cut distinction between the Twelve and the disciples, since such a separation cannot be maintained for the subsequent passages (Mark 6:35-44; 7:17; 9:28,10:10). Insofar as Mark does not stress the apostolic character of the Twelve, even though he is aware of it (see 3:14 and 6:30), he clearly is not concerned with the the*logical foundation of apostolic ministry. He primarily understands the Twelve as disciples and attributes to them no distinctive function and mission other than discipleship. The mission of the Twelve to do what Jesus did is therefore, according to Mark, not restricted to the Twelve but is a mission given to all disciples.

The second part of the Gospel therefore stresses again and again that the disciples have to suffer the same consequences that Jesus had to suffer for his preaching and mission. Just as the way of Jesus led to suffering and death, so does the way of the true disciple. Connected with each passion prediction are statements stressing that no possibility of discipleship exists apart from taking upon oneself its consequence of suffering. Yet, again and again, the Twelve with their leading spokesman, Peter, show that they do not understand and even reject Jesus' insistence on suffering discipleship.

The twelve disciples who were called "to be with his companions" (Mark 3:14), desert Jesus in his hour of suffering (14:50), and Peter denies him three times (14:66-72). They are not found under the cross of Jesus, nor at his burial, and it remains unclear whether they receive the message of the Resurrection (Mark 16:7-8). In marked contrast to the twelve disciples, the wo/men disciples who followed Jesus from Galilee to Jerusalem (see 15:40) remain faithful until the end.

Not the Twelve, but the wo/men disciples prove to be the true disciples of Jesus in Mark. The wo/men not only accompany Jesus on his way to suffering and death but they also *do* what he had come to do, namely, to serve (*diakonein*, see 10:42-5 and 15:41). While the twelve disciples are unable to understand and to accept Jesus' teaching that he must suffer, it is a wo/man who shows such perception and acts accordingly (14:3-9). In Mark her action is the immediate cause for the betrayal of Jesus by one of the Twelve (14:10). This contrast between the Twelve and the wo/men disciples would suggest that in Mark's church the apostolic wo/men were considered to have been the exemplary disciples of Jesus who had their place among the leaders of the Jesus movement in Palestine.[22] In Mark's the*logical perspective, the wo/men disciples are the functional successors of Jesus and they continue Jesus' mission and ministry in the "new family" of G*d. Far from being the exemplars of apostolic discipleship, the Twelve are the negative blueprint of right discipleship.

Luke's The*logical Accentuation

Since Luke-Acts has formed our the*logical understanding and historical imagination of early Christian beginnings, its identification of the Twelve with the apostles has greatly influenced Christian the*logical and historical self-understanding. Nevertheless, the Lukan redaction still views the circle of the Twelve as belonging to the time of Jesus and to the very beginnings of the Christian movement. The Twelve's legitimization is rooted in their companionship with Jesus and in their witness to the resurrection. They have special eschatological (Q) and historical (Mark) functions *vis-à-vis* Israel.

It is debatable whether Acts 1:21²³ makes maleness explicitly a precondition for replacing a member of the Twelve. According to Luke the position of Judas can be taken "Out of the men *(anēr)* who have been with us the whole time that the Lord Jesus was living with us, from the time John was baptizing until the day when he was taken up from us." Thus, according to Luke-Acts only one of the original disciples of Jesus who were, together with the Eleven, witnesses to the Resurrection could replace Judas, who was one of the Twelve. However, it is not clear whether *anēr* is used in 1:21 in a grammatically generic or in a gender specific masculine sense, since Acts often uses the address "men, brothers" (1:16; 23:29; 2:37; 7:2; 13:15; 13:26,38; 15:7,13; 22:1,6; 28:17) in a grammatically generic-inclusive sense for addressing the whole community, even when wo/men are present (see 1:14 and 1:16).

It could, however, also be argued to the contrary that because of his the*logical understanding of the Twelve, Luke maintains that only one of the *male* followers of Jesus is eligible to become one of the Twelve, since Luke 8:1-3 clearly distinguishes between the wo/men disciples of Jesus and the Twelve. Differing from its Markan source, the Gospel of Luke has the wo/men disciples serve Jesus and the Twelve. It qualifies their *diakonein* insofar as it specifies that the wo/men disciples served them—that is, Jesus and the Twelve—with their possessions. Just as wealthy wo/men provided patronage for Jewish missionary endeavors, so, according to Luke, wealthy Christian wo/men support the ministry of Jesus and of the twelve apostles. Luke then seems to limit the leadership role of wo/men in the Christian missionary movement to that of benefactors.²⁴

However, Luke-Acts precludes the notion that the Twelve could have appointed a line of successors, since Luke's the*logical perspective assigns only a very limited function to the twelve apostles. The Twelve are mentioned for the last time in Acts 6:2ff, and they disappear altogether after chapter 15. It is, moreover, curious that most passages in Acts speak only of the work of one of them, Peter. Luke-Acts does not characterize the Twelve as missionaries, and there is little evidence in Acts that they were at all active outside Jerusalem. In Acts the apostle par excellence is Paul, who clearly was not one of the Twelve.

Luke knows likewise that the Twelve were not the official local ministers of the Jerusalem church or any other church. According to Paul and Acts, the leadership of the Jerusalem church was in the hands of James, the brother of the Lord, who was not one of the Twelve. Moreover, the Twelve as a group were not replaced when they died (see Acts 12:2). The twelve apostles had no successors. Thus it is evident that Luke knows only of a very limited function for the Twelve in the origins of the Christian movements. Their significance appears to be limited to the very beginnings of the church and to its relationship to the chosen people of Israel.

Following Mark, Luke seems to historicize their eschatological-symbolic function *vis-à-vis* Israel that the Twelve had in his tradition. He limits their activity to the mission within Israel. After the gentile mission is under way, the Twelve disappear from the historical scene. The elders and bishops in Acts are not understood as successors of the Twelve. They are either appointed by Paul and Barnabas (14:23) or directly called by the Holy Spirit (20:28).

In conclusion, it needs to be stressed that according to Luke-Acts the historical and symbolic function of the Twelve was not continued in the ministries of the church. Neither their eschatological-symbolic and historical-missionary function *vis-à-vis* Israel nor their function as eyewitnesses of the ministry and resurrection of Jesus is constitutive for the ministry of the church. If Luke should have required that the replacement of Judas must be a male follower of the historical Jesus, then this does not say anything about maleness as an essential requirement for the ordained priesthood or episcopacy in the church, since Luke does not envision any "apostolic succession" of the Twelve. The the*logical problem at hand is then whether the the*logical construct of "apostolic succession" can be maintained today in view of the historical recognition that the twelve apostles had no successors.

The historical-the*logical issue at stake is therefore not whether wo/men can be appointed as successors of the apostles, since Jesus did not call any wo/man disciple to be a member of the circle of Twelve. Rather the the*logical issue at hand is whether the discipleship of equals will be realized by the *ekklēsia*, the democratic assembly of *all* citizens in the church. As long as such a vision of the *ekklēsia of wo/men* has not become a reality, apostolic calling engages wo/men and men in the struggle for the transformation of the patriarchal church into the discipleship community of equals.

NOTES

[1] For this expression, see my book *In Memory of Her: A Feminist The*logical Reconstruction of Christian Origin*, (Crossroad: New York, 1983); see also R. L. Sider, "Toward a Biblical Perspective on Equality," *Interpretation* 43 (1989): 156–69.

[2] For Dr. Patricia Brennan in deep appreciation for her vision.

[3] For such an argument, see L. W. Countryman, "Christian Equality and the Early Catholic Episcopate," *ATR* 63 (1981): 115.

[4] See my article "Die Anfänge von Kirche, Amt, und Priestertum in feministisch-theologischer Sicht," in Hoffman, *Priesterkirche: Theologie der Zeit* 3 (Patmos: Düsseldorf, 1987), 62–95.

[5] See the epilogue in Dieter Georgi, *The Opponents of Paul in Second Corinthians* (Philadelphia: Fortress Press, 1986), 362, and Elisabeth Schüssler Fiorenza, ed., *Aspects of Religious Propaganda in Judaism and Early Christianity* (Notre Dame: Notre Dame University Press, 1976).

[6] For a discussion of such a positivist approach, see "Text and Reality—Reality as Text: The Problem of a Feminist Historical and Social Reconstruction Based on Texts," *Studia Theologica*

43 (1989): 19–34, and my Society of Biblical Literature presidential address, "The Ethics of Interpretation," *JBL* 107 (1988), 3–17.

7 See my articles "The Twelve" and "The Apostleship of Women in Early Christianity," in L. and A. Swidler, eds., *Women Priests: A Catholic Commentary on the Vatican Declaration* (New York: Paulist, 1977), 114–22, 135–40. J. A. Kirk, "Apostleship since Rengstorf," *NTS* 21 (1974/75), 260; Andrew C. Clark, "Apostleship: Evidence from the New Testament and Early Christian Literature," *Vox Evangelica* 19 (1989): 49–82.

8 For a general discussion of the problem, see B. Rigaux, "The Twelve Apostles," *Concilium* 34 (1968): 5–15; "Die 'Zwölf' in Geschichte und Kerygma," in Ristow-Matthiae, ed., *Der Historische Jesus und der kerygmatische Christus*, 2nd ed. (Berlin, 1961), 468–86; G. Klein, *Die Zwölf Apostel: Ursprung und Gehalt einer Idee*, Forschungen zur Religion und Literatur des Alten und Neuen Testaments 59 (Göttingen: Vandenhoeck and Ruprecht, 1961); J. Roloff, *Apostolat—Verkündigung—Kirche* (Gütersloh: Mohn, 1965); R. Schnackenburg, "Apostolicity: The Present Position of Studies," *One in Christ* 6 (1970): 243–73; V. Taylor, *The Gospel according to Saint Mark*, 2nd ed. (London: Macmillan, 1966), 619–27; A. Vögtle in *Lexikon für Theologie und Kirche*, vol. 9, 2nd ed. (Freiburg: Herder, 1966), 1443; H. D. Betz, *Galatians*, Hermeneia (Fortress Press: Philadelphia, 1979), 74.

9 See my book, *Priester für Gott: Studien zum Herrschafts und Priestermotiv in der Apokalypse* (Münster Aschendorff, 1972).

10 For a discussion of the text and of the secondary literature, see Joseph A. Fitzmyer, *The Gospel according to Luke*, Anchor Bible 28AB (Doubleday, Garden City, 1985), 613–21.

11 For extensive bibliographic information see H. Conzelmann, *1 Corinthians*, Hermeneia (Philadelphia: Fortress Press, 1975), 251–54.

12 For an extensive discussion and literature see H. Merklein, *Das kirchliche Amt nach dem Epheserbrief*, Studia Antoniana (München, Kösel, 1973), 273–8.

13 For a discussion of the original Q-form and the Matthean and Lukan redaction, see Fitzmyer, 1413ff.

14 Q is used to designate the source of the material that is common to Matthew and Luke but is not found in Mark. Since the material is almost wholly teaching material, Q is often called "Sayings-source" or "*Logia*" source.

15 However, Christian feminists must learn to read such information in an anti-patriarchal fashion rather than perpetuate scholarly anti-Jewish readings. See Judith Plaskow, *Standing Again at Sinai: Judaism from a Feminist Perspective* (Harper and Row, New York, 1990).

16 For a comprehensive interpretation of Revelation, see my book *Revelation: Vision of a Just World* (Fortress Press, Minneapolis, 1991).

17 G. Lohfink, *Jesus and Community: The Social Dimension of Christian Faith* (Philadelphia: Fortress Press, 1984), 10. See also Ulrich Luz, *Das Evangelium nach Matthäus II* (Zürich: Neukirchener, 1990), 74–161.

18 See J. Coutts, "The Authority of Jesus and the Twelve in Saint Mark's Gospel," *Journal of Theological Studies* 8 (1957), 111–18; K. G. Reploh, *Markus—Lehrer der Gemeinde*, Stuttgarter biblische Monagraphien 9 (Stuttgart: Katholisches Bibelwerk, 1969), 43–58; K. Stock, *Boten aus dem Mit-Ihm-Sein: Das Verhältnis zwischen Jesus und den Zwölf nach Markus*, Analecta Biblica 70 (Rome: Biblical Institute Press, 1975); G. Schmahl, "Die Berufung der Zwölf im Markusevangelium," *Trierer theologische Zeitschrift* 81 (1972): 203–313; R. Pesch, *Das Markusevangelium*, 1. Teil, Herders theologischer Kommentar zum Neuen Testament 2/1 (Freiburg: Herder, 1976), 202–9, 325–32.

19 See K. Kertelge, "Die Funktion der 'Zwölf' im Markusevangelium," *Trierer theologische Zeitschrift* 78 (1969): 193–206.

20 See Ched Myers, *Binding the Strong Man: A Political Reading of Mark's Story of Jesus* (Maryknoll: Orbis, 1988), 164, who stresses the political dimension of this symbolic act: Jesus forms a "kind of vanguard 'revolutionary committee.'"

21 Against K. Stock, who ascribes to the Twelve a special function, namely to represent and to continue his work. See, however, K. G. Reploh, 47, who maintains that the Twelve are included among the disciples. They have no special function distinctive to the disciples, but they are the origin and beginning of the whole church. See also U. Luz, who warns not to restrict the

commissioning of the twelve disciples to a limited historical circle and thereby to excuse the *ekklesia* from practicing the ethos of discipleship.

[22] See J. Achtemeier, *Mark*, Proclamation Commentary (Philadelphia: Fortress Press, 1975), 92–100.

[23] For Acts 1:15-26, see E. Haenchen, *The Acts of the Apostles* (Philadelphia: Westminster, 1971), 157–65.

[24] For a different interpretation, see H. Conzelmann, *The Theology of Saint Luke* (London: Faber and Faber, 1961), 47n1: "Features from the primitive community have naturally been projected back. Just as the male followers are turned into apostles, so the female followers are turned into deaconesses (v.3)." F. W. Danker, *Jesus and the New Age*, rev. ed. (Philadelphia, Fortress Press, 1988), 172, on the other hand stresses that the women are to "be included within the class of benefactors that was so esteemed in Mediterranean society," but he does not reflect on the Lukan redactional tendencies that determine this inclusion. For a feminist analysis of such tendencies, see my book *But She Said* (Beacon, Boston, 1992).

15

Resisting Violence—Engendering Easter

In this time before Holy Week and Easter we are poised to commemorate not only the suffering and execution of Jesus condemned to death as an insurrectionist by the Romans but also that of all those who seek justice and whose bodies or souls are being destroyed in the process.[1] We have gathered in this sacred space at a time when right-wing reactionary voices in society and religion seem to be increasing day by day and when it becomes harder and harder to keep the Easter dream of life in fullness alive. We are gathered here to resist despair in the face of violence and to empower each other with the life-giving word of Divine Wisdom.

The Passion and Easter story, however, cannot be told without also telling the story of Mary of Magdala, the primary witness of Jesus' crucifixion and resurrection, who was sent as apostle to the apostles. According to tradition she was the first one to spread the good news of Easter. The following historical scenario is most likely: Most of the Galilean disciples of Jesus fled after his arrest from Jerusalem and went back home to Galilee. Some of Jesus' wo/men disciples, foremost among them Mary of Magdala, did not flee after his arrest but stayed in Jerusalem for his execution and burial. These Galilean wo/men were also the first to articulate their conviction that G*d did not leave the executed Jesus in the grave but raised him from the dead. The early Christian message that "Jesus the Nazarene who was executed on the cross and was raised in glory" is revealed first to the Galilean wo/men disciples of Jesus.

Those wo/men disciples who remained in the capital probably sought to gather together the dispersed disciples and friends of Jesus who lived in and around Jerusalem. Some of these in all likelihood moved back soon to Galilee, their native country. Such a reconstruction of the events after the death and resurrection of Jesus is historically plausible, since it might have been easier for the wo/men of the Jesus movement to go "underground" than for the men. By keeping alive the good news of G*d's life-giving power in the resurrection of Jesus the executed one, the Galilean wo/men continued the *basileia* movement of which Jesus was a part.

Yet Mary of Magdala's story also bespeaks the misogynism that wo/men face who dare to assume leadership. In Christian the*logy, Mary of Magdala, the apostle, has been turned into the repentant sinner and "most chaste" whore, the sexuate wo/man who is in love with Jesus and teaches him feminine ways of being. This stereotype of Mary Magdalene was solidified by Pope Gregory the Great (540-604). He offered Mary Magdalene as the example of repentance and conversion to the people of Rome suffering from famine, plague, and war. As Susan Haskins writes: "And so the transformation of Mary Magdalene was complete. From the Gospel figure, with her active role as the herald of the New Life—the Apostle to the Apostles—she becomes the redeemed whore and Christianity's model of repentance, a manageable and controllable figure and effective weapon and instrument of propaganda against her own sex."[2]

Today, Christian the*logians no longer emphasize the sinfulness of the Magdalene but they degrade her leadership by insisting that wo/men cannot be ordained because Jesus chose only men as apostles. Popular culture continues to reinforce this stereotype in books such as Niko Kasantzakis's *The Last Temptation of Christ*, in films such as Martin Scorsese's adaptation of that book, or in musicals such as *Jesus Christ Superstar* by Andrew Lloyd Webber and Tim Rice. Mary Magdalene has become degraded from an apostle and witness to new life to a symbol of female sinfulness and feminine love for a great man.

Despite such disparagement, the age-old tradition of Mary's Easter witness and her mission to the male apostles, the "brothers," still survives. Thankfully, because of feminist research it is gaining new strength today. She has become for many wo/men the symbol of hope that challenges those who fear freedom and lack the courage to stand up against injustice. Hers and the other wo/men's testimony to the empty tomb was and still is used in the Easter liturgy and is the most frequently depicted image in early Christian art. Hippolytus of Rome, who lived around 170 to 235 CE, for instance, refers to the tradition of Mary's apostleship that was still known later in the Middle Ages: "So that the wo/men did not appear liars but bringers of the truth, Christ appeared to the [male] apostles and said to them: It is truly I who appeared to these wo/men and who desired to send them to you as apostles."[3]

Several hundred years later, Gregory of Antioch—a contemporary of Gregory the Great (d. 593)—still expressed the same understanding when he has Christ saying to the wo/men: "Be the first apostles to the apostles. So that Peter learns that I can choose even wo/men as apostles."

I have invoked here the figure of Mary of Magdala as an example of wo/men's leadership in early Christianity. The image of her I like best is found in Grace Episcopal Cathedral of San Francisco. The modern artist has painted her as a wo/man of color holding in her hand an Easter egg as the symbol of new life. She is a witness to the fullness of life in the midst of injustice and death.

We are called to be an Easter people, followers of Mary of Magdala, we are church, the *ekklēsia* of wo/men. We have come together because we hunger and thirst for justice. We have gathered here to gain strength in solidarity and to realize that we are not alone and powerless. We have come together here to celebrate the liberating vision of Easter, the message of new life and of liberation from the dehumanizing, death-dealing powers of anti-Judaism, racism, misogynism, homophobia, and many more -isms. We have come together here as the *ekklēsia* of wo/men, as people of G*d.

The Greek word *ekklēsia* can be rendered as "assembly, gathering or congress of full citizens. In the Pauline literaturem the expression *ekklēsia* is the very name for the Christian community. Hence, the best translation of *ekklēsia* is not "church." Rather it is best understood in light of the political notions of "public assembly" or democratic congress of full decision-making citizens." The word "synagogue" has the same valence and means the "congregation of the people of G*d." The very self-description of the early Christian messianic communities who gathered in the name of Jesus was a political-democratic one. Only when one realizes how fundamental this radical democratic spirit was to the self-understanding of the early Christian communities can one appreciate the break in Christian self-understanding that took place when the church adopted the administrative organizational structures of the Roman empire that were monarchical-hierarchical.

Although the word *ekklēsia* is usually translated in English as "church," the English word "church" derives from the Greek word *kyriakē*, that is, belonging to the *kyrios* (that is, the lord/ master/ father/husband), but not from the Greek term *ekklēsia*. The translation process, which has transformed "*ekklēsia*/congress" into "*kyriakē*/church," indicates a historical development that has privileged the hierarchical form of church. This "church" is characterized by hierarchical structures, represented by men, and divided into a sacred two-class system of the ordained and the laity. This two-class system spells second-class citizenship for those who are not clerics.

The radical equality of the *ekklēsia* of wo/men is the*logically grounded in the fact that we are all created in the image of G*d and have received the multifaceted gifts of the Spirit. In all our differences wo/men represent the Divine here and now because we are made in G*d's very own image and likeness. We are white and black, male and female, American, European, Asian, or African, young and old, able bodied and differently abled, gay and straight, immigrants and natives. We are wise and foolish, theoretical and practical, courageous and timid, beautiful and not so beautiful, eloquent and taciturn, smart and clever, strong and weak. We are endowed with a variety of talents and gifts, experiences and hopes, faith and love. We are the image of G*d!

Every one of us is made in G*d's very own image. G*d who created people in the divine image has gifted and called every one of us differently. The divine image is neither male nor female, white or black, rich or poor but multicolored and multi-gendered and more. We, the people, are G*d's visible representatives. Created in the Divine image we are equal. We are equal not only on grounds of creation but also on grounds of baptism. We are G*d's people, called and elect, holy in body and soul, gifted with the Spirit. In the words of 1 Peter, we "are a chosen race, a royal priesthood, a holy nation, G*d's very own people." As a richly gifted people we are the body of Christ in whom religious, racial, class, ethnic, and sexual status differences no longer exist. As a pilgrim people we may fail again and again, but we continue to struggle for living in fullness and for realizing our calling to the discipleship of equals. As the discipleship of equals we are church, the *ekklēsia* of wo/men in process.

We are called to be an Easter people, followers of Mary of Magdala; we are church, the *ekklēsia* of wo/men. Like Mary of Magdala and the other wo/men disciples we are commissioned to go and tell the "brothers" that they must abandon their compulsion to control and their fear of wo/men's autonomy and creativity. Jesus is going ahead to Galilee. Only among the people will they meet him. Whereas according to Matthew the male group of the twelve is sent by the Resurrected One to preach the gospel to the whole world, the wo/men apostles are sent to the male disciples to proclaim the good news of the Living One. They are called to empower the community of the Living One.

The Gospel traditions still transmit some of the names of the Galilean wo/men disciples who were sent as apostles to the apostles. These wo/men are not only said to be the first who proclaimed Jesus' resurrection, but they are also characterized as the primary witnesses to Jesus' execution and burial. Mary of Magdala was the most prominent of the Galilean disciples. According to tradition she was the first one to spread the good news of Easter.

The following historical scenario is most likely. Most of the Galilean disciples of Jesus fled after his arrest from Jerusalem and went back home to Galilee. Some of Jesus' wo/men disciples—foremost among them Mary of Magdala—did not flee after his arrest but stayed in Jerusalem for his execution and burial. These Galilean wo/men were also the first to articulate their conviction that G*d did not leave the executed Jesus in the grave but raised him from the dead. The early Christian confession that "Jesus the Nazarene who was executed on the cross was raised" is revealed first to the Galilean wo/men disciples of Jesus.

Those wo/men disciples who remained in the capital probably sought to gather together the dispersed disciples and friends of Jesus who lived in and around Jerusalem. Some of these wo/men in all likelihood soon also moved back to Galilee, their native country. Such a reconstruction of the events after the death and resurrection of Jesus is historically plausible, since it might have been easier for the wo/men of the Jesus movement to go "underground" than for the men. By keeping alive the good news of G*d's life-giving power in the resurrection of Jesus the executed one, among the followers and friends of Jesus, the Galilean wo/men continued the movement initiated by Jesus.

The apostleship of Mary of Magdala is corroborated by writings that did not make it into the canon. For instance, the writing *Sophia of Jesus Christ*, which is dated in the early second century, relates that the redeemer appeared to the twelve and the seven wo/men disciples who had followed him from Galilee to Jerusalem. Among the wo/men disciples only Mary Magdalene is singled out by name. The teachings of the Resurrected One conclude: "From that day on his disciples began to preach the Gospel of G*d, the eternal Father." The *Gospel of Thomas*, which is dated in the late first century, in turn alludes to the antagonism between Peter and Mary of Magdala, a theme more fully developed in the *Gospel of Mary (Magdalene)*, which is dated in the second century CE.

Mary of Magdala and the other wo/men apostles were told by the angel: "Go and tell the disciples that Jesus has risen." The male apostles did not believe them because they were women. Just as the wo/men apostles so also Christian feminists today are not heard and believed. As the Gospel text elaborates, such disbelief is caused by religious and cultural prejudices against wo/men rather than by fidelity to the gospel.

One can already detect in the Gospels this prejudice against wo/men and the tendency to downplay the crucial witness of the wo/men disciples. Mark's shorter ending leaves it unclear whether the wo/men acted on the angelic command. John tells the story in such a way that it is Peter and not Mary who receives the message that Jesus was raised from the dead. Luke stresses that "the words of the wo/men seemed to the eleven an idle tale and they did not believe them" (Luke 24:11).

The *Epistola Apostolorum*, an apocryphal document of the second century, also underscores the skepticism of the male disciples. In this version either Mary Magdalene and Sara or Martha and Mary are sent to announce to the apostles that Jesus has risen. However, the apostles did not believe them, even when Jesus himself corroborates their witness. Only after the eleven touch him do they know that "he has truly risen in the flesh."

In the third-century writing *Pistis Sophia* Mary Magdalene and John have a prominent place among the other disciples. Jesus himself stresses that these two will surpass all his disciples. Other wo/men disciples mentioned are Mary the mother of Jesus, Salome, and Martha. Mary Magdalene asks thirty-nine out of forty-six questions and plays a major role in giving interpretation. Peter's hostility toward her is apparent throughout the whole work. He objects, "My Lord, we shall not be able to endure this wo/man, for she takes our opportunity and she has not let any of us speak, but talks all the time herself." Mary in turn complains that she hardly dares to interpret the revelations received, because Peter who "hates the female race" intimidates her so much. However, she is told that anyone who receives insights and knowledge is obliged to speak, no matter whether one is a wo/man or a man. This argument between Peter and Mary Magdalene clearly reflects the debate in the early church on whether wo/men are the legitimate transmitters of apostolic teaching and tradition.

This conflict between Peter and Mary Magdalene is even more pronounced in the second-century *Gospel of Mary* that was discovered only at the end of the nineteenth century and is attributed by most scholars to Mary Magdalene. At the end of the first part, Mary Magdalene exhorts the disciples to go and proclaim the gospel despite their fear and anxiety. After the departure of Jesus the disciples are not willing to do so because they worry that they might suffer the same fate as did Jesus. Mary Magdalene assures them that the Savior will protect them and that they should not be afraid because he has made them manly.

The second part of this Gospel begins with Peter asking Mary Magdalene to share with them the revelation she has received from the Savior "who loved her more than other wo/men." But Peter and Andrew react with unbelief when she tells them about a vision she has received. Peter articulates the objection of the male disciples: "Did he then speak privily with a wo/man rather than with us and not openly? Has he preferred her over and against us?" Mary is offended and insists, weeping, that she has not invented her visions nor lied about the Savior. Levi comes to her defense and rebukes Peter: "Peter, you have ever been of hasty temper. Now I see you do exercise yourself against the wo/man like the adversaries. But if the Savior has made her worthy, who then are you to reject her? Certainly the Savior knows her well enough. Let us rather be ashamed, put on the perfect Man, as he has charged us, and proclaim the Gospel."

The conflict of authority between the tradition that proclaims Mary of Magdala as the first witness to the resurrection and the tradition that ascribes this apostolic preeminence to Peter becomes apparent if one compares the Easter stories of the Gospels and the resurrection tradition incorporated in 1 Cor. 15:3-6, which reads: "For I handed on to you as of first importance what I in turn had received: that Christ died for our sins in accordance with the scriptures, and that he was buried, and that he was raised on the third day in accordance with the scriptures, and that he appeared to Cephas, then to the twelve. Then he appeared to more than five hundred brothers at one time, most of whom are still alive, though some have died. Then he appeared to James, then to all the apostles. Last of all, as to one untimely born, he appeared also to me" (1 Cor. 15:3-8 NRSV).

This text does not mention wo/men at all but gives the place of eminence to Peter and the twelve. The enumeration of the various appearances of the Resurrected One—to Peter, the twelve, James, five hundred brethren, the apostles, and Paul—legitimates a male chain of authority. Paul quotes this tradition here because he wants to justify his own apostolic authority by asserting that he has seen the resurrected Christ. Such a proof was necessary because Paul could not claim to have known and been a disciple of Jesus himself.

The Gospel narratives about the passion and resurrection of Jesus of Nazareth are basically structured in the same way as the nucleus of 1 Cor. 15:3-5. However, the resurrection proclamation in the Easter stories differs from the early Christian confession quoted by Paul in three important ways:

First, the Easter message in the Gospels is given first to Mary of Magdala and to the other wo/men who have come to the gravesite.

Second, the message of the angel in Mark 16:6 ("Do not be afraid. You seek Jesus of Nazareth who was crucified. He was raised. He is not here . . . But go tell his disciples and Peter that he is going before you to Galilee; there you will see him as he told you" [see also Matt. 28:5-6].) speaks about the death of Jesus not in general terms but specifically as an execution by crucifixion. Moreover, the testimony "he was buried" in 1 Corinthians 15 is positively stated in the resurrection stories of the Gospels as "he is not here," that is, in the place where Jesus was buried, and the proclamation "he was raised" is the "proof" for it.

Third, the Easter message of the Gospels is a proclamation that requires action rather than a statement of confession. It is future oriented rather than backward looking: the wo/men "seek" Jesus among the dead but are told that the tomb is empty.

Hence, we must be careful not to read the Easter message of Mark 16:6 in light of Luke's account of the ascension tradition, according to which Jesus absents himself in Divine glory by returning from earth to heaven. We also must avoid understanding the "empty tomb" story in a literalist and rationalist modernist fashion debating whether the miracle of the empty tomb has actually happened. Whereas modern liberal scholarship questions whether such a miracle could have happened, liberation the*logians ask what kind of well-being was brought about by the miracle.

The miracle of resurrection spells hope. It means that Jesus, The Living One, goes ahead of us. The Living One can be found only in the experience that he opens up a future for us. The Gospels ascribe the proclamation of this "revelatory" experience and of the future-oriented "empty tomb" message primarily to wo/men, whereas the Pauline tradition associates the confessional articulation of resurrection primarily with men, which served as visionary legitimization of their authority.

The Gospel of "Matthew" combines both traditions—that of the "empty tomb" narrative and that of visionary legitimization—with each other but gives primary place to the wo/men witnesses. The text prohibits such a misreading, not only by connecting the visionary experience of the Resurrected One with the "open space" of the "empty tomb" and the "open road" pointing ahead to Galilee. It also does so by entrusting the resurrection proclamation to the witness of wo/men. With the assertion that the tomb is "empty," it insists on the bodily, material reality of resurrection as well as on the vindication of unjust suffering and death In this way the proclamation that "Jesus is the Living One who was vindicated and not left in death" is safeguarded from a spiritualized misreading.

It is difficult to say which tradition, that of the "empty tomb" associated with wo/men or that of the "visionary experience" authorizing men, was primary. Whatever the case might have been historically, to privilege the "wo/men's tradition" can inspire our own meaning making today in the face of societal and religious violence. The texts of the "empty tomb" tradition take suffering and death seriously but do not see them as having the "last word" or grant to suffering a religious-the*logical value in itself. Since G*d was absent in the execution of Jesus, the wo/men's presence under the cross is a witness to this absence. The tomb is the brutal final reality that eclipses G*d and vitiates all possibilities for the future. But the "tomb is empty!"

In contrast to the Gospels, the "visionary appearance" tradition of 1 Cor. 15:3-8 appeals to the male witnesses as authorities. Jesus is "absent"; he has gone back to heaven. His presence is only available in visionary form to a few: to male apostles, prophets, and specially gifted "spiritual" people. His death is no longer seen as an execution but as a "sacrificial atonement," no longer an indictment of brutal force but a willingly accepted victimization. The torture of crucifixion no longer indicts the political reality of imperial power and systemic victimization but has becomes a religious symbol. It valorizes all those the*logies that understand human suffering and victimization as "revelatory" of a higher, more important reality and of a greater, more valuable life as the life and well-being of those who are "crucified" daily.

In contrast, a critical spirituality of liberation engendered by the witness of Mary of Magdala and the wo/men disciples insists that G*d and the Resurrected One can only be found among the living ones. The Living One is not to be found among the dead. The Korean feminist the*logian Chung Hyun Kyung quotes a reflection by an Indian wo/man from a famine-stricken area as an example for such a spirituality that celebrates the Living One in a sociopolitical context of starvation: "Without food, there is no life. When starving people eat food, they experience G*d 'in every grain.' They 'know' and 'taste' G*d when they chew each grain. Food makes them alive. The greatest love of God for the starving people is food. When the grain from the earth sustains their life, they discover the meaning of the phrase, 'For God so loves this world.' When God gives them food through other concerned human beings, God gives them God's 'beloved child,' Jesus Christ."[4]

The stories of the "empty tomb" are ambiguous and open ended. They invite us to cultivate a spirituality that is inspired rather than threatened by such religious openness. They leave unknown what actually happened to the body of Jesus. In the face of the empty tomb the search for orthodox control and scientific certainty becomes questionable. Instead the story of the empty tomb valorizes a compassionate practices of honoring those who are unjustly killed in body or spirit. The empty tomb story celebrates wo/men as faithful witnesses who do not relinquish their commitment and solidarity with those who fall victim in the struggle against dehumanizing powers. Most importantly, it affirms that Jesus' struggle has not ended with execution and death. The tomb is empty!

The Living One is not going "away," to live in heavenly glory, not leaving us to struggle on our own. The "empty tomb" does not signify absence but presence: it announces the presence of the Resurrected One. According to Matthew the Resurrected One is present in the "little ones," in the struggles for survival and justice of those who are impoverished, hungry, imprisoned, tortured, and killed today. The Living One is going ahead—not going away— so the wo/men in the Gospels and we with them are told. Fear of brutal violence could not stop the witness of Mary of Magdala and the other wo/men. Neither will it stop us.

NOTES

[1] This sermon was given in Tokyo, Japan. I want to thank Dr. Satoko Yamaguchi for inviting me, organizing my visit to Japan, and preparing the lectures for publication. I am deeply grateful to her for introducing me to the Christian feminist community in Japan. The following literature has been consulted for this address/sermon: Susan Haskins, *Mary Magdalen. Myth and Metaphor* (New York: Harcourt Brace, 1994); Jane Schaberg, *The Resurrection of Mary Magdalene: Legends, Apocrypha and the Christian Testament* (New York: Continuum, 2002); Ann Brock, *Mary Magdalene, the First Apostle: The Struggle for Authority* (Cambridge: Harvard University Press, 2002); Karen King, *The Gospel of Mary of Magdala: Jesus and the First Woman Apostle* (Santa Rosa: Polebridge, 2003); Elaine Wainwright, *Toward a Feminist Critical Reading of the Gospel according to Matthew*, BZNW 60 (Berlin: de Gruyter, 1991), 284–318; Chung Hyun Kyung, *Struggle to be the Sun Again: Introducing Asian Women's Theology* (Maryknoll: Orbis, 1990); and Satoko Yamaguchi, *Mary and Martha: Women in the World of Jesus*, (Maryknoll: Orbis, 2002).

[2] Susan Haskins, *Mary Magdalene*, 96–97.

[3] Ibid., 65n15.

[4] Chung Hyun Kyung, *Struggle to Be the Sun Again*, 73.

16

Liberation, Unity, and Equality in Community

New Testament Case Studies

Introduction: An Incarnational Approach

The method suggested for this consultation sponsored by the Faith and Order department of the World Council of Churches in 1985 is not platonic or do-cetist but incarnational. Case studies about the relations of wo/men and men in society and church are the*logical reflections on very concrete experiences and ecclesial situations. Such a the*logical method is incarnational insofar as it does not begin with timeless ideas, principles, or doctrines but seeks to discover divine presence and salvation in and through the communal, social-political life-praxis of the church, and to name it the*logically.

This method rests on an understanding of the*logy "as emerging from the interaction between what we make of the Christian story and tradition and what we make of contemporary life. It is at these points of interaction that G*d is to be encountered and discovered."[1] In preparing these Bible studies, then, I sought consciously to follow this approach by analyzing three New Testament texts—Luke 13:10-17, Gal. 3:28, 1 Timothy, and Mark—in terms of their actual historical-social-ecclesial settings. Rather than elaborating theoretically my own the*logical hermeneutics of liberation, I decided to actualize it in the process of interpretation. The following is a summary account of these New Testament case studies in terms of a critical feminist the*logy of liberation.[2]

Luke 13:10-17: The Wo/man Bent Double and the Bondage of Wo/men

Only Luke's Gospel has the story of the wo/man who was bent over and could not stand upright (Luke 13:10-17).[3] She came to praise G*d in the synagogue where Jesus was teaching. In distinction to other miracle stories the wo/man makes no request for healing; it is Jesus who calls her and lays hands upon her. The wo/man straightens (literally "was straightened up," using the so-called divine passive construction), lifts up her head, stands upright, and continues to praise G*d. The story is simple: the wo/man was bent double, she had suffered from a "spirit of infirmity" for eighteen long years. She hears the call, feels the touch of Jesus, and experiences wholeness and freedom. As a liberated wo/man she stands upright and praises G*d, who has freed her from her bondage.

This story is connected with a controversy dialogue.[4] The leader of the synagogue objects that it was not necessary to break the Sabbath Torah. Jesus' response does not argue that he broke the Sabbath Torah in order to save life, since the illness was not fatal. Rather he did so in order to make the wo/man healthy and to free her from her infirmity. The point of comparison is: just as it is permitted to care for household animals on the Sabbath, so one can act for the welfare of a daughter of Israel. What is puzzling is that Jesus seems not to have heard the objection of the "ruler of the synagogue," whose precise point was that there are six days on which one could be healed. If the wo/man was bent double for eighteen long years, why could Jesus not wait a day longer?

The dialogue startles, and leads us to ask: Why *did* Israel observe the Sabbath? Since the Babylonian Exile, Sabbath observation was the ritual celebration of G*d's creation and Israel's election. While the head of the synagogue insists on a complete rest from work, Jesus heals the wo/man so that she is able to fulfill the purpose of the Sabbath — to praise G*d the creator of the world and the liberator of Israel. This means that a final aspect of this healing controversy is significant. This daughter of Israel was in the power of Satan, in a bondage that deformed her whole bodily being for eighteen long years. In freeing her from her bondage, G*d's power of salvation becomes manifest.[5]

The salvation of G*d's *basileia* (kingdom)[6] becomes available experientially whenever Jesus casts out demons, heals the sick and ritually unclean, or tells stories about the lost who are found, about the uninvited who are invited, or about the least who will be first. The power of G*d's new creation is realized in Jesus' table community with the poor, the sinners, the tax collectors, the prostitutes — with all those who do not "belong" because they are cultically deficient in the eyes of the pious and righteous. For Jesus and his movement the *basileia* does not spell cultic holiness but human wholeness. It is like the dough that has been leavened but not yet transformed into bread, like the fetus in the womb not yet transformed in birth to a child.

Although the future of G*d's new world can be experienced already in Jesus' healings, parables, and inclusive discipleship community, Jesus and his first followers, wo/men and men, nevertheless still hope and expect the future inbreaking of G*d's *basileia* when death, suffering, and injustice will finally be overcome. The Jesus movement's praxis and vision of the *basileia* is the mediation of G*d's future into the structures and life experiences of its own time and people. But this future is available to *all* members of the people of G*d; everyone is invited. Not the holiness of the elect but the wholeness and happiness of all is the central vision of the Jesus movement. The healing of the wo/man bent double reveals, and makes experientially available, the caring presence and power of the *basileia* at work in the words and praxis of the Jesus movement. Despite opposition from the religious leadership the common people recognize the wonderful things that have happened in their midst.[7]

I have chosen this text to begin our biblical reflections because this story has become one of the key texts of the wo/men's movement in the church. The wo/man bent double has become a paradigm for the situation of wo/men, not only in society but also in the church. We usually read biblical texts either as a confirmation of, or as a challenge to, our own Christian self-understanding.[8] If Christian the*logians and preachers identify with Jesus they will read the passage antisemitically, get angry with the leader of the synagogue, and feel religiously and morally superior to Judaism. Should churchmen identify with the leader of the synagogue, however, then they would find his statement to the crowd ("There are six days when one has to work; come on one of these to be cured") to be reasonable church policy—biblical or ecclesiastical law and tradition, after all, cannot be changed just because a wo/man is in bondage and is not able to stand upright. Reading the story in this way should give pause to ecclesiastical officials who use the Bible, tradition, ecumenical the*logy, and church unity to exclude wo/men from ecclesial and liturgical leadership, and thereby make it impossible for more and more wo/men to praise G*d today.

KYRIARCHY: CULTURE BENT DOUBLE AND THE BONDAGE OF WO/MEN

A feminist the*logical reading of this story must translate it into the language and structures of our own time. The miracle story understands the illness of the wo/man as bondage that was caused by Satan. Early Christian the*logy sees the world and human beings as caught up in the struggle between the life-destroying powers of evil and the life-giving power of G*d.[9] While in the last analysis these evil powers cannot frustrate the life-giving purpose of G*d, their power is still real and has its effects in the present world. Their hostility against life and human wholeness is expressed in their attempt to enslave human beings and ultimately in their crucifixion of Christ. Apocalyptic New Testament the*logy explains the execution of Jesus as caused by these cosmic and political powers, but not as willed by G*d.

Much Western New Testament scholarship, under the influence of Rudolf Bultmann, has sought to "demythologize" this apocalyptic language of mythic powers. In the process it is translated into the categories of existentialist philosophy; it is individualized and depoliticized.[10] A critical feminist the*logy of liberation, however, does not seek to demythologize this apocalyptic language but to translate it into sociopolitical language.

I have renamed patriarchy as kyriarchy, as a complex system of structural dependencies and individual oppressions, as the life-destroying power of Western society and religion. Kyriarchy is not to be understood solely in terms of male supremacy and misogynist sexism[11] but must be seen in terms of the systemic interaction of racism, classism, and sexism in Western militarist societies.[12] This Western understanding of kyriarchy was first articulated in Aristotelian political philosophy.[13] Aristotle did not define kyriarchy simply as the rule of all men over all wo/men, but as a gradated male status system of domination and subordination, authority and obedience, rulers and subjects in household and state. Wives, children, slaves, and property were owned and at the disposal of the freeborn Greek male head of the household. He was the full citizen who determined public life.[14] Since the democratic ideal invites the participation of all citizens, Aristotle has to legitimate the exclusion of freeborn wo/men and Greek-born slaves from democratic government.[15] Therefore, he defines their "nature" in terms of their subordinate status and social function, in order to argue that their "nature" does not make them fit to rule.

This basic contradiction between the democratic claim to the full equality of all human beings and their subordinate position in the kyriarchal structures of household and state has also defined Western Euro-American notions of democracy.[16] Although kyriarchy has been modified in the course of history, it has not been replaced by private or state capitalism. In feudalistic and slave societies freeborn wo/men as well as wo/men serfs and slaves were legally, economically, and sexually subject to the lord of the castle or the master of the house; in capitalist global kyriarchy all wo/men become dependent on the male heads of households.[17] Wo/men's social status is defined by the class, race, and nationality of the men to whom we belong.

Capitalist kyriarchy has generated a separate system of economics for wo/men: on the one hand, child-rearing and household maintenance are considered as wo/men's "natural vocation" (and therefore are not remunerated); on the other hand, wo/men's work outside the home is paid less because it is assumed that men are the breadwinners of the family. Moreover, wo/men's economic dependence is reinforced through "feminine" education and sexual violence in and outside the home.[18]

Insofar as the Aristotelian pattern of kyriarchal submission has been incorporated in the New Testament in the form of the household-code texts,[19] it has influenced Christian self-understanding and community throughout the centuries. The*logians such as Augustine[20] or Thomas of Aquinas[21] have woven this Aristotelian construct of the inferior human "natures" of slaves and freeborn wo/men into the basic fabric of Christian the*logy. Just as societal kyriarchy, so also religious Christian kyriarchy has defined not only wo/men but also subjugated peoples and races as "the other," as "nature" to be exploited and dominated by powerful men. It has defined wo/men and colonialized peoples not just as "the other" of white men, but also as subordinated and subjected to them. Obedience, economic dependence, and sexual control are the sustaining force of societal and ecclesiastical kyriarchy.

Such kyriarchal Christian the*logy has provided religious legitimizations of racism, colonialism, classism, and hetero/sexism in society and church. It has not only encouraged the sacrifice of people to authoritarian systems but also the exploitation of the earth and its resources. Its posture of divine domination and absolute power over the "other" has legitimated an imperialism and militarism that have brought us to the brink of nuclear annihilation.[22]

In short, a critical feminist the*logy of liberation names the*logically the kyriarchal bondage of wo/men in Western society and church.[23] Kyriarchy inculcates and perpetrates not only sexism but also racism and property-class relationships as basic structures of wo/men's oppression. In a kyriarchal society or religion all wo/men are bound into a system of male privilege and domination, but impoverished third-world wo/men constitute the bottom of the oppressive kyriarchal pyramid. Kyriarchy cannot be toppled except when the basis or bottom of the kyriarchal pyramid—which consists of the exploitation of multiply oppressed wo/men—becomes liberated.[24]

The black feminist poet June Jordan articulates this goal of feminist liberation not so much as freedom from men, but as a movement *into* self-love, self-respect, and self-determination. Such a self-love and self-respect, she argues, has the strength to love and respect wo/men who are "not like me" and to love and respect men "who are willing and able, without fear, to love and respect me."[25] Just as Jesus, who was born with the privileges of a Jewish male, focused attention on the wo/man bent double and insisted that she must be healed, so Christian men must recognize the kyriarchal exploitation and oppression of wo/men in society and church. They must not only reject all the*logies of subordination or of "wo/men's special nature and place" as kyriarchal ideologies, but must also relinquish their kyriarchal privileges and join wo/men in our struggle to end kyriarchal exploitation and bondage.[26]

Recognizing ourselves in the story of the wo/man bent double, we wo/men must identify ourselves *as wo/men* deformed and exploited by societal and ecclesiastical kyriarchy. Those of us who are privileged in terms of race, class, culture, and education must realize that as long as a single wo/man is not free, no wo/man is able to overcome kyriarchal infirmity and bondage. Just as the wo/man bent double did not ask for healing from the man Jesus, but came to the synagogue to praise G*d, so Christian wo/men must realize that our liberation will not come from the men in the churches.

As long as we who are privileged in terms of race, class, culture, or education identify with men who hold positions of power in society and church—

rather than with our sisters living on the bottom of the kyriarchal pyramid— we will not be able to realize that we suffer from the same kyriarchal bondage. Only when we see ourselves and our daughters in the wo/men who are today bent double in our midst, will we be able to articulate the*logically a vision of G*d's salvation and community that enables all wo/men to become free from kyriarchal dehumanization. Mutuality between wo/men and wo/men, wo/men and men is only possible when, in a feminist conversion, we reject the structural evil of kyriarchy and our personal collaboration in it.[27] The "preferential option for the poor" must be spelled out as a commitment to the liberation struggle of wo/men, since the majority of the poor are wo/men and children dependent on wo/men.

EQUALITY IN THE SPIRIT: THE BASIS OF CHRISTIAN COMMUNITY

Western kyriarchy was not invented by Christianity and the struggle against kyriarchal dehumanization was not initiated by Christians.[28] However, I would argue that the struggle with kyriarchal structures is constitutive for Christian faith and community from its very beginnings. Some exegetes have maintained to the contrary that the early Christian missionary movement outside Palestine was not in conflict with its society, but was well integrated into it. The radicalism of the Jesus movement was supposedly assimilated by the urban Hellenistic communities into a family-style "love patriarchalism," which perpetuated the hierarchical relationships of the patriarchal Greco-Roman household in a softer, milder form.[29]

However the textual basis for such a contention is not derived from the early Pauline literature but only from Acts, which was written at the end of the first century when Christian writers (for apologetic reasons) began to advocate the Aristotelian kyriarchal pattern of submission. It is not the patriarchal household, but the more egalitarian community structures of private *collegia* or cultic associations, which provided the organizational models for the early Christian missionary movement in the Greco-Roman cities.[30] This movement was suspect to Greco-Roman authorities not only because it accorded wo/men and slaves equal standing, but also because it was a religious cult from the Orient. Because it admitted *individuals* irrespective of their status in the patriarchal household, it stood in conflict with Greco-Roman kyriarchal society.

The the*logical self-understanding of this movement is rooted in the experiences of the Spirit. While the experience of G*d's gracious goodness in the ministry and life of Jesus is fundamental for the Jesus movement and its vision, the experience of the power of the Spirit is basic for the Christian missionary movement and its vision.[31] G*d did not leave Jesus in the power of death but raised him "in power" so that he becomes "a life-giving Spirit"

(1 Cor. 15:45). Christ is preached to Jews and Greeks as the "power of G*d" and the "sophia of G*d" (1 Cor. 1:24). The *basileia* of G*d does not consist in "mere talk" but in "power" (1 Cor. 4:20). Those who are "in Christ" are "filled with the Holy Spirit." Those who have been baptized into Christ, live by the Spirit (Gal. 5:25)—they are "pneumatics," Spirit-filled people (Gal. 6:1). Both wo/men and men have received spiritual gifts for the up-building of the body of Christ, the church. In the second century Justin still can assert that among the Christians *all*—wo/men and men—have received charisms from the Holy Spirit. This "equality" in the Spirit is summed up by the early Christian movement in the words of Galatians 3:28, which is today generally understood as a pre-Pauline baptismal confession.[32]

GALATIANS 3:28: AN INCARNATIONAL APPROACH

Traditional ecclesiology has often overlooked or explained away the ekklesial character of Gal. 3:28. Some the*logians still maintain that wo/men have a different role from men in the order of creation and redemption: in creation or in the natural order of society wo/men are assigned a position of subordination by G*d, while in the order of redemption all have equal standing. With respect to baptism and the gifts of the Spirit all are equal before G*d. But the sociological implications of this equal standing before G*d must not be applied either to society or the ministry of the church; it is given only in heaven or postponed until the eschatological future. While traditional the*logy insisted on the subordination and inferiority of wo/men, slaves, and Jews in society and church, the more recent "the*logy of wo/man" proceeds from the assumption of "equal but different" that postulates the ontological complementarity of wo/man and man. It is striking, however, that this the*logy no longer insists on a ontological symbolic" difference of race or class, but only on the symbolic difference of sex, which still must be lived out by wo/men in "subordination."[33]

Over and against such an interpretation of Galatians 3:28, which restricts equality and oneness to the soul or to one's standing before G*d, an incarnational the*logy insists that what happens in Christ through baptism manifests itself in the social dimensions of the church. In his commentary on Galatians Hans Dieter Betz observes that commentators "have consistently denied that Paul's statements have political implications." According to Betz they are prepared to state the opposite of what Paul actually says in order to preserve a "purely religious" interpretation. In doing so they can strongly emphasize the reality of equality before G*d sacramentally, and at the same time "deny that any conclusions can be drawn from this in regard to the ecclesiastical offices (!) and the political order."[34] The exegetical discussion linking Galatians 3:28 and the household code tradition,[35] however, points to a historical-political dynamic that does not come to the fore when it is forced into the traditional oppositions between "order of creation" and "order of redemption" on the one hand, and between "enthusiastic excess or gnostic heresy" and "Pauline the*logy or New Testament orthodoxy" on the other.

Understood as a baptismal confession, Galatians 3:28 expresses the ekklesial self-understanding of the early Christian missionary movement. In baptism Christians entered into a kinship relationship with people coming from very different racial, cultural, and national backgrounds. These kyriarchal status differences, however, do not determine the social structures of the community. Therefore both Jewish and gentile wo/men's status and role were drastically changed, since kyriarchal household structures did not determine the social structures of the Christian community.

This seems to be stated explicitly in the final pairing of the baptismal confession: "there is no male and female." This last pair differs in formulation from the preceding two, insofar as it does not speak of opposites but of male *and* female. Exegetes have speculated a good deal about the fact that "male and female" are used here, rather than "man and wo/man." It is sometimes argued that not only "the *social* differences [roles] between men and wo/men are involved but the *biological* distinctions" as well. Therefore, it is conjectured that Gal. 3:28 is gnostic and advocates androgyny.[36]

This argument, however, overlooks the fact that designations of the sexes in the neuter can simply be used in place of "woman and man."[37] Such designations do not imply a denial of biological sex differences. Galatians 3:28 probably alludes here to Gen. 1:27, where humanity created in the image of G*d is qualified as "male and female" in order to introduce the theme of procreation and fertility. Jewish exegetes understood "male and female," therefore, primarily in terms of marriage and family. Galatians 3:28 then does not assert that there are no longer men and wo/men in Christ, but that kyriarchal marriage relationships between male and female are no longer constitutive of the new community in Christ. Irrespective of their kyriarchal status in the household, persons will be full members of the Christian movement in and through baptism. Wo/men and men in the Christian community are not defined by their sexual procreative capacities or by their religious, cultural, or social gender-roles, but by their empowerment by the Spirit.

Not only sex or gender roles were considered in antiquity to be grounded in biological nature but also cultural, racial, and social differences. Although most would concede today that racial or class differences are not natural or biological (but rather cultural and social), gender differences are still proclaimed as given by nature or ordained by G*d. However, feminist studies have amply documented that most perceived gender differences are cultural-social.[38] We are socialized into gender roles as soon as we are born. Every culture gives different symbolic significance and derives different social roles from the human biological capacities of sexual intercourse, childbearing, and lactation. Sexual dimorphism and strictly defined gender roles are products of a kyriarchal culture, which maintain and legitimize structures of control and domination, that is, the exploitation of wo/men by men.

Galatians 3:28 does not only proclaim the abolition of religious-cultural divisions, and the exploitation wrought by institutional slavery, but also domination based on kyriarchal gender divisions. It asserts that within the Christian community no structures of dominance can be tolerated. Galatians 3:28 is therefore best understood as a communal Christian self-definition rather than as a statement about the soul of the individual. It proclaims that in the Christian community all distinctions of religion, race, class, nationality, and gender are insignificant. All the baptized are equal; they are one in Christ. Being baptized into Christ means entering the sphere of the resurrected One, the life-giving Spirit whose reality and power are manifested in the Christian community. It is not anthropological oneness but ecclesiological oneness or unity in Christ Jesus that is the goal of Christian baptism. The unity of the church comes to the fore in the ecclesial equality of all those baptized. Such equality is not restricted to baptism, but determines the organizational structures of the church.

The Household-Code Texts and Galatians 3:28: Subordination versus Equality in the Spirit

Insofar as the Christian community did not withdraw from society the early Christian missionary movement provided the experience, for those who came in contact with it, of alternative community in the midst of the Greco-Roman city. As an alternative association that accorded freeborn wo/men and slave initiates equal status and access to leadership roles, the Christian missionary movement was a "conflict movement" standing in tension with the kyriarchal institutions of slavery and family. Since Christians admitted to their membership freeborn wo/men as well as slave wo/men who continued to live in pagan households, tensions could arise not only within the community but even more so with respect to the larger society. The prescriptive post-Pauline exhortations of the household-code texts testify to these tensions. They seek to lessen these tensions in the face of accusations and harassment that Christians had to endure in Asia Minor.[39]

These household-code injunctions, which demand the subordination of slave and freeborn wo/men and young people, may also express the interests of the "owner and patron class," as some exegetes have suggested.[40] They could reflect the interests of Christian husbands and slave masters, heads of households, who felt that their prerogatives were being undermined. Of course it is difficult for us to decide whether or not such motivations played a role in these modifications of the Christian baptismal self-understanding. It is hard to know which admonitions to subordination were due to a genuine concern for the Christian group's embattled situation, and which arose from a defense of kyriarchal dominance couched in the*logical terms. We hear only one side of the story; the the*logical counterarguments by slaves or wo/men have not survived in history.[41]

To assume that such kyriarchal interests were at work is historically plausible, to the extent that the baptismal declaration of Gal. 3:28 runs counter to the general acceptance of male religious privilege among Greeks, Romans, Persians, and also Jews of the first century CE. It was a rhetorical commonplace that Hellenistic man was grateful to the gods because he was fortunate enough to be born a human being and not a beast, a Greek and not a Barbarian, a freeman and not a slave, a man and not a wo/man. Conversion and baptism into Christ, therefore, implied for privileged men a much more radical break with their former social status and religious self-understandings than it did for freeborn and slave wo/men.

While the baptismal declaration cited in Gal. 3:28 offered a liberating religious vision to freeborn and slave wo/men, it denied, within the Christian community, all male religious prerogatives based on kyriarchal status. Just as Jewish men had to abandon the notion that they alone were the chosen of G*d, so masters had to relinquish their power over slaves, and husbands, their power over wives and children. And for men, conversion to the Christian movement also meant relinquishing their religious prerogatives, since their social-political kyriarchal privileges were, at the same time, religious privileges.

It is often argued that it was impossible for the tiny Christian group to abolish the institution of slavery and other social hierarchies. That might have been the case or it might not. However, what is often overlooked is that relinquishment of religious male prerogatives within the Christian community *was* possible, and that such a relinquishment included the abolition of social privileges as well. Legal-societal and cultural-religious kyriarchal status privileges were no longer valid for Christians.[42] Insofar as this egalitarian Christian self-understanding did away with all kyriarchal privileges of religion, class, and caste, it allowed not only gentiles but also slave and freeborn wo/men to exercise leadership functions within the missionary movement.

It is also true that the pre-Pauline baptismal formula of Gal. 3:28 does not reflect the same notion of anthropological unification, and the same androcentric perspective, that has determined the understanding of equality found in later gnostic and patristic writings. According to various gnostic and patristic texts, becoming a disciple means for a wo/man becoming "male," "like man," and relinquishing her sexual powers of procreation, because the male principle stands for the heavenly, angelic, divine realm; whereas the female principle represents either human weakness or evil.[43] While patristic and gnostic writers could express the equality of Christian wo/men with men only as "manliness" or as abandonment of wo/men's sexuality, Gal. 3:28 does not extol maleness but the oneness of the body of Christ, the church, where all kyriarchal social, cultural, religious, national, and gender divisions, as well as all structures of domination, are rejected. Not the "love-patriarchalism" of the post-Pauline school but the ecclesial self-understanding of "equality in Christ" expresses the vision and praxis of the early Christian movement in the Greco-Roman world.

The Vision of Mark's Gospel: Equality in the Spirit, Discipleship, and Suffering

That this vision and praxis is still alive at the beginning of the second century is apparent not only from the prescriptive household-code texts, which advocate kyriarchal submission over and against an egalitarian ecclesial praxis, but also from the Gospels. Independent of each other, the evangelists called Mark and John have gathered traditional materials and stories about Jesus and his first followers and molded them into the Gospel form. They did so not because of antiquarian interest in the life of Jesus—now past—but because they believed that the resurrected One was, at that very moment, speaking to their communities through the words and deeds of Jesus of Nazareth.

Both Mark and John[44] emphasize service and love as the core of Jesus' ministry and as the central demand of discipleship. The Gospel of Mark was written at approximately the same time as Colossians, which marks the beginnings of the kyriarchal household-code trajectory, or line of development. The final redaction of the Gospel of John emerges at about the same time as the Pastoral Epistles and the letters of Ignatius, and might address the same communities in Asia Minor. It is, therefore, significant that the first writers of the Gospels articulate a very different vision of Christian discipleship and community than that presented by the writers of the injunctions to kyriarchal submission, although both address Christian communities in the last third of the first century.

Discipleship in Mark is understood as a literal following of Jesus and of his example. Mark's christological emphasis, however, is on the necessity of Jesus' suffering, execution, and death. Suffering is not an end in itself, but it is the outcome of Jesus' life-praxis of solidarity with the social and religious outcasts of his society. The threefold announcement of Jesus' suffering in Mark 8:22–10:52 is followed each time by the disciples' misunderstanding and by Jesus' call to discipleship as a following on the way to the cross. Just as rejection, suffering, and execution as a criminal are the outcome of the preaching and life-praxis of Jesus, so will they be the fate of the true disciple. In Mark's view this is the crucial christological insight that determines both Jesus' ministry and Christian discipleship.[45]

This the*logy of suffering is developed for Christians who are persecuted, handed over to Sanhedrins, beaten in synagogues, and standing trial before kings and governors "for Jesus' sake" (Mark 13:9). Such persecutions are instigated by their closest relatives and friends: "Brother will betray brother to death, and the father his child; children will rise against their parents and have them put to death" (Mark 13:12). Thus the Markan Gospel situates the persecutions and sufferings of its community in the context of tensions within their own households. While the writers of 1 Peter or the Pastoral Epistles seek to lessen these tensions by advocating adaptation to the dominant kyriarchal Greco-Roman society, the Markan Jesus clearly states that giving offense and experiencing suffering must not be shunned. A true disciple of Jesus must expect suffering, hatred, and persecution.

In conclusion, I have read Mark's the*logy in light of early Christian developments at the end of the first century, not by construing hypothetical "heretical opponents," but by placing this Gospel in the context of other New Testament writings. The Markan community gathers in house-churches. It struggles to avoid the kyriarchal pattern of dominance and submission that characterizes its sociopolitical environment. Those who are the farthest from the center of religious and political power—slaves, children, poor, gentiles, wo/men—become the paradigms of true discipleship.

Most of our New Testament literature was written to Christian communities in the last third of the first century or at the beginning of the second. These communities seem to have experienced tensions with (and even persecutions by) their kyriarchal Greco-Roman society. These tensions were not only religious but also social-political. In order to lessen the threat of persecution, the post-Pauline writers sought to lessen these tensions between the Christian community and Greco-Roman society, by adapting the alternative Christian missionary movement to the kyriarchal structures and values of their Greco-Roman environment and Asian culture.

The writers of the primary Gospels, Mark and John, choose a different approach. Written around the same time as Colossians and Ephesians, Mark's Gospel insists that suffering and persecutions engendered by an alternative form of community and lifestyle must not be avoided. Whereas the advocates of the household-code texts appeal to Paul or Peter to legitimize their injunctions for submission and adaptation to Greco-Roman kyriarchal structures, the writers of Mark's and John's Gospels appeal to Jesus himself to support their stress on love and service, a love and service that is demanded not from the slaves and the lowliest in the community but from masters and would-be leaders, not from wo/men but from men.

While for apologetic reasons the post-Pauline writers seek to limit freeborn and slave wo/men's leadership in the community to roles that are culturally and religiously acceptable, the evangelist known as Mark insists on "equality from below" in the familial community of disciples and therefore highlights the paradigmatic discipleship of the apostolic wo/men followers of Jesus. In historical retrospective, the post-Pauline writers' the*logical stress on the submission of the subordinate members in kyriarchal household and church has won out over the early Christian vision and praxis of the discipleship community of equals.

However, this historical success of the Greco-Roman societal pattern of kyriarchal submission must not be justified the*logically today just because it can claim a longer tradition. Rather it must be assessed the*logically in terms of the early Christian vision of the discipleship of equals. By insisting on it the writer of Mark's Gospel, like other New Testament writers, has kept this vision alive in the church. The inclusion of this vision into the canon has spawned reform movements throughout the centuries. It has made it impossible for Christian churches to forget Jesus' invitation to realize the discipleship community of equals. Church unity and community must not be bought at the expense of this vision. Only when the church rejects all kyriarchal structures of domination and exploitation will it be able to offer a vision of community for a human future that is not sustained by domination and exploitation.

NOTES

[1] Mary Tanner, "Unity and Renewal: The Church and the Human Community," *Ecumenical Review* 36, (1984): 254.

[2] See my articles "Feminist Theology as a Critical Theology of Liberation," *Theological Studies* 36 (1975): 606–26, and "Claiming the Center: A Critical Feminist The*logy of Liberation," *Women's Spirit Bonding*, ed. M. Buckley and J. Kalven, 293–309 (New York: Pilgrim, 1984). See also I. Carter Heyward, "An Unfinished Symphony of Liberation," *Journal of Feminist Studies in Religion* 1, no. 1 (1985): 99–118; Renate Rieger, "Inhaltliche und methodische Voraussetzungen einer Feministischen Theologie als Befreiungsthelogie," *Schlangenbrut* 13 (1985): 26–30.

[3] See J. Wilkinson, "The Case of the Bent Woman in Luke 13:10-17," *Evangelical Quarterly* 49 (1977): 195–205; J. Fitzmyer, *The Gospel according to Luke 10–24*, Anchor Bible 28A (Garden City: Doubleday, 1985), 1009–1014.

[4] For a review of the Sabbath-healing controversies, see C. Dietzfelbinger, "Vom Sinn der Sabbatheilungen Jesu," *Evangelische Theologie*, 38 (1978): 281–97; A. Hultgren, *Jesus and His Adversaries* (Minneapolis, Augsburg, 1979), 111–15; L. Schottroff and W. Stegemann, *Jesus von Nazareth: Hoffnung der Armen*, (Stuttgart, Kohlhammer, 1978), 15–28.

[5] The structural analysis of Antoinette C. Wire, "The Structure of the Gospel Miracle Stories and Their Tellers," *Semeia* 11 (1978): 83–113, shows that the structure of the New Testament miracle story consists in a juxtaposition of an oppressive situation and the breaking open of it.

[6] For a review of the literature on the *basileia* (kingdom) message of Jesus and its interpretation in Christian literature, see N. Perrin, *Jesus and the Language of the Kingdom: Symbol and Metaphor in New Testament Interpretation* (Philadelphia: Fortress Press, 1976), 15–88. See also his earlier book *The Kingdom of God in the Teaching of Jesus* (Philadelphia: Westminster, 1963) and W.G. Kümmel, *The Theology of the New Testament* (Nashville: Abingdon, 1973), 32–39.

[7] For such an interpretation and bibliographical documentation, see my book *In Memory of Her: A Feminist The*logical Reconstruction of Christian Origins* (New York: Crossroads, 1983), 105–59.

[8] For an elaboration of this hermeneutical perspective, see J. Sanders, "Hermeneutics," *The Interpreters Dictionary of the Bible: Supplementary Volume* (Nashville: Abingdon, 1976), 402–7.

[9] For a review of the New Testament materials but with a somewhat different approach, see Walter Wink, *Naming the Powers: The Language of Power in the New Testament*, vol. 1 (Philadelphia: Fortress Press, 1984). See also my book *The Book of Revelation: Justice and Judgment* (Philadelphia: Fortress Press, 1985), for an apocalyptic the*logy of power.

[10] For an excellent critique of R. Bultmann's program, see Dorothee Sölle, *Political Theology* (Philadelphia, Fortress, 1974).

[11] See, for example, Elisabeth Wendel Moltmann, *Das Land wo Milch und Honig fliesst: Perspectiven einer feministischen Theologie*, STB Seibenstern 486 (Gütersloh: Mohn, 1985), 37–50.

[12] Feminist literature often uses the term patr*iarchy* as synonymous with "sexism" or "androcentric dualism." However such understanding of patriarchy in terms of male-female dualism or masculine privilege cannot explain the interaction of racism, classism, sexism, and imperialist militarism in modern industrialized societies. For a discussion of the different meanings of patriarchy in feminist literature see V. Beechy, "On Patriarchy," *Feminist Review* 1 (1979), 66–82.

[13] E. Baker ed., *The Politics of Aristotle* (New York: Oxford University Press, 1962); L. Lange, "Woman Is Not a Rational Animal: On Aristotle's Biology of Reproduction"; E. V. Spellman, "Aristotle and the Politization of the Soul"; and J. Hicks, "The Unit of Political Analysis: Our Aristotelian Hangover." All three articles are in S. Harding and M. B. Hintikka eds., *Discovering Reality: Feminist Perspectives on Epistemology, Metaphysics, Methodology, and Philosophy of Science* (Boston: Reidel, 1983), 1–43.

[14] E. C. Keuls, *The Reign of the Phallus: Sexual Politics in Ancient Athens* (New York, Harper and Row, 1985).

[15] The contradiction between the kyriarchal social structures and the democratic ideals of the Athenian city-state has been pointed out especially by M. B. Arthur, "Women in the Ancient World," in *Conceptual Frameworks of Studying Women's History* (New York: Sarah Lawrence College Press, 1975), 1–15; "Liberated Women: the Classical Era," in R. Bridenthal and C. Koonz, eds., *Becoming Visible: Women in European History* (Boston: Mifflin, 1977), 60–89.

[16] See especially the study of Susan Moller Okin, *Women in Western Political Thought* (Princeton: Princeton University Press, 1979); and H. Schröder, "Feministische Gesellschaftstheorie," and "Das Recht der Väter," in L. F. Pusch, ed., *Feminismus: Inspektion der Herrenkultur* (Frankfurt: Suhrkamp, 1983), 449–506.

[17] See Z. L. Eisenstein, *The Radical Future of Liberal Feminism* (New York, Longman, 1981); H. Hartmann, "Capitalism, Kyriarchy, and Job Segregation by Sex," in Abel and Abel, eds., *The Signs Reader: Women, Gender, and Scholarship* (Chicago: Chicago University Press, 1983), 193–225; and D. K. Lewis, "A Response to Inequality: Black Women, Racism, and Sexism," 169–99, on the double and triple jeopardy of poor and minority women.

[18] The literature on sexual violence against women and children is too extensive to be listed here. See, for example, K. Barry, *Female Sexual Slavery* (New York: Avon, 1979); F. Rush, *The Best Kept Secret: Sexual Abuse of Children* (New York: McGraw Hill, 1980), and the review of the literature by W. Brines and L. Gordon, "The New Scholarship on Family Violence," *Signs* 8 (1983): 490–531.

[19] Such texts of kyriarchal submission are: Rom. 13:1-7; Col. 3:18—4:1; Eph. 5:22—6:9; 1 Pet. 2:18—3:7; 1 Timothy 2:11-15; 5:3-8; 6:1-2; Titus 2:2-10; 3:1-2; 1 Clement 21:6-8; Polycarp 4:2-6:1; Didache 4:9-11; Barnabas 19:5-7. See my discussion of these texts and their interpretation in *Bread Not Stone: The Challenge of Feminist Biblical Interpretation* (Boston: Beacon, 1984), 65–92.

[20] See K. Thraede, "Augustin—Texte aus dem Themenkreis 'Frau,' 'Gesellschaft,' und 'Gleichheif,'" *Jahrbuch für Antike und Christentum* 22 (1979): 70–97.

[21] See K. E. Borresen, *Subordination and Equivalence: The Nature and Role of Women in Augustine and Thomas of Aquinas* (Washington, DC: University of America Press), 1981.

[22] See the trenchant criticism of life-destroying structures in Christianity by M. Daly, *Beyond God the Father: Toward a Philosophy of Women's Liberation* (Boston: Beacon, 1973), and *Gyn/Ecology: The Metaethics of Radical Feminism* (Boston: Beacon, 1978); Rosemary Radford Ruether, *New Woman,*

New Earth: Sexist Ideologies and Human Liberation (New York: Crossroads, 1975); B. Wildung Harrison, *Making the Connections: Essays in Feminist Social Ethics* (Boston: Beacon, 1985); E. Sorge, "Feministische Theologie mit oder ohne Göttin?," *Schlangenbrut* 12 (1986): 14–21; and the contributions of Ynestra King, "Making the World Live: Feminism and the Domination of Nature," and M. Condren, "Patriarchy and Death," in Buckley and Kalven, eds, *Women's Spirit Bonding*, 56–64 and 172–89.

[23] See my "Breaking the Silence—Becoming Visible," in Elisabeth Schüssler Fiorenza and M. Collins, eds., *Women Invisible in Church and Theology*, Concilium 181 (Edinburgh, T and T Clark, 1975), 3–16.

[24] See bell hooks, *Feminist Theory: From Margin to Center* (Boston: South End, 1984), and the articles on "Racism, Pluralism, Bonding," in Buckley and Kalven, 67–136.

[25] June Jordan, *Civil Wars* (Boston, Beacon, 1981), 143.

[26] Katie G. Cannon, "The Emergence of Black Feminist Consciousness," in L. Russell ed., *Feminist Interpretation of the Bible* (Philadelphia: Westminster, 1985), 30–40; D. Williams, "Women's Oppression and Life-Line Politics in Black Women's Religious Narratives," *Journal of Feminist Studies in Religion* 1, no. 2 (1985): 59–72.

[27] See my "Sexism and Conversion," *Network* 9 (1981): 15–22; and Cooey, "The Power of Transformation and the Transformation of Power," *Journal of Feminist Studies in Religion* 1, no. 1 (1985): 23–26.

[28] Neither should Jesus be understood over against Jewish "kyriarchy," an interpretation also found in feminist literature. See most recently E. Sorge, *Religion und Frau: Weibliche Spiritualität im Christentum* (Stuttgart: Kohlhammer, 1985), and her articles in *Schlangenbrut*. J. Plaskow, a Jewish feminist, has consistently deplored the anti-Judaism in Christian feminist writings; see, for example, "Christian Feminism and Anti-Judaism," *Cross Currents* 28 (1978): 306–15; and "Blaming Jews for Patriarchy," *Lilith* 7 (1980): 11–17. For the leadership of Jewish wo/men in the synagogue see B. Brooten, *Women Leaders in the Ancient Synagogue*, Brown Judaic Studies 36 (Chico: Scholars, 1982).

[29] See, for example, Gerd Theissen, *Sociology of Early Palestinian Christianity* (Philadelphia: Fortress Press, 1978), and *The Social Setting of Pauline Christianity: Essays on Corinth* (Philadelphia: Fortress Press, 1982). What Theissen calls "love patriarchalism," B. Malina terms "maternal-uncle-archy" or "emarchy" within dominantly patriarchal or patrilineal societies, *Christian Origins and Cultural Anthropology: Practical Models for Biblical Interpretation* (Atlanta: John Knox, 1986). Yet neither Theissen nor Malina questions critically the sociological or anthropological models that are assumed by their own model for the reconstruction of early Christian history.

[30] For a discussion of the different organizational forms available, see A. J. Malherbe, *Social Aspects of Early Christianity* (Philadelphia: Fortress Press, 1983); Wayne A. Meeks, *The First Urban Christians: The Social World of the Apostle Paul* (New Haven: Yale University Press, 1983); J. E. Stambaugh and D. L. Balch, *The New Testament in Its Social Environment* (Philadelphia: Westminster, 1986).

[31] For a fuller elaboration and bibliography, see *In Memory of Her*, 160–204. See also G. Lohfink, *Jesus and Community: The Social Dimension of Christian Faith* (Philadelphia: Fortress Press, 1984).

[32] For a discussion of the literature see H. D. Betz, *Galatians*, Hermeneia (Philadelphia: Fortress Press, 1979); H. Paulsen, "Einheit und Freiheit der Söhne Gottes—Gal. 3:26-29," *ZNW* 71 (1980): 74–95, and *In Memory of Her*, 205–41.

[33] For a critique of such interpretations developed especially in the controversy around women's ordination, see Krister Stendahl, *The Bible and the Role of Women* (Philadelphia: Fortress Press, 1966).

[34] Betz, *Galatians*, 189.

[35] For example, J. E. Crouch, *The Origin and Intention of the Colossian Haustafel*, FRLANT 109 (Göttingen: Vandenhoeck und Ruprecht, 1972), speaks of "enthusiastic excesses" of slaves and women inspired by Gal. 3:28. Different is D. Lührmann, "Wo man nicht mehr Sklave und Freier ist: Überlegungen zur Struktur frühchristlicher Gemeinden," *Wort und Dienst* 13 (1975): 53–83.

[36]See, for example, Wayne A. Meeks, "The Image of the Androgyne: Some Use of a Symbol in Earliest Christianity," *History of Religions* 13 (1974): 165–208.

[37]For textual material, see M. de Merode, "Une théologie primitive de la femme?," *Revue théologique de Louvain* 9 (1978): 176–84.

[38]The literature on the topic is vast, although biblical scholars are for the most part unaware of it. For a review of the discussion, see A. Oakely, *Subject Women* (New York: Pantheon, 1981); A. M. Jaggar, *Feminist Politics and Human Nature* (Totowa: Rowman and Allanheld, 1983); Lewontin/Rose/Kamin, eds., *Not in Our Genes: Biology, Ideology, and Human Nature* (New York: Pantheon, 1984); C. Burton, *Subordination: Feminism and Social Theory* (Winchester: Allen and Unwin, 1985).

[39]C. F. K. Thraede, "Zum historischen Hintergrund der Haustafeln des Neuen Testaments," *JAC Ergänzungsband* 8 (1981): 359–68; D. Lührmann, "Neutestamentliche Haustafeln und Antike Ökonomie," *NTS* 27 (1981): 83–91; D. L. Balch, *Let Wives Be Submissive: The Domestic Code in 1 Peter*, SBLM 26 (Chico: Scholars, 1981).

[40]See, for example, E. A. Judge, *The Social Pattern of Christian Groups* (London: Tyndale, 1969), 60–71.

[41]However, S. L. Davies, *The Revolt of the Widows: The Social World of the Apocryphal Acts* (Carbondale: Southern Illinois University Press, 1980), and D. R. MacDonald, *The Legend and the Apostle: The Battle for Paul in Story and Canon* (Philadelphia: Westminster, 1983) argue that such counterarguments are still found in the Apocryphal Acts.

[42]See, for example, D. C. Verner, *The Household of God: The Social World of the Pastoral Epistles*, SBLDiss 71 (Chico: Scholars, 1983), for the literature.

[43]See E. H. Pagels, *The Gnostic Gospels* (New York: Random, 1979); G. H. Tavard, *Woman in Christian Tradition* (Notre Dame: Notre Dame University Press, 1973).

[44]For discussion of the literature and interpretation, see *In Memory of Her*, 316–42.

[45]For literature and discussion of Mark, see introductions to the New Testament, for example, Helmut Koester, *Introduction to the New Testament*, vol. 2, *History and Literature of Early Christianity*, (Philadelphia: Fortress Press, 1982), 164–71.

17

Bread/Rice of Wisdom

Interpretation for Liberation

In the past decade or so, Christian feminist the*logians have rediscovered the significance of Divine Wisdom-Sophia as the other name and face of the Creator G*d. Although biblical scholarship has pointed to the importance of the biblical wisdom traditions for quite some time, it has been feminist the*logy and liturgy that have made Divine Wisdom present and recognizable again among the people of G*d. Divine Wisdom is not exclusive of other religious traditions but is at work in different ways among all peoples, cultures, and religions. Divine Wisdom teaches justice, prudence, and well-being. She embraces creation in its living beauty and manifold variety and sustains everything and everyone. She is present as the Wise Wo/man of the ancients and indigenous peoples or as a Wisdom Goddess in diverse religions. As her messengers, feminist the*logians seek to extend her invitation and make her voice heard among her people.

> Wisdom has built her house
> She has set up her seven pillars
> She has slaughtered her beasts
> She has mixed her wine
> She has also set her table
> She has sent out her wo/men servants
> to call from the highest places in the town . . .
> Come eat of my bread
> and drink of the wine I have mixed.
> Leave foolishness and live
> and walk in the way of Wisdom.[1]

This lecture will explore how feminist the*logians as the "wo/men servants" of Divine Wisdom seek to "walk in her ways" by positioning biblical interpretation within a justice-seeking community. In her name we develop the*logy as sophialogy, as a wisdom theory—that is, as a new way of seeing or comprehending the world and the Divine.[2] To that end we seek to overcome the centuries of wo/men's silencing and second-class citizenship in society, religion, and church. In a first step I will explore how their search for different methods, frameworks, and approaches of interpretation attempts to render the Scriptures as the nourishing bread of Wisdom rather than as the stone that upholds wo/men's oppressions. In a second step I will then attempt to display how such a critical interpretation for liberation or sophialogical hermeneutics works.

In short, in this chapter I will engage such a critical sophialogical hermeneutics for a historical reading of the Gospel story of the Syrophoenician or Canaanite wo/man and its diverse interpretations. I will also attempt to show how the meaning of a biblical *text* is determined by contemporary sociocultural practices. Both of my arguments seek to introduce the never-ending process of a feminist biblical interpretation for liberation to which Divine Wisdom invites us today. They circle around the problem of how to articulate a Wisdom-vision of biblical identity, community, and praxis that is not exclusivist, triumphalist, or oppressive but helps to create a common religious ground for a worldwide feminist praxis of solidarity in the twenty-first century.

Such a sophialogical theory or vision has been articulated by Anna Julia Cooper, an African feminist foresister, more than a hundred years ago:

> It is not the intelligent woman versus the ignorant woman; nor the white woman versus the black, the brown, and the red—it is not even the cause of woman versus man. Nay, it is woman's strongest vindication for speaking that the world needs to hear her voice. It would be subversive of every human interest that the cry of one half of the human family be stifled. Woman . . . daring to think and move and speak—to undertake to help shape, mold, and direct the thought of her age, is merely completing the circle of the world's vision. Hers is every interest that has lacked an interpreter and a defender. Her cause is linked with that of every agony that has been dumb—every wrong that needs a voice. . . . The world has had to limp along with the wobbling gait and one-sided hesitancy of a man with one eye. Suddenly the bandage is removed from the other eye and the whole body is filled with light. It sees a circle where before it saw a segment. The darkened eye restored, every member rejoices with it.[3]

A critical sophialogy of liberation, I submit, seeks to articulate such a different theo-ethical vision and religious imagination, in order to correct and complete the world's and the church's one-sided vision. It seeks to restore the world's full spiritual vision by correcting the fragmentary circle of religious vision and by changing our one-sided and biased perception of the Bible as the Word and G*d.

BIBLICAL TEXT AND INTERPRETATION AS A SITE OF STRUGGLE

It is a common popular misunderstanding that feminist biblical interpretation focuses primarily on stories and texts about "woman in the Bible" or that it is only of interest to wo/men. Such a misconception overlooks that feminist biblical readings committed to the struggle for changing structures of domination cannot limit themselves simply to androcentric (that is, male-centered) or better kyriocentric (that is, elite male, slave-master, lord, father, centered) texts about wo/men. They also cannot identify uncritically with the wo/men characters of the Bible because these often represent the kyriocentric values and perspectives of their authors. Rather, feminist liberationist biblical studies first of all have to unmask and highlight the kyriocentric character of all biblical texts and their ideological functions for inculcating and legitimating the kyriarchal (that is, rule of the slavemaster, lord, father, husband) determined social order. Hence, they adopt methods of interpretation that can demystify kyriocentric scriptural texts and empower wo/men to resist the spiritual kyriarchal authority of the text over them.

A critical feminist interpretation for liberation that reads the Bible with the lens and in the context of wo/men struggling for changing the oppressive kyriarchal structures of religious, cultural, and societal texts and institutions therefore must be distinguished from both apologetic the*logical wo/men's studies and academic wo/man's or gender studies. Popular and academic biblical readings by wo/men, reading the Bible as a woman and from the perspective of wo/men, as well as biblical interpretation in terms of gender are not simply identical with the interpretation of a critical feminist hermeneutics, insofar as these modes of reading do not problematize their pre-given cultural-religious gender lens of interpretation.

This crucial methodological difference in the approach of wo/men or gender readings of the Bible and those of a critical feminist interpretation for liberation is not understood when it is argued that a critical feminist liberation the*logical interpretation remains entrapped in the doubt and skepticism of the Enlightenment. It allegedly moves from a hermeneutics of suspicion to a "reclaiming of the text" rather than starting with "reading a text naively, opening ourselves to its dynamic in the way children listen to stories."[4] Instead of putting the proverbial feminist label on all biblical texts, "Caution: could be dangerous to your health and survival," an approach that is primarily interested in the recuperation of Bible and tradition rather than in the conscientization of wo/men warns: "If we begin reading Scripture in a suspicious frame of mind presupposing its androcentrism (or whatever), our interpretation can become entrapped, at best in a 'neutral' reading that ignores the place of faith and the Spirit, and at worst in negativity, prejudice, self-projection, and the desire for control."[5]

Yet, such a warning does not recognize that a "hermeneutics of sus-picion" has its roots not in the rationalism of the Enlightenment but in Christianity's emancipatory impulses as well as a realistic acknowledgment of sinful structures and people. It also overlooks the careful distinction between androcentrism/ kyriocentrism as a symbolic/linguistic ideological system and patriarchy/kyriarchy as a sociopolitical system of dominations and subordin-ations. Since andro-kyriocentrism is a property of biblical language, grammar, and text, feminist critical readings do not presuppose "androcentrism" but seek to recognize, analyze, and deconstruct it in the act of reading.

As long as Scripture is used not only against wo/men struggling for emancipation and in support of kyriarchy[6] but also to shape wo/men's self-understandings and lives, a feminist biblical interpretation has to enable wo/men to engage texts critically, to reclaim their spiritual authority for adjudicating what they read, and to value the process of biblical readings as a process of conscientization. Hence, a critical feminist interpretation for liberation does not understand the Bible as a prescriptive blueprint of G*d's revelation but rather as an open-ended paradigm or a multilayered parable of Divine Wisdom-Sophia.

In its search for justice and liberation feminist biblical interpretation confronts two seemingly contradictory hermeneutical insights. On the one hand, the Bible is written in androcentric language, has its origin in the patriarchal cultures of antiquity, and has functioned throughout its history for inculcating misogynist mind-sets and oppressive values. On the other hand, the Bible has also been experienced as inspiring and authorizing wo/men and other non-persons in their struggles against kyriarchal oppressions.

Christian liberationist studies from the perspective of wo/men have made this latter point by stressing that the Bible and religion have not just served to oppress wo/men. Rather, in the experience of their communities religions and Scriptures also have authorized and energized wo/men in their struggles for liberation. Whereas those feminist scholars who seek to defend biblical religion tend to downplay its kyriocentric-kyriarchal character, postbiblical feminists tend to declare the contention that the Bible has been read by wo/men in a liberating way as an instance of "false consciousness." Feminist biblical studies in one way or the other presuppose and continue to wrestle with this either-or alternative.

A critical interpretation for liberation, I have argued in the past twenty years or more, must not deny or ignore this feminist conflict and debate but must reconceptualize feminist biblical studies and the Bible as sites of struggle. Biblical interpretation and biblical texts are best understood as a feminist site of struggle over the production of oppressive or liberative meaning and author-ity. Therefore, a feminist sophialogy must articulate the religious-the*logical agency of wo/men and underscore wo/men's authority to participate in the critical construction and assessment of religious, biblical, and the*-ethical meanings. In reclaiming the authority of wo/men as religious-the*logical subjects for shaping and determining biblical religions, my own feminist work has attempted to reconceptualize the act of biblical interpretation as a moment in the global praxis for liberation.

A critical feminist interpretation for liberation conceptualized as a site of struggle over meaning and authority/power is best understood as an actualization of the *ekklēsia* of wo/men at work, understood as a "congress" of ecumenical, interreligious, multicultural, and global voices. By interfacing the particular struggles of wo/men in society with those in the Christian churches and other world religions, it seeks to transform traditional the*logical discourses. Just as other religious feminists desire to change their own kyriarchal religious homebase, so Christian feminists attempt to do so by introducing wo/men as new thinking and speaking subjects into the*logy and the study of religion. By critically reflecting on their own location within institutionalized biblical religions and the academy, feminist biblical interpreters are able to claim their own religious voice, heritage, and community in the struggle for liberation.

By focusing on the struggles and survival of those women who live at the bottom of the kyriarchal pyramid, Christian feminists can glimpse the power of Divine Wisdom because wo/men struggling at the bottom of the kyriarchal pyramid for survival and well-being reveal the fulcrum of dehumanizing oppression threatening every wo/man. Hence, a feminist critical interpretation for liberation commences with a systemic sociocultural analysis and reflection on the experience of wo/men on the bottom of society and religion. It insists on the hermeneutical priority of feminist struggles in order to be able not only to disentangle the ideological (religious-the*logical) functions of biblical texts for inculcating and legitimating the kyriarchal order but also to explain their potential for fostering justice and liberation.[7]

Feminist literary critics have pointed out that readers do not engage texts in "themselves." Rather, insofar as readers have been taught how to read, they activate reading paradigms.[8] Both professional and nonprofessional readers draw on the "frame of meaning"[9] or contextualization provided by shared symbolic-religious constructions of social-cultural worlds. Feminist biblical interpretations that prioritize wo/men's struggles against multiplicative oppressions are able to become conscious of the ways in which their readings are determined by such malestream doctrinal, the*logical, spiritual, or theoretical frameworks.

Moreover, reading paradigms organize the practice of reading insofar as they relate texts, readers, and contexts to one another in specific ways. For example, whereas a dogmatic reading paradigm relates biblical texts, readers, and contexts in terms of church doctrine, a historical reading paradigm seeks the text's "original" meaning and social situation, and a literary analytic paradigm traces the narrative strategies and symbolic world constructions of biblical texts. Thus a dogmatic reading, for instance, of the story of the Syrophoenician wo/man will insist that Jesus is without sin and therefore cannot be thought of as prejudiced, whereas a historical reading paradigm will try to ascertain whether the encounter between Jesus and the wo/man really took place, and a literary analysis will trace the different narrative or rhetorical strategies inscribed in the text. If however, reading paradigms establish different relations between texts, readers, and contexts, then the different meanings of a text cannot be adjudicated in terms of "the true meaning of the text itself." Rather they must be assessed ethically and politically in terms of their implications and consequences for the struggle to transform kyriarchal relations of oppression.

In order to become accountable to and promote the well-being of wo/men at the bottom of the kyriarchal pyramid of oppression and exploitation, a critical feminist interpretation for liberation also pays special attention to the kind of socio-symbolic worlds and moral universes that biblical texts and their interpreters construct. Consequently, a critical feminist reading does not subscribe to one single reading strategy and method but employs a variety of theoretical insights and methods for interpreting the Bible. It does not understand biblical interpretation in positivist but rather in rhetorical terms. Such a critical rhetorical understanding of interpretation investigates and reconstructs the discursive arguments of a text, its socioreligious location, and its diverse interpretations in order to underscore the text's oppressive as well as liberative performative actions, values, and possibilities in ever-changing historical situations.

Finally, such a critical feminist sophialogy of reading[10] that understands the Bible and biblical interpretation as a site of struggle over authority and meaning engages in biblical interpretation not only as a the*logical but also as a cultural-religious practice of resistance and transformation. Historical and religious meaning is always sociopolitically constructed insofar as biblical interpretation is located in social networks of power/knowledge relations that shape society, university, and biblical religions. Biblical texts are argument- ative texts, produced in and by particular historical debates and struggles. By deconstructing the kyriarchal rhetorics and politics of subordination inscribed in Scripture, feminist interpretation is able to generate new possibilities for the ever-new articulation of religious identities and emancipatory practices.

THE SYROPHOENICIAN WO/MAN

A cursory reading of the story of the Syrophoenician wo/man and its diverse interpretations may serve as an example for what I mean by conceptualizing "biblical text and interpretation as a site of struggle over meaning." This Gospel story can be read as an *ideo-story*, whose "representational makeup promotes concreteness and visualization" for rhetorical ends.[11] Since the narrative of an ideo-story is not closed but open, it not only allows readers to elaborate the main characters in an imaginative and typological fashion but also reads differently in diverse sociocultural contextualizations.

Whether one situates this story's rhetorical practice in the life of Jesus, or in that of the early church, or limits its present narrative context in Mark's or Matthew's Gospel, Jesus is seen in it as engaging in an argument that discloses religious prejudice and exclusivist identity because he is quoted as saying: "It is not right to take the children's bread and throw it to the dogs." The wo/man, in turn, is characterized ethnically and culturally as a religious outsider, who enters the kyriocentric the*logical argument, turns it against itself, and achieves the well-being of her little daughter.

Two different forms of this story are found in the Gospels of Mark and Matthew. It is absent in the Gospel of Luke, even though Luke is generally praised in malestream exegesis for favoring stories about wo/men. In Mark 7: 24-30 the wo/man's identity is marked through linguistic/cultural (Greek) as well as national/racial (of Syrophoenician origin) characterizations. The text does not recognize the wo/man either by her own name or by that of her father or husband. Rather she is characterized by her cultural, religious, and ethnic location as an outsider who enters the house into which Jesus has withdrawn. Her daring and disruptive initiative is fueled by her interest in the well-being of her daughter.

However, the story in its present form does not tell the miracle but centers on the argument of Jesus rejecting her petition because she is a cultural, religious, and national outsider. Nevertheless the wo/man does not give in but takes up Jesus' insulting saying and uses it to argue against him. She wins the controversy because Jesus, convinced by her argument (*dia touton ton logon*), announces her daughter's well-being.

A critical-historical reading that traces the transmission of this story in the pre-Markan tradition makes it possible to see how rhetorical arguments may have shaped the genesis of this narrative. The story might have begun as a simple Galilean miracle story that was told about a wo/man asking Jesus to exorcise her daughter, with Jesus granting her request. In the process of the retelling of this miracle story at a second stage, the opposition between Syro-Phoenician-Greek-female on the one hand and Jesus-Galilean-male on the other was probably introduced.

Moreover, the parabolic saying about food-children-table-dogs now plays on an "ironic" double meaning, in case Jesus speaks of street dogs and the wo/man of house dogs. The addition of this saying not only inscribes the opposition between Jew and Gentile. It also ascribes an offensive, exclusivist attitude to Jesus, an attitude that the argument of the Syro-Phoenician wo/man challenges and overcomes. As a third stage of transmission, this story probably was taken over by Mark and tied into the Gospel narrative through the introduction in verse 24 and the qualifying addition of "first" in verse 27.

Another version of this story is found in Matthew's Gospel. In Matthew's version (15:21-28) the two protagonists remain embroiled in the argument about food-children-master's table-house dogs. Matthew changes the story's the*logical dynamics in significant ways by both adding the saying "I was only sent to the lost sheep of Israel" and introducing the disciples as those who want to get rid of the wo/man. Thus in Matthew both the characterization of the protagonists and the plot of the story is changed. The wo/man is consistently rebuffed not only by Jesus but also by his disciples. She is characterized with the archaic term "Canaanite," which reminds the reader of Israel's long struggle with Canaan's cultic heritage. The wo/man not only enters the public domain, but she does so speaking loudly [*krazein*].

Matthew's text concludes with Jesus praising the wo/man's "great faith" and Mark's with announcing that her daughter is freed from the demon because of her word or because of her teaching. Although this is one of the few Gospel stories in which a wo/man character is accorded "voice," in both versions the final promise gives to Jesus the last word and underscores that the authority of the text rests with the "master" voice of Jesus. The wo/man's argument serves to enhance its discursive resonance. Standard scholarly commentaries also tend to engage in an apologetic defense of the master Jesus[12] if they comment at all on the wo/man and her significance. Thus they amplify the marginalizing tendencies not only of the biblical text but also reinscribe it into critical scholarship.[13]

Read in a kyriocentric—that is, master-centered—frame, the story functions as one more variation of wo/man as outsider in the symbolic worlds and social constructions of male discourse. A substantial part of the Markan manuscript tradition seeks to portray the Syrophoenician as an example of humble submissiveness by inserting "yes" into the text,[14] to play down the "but" that the wo/man speaks so that the text now reads: "But the wo/man answered and said, yes Lord" (Mark 7: 27). Moreover, both Gospel texts contrast the wo/man outsider with the master figure of Jesus who, according to Mark, has withdrawn inside the house, while in Matthew he is surrounded by his (male) disciples. Whereas Matthew calls her by the antiquated scriptural name Canaanite, Mark elaborately characterizes the wo/man as a Greek who was a Syrophoenician by birth. Not only by virtue of her gender, but also because of her ethnicity and cultural-religious affiliation, the wo/man enters the site of canonical male discourse as a "triple" outsider.

History of Interpretation

The history of interpretation[15] of this story is variegated. To my knowledge the first retelling of the story in the early church emerges in a less-known Jewish-Christian extracanonical writing called the Pseudo-Clementine Homilies. The Pseudo-Clementine Homilies are thought to have been composed during the third and fourth centuries, but have probably incorporated older traditions.[16] They tell the story of Clement of Rome who accompanied Peter on his missionary journeys. In their retelling (Ps. Clem. Hom. II,19,1-3), the wo/man for the first time receives a name. She is called in Latin "Justa," which means the "just one," and is characterized as a well-educated upper class wo/man. In this version of the story Justa is joined by the disciples in asking Jesus to heal her daughter. But Jesus replies in the negative: "It is not permitted to heal the gentiles who are similar to dogs in that they use all kinds of food and do all kinds of things, since the table in the *basileia [the commonweal of G*d]* is given to the children of Israel." The text underscores that the wo/man responds positively. I quote: "But hearing this she wanted to participate in the table like a dog, namely in the crumbs from the table, abandoned her previous customs, in that she ate in the same manner as the sons of the kingdom and achieved, as she desired, the healing of her daughter." Although Justa does not persuade Jesus to change his prejudice, she is persuaded by Jesus to change her lifestyle. Justa converts to Judaism. She becomes the righteous one.

In the subsequent history of interpretation two rhetorical strategies compete with each other. The salvation historical approach employs the allegorical method of interpretation. In this reading the healing from a distance corresponds to the situation of the pagans, the dogs under the table are analogous to the gentiles, the children stand for Israel, the bread of the children signifies the gospel, and the table signifies sacred Scripture. Such allegorical interpretations spiritualize and the*logize the story in such a way that it can be read in a salvation historical sense. The wo/man is seen as a Proselyte interceding for the salvation of the gentiles who are saved not through the encounter with the historical Jesus but through his word. Yet, this interpretation carries anti-Jewish overtones: Whereas the Jews were the children and the Gentiles were the dogs in the days of Christ, now in the time of the church the opposite is the case: the Jews have killed the prophets and Jesus has become dogs.

While the salvation historical reading is anti-Jewish, the exhortative reading approach focuses on the paradigmatic behavior of the wo/man, especially on her exemplary faith, which is differently understood in different confessional historical contextualizations. Interpretations of the early church, medieval times, and the Catholic Counter-Reformation understand faith as a virtue that is expressed as modesty, perseverance, reverence, prudence, trust, and especially as meekness and humility. According to this interpretive strategy, the wo/man's faith comes to the fore as humbleness especially in Mark 7:27 where she does not reject Jesus' calling her a dog, but accepts it saying, "Yes, Lord." Yet, whereas medieval exegesis thought that her humble behavior exhibits a "masculine" stance, modern exegesis stresses that her humble acceptance of grace expresses her "feminine soul." The interpretation of the Reformation in turn understands her faith as "feminine surrender" rather than as humility. Now the story becomes a doctrinal discourse on the topic of submissive faith. Faith consists in the unconditional surrender to the Lord, which expresses itself in repeated intercessions and persevering prayer. It consists in the recognition that the self is nothing except for its trust in Jesus, the Lord.

Finally, colonialist "missionary" discourses have underscored the wo/man's subservient behavior as an example to be imitated. In her new book *Discovering the Bible in the Non-Biblical World* the Chinese scholar Kwok Pui-lan, for instance, points to the use of this story for colonialist ends.[17] She highlights that just as the gentile wo/man so also colonialized peoples were expected to be as subservient, obedient, and loyal as a "devoted dog would be." The Western construction of the alien "other" in feminine terms resorts to biblical wo/men and "feminine" virtues in order to inculcate Western values of domination. Moreover, Kwok argues, such a colonialist interpretation contrasts Jesus' attitude toward wo/men with the understanding of wo/manhood in non-Christian cultures in order to prove their inferiority and the superiority of Christianity. Such a colonialist use of biblical wo/men's stories parallels their anti-Jewish interpretation by Christian apologetic discourses.

CONTEMPORARY INTERPRETATIONS

Most contemporary commentators are troubled by the response of Jesus in Mark, a response that reveals his biased partiality. Their interpretations are concerned with changing the prejudicial tenor of the story by either declaring Jesus' response in Mark as historically inauthentic, by explaining away his religious-ethnic prejudice and exclusivity, by resorting to features of the Matthean version or by adducing anti-Jewish or folklorist considerations. They argue, for instance, that Jesus does not intend an insult to the wo/man but only wants to test her faith, that he rebukes her because he needed his meal and rest, that he was instructing his disciples and not the wo/man, that he muttered this harsh word under his breath, or even that it was the wo/man who first mentioned dogs since she knew how Jews regarded her people so that Jesus merely responded to her word. Others suggest that the saying might have roots in rabbinic oral teachings or reflect a Jewish proverb ordering who eats first in a Jewish household. Some in turn explicate that Jesus used the diminutive of "dog" [*kynarion*] in order to soften this allegedly widely-known Jewish label for gentiles or that the wo/man is thereby characterized as a cynic philosopher. All these arguments seek to diminish the insult of the saying on the lips of Jesus by giving good reasons for Jesus' prejudicial words. In short, rather than critically assessing and ethically evaluating the kyriarchal politics of the text for Christian identity formation, they try to explain away its cultural-religious bias.

In my book *In Memory of Her*, I have proposed that the story's controversy is best situated historically in Galilean missionary beginnings. Although the Syrophoenician respects the primacy of the children of Israel, she nevertheless makes a the*logical argument against limiting the Jesuanic inclusive table-community and discipleship of equals to Israel alone. That such a historical argument is placed in the mouth of a wo/man, I argued, gives us a clue to the historical leadership of wo/men in opening up the Jesus movement to Gentiles. Thus the story of the Syrophoenician makes wo/men's contributions to one of the most crucial transitions in early Christian beginnings historically visible. Although I was concerned with the historical reconstruction of an inner-Christian debate about the mission to Gentiles, my interpretation has been misused for deflecting a critical the*logical discussion and ethical evaluation of the prejudice and discriminatory stance that the text ascribes to Jesus.

A *sociohistorical* reading has developed and in turn contextualizes the story of the Syrophoenician not in terms of early Christian the*logical debates or Jewish purity laws, but rather in terms of inner-Jewish ethnic and class conflicts. This sociocritical reading emphasizes that the story's first teller and audience were familiar with the tensions between Jews and Gentiles in the villages of the Tyrian-Galilean border regions. The description of the Syrophoenician as Greek characterizes her as an educated upper class wo/man who asks Jesus for help. This characterization underlines the "social" clash between her and Jesus, who is portrayed, by contrast, as an itinerant preacher and exorcist from the backwaters of Galilee.

In the context of such sociocultural status difference, Jesus' retort must have been heard, so the German scholar Gerd Theissen argues, as follows: Let the poor people in the Galilean backwaters be satisfied. For it is not just to take away food from the poor people in the Galilean villages and to give it to rich Gentiles in the cities. This reading situates the story of the Syrophoenician within an inner-Jewish debate, the conflict between poor Galilean villagers and rich Gentile citizens. It does not exculpate Jesus because he is seen as expressing the resentment of the underprivileged population. Yet again, this reading does not confront ethically and the*logically the prejudicial saying ascribed to Jesus but ascribes it to the resentment of the underprivileged.

Whereas a sociohistorical contextualization stresses the contrast between poor villagers and rich city folk, a sociocultural reading emphasizes ethnic identity as key to the saying of Jesus. The Japanese interpreter Hisako

Kinukawa contextualizes the story of the Syro-Phoenician not within debates on the equal participation of gentiles in early Christian beginnings but within Israelite purity regulations. She does so in order to draw out parallels between the understanding of ethnic exclusivism and national integrity in first century Judaism and in Japan today.[18] Kinukawa rejects other feminist interpretations that emphasize the audacity of the wo/man and instead stresses her alien status. She points out that the Israelites "excluded foreigners from their ethnic borders in order to retain their purity of blood. . . . Geographically, they were defenseless against foreign invasions and were invaded by one foreign power after another. Thus it seems natural for Jesus as a Jew to defend his people and not to want to dilute their ethnic integrity."[19]

The *gender* reading of Sharon Ringe in turn focuses on the wo/man as widowed, divorced, or never married, as totally alone and isolated from family support. When we meet her she is left with only a daughter who is a further liability in her society's terms. Nevertheless, for the sake of her daughter, the Syro-Phoenician breaks custom and stands up to the visiting rabbi and miracle-worker. Such a single-minded focus on gender relations rejects the interpretation of the original story in terms of either cultural class or early Christian missionary conflicts. Instead, Ringe argues that the story's significance is christological. The story could not have been invented by the church because of its shocking portrait of the man Jesus. Rather than inventing such a story, it is more likely that the early church tried to make the best out of a bizarre tradition that must have preserved the memory of an incident in the life of Jesus "when he was caught with his compassion down."[20] Only in the Markan retelling, according to Ringe, does the story become a story about Jews and Gentiles.

ETHICAL EVALUATION

To sum up my exercise: I hope that I have succeeded in showing how a critical feminist interpretation for liberation explores, problematizes, and assesses different readings paradigms and hegemonic interpretations. Its goal is to unmask biblical texts and reading that foster an elite "feminine," racist exclusivist, dehumanizing colonialist or Christian anti-Jewish inscription of cultural-religious identity. Thus, it revisions biblical interpretation as an argumentative, persuasive and emancipatory praxis that destabilizes, proliferates, and energizes critical readings for liberation in particular sociohistorical-religious contexts. In so doing, it seeks to undermine a fundamentalist mode of biblical reading that claims to be the only correct or true one. It thereby attempts to overcome a kyriarchal identity formation that invokes the authority of G*d for biblical texts that reinscribe prejudice and dehumanization.

I hope to have shown that a critical evaluative process of interpretation for liberation does not reduce the historical and textual richness of the Bible in general and of the story of the Syro-Phoenician in particular to abstract the*logical or ethical principle, timeless norm, or ontologically immutable archetype that is to be accurately repeated and translated from generation to generation. As my cursory discussion of the Syro-Phoenician's story has indicated biblical texts and their interpretations continue to reinscribe in the name of G*d religious prejudice and relations of oppression if their kyriarchal rhetoric and religious identity formation is not only accepted without question but also legitimated in the process of interpretation. Therefore, the primary the*logical task of a critical emancipatory hermeneutics consists in scrutinizing and marking biblical texts and interpretations as to how much they promote a kyriarchal ethos and dehumanizing religious vision that legitimate injustice and oppression.

When trying to assess whether the story of the Syro-Phoenician advocates kyriachal values and visions, participants in my classes and workshops usually disagree. Those arguing that the narrative is not kyriarchal point to the fact that the wo/man is the major protagonist in this story, that her argument convinces Jesus, and that her daughter was healed. "But at what cost?" other students ask. The wo/man does not challenge the ethnic-religious prejudice of Jesus but confirms it with "Yes, Lord." She does not argue for equal access; she begs for crumbs. Thus she accepts second-class citizenship, which she herself has internalized. She acts like a dog who is grateful even when kicked. Hence it is not surprising that commentators praise her for her humble submission. This is indeed a sacred text that advocates and reinscribes kyriarchal power-relations, anti-Jewish prejudices, and wo/men's cultural "feminine" identity and submissive behavior.

In one of these debates, when we came to this impasse in the discussion, Renee, an African American Baptist student chided us for not taking seriously the wo/man's situation of powerlessness and the ironic cast of her words. Maria, a Hispanic student countered that according to Theissen the wo/man was upper class, urban, and well-educated. Nevertheless, the first student persisted: Even as a privileged educated wo/man she remains a religious outsider, a despised foreigner, and a female who dares to disrupt the discourse of men. If she wants to achieve what she has come for, she needs to "play the game." Readers miss the irony of the story—she argued—if they do not see that the wo/man humors the great religious man in order to get what she wants. The wo/man from Syro-Phoenicia wins the argument, her daughter is liberated.

In a socioeconomic and cultural-political global situation of increasing exploitation and repression, feminist biblical interpretation must continue to articulate an emancipatory politics of meaning that do not vilify and block access to the table. It can do so, however, only if it overcomes its exclusivist kyriarchal formations and articulates a vision of faith and hope in a liberating G*d who is justified (*edikaiothē*) by all Her children" (Luke 7:35). Once again, the Syro-Phoenician challenges us to set liberating argument and praxis against the word that dehumanizes and excludes.

NOTES

[1] Prov. 9:1-6.

[2] See my introduction to *The Power of Naming: A Concilium Reader in Feminist The*logy* (Maryknoll: Orbis, 1996).

[3] Anna Julia Cooper, *A Voice from the South*, 1892; rep. in Schomburg Library of Nineteenth-Century Black Women Writers (New York: Oxford University Press).

[4] Dorothy Lee, *Claiming Our Rites*, 81.

[5] Ibid., 82.

[6] Elizabeth Cady Stanton, ed., *The Woman's Bible*, 2 vols. (1884/1888); rep. Seattle: Coalition Task Force on Women and Religion, 1984.

[7] Although Anthony C. Thiselton, *New Horizons in Hermeneutics: The Theory and Practice of Transforming Biblical Reading* (London: HarperCollins, 1992), 449, in his discussion of my work claims that "what is at stake is hermeneutical theory" he does not bother to discuss *Bread Not Stone* but rather focuses on a particular exegetical topic regarding women's witness to the resurrection discussed in *In Memory of Her*. In so doing he seeks to show that I did not take all possible interpretations into account. Yet such a criticism overlooks the limits set by my choice of genre for this work and mistakes a work of historical reconstruction for one of hermeneutical critical theory. The interests driving his misreadings come to the fore not only in his emotionally laden comparison of my own work with that of Susanne Heine. Although Heine's work has appeared later and is dependent on my own work, albeit without acknowledging it, she finds Thiselton's favor because she attacks the work of other feminists. It also comes to the fore in his repeated question as to how much a given tradition can undergo transformation before it ceases to be *this tradition* as well as in the question of whether the transformation of which I speak comes "into being by imposing one's community values upon another in a hermeneutic of conflict, or by progress toward a universal commitment to a transcendental critique of justice and of the cross which speaks from beyond given context-bound communities in a hermeneutic of openness?" Obviously, Thiselton is not able to understand either commitment to wo/men as a universal stance nor feminist struggle as a commitment to a "transcendental critique of justice" or to the "cross" as the symbolic expression of such struggle.

[8] Annette Kolodny, "Dancing through the Minefield: Some Observations on the Theory, Practice, and Politics of Feminist Literary Criticism," in *Feminist Criticism: Essays on Women, Literature, Theory*, ed. Elaine Schowalter (New York: Pantheon, 1985), 153.

[9] For the expression "frame of meaning," see Anthony Giddens, *New Rules of Sociological Methods: A Positive Critique of Interpretative Sociologists* (New York: Basic, 1976), 64.

[10] It is curious that Gerald West, *Biblical Hermeneutics of Liberation Modes of Reading the Bible in the South African Context* (Pietermaritzburg: Cluster, 1991), does not discuss this process model of interpretation although (or because?) he is interested in the "interface between biblical studies and the ordinary reader." Instead, he tries to limit my hermeneutical proposal to a "reading behind the text," pointing out its similarity to Itumeleng Mosala's approach—*Biblical Hermeneutics and Black Theology in South Africa* (Grand Rapids: Eerdmans, 1989)—although Mosala's work not only has appeared later but also uses a Marxist rather than feminist analysis. It seems that even in a *Hermeneutics of Liberation*, the "ordinary reader" remains male.

[11] Mike Bal, *Death and Disymmetry: The Politics of Coherence in the Book of Judges* (Bloomington: Indiana University Press, 1987), 11.

[12] See, for instance, Herman C. Waetjen, *A Reordering of Power: A Socio-Political Reading of Mark's Gospel* (Minneapolis: Fortress Press, 1989), 135, explains Jesus' ethnocentric refusal as

"Jesus' passionate dedication to the fulfillment of Jewish need." Although Waetjen notes the weak manuscript attestation of "yes," he bases his interpretation on it: "She affirms the validity of his proverb by acknowledging Jewish priority. She does not want to deprive the children of their bread."

[13] For a feminist reading see Monika Fander, *die Stellung der Frau im Markusevangelium unter besonderer Berücksichtigung kultur und religionsgeschichtlicher Hintergrunde*, MthA 8 (Altenbetge: Telos, 1989), 75, who argues that the "but" [*de*] in v. 28 places the response of the woman in the center of attention. Moreover the doubling of the verb [*apekrithei kai legei*] places an additional emphasis on her speech act.

[14] The word "yes" [*nai*] is not found anywhere else in the Gospel and is missing from important manuscripts such as Papyrus 45. See T. A. Burkill, *New Light on the Earliest Gospel* (Ithaca: Cornell University Press, 1972), 72n3.

[15] For the material in this section, see U. Luz, *Das Evangelium des Matthaus*, 2. Band: Matt. 8-17 (Einsiedeln: Neukirchener, 1990), 431.

[16] Helmut Koester, *Introduction to the New Testament*, 2:205.

[17] Kwok Pui-lan, *Discovering the Bible in the Non-Biblical World* (Maryknoll: Orbis, 1995), 71–83.

[18] Ibid., 61.

[19] Hisako Kinukawa, *Women and Jesus in Mark* (Maryknoll: Orbis, 1994), 61.

[20] Sharon Ringe, "A Gentile Woman's Story," in L. Russell, ed. *Feminist Interpretation of the Bible* (Philadelphia: Westminster, 1985), 68.

18

Wisdom's "Dance"

Practicing a Critical Feminist Interpretation

In the last thirty years or so, feminist biblical studies[1] have been established as a new field of learning with its own publications and methods.[2] It is taught in schools, colleges, and universities and is practiced by many scholars in different parts of the world. While feminist biblical studies was not in existence more than thirty years ago, today it is a blooming field of inquiry with many different voices and directions. Hence one would assume that critical feminist biblical studies is accepted not only as a serious academic field but also as a method used in preaching and teaching. However, this is often not the case and various reasons could be adduced to explain the situation.

In the following chapter, I want to outline the hermeneutical strategies and steps that constitute the critical feminist process of conscientization or coming into consciousness. This is hard to sketch on paper because it requires a process of "doing" and action that is different in every concrete situation of interpretation.[3]

A CRITICAL FEMINIST EMANCIPATORY INTERPRETATION

Since there are so many different articulations of feminism, I want to underscore again that my own methodological approach is that of a critical feminist interpretation for liberation:

- It is *critical* because it understands text as rhetorical communication that needs to be evaluated rather than accepted or obeyed.
- It is *feminist* insofar as it focuses on wo/men and their well-being.
- It is liberationist or emancipatory because it works with a systemic analysis of the intersecting structures of domination. Since *patriarchy*—which has been and still is used to designate such structures of domination—usually is understood in terms of gender, I have coined the word *kyriarchy*, that is: *the domination/rule of the emperor, lord, slave-master, father, husband, of elite propertied educated men* as an analytic category to communicate the complex interstructuring of dominations.

275

- Its goal of a critical feminist emancipatory interpretation is not just understanding but change and transformation. It seeks to change not only the ways the Bible is read and understood but also to transform wo/men's self-understanding and cultural patterns of dehumanization.

Although there are rather variegated and theoretically different articulations of feminist biblical studies, all of them stress the agency and authority of wo/men to read Scripture differently. Moreover, most of them would agree on the following seven points:

- The Bible is written in androcentric/kyriocentric[4] language.
- The Bible came into being in patriarchal/kyriarchal societies, cultures, and religions.
- The Bible is still proclaimed and taught today in patriarchal/kyriarchal societies and religions.
- Wo/men who until very recently have been excluded from official academic or religious biblical interpretation must be acknowledged as subjects of interpretation.
- Biblical texts and interpretations are rhetorical communications shaped by their sociopolitical-religious contextualizations.
- If read critically the Bible can be a resource in the struggles for emancipation and liberation.

In short, the objective and goal of a critical feminist biblical interpretation is not just a better understanding of the Bible. Its primary goal is the *conscientization of biblical readers.* Critical conscientization is possible *because* wo/men participate at one and the same time both in the specifically "feminine" cultural discourse of submission, inadequacy, inferiority, dependency, and irrational intuition and in the generic "masculine-human" discourse of subjectivity, self-determination, freedom, justice, and equality. Christian wo/men participate at one and the same time both in the biblical discourse of subordination and prejudice as well as in that of the discipleship of equals. If such a cultural and religious alternative discursive location becomes conscious, it allows the feminist interpreter to become a reader resisting the persuasive power of the kyriocentric biblical text.

When wo/men recognize our contradictory ideological position in a grammatically kyriocentric language system, we can become readers resisting the *lord-master-elite male* identification of the andro-kyriocentric, racist, heterosexist, classist, or colonialist text. However, if this contradiction is not brought into consciousness, it cannot be exploited for change but leads to further self-alienation. For change to take place, subordinated people must concretely and explicitly claim as their very own the human values and democratic visions that the kyriocentric text reserves solely for elite, educated, and propertied men.

In short, a critical feminist biblical interpretation, which I have elaborated in *In Memory of Her*[5] and *Bread Not Stone*,[6] theorized in *But She Said*[7] and *Sharing Her Word*,[8] and pedagogically explicated in *Wisdom Ways*[9] is best understood as a practice of rhetorical inquiry that engages in the formation of a critical historical and religious consciousness. Whereas hermeneutical theory seeks to understand and appreciate the meaning of texts, rhetorical interpretation and its theo-ethical interrogation of texts and symbolic worlds pays close attention to the kinds of effects not only biblical discourses but also biblical readers produce and how they produce them. Only a complex model of a critical process of feminist interpretation for liberation[10] can overcome the hermeneutical splits between sense and meaning, between explanation and understanding, between critique and consent, between distanciation and empathy, between reading the text "behind" and "in front of" the text,[11] between the present and the past, between interpretation and application, between realism and imagination.

THE DANCE OF INTERPRETATION

Consequently, a critical feminist biblical interpretation engages in a complex and exhilarating process of interpretation. Feminists have used different rhetorical metaphors and comparisons for naming such an emancipatory process of interpretation: "Making visible," "hearing into speech," "finding one's voice." I myself have favored metaphors of movement such as turning, walking, way, dance, ocean waves, or struggle. Since Plato attacked rhetoric as "mere cookery," I sometimes have borrowed this metaphor and spoken of biblical rhetorical interpretation as baking bread, mixing and kneading milk, flour, yeast, and raisins into dough, or as cooking a stew, utilizing different herbs and spices to season the potatoes, meats, and carrots, which, stirred together, produce a new and different flavor.

However, the metaphor of the dance seems best to express the method of feminist biblical interpretation. Dancing involves body and spirit, it involves feelings and emotions, and it takes us beyond our limits and creates community. Dancing confounds all hierarchical order because it moves in spirals and circles. It makes us feel alive and full of energy, power, and creativity. Moving in spirals and circles, critical feminist biblical interpretation is ongoing; it cannot be done once and for all but must be repeated differently in different situations and from different perspectives. It is exciting because in every new reading of biblical texts a different meaning emerges. By deconstructing the kyriarchal rhetoric and politics of inequality and subordination inscribed in the Bible, feminist interpreters are able to generate ever fresh articulations of radical democratic religious identities and emancipatory practices. Such an emancipatory process of biblical interpretation has as its "doubled" reference point both the interpreter's contemporary presence and the biblical past.

Whether one thinks of the emancipative interpretive process as baking bread or as a hearty stew or a joyful dance, crucial ingredients, spices, strategies, or moves in a critical process of a multicultural feminist interpretation are:

- experience and recognition of social-ideological location
- critical analysis of domination (kyriarchy)
- suspicion of kyriocentric texts and frameworks
- assessment and evaluation in terms of a scale of feminist emancipative values
- creative imagination and vision
- reconstruction or remembering,[12]
- transformative action for change

These interpretive practices are not to be construed simply as successive independent methodological steps of inquiry or as discrete methodological rules or recipes. Rather they are best understood as interpretive moves and movements, as strategies that interact with each other simultaneously in the process of "making meaning" out of a particular biblical or any other cultural text in the context of the globalization of inequality. This "dance of interpretation" is taking place on a dual level of interpretation: on the level of *biblical texts* and on the level of *contemporary meaning making* in kyriarchal situations.

Such an interpretation continually moves between the present and the past, between realism and imagination. It moves, spirals, turns, and dances in the places found in "the white spaces between the black letters" of Scripture—to use a metaphor of Jewish interpretation. Hence, it is very difficult to boil down such a dynamic process of interpretation to a logical consecutive description. If I try to do so here, I hope readers will not see my attempt as transcript of a process but see it more like a basic instruction in dance steps, which they must execute in their own manner in order to keep dancing. We will try out these dance—steps by looking at 1 Peter 2:9—3:7 in terms of a feminist rhetorical analysis that enacts the hermeneutical strategies of a critical feminist interpretation.

First Peter

The Christian Testament writing called 1 Peter was written at the end of the first century CE and is addressed to "resident aliens" who live in the Roman Province of Asia Minor. They are portrayed as a marginalized group who experiences harassment and suffering. This pseudonymus epistle is a rhetorical communication in the form of a circular letter between those who live in the metropolitan center of imperial Rome, which is the*logically camouflaged as Babylon, and those who live in Asia Minor as colonial subjects.

The argument of 1 Peter moves from an elaboration of the theoretically high but sociopolitically precarious status of the recipients (1:15- 2:10) to the central part of the letter addressing the problem as to how to behave in a politically correct manner (doing good) with regard to the imperial-colonial authorities, especially if one is a subordinate member of the household (2:11-3:12). The rhetorical strategy then shifts to a more general argument addressing all the intended recipients about "good" behavior in public and the "honorable sufferings" to be expected (3:13-4:11). Finally, the argument climaxes with admonitions regarding the exercise of leadership in the "household of G*d" (4:12-5:11).

Central to the rhetoric of the letter is the image of the household (Gk. *oikos*). In the rhetoric of 1 Peter, the Christian community is called "the household of G*d," and G*d is understood as its Father (*pater familias*) in analogy to the Roman emperor. The injunction to subordination is used five times in 1 Peter. Four times it addresses a group of people: everyone in 2:13, household slaves in 2:18, wives in 3:1, and younger people or neophytes in 5:1. Only once is it used in a descriptive praise statement in 3:22, which says that angels, authorities, and powers were made subject to Jesus Christ who "has gone into heaven and is at the right hand of G*d." This last statement makes it clear that the Greek verb *hypotassein* expresses a relation of ruling and power.

In sum, 1 Peter's Roman colonial rhetoric of subjection advocates the submission of the subaltern migrants and noncitizens in Asia Minor and specifies as problem cases the unjust suffering of slave wo/men and the marriage relationship between freeborn Christian wives and their Gentile husbands. Commentators agree that the context of the letter is one in which Jews and "*Christianoi*/Messianists" were seen as seditious and as threat to the colonial religious, cultural, and political Roman imperial "customs." The conversion of slave wo/men, freeborn ladies, and younger people in which the master of the house did not convert constituted already an offense against the "ancestral" laws and customs.

According to Roman laws and customs, the *pater familias*—like the emperor who was called the supreme Father of the empire (*pater patriae*)—had absolute power over his subordinates in the household and determined the religion of its members. Hence, it was generally accepted as a matter of good civil order that slave wo/men, freeborn wo/men, and all other members of the household practiced the religion of the master and lord of the house. The letter writer is concerned with "honor," construes the "house of G*d" not as temple but as "household," advocates submission, and the hegemonic ethos of "doing good," so that the recipients will not be attacked as wrongdoers. Hence, he advocates *accommodation* to the kyriarchal order of house and state for missionary purposes as long as such *accommodation* does not interfere with their "Christian" calling.

Because of feminist work most recent scholarship on 1 Peter is aware of the problematic ethical-political meaning and sociohistorical effects of the letter's subordination discourse on contemporary society and church. Thus, commentators tend to focus less on the hermeneutical problems posed by the Jewish language of the letter, by the injunction to political subjection or by the use of the example of Christ to pacify suffering slaves, than on the demand for the subordination of wo/men. In response to feminist interpretation malestream exegetes feel compelled to write a special hermeneutical excursus[13] or to articulate special hermeneutical rules[14] for reading texts of submission today, in order to eliminate or mitigate the problems that modern hearers/readers have with this text.

They also seek to do so by translating the Greek word *hypotassein* with "accept the authority," "defer to," "show respect for," "recognize the proper social order," or "participate in," "be involved with," "be committed to" rather than with "subordinate yourselves." Although such an apologetic translation is primarily concerned with not offending "wo/men" and "liberal" readers/hearers, it conceals the elite male character of subordination that in 1 Peter is "the*logized." Such a defensive reading takes the side of the author and his rhetoric of submission rather than that of those whose subjection he advocates in the*logical terms.

The Hermeneutical Dance Movements

We begin the hermeneutical dance by engaging in a *hermeneutics of experience* and ask what the experience and reaction of the recipients in the first century could have been when they read or heard the author's admonitions. A critical feminist interpretation in turn reads the text from the perspective of the recipients and takes the side of freeborn and slave wo/men as well as the whole community of resident aliens. The rhetorical tension between the lofty address of the recipients and the ethos of submission that is inscribed in the letter seems to indicate a "rhetorical debate" in the community about what the "will of G*d" demands from Christians living under Roman rule. Slave wo/men for instance could have argued that it was "G*d's will" to be treated justly as members of G*d's elect people rather than to suffer patiently the sexual abuse and cross mistreatment at the hands of their masters. Hence, it was justified to run away, if their masters treated them harshly. Freeborn well-to-do wives could have argued that it was their Christian calling to proclaim the "good news" to their Gentile husbands. If they could not convert them to the lifestyle of the elect people of G*d, it was the "will of G*d" to separate from them by divorcing them. They could have bolstered their argument with reference to Paul who supported the "marriage free" state of wo/men.

All of the members of the community could have argued that the covenant of G*d demanded that they separate from Gentile society and resist Roman imperial culture because their "low class" status as noncitizens and migrants had been changed in and through their conversion. They now were bound together in love and respect and formed a royal priesthood and holy nation, a temple of the Spirit. In consequence, they could not possibly pay obeisance to the emperor, his governors, and other cultural institutional authorities, a political strategy also espoused by the book of Revelation. Thus they could have advocated a separatist stance that would not totally avoid but maybe reduce harassment and suffering, since they would not have to mix daily with their Gentile neighbors. Such an interpretation is possible if one reads the arguments of 1 Peter as part of a broad-based argument in early Christian communities.

Engaging in a hermeneutics of experience one would ask questions on the level of *contemporary meaning making* such as: What is our experience with this text today? Is it preached or emphasized at certain occasions? How does it reinforce contemporary prejudices? Which statements appeal to you and why? Which do you reject? This step compels us to look at our own experience and reaction when reading 1 Peter 2:9—3:7. While the oppressive social system of overt slavery is no longer practiced today, the international sex-trade is booming and lucrative. Thousands of wo/men and children are forced or duped into it. Many will feel guilty fearing the wrath of G*d because of their sinfulness. In a similar fashion, millions of wo/men stay in abusive marriage relationships. They blame themselves for provoking violence because they are not obedient and submissive. Christian wo/men readers who have been socialized into a literalist reading of the Bible as the word of G*d will therefore understand 1 Peter as telling them that they should accept abuse, suffering, and beatings from their husbands as the will of G*d. When they experience domestic violence and abuse, they blame themselves and accept it as their fault. Many ministers underscore that we should suffer just as Christ has suffered when preaching this text. Hence, it is important that feminist Bible study groups and the*logical education get in touch with such experiences of suffering and abuse and critically reflect on them in terms of a hermeneutics of domination.

A *hermeneutics of domination* analyzes the kyriarchal structures of domination and investigates how they are inscribed in the text by the author and how we reinscribe them in our contemporary readings. Engaging this strategy one would ask questions on the level of text such as: Does this text reflect Christian and Roman imperial societal values? Is its call to suffering and subordination "the word of G*d," or does it reflect values of the time that reinforce domination and oppression? Hence, it is important to show that this text reflects values of Roman imperial domination, which the author legitimates with reference to the suffering of Christ when admonishing slave wo/men and with references to the holy wo/men of the past (such as Sarah) when admonishing wives.

This hermeneutical step also explores the second level of contemporary meaning making and asks: Into what kind of structures of domination and subordination are we socialized today? In order to do so, one needs to become schooled in systemic social-ideological analysis. Bible study groups have to learn how to critically reflect on their social-religious location and ideological context. How are we shaped by our kyriarchal socializations, privileges, and prejudices that inscribe systemic racism, heterosexism, class discrimination, and nationalism? How do such socialization, privileges, and prejudices determine our readings of this text? How does 1 Peter function as ideological legitimization today? Both legitimizations of kyriarchal subordination that are inscribed in the text—the christological and the scriptural appeal—are ideological because they justify structures of domination. Hence a hermeneutics of suspicion and evaluation are called for.

A hermeneutics of suspicion is necessary not only because of the kyriarchal structures of domination inscribed in the text and legitimated today by the authority of the Bible. It is also necessary because of the grammatically kyriocentric language of 1 Peter. For instance, in studies about "wo/men in the Bible," usually only the admonitions for wives are understood as speaking about wo/men. Thereby it is overlooked that the admonitions to slaves also are addressed to wo/men, since the term *slave* includes slave men and wo/men. Hence, the admonition must be read as also addressed to slave wo/men since the generic masculine could be used as inclusive. Thus in a "normal" reading of the text that is not aware of kyriocentric language, slave wo/men are erased from historical and contemporary consciousness. Or to give another example from 1 Peter: The community is defined by the masculine term "brotherhood," although the admonition of freeborn wives indicates that wo/men were active members of the community.

Hence, a feminist hermeneutics of suspicion must problematize kyriocentric language on both the level of text and on the level of contemporary meaning making because such language makes marginalized wo/men doubly invisible. For instance, today affirmative action job advertisements will invite "African Americans, Native Americans, Asian Americans, and wo/men" to apply, as if African Americans, Native Americans, and Asian Americans are only men and not also wo/men. How one understands kyriocentric language determines one's understanding of early Christianity and of our world today. However, a hermeneutics of suspicion does not only scrutinize language but also lays open the kyriarchal-ideological-the*logical tendencies of the text and also those of contemporary interpretations. It lays open for critical scrutiny, for instance, the the*logy of suffering that is preached to slave wo/men and inscribed in 1 Peter, or it questions the ethical injunctions to subordination as part of the kyriarchal ethos of the Roman Empire. Hence, it calls for a hermeneutics of evaluation.

A *hermeneutics of evaluation* explores the ideological mechanisms identified by a hermeneutics of suspicion and assesses them in terms of a feminist scale of values. It asks how much a text contributes to or diminishes the emancipation and well-being of every wo/man. Does, for instance, the appeal to the suffering of Christ contribute to the well-being of slave wo/men to whom it is addressed? Does the appeal to Sarah's obedience persuade Christian wo/men today to submit to male "headship" or domestic violence?

In order to adjudicate the ethical implications and impact of biblical texts and their interpretations in the past and in the present, we need a feminist scale of values and visions. Since the values articulated by feminists are context and theory dependent, they cannot be fixed once and for all but must be discussed and debated. Hence, feminist biblical interpretation cannot do its work without simultaneously engaging in a critical feminist the*logy and ethics. The academic disciplinary divisions between biblical studies, the*logy, ethics, and ritual break down in the dance of interpretation.

Such a scale of values and visions cannot just be derived from disciplined reasoning but presupposes the vision of a different world and church. We may not yet experience the realization of such a different world of well-being, but it lives in our dreams and hopes that inspire us to continue the struggles for the well-being of all without exception.

A *hermeneutics of creative imagination* seeks to "dream" a world of justice and well-being different from that of kyriarchal domination. As Toni Morrison so forcefully states in her novel, *Beloved*: "She did not tell them to clean up their lives or to go and sin no more. She did not tell them they were the blessed of the earth, its inheriting meek or its glory bound pure. She told them that the only grace they could have was the grace they could imagine. That if they could not see it, they would not have it."[15]

Such an envisioning of an alternative reality is only possible if we have some experience of it. Wo/men who have not experienced radical egalitarian love cannot imagine it. Wo/men who have experienced religion only as oppressive and discriminatory but not also as promoting justice and equality cannot imagine its grace. This insight also applies to the level of text. If we do not discover visions of equality and well-being inscribed in biblical texts, we cannot imagine the early Christian life and world differently. Hence, it is important to discover the visions of justice, equality, dignity, love, community, and well-being also inscribed in the biblical text. We do so not in order to show that the Bible is liberating or to explain away or to deny the inscriptions of kyriarchal domination in it, but rather we need to do so in order to be able to read the kyriarchal text agaist the grain.

Feminist interpretation can only imagine a different world of 1 Peter if it focuses on these statements and visions that express a self-identity different from that of domination. Slave wo/men and wives who are told— "you are a chosen race, a royal priesthood, a holy nation, G*d's own people, in order that you may proclaim the mighty acts of him who called you out of darkness into his marvelous light. Once you were not a people, but now you are G*d's people" (2:9-10)—will have heard this message differently than elite propertied men, since kyriarchal culture told them that they were non-persons. Slave wo/men who understood themselves as a royal priesthood and chosen race might have claimed their new self-identity and argued that their conversion abolished their slave status; freeborn wo/men might have insisted to "proclaim" in the community the great deeds of the One who had called them and objected to living with husbands who did not heed the call.

Thus a *hermeneutics of historical reconstruction and memory* presupposes and substantiates a hermeneutics of imagination. It uses the tools of historiography to reconstruct the struggles of slave wo/men and freeborn wo/men against kyriarchal domination inscribed in early Christian literature in general and 1 Peter in particular. It reconceptualizes and rewrites early Christian history as feminist history and memory. It does so not from the perspective of the historical winners but from the perspective of those who struggled against kyriarchal domination. It does so by placing freeborn wo/men and slave wo/men in the center of its attention. In so doing it changes our image of early Christianity, of church and world today, and of ourselves.

Thus the dance of interpretation culminates in a *hermeneutics of change and transformation*. When seeking future visions and transformations, we can only extrapolate from present experience, which is always already determined by past experience. Hence, we need to analyze the past and the present, biblical texts and our world in order to articulate creative visions and transcending imaginations for a new humanity, global ecology, and religious community. Yet, I submit, only if we are committed to work for a different future, more just future, will our imagination be able to transform the past and present limitations of our vision.

A critical rhetorical-emancipative process of interpretation challenges practitioners of biblical studies and readers of the Bible to become more theo-ethically sophisticated readers by problematizing both the modernist ethos of biblical studies and their own sociopolitical locations and functions in global structures of domination. At the same time it enables them to struggle for a more just and radical-democratic *cosmopolitan* articulation of religion in the global cosmopolis or *ekklesia* of wo/men.

To sum up my argument: I have suggested that a critical rhetorical feminist method and hermeneutical process is best understood as wisdom-praxis. Wisdom's spiraling dance of interpretation seeks to serve public the*logical deliberation and religious transformation. It is not restricted to Christian canonical texts but can be and has been explored successfully by scholars of traditions and Scriptures of other religions. Moreover, it is not restricted to the biblical scholar as expert reader. Rather, it calls for transformative and engaged biblical interpreters who may or may not be professional readers. It has been used in graduate education, in parish discussions, in college classes, and in work with illiterate wo/men.

The Swiss theologian Regula Strobel sums up her pastoral experience with people who, in parish Bible study groups, have engaged or "danced" this feminist wisdom dance of interpretation. She writes that people who have worked with such a critical multifaceted wisdom process of interpretation have

> changed in an impressive way. In the beginning they still sought the authority of the theologian, who was to decide how a biblical text is correctly understood and interpreted. Increasingly they learnt to understand themselves as subjects not only of biblical readings. On the basis of their experiences they have formulated what was liberatory and what was oppressive. They eschewed the pressure to derive all decisions from the Bible or the attitude of Jesus. For they experienced as meaningful and supportive, as the criterion for decision and action everything that contributes to the liberation and life in fullness of wo/men and other disadvantaged persons. Thereby they could read even ambiguous Bible texts and be nourished by the liberating aspects without taking over the oppressive ones.[16]

In and through such a critical rhetorical process of interpretation and deliberation, biblical texts such as 1 Peter can be critically investigated and become sites of struggle and conscientization. Patricia Hill Collins has dubbed such a praxis of change and transformation visionary pragmatism. Feminist visionary pragmatism points to an alternative vision of the world but does not prescribe a fixed goal and end point for which it then claims universal truth.[17]

In such a process of imaginative pragmatism, one never arrives but always struggles on the way. This process reveals how current actions are part of a larger, meaningful struggle. It demonstrates that ethical and truthful visions of self-affirmation and community cannot be separated from the struggles on their behalf. One takes a stand by constructing new knowledge and new interpretations. While vision can be conjured up in the historical imagination, pragmatic action requires that one remain responsive to the injustices of everyday life. If religion and biblical interpretation are worth anything, they must inspire such visionary pragmatism in the everyday struggles for justice and the well-being of all.

I hope I am able to give here an impression of how a critical feminist interpretation of Scripture[18] seeks to do the work of Divine Wisdom in ourselves and in the world—bringing about and fomenting radical change, searching for lost and buried emancipatory biblical traditions, and insistently struggling for justice without ever giving up this struggle. Divine Wisdom-Sophia calls her wo/men messengers today from all corners of the earth to search like She does for their lost, submerged, and forgotten liberating heritage; to unfailingly assert the rights of the disenfranchised and to seek for justice in kyriarchal systems of domination. A critical feminist interpretation seeks to hear Her call and act in the power of Wisdom-Spirit, fomenting the radical change that is demanded by the vision of G*d's dream of a world of well-being and salvation.

NOTES

[1] See, for example, Janice Capel Anderson, "Mapping Feminist Biblical Criticism," *Critical Review of Books in Religion* 2 (1991): 21–44; Elizabeth Castelli, "Heteroglossia, Hermeneutics, and History: A Review Essay of Recent Feminist Studies of Early Christianity," *The Journal of Feminist Studies in Religion* 10, no. 2 (1994): 73–8. Luise Schottroff, S. Schroer, and M. T. Wacker, *Feminist Interpretation: The Bible in Women's Perspective* (Minneapolis: Fortress Press, 1998); Musa W. Dube, ed., *Other Ways of Reading: African Women and the Bible* (Atlanta: SBL, 2002); Silvia Schroer and Sophia Bietenhard, eds., *Feminist Interpretation of the Bible and the Hermeneutics of Liberation* (New York: Sheffield, 2003). For Jewish feminist interpretations see the work of Esther Fuchs, Ilana Pardes, Adele Reinhartz, Tal Ilan, Amy Jill Levine, Cynthia Baker, or Alicia Suskin Ostriker and many others. See also Esther Fuchs, "Points of Resonance," in *On the Cutting Edge*, ed. Jane Schaberg, Alice Bach, and Esther Fuchs (New York: Continuum, 2004), 1–20. For Muslim feminist hermeneutics, see Amina Wadud, *Qur'an and Woman: Rereading the Sacred Text from a Woman's Perspective* (Oxford: Oxford University Press, 1999); Barbara F. Stowasser, *Women in the Qur'an: Traditions and Interpretations* (New York: Oxford University Press, 1994); Asma Barlas, "Believing Women," in *Islam: Unreading Patriarchal Interpretations of the Qur'an* (Austin: University of Texas Press, 2002).

[2] See also my contribution in Ann Braude, ed., *Transforming the Faith of Our Fathers* (New York: Palgrave 2004), 135–56; and Elisabeth Schüssler Fiorenza, ed., *Searching the Scriptures: A Feminist Introduction* (New York: Crossroad, 1993).

[3] Elisabeth Schüssler Fiorenza, Katie G. Cannon, Jane Schaberg, and David Barr, "Pedagogy and Practice: Using Wisdom Ways in the Classroom," *Teaching Theology and Religion* 6 (2003), 208–10, 225–26. For such a process see also John Lanci, "To Teach without a Net," in *Walk in the Ways of Wisdom: Essays in Honor of Elisabeth Schüssler Fiorenza*, ed. Cynthia Briggs Kittredge, Melanie Johnson-Debaufre, and Shelly Matthews (Harrisburg: Trinity International, 2003), 58–73. For feminist pedagogy, see Katie G. Cannon, Kelly Brown Douglas, Toinette M. Eugene, Cheryl Townsend Gilkes, "Living It Out: Metalogues and Dialogues—Teaching the Womanist Idea"; *Journal of Feminist Studies in Religion* 8:2 (Fall 1992): 125–52; Fawzia Ahmad, Living It Out: "Engaging a New Discourse: Teaching 'Women in Islam' in the American University Classroom." *Journal of Feminist Studies in Religion* 18, no. 2 (2002): 131–40; Amy Richlin, "Teaching Religion and Feminist Theory to a New Generation," in *Journal of Feminist Studies in Religion* 14, no. 2 (1998): 124–31; Rebecca S. Chopp, *Saving Work: Feminist Practices of Theological Education* (Louisville: Westminster John Knox, 1995).

[4] *Kyriocentrism* is a name for the linguistic-cultural-religious-ideological systems and intersecting discourses of race, gender, heterosexuality, class, imperialism, and other dehumanizing discourses that legitimate, inculcate, and sustain *kyriarchy*, that is, multiplicative structures of domination.

[5]Elisabeth Schüssler Fiorenza, *In Memory of Her: A Feminist The*logical Reconstruction of Christian Origins*, 2nd ed. (New York: Crossroad, 1983).

[6]*Bread Not Stone: The Challenge of Feminist Biblical Interpretation* (Boston: Beacon, 1985).

[7]*But She Said: Feminist Practices of Biblical Interpretation* (Boston: Beacon, 1992).

[8]*Sharing Her Word: Feminist Biblical Interpretation in Context* (Boston: Beacon, 1998).

[9]*WisdomWays: Introducing Feminist Biblical Interpretation* (Maryknoll: Orbis, 2001).

[10]See especially *But She Said*, 51–76 and 195–218, for the elaboration of this process with reference to a particular text.

[11]For such a hermeneutical reading, see Sandra Schneiders, *The Revelatory Text: Interpreting the New Testament as Sacred Scripture* (New York: HarperSanFrancisco, 1991).

[12]See Elisabeth Schüssler Fiorenza, "Re-Visioning Christian Origins: *In Memory of Her* Re-visited." *Christian Beginnings: Worship, Belief, and Society*, edited by Kieran O'Mahony, 225–50 (London: Continuum, 2003).

[13]See, for instance, M. Eugene Boring, *1 Peter*, ANTC (Nashville: Abingdon, 1999).

[14]John H. Elliott, *1 Peter: A New Translation with Introduction and Commentary*, AB (New York: Doubleday, 2000); Paul J. Achtemeier, *1 Peter*, Hermeneia (Minneapolis: Fortess Press, 1996).

[15]Toni Morrison, *Beloved* (New York: Knopf, 1987), 88.

[16]Regula Strobel, "Brot nicht Steine," *Fama* 14, no. 2 (1998): 11 (my translation).

[17]Patricia Hill Collins, *Fighting Words: Black Wo/men and the Search for Justice* (Minneapolis: University of Minnesota Press, 1998).

[18]See Elisabeth Schüssler Fiorenza and Kwok Pui-Lan, eds., *Women's Sacred Scriptures* (Maryknoll: Orbis, 1998).

19

Claiming the Word

Charting Global Feminist Biblical Studies

Now that feminist biblical studies[1] have come of age and are moving toward the future it is timely to assess this field of study and its prospects in a global context. Such a worldwide context reveals at one and the same time the exploitation of wo/men around the world and the feminist affirmation of cultural particularities and wo/men's networking in solidarity to bring about change and transformation. I will therefore first discuss my understanding of critical global feminist biblical studies, then go on to sketch their genealogy, look thirdly at the danger of academizing and scientizing feminist biblical studies, and finally argue that feminist biblical interpretation needs to be constantly reshaped in the interest of "dissident"[2] global solidarity.

As I have argued throughout this book, I understand feminist biblical studies as an important scientific area of research that seeks to produce knowledge in the interest of wo/men[3] who by law and custom have been marginalized and exploited as well as excluded from scientific the*logy and biblical interpretation for centuries. Although wo/men have interpreted Scriptures and shaped religions throughout the centuries,[4] they could not do so officially and their work often has been forgotten. Hence, I want to distinguish feminist biblical studies as an academic area of study from feminist biblical interpretation that is the domain of all feminists in biblical religions. If feminist biblical studies do not want to be beholden to the kyriarchal academy, I have argued in these pages, they have to adopt a critical feminist hermeneutics and the*logical ethos of liberation as their theoretical framework and approach of inquiry in order to be able to learn from and serve wo/men in biblical religions.

While throughout Christian history wo/men have interpreted the Bible, feminist biblical studies in their academic incarnation are of very recent vintage. Moreover, their ethos is always in danger of being co-opted by the reigning academic paradigm of interpretation. Such academic incorporation raises difficult questions. By the*logical ethos I do not mean a dogmatic or ecclesiastical worldview but the disciplined critical reflection on how discourses about the Divine and religion interrupt globalizing discourses of dehumanization or inspire discourses of well-being. In addition, I would insist that even studies that call themselves *feminist* must be analyzed as to whether their goals are emancipatory and their theoretical assumptions interrupt global discourses of domination.[5] In the face of globalization feminist scholars cannot subscribe to a "so-called" value-detached, neutral, objectivist-scientific investigation, because scientific interpretation and knowledge are always already enmeshed in structures of domination and exploitation. Such structures of domination and subordination engender kyriarchal domination and kyriocentric[6] discourses of dehumanization.

A Critical Global Feminist Analytic

Structures of domination and subordination throw into question the dualistic conceptualization of wo/men's studies in terms of gender as the basic feminist category of analysis. Alice Duer Miller's witty jingle expresses the understanding of feminism in terms of gender dualism well:

> Mother, what is a feminist?
> A feminist, my daughter
> Is any woman now who cares
> To think about her own affairs
> As men don't think she oughter.[7]

In this understanding, feminism is the rejection of male control and the affirmation of female independence. Such a conceptualization of domination in terms of gender or patriarchy/androcentrism, however, does not suffice in a global context. In such a context the analytic category of gender/patriarchy/androcentrism understood as men's domination over wo/men must be inflected in and through an analytic that can articulate the intersecting structures of domination and prejudice. Wo/men are not just defined by gender, but also by race, class, nationality, age, sexuality, and imperialism. Hence, the obfuscating ideological character of androcentric language must become conscious.

To make conscious the power of kyriocentric language and discourse in general and biblical language[8] in particular, I use the expression *wo/men* always in an inclusive way and invite readers to engage in a spiritual-intellectual exercise that reverses the usual linguistic practice. In a Western kyriocentric, grammatically male-determined language system such as English, masculine terms like *men*, *he*, and *mankind* are used as generic terms for human beings and are therefore presumed to include wo/men. Simply by learning how to speak, men experience themselves as central and important whereas wo/men learn that we are not directly addressed but are subsumed under male terms.

In a grammatically androcentric (that is, male-centered) language system wo/men always have to think twice and to deliberate whether we are meant or not when we are told, for example, that "all men are created equal" or that we are "sons of G*d." In a kyriocentric language system we have to ask which wo/men are meant when we speak of wo/men. To lift into consciousness these androcentric language mechanisms, I use wo/men as inclusive of men, s/he as inclusive of he, and fe/male as inclusive of male. Thereby I invite male readers to deliberate and adjudicate whether they are also meant when I refer, for instance, to *globalized wo/men*. Since the limits of our language are the limits of our world, I recommend this "thinking twice" approach as a good spiritual exercise for the next hundred years or more.

Religious and biblical language tells us that we are made in the image of G*d, who is generally understood as male. Wo/men thereby internalize that the Divine is male and not female. Simply by learning to speak or to pray, wo/men learn that we are marginal, insignificant, "second-class citizens" in society and religion. It seems to me, therefore, that only those two-thirds world feminist scholars who have not been socialized into a Western androcentric language system, because the languages of their native countries are not gendered, can break this power of male-centered language over us; but they still have to be alert to kyriocentric language, which is status dependent. Scholars who have grown up in a language system that, for instance, is a *status system* are able to make significant contributions to feminist translation, thought, and the*logy, although feminist research in this area is still very much lacking.[9]

At the same time, by problematizing *woman* throughout my writings, I want wo/men to pause and ask which wo/men are meant—since not all wo/men are the same and the differences between wo/men are as great or often even greater than those between wo/men and men of the same race, class, or ethnic group. Wo/men are not a unitary group and do not have a feminine nature and essence in common. Wo/men are not a different human species from men, nor are we all the same. Rather, wo/men come in all sizes, shapes, and colors. What it means to be a "woman" is different in Europe, Africa, or Asia. It means something different when you are black or white, young or old. It means something different if you have grown up in a pueblo or in an academic environment. It means something different if you are a beauty queen or differently abled, a girl or a mother. It means something different if you are a student or a teacher, the lady of the house or her slave.

Wo/man or wo/men is an unstable fragmented category and one cannot assume that all wo/men are similar in their hopes and desires. Hence it becomes important to ask which wo/men come to mind when one speaks of a "woman's perspective." Are they right-wing or feminist, black or white, native or foreign? Wo/men as much as men are socialized into the mind-sets and world-views of the dominant culture. We are not better human beings or able to envision a different future just because we are "wo/men." Changing language patterns is a very important step toward the realization of a new consciousness. Not femininity or "woman" but wo/men's rich diversity must constitute the feminist perspective and theoretical framework of a "global reading" of the Bible.

Such a critical understanding of language requires that we conceptualize feminist biblical studies as a critical rhetoric of inquiry[10] that treats biblical texts and scholarly interpretations as arguments rather than as descriptive statements or the*logical doctrines. It investigates both what biblical texts and interpretations mean and what they do. Such an understanding of biblical texts as rhetorical overlaps with Edward Said's view that "Texts are worldly, to some degree they are events, and even when they appear to deny it, they are nevertheless a part of the social world, human life, and of course the historical moments in which they are located and interpreted,"[11] but it accentuates this insight in a critical feminist mode. I understand, therefore, feminist biblical studies as an important scientific area of research that seeks to produce knowledge in the interest of wo/men who by law and custom have been marginalized and exploited as well as excluded from scientific the*logy and biblical interpretation for centuries.

Although some strains of postmodernism and postfeminism are adamant in their rejection of speaking about "social structures of domination" and focus on ideology instead,[12] I maintain that a critical feminist hermeneutics cannot relinquish the analysis of structures of domination.

In the face of wo/men's globalized inequality, a strong feminist movement is called for that does not understand wo/men's oppression just in terms of gender dualism or the domination of all wo/men by all men but in terms of intersecting, multiplicative structures and discourses of domination—racism, heterosexism, poverty, imperialism, ethnocentrism, and ageism—and insists on the revalorization of *differences* and not just of *gender difference*. Therefore it becomes necessary to focus specifically on the struggles of multiply oppressed wo/men for self-determination and justice in society and religion, which leads to a different self-understanding and vision of the world.

Such a critical feminist liberationist approach engages a "doubled" analysis of power, one that conceptualizes power as structural-pyramidal—or more precisely as kyriarchal relations of domination—and one that understands power horizontally as an ideological network of relations of domination. Both modes of power, the vertical and the horizontal, are at work in capitalist globalization. The kyriarchal (that is, imperial) pyramid of domination is structured by race, gender, sexuality, class, empire, age, and religion, which are intersecting systems that have multiplicative effects of dehumanizing exploitation and othering subordination.

In working with a social analytic of domination and liberation I prefer a *status* rather than an *identity* model of inquiry that is able to examine the institutionalized structures and value patterns of domination for their effects on the relative status of social actors both in a given society and in a text. If such status inscriptions constitute persons as peers, capable of participating on a par with each other, then we can speak of status equality or grassroots democracy. If they do not do so, then we speak of domination and subordination. Wo/men's struggles for radical democratic equality seek to abolish relations of domination and to establish those of subordinated status as full partners and peers with equal rights and responsibilities.

In the days of postfeminism and the "war on feminism" (*New York Times*) by the Christian right it is often argued that wo/men are not discriminated against or oppressed, that feminist rhetoric and not discriminatory structures turn wo/men into victims. I am frequently told by young wo/men that they cannot connect with a critical feminist interpretation for liberation because they do not feel disadvantaged and have not experienced discrimination.[13] They are convinced that feminist struggles were won by their mothers or grandmothers.

I generally respond to such interlocutors that if they come from a middle-class, white, racially and nationally privileged background, it is quite understandable that they have not yet experienced oppression or even discrimination. Yet, anyone who knows how to read the newspapers or gets involved in religious or university politics[14] soon will learn that feminist struggles are not yet over. Feminist the*logy and biblical studies are still very controversial and far from being accepted by leaders in religion and academy.

A glance at statistical data on wo/men's situations in the United States and around the world can easily document that wo/men as a group are disadvantaged worldwide in and through the processes of globalization. Wo/men still earn only two-thirds of what men in similar situations earn; the majority of people living in poverty are wo/men; violence against wo/men and gynecide, that is the killing of wo/men, is on the increase; sexual trafficking, various forms of forced labor, illiteracy, migration, and refugee camps spell out globally wo/men's increasing exploitation.

Economic globalization was created with the specific goal, to give primacy to corporate profits and values and to install and codify such market values throughout the world. It was designed to amalgamate and merge all economic activities around the world within a single model of global monoculture. In many respects wo/men are suffering not only from the globalization of market capitalism but also from their sexual exploitation instigated by such market capitalism.

The Human Rights Watch *World Report* extensively documents the systemic inequality, abuse, violence, discrimination, starvation, poverty, neglect, and denial of wo/men's rights that afflict the lives of wo/men around the globe.[15] Hence, the experience of white middle- or upper-class American wo/men is not typical and does not adequately comprehend the extent of wo/men's oppression worldwide. A global feminist biblical hermeneutics, therefore, must critically look at its politics of location. While it is important that we recognize our social location and celebrate our particular cultural-religious differences, we also need to be wary of the global-capitalist ethos of fragmentation and competition that prevents our solidarity.

In and through cultural, political, and religious discourses, the social structures in which we are positioned are interpreted. Since we cannot stand outside the interpretive frameworks available in our society and time, we "make sense" out of life with their help. For instance, one wo/man might be influenced by neoconservatism and believe that her social position results from the fact that she worked harder in life than the wo/man on welfare who lives down the street. Another wo/man influenced by right-wing religious fundamentalism might make sense of her situation by believing that she is blessed by G*d because of her virtuous life, whereas the unmarried mother on welfare has gravely sinned and therefore is punished. Again another wo/man might think that her success as a wife and mother is due to her feminine attractiveness and selfless dedication to her husband and children and that the fate of the wo/man on welfare is due to her lack thereof.

If we always have to resort to existing interpretive discourses and frameworks for making sense of our lives or of biblical texts, then the importance of social movements for justice becomes obvious. Since malestream[16] hegemonic discourses provide the frameworks in which we "make meaning" in oppressive situations, feminist discourses must provide interpretive frameworks that illuminate not only the choreography of oppression but also the possibilities for a radical democratic society and religion.[17] We are able to articulate an emancipatory self- and world-understanding only within the context of radical democratic movements, which shape theories that help us exploit the contradictions existing between diverse socio-hegemonic discourses.

Here the distinction between a wo/man's *structural position* and her *subject position* becomes important. Every individual is *structurally* positioned by birth within social, cultural, economic, political, and religious structures of domination. No one chooses to be born white, black, Asian, European, mixed race, poor, healthy, male, or female. We always find ourselves already positioned by and within structures of domination and the chances we get in life are limited by them. For example, wo/men are not poor or homeless because we have low motivation, faulty self-esteem, or poor work habits. Rather wo/men are poor or homeless because of our *structural position* within relations of domination.

Unlike a *structural position* a *subject position* is variable, open to intervention, and changeable but also limited by hegemonic structures of domination. According to the theorists Ernest Laclau and Chantal Mouffe, "A 'subject position' refers to the ensemble of beliefs through which an individual interprets and responds to her structural positions within a social formation.

In this sense an individual becomes a social agent insofar as she lives her structural positions through an ensemble of subject positions."[18]

The relationship between a *subject position* and a *structural position* is quite complex since our self-understandings are always already determined by our *structural position* with its rewards and pressures. Thus a person might be theoretically able to live her structural position through a wide range of subject positions, but practically might be restricted to a rigidly defined and closed set of available interpretive frameworks. Hence, the importance of emancipatory movements for articulating different interpretive frameworks.

Feminist critical theory has made a range of such interpretive frameworks and categories available to wo/men for shaping our *subject positions*.[19] It has provided various social analytics for diagnosing and changing wo/men's structural positions in and through the articulation of different *subject positions*. Key analytic concepts and categories with which to read in a feminist fashion have been developed either as reverse discourse to the binary intellectual framework of systemic dualisms or in a critical liberationist frame. Feminist biblical studies also have shared in this intellectual process.

GENEALOGY OF FEMINIST BIBLICAL STUDIES

While academic feminist biblical studies are of recent vintage, the study of wo/men in the Bible was already flourishing when I started to study the*logy in the late 1950s. Just as according to Virginia Woolf the library shelves were filled with books written by men *about wo/men*,[20] so also the religious libraries had a great array of tracts on "wo/men in the Bible." These were either moralistic tales to inculcate the standards of Christian femininity with the help of biblical wo/men characters and saints, or they were written to legitimate wo/men's exclusion from or admission to ordination. Others again were apologetic in tone, arguing that Jesus and Christian religion has liberated wo/men. Such portrayals of Jesus and his liberation of wo/men were often used for missionary purposes or served antifeminist and anti-Jewish interests.

Like the study *about wo/men*, so also *wo/men's biblical studies*—in which wo/men are not just objects but also subjects of interpretation—have a long history starting with antiquity and continuing throughout the middle ages and modernity. In the nineteenth century, Sojourner Truth, Anna Maria Stewart, and the Grimkè sisters, for instance, claimed such authority of interpretation in the struggle for the abolition of slavery, Elizabeth Cady Stanton edited the Woman's Bible,[21] and Antoinette Blackwell wrote a scientific paper on 1 Corinthians. However, the wo/men scholars of the time were, according to Cady Stanton, not willing to collaborate in the project of the *Woman's Bible*.[22]

Many feminists were and still are convinced that the Bible and religion are anti-wo/men and hence must be rejected as hopelessly patriarchal. Biblical interpretation is the domain of believers but not the task of feminists. Yet, already in the nineteenth century Elizabeth Cady Stanton pointed to the pitfalls of such a feminist attitude. She maintained that feminists must concern themselves with the Bible and religion because many wo/men still believe in them. She also pointed out that one cannot reform one segment of patriarchal society without reforming the whole. If feminists are concerned with the liberation of wo/men, then they must take account of the fact that many wo/men not only consult the Bible as an inspiring authority but also value and transmit it as a source of strength and hope. Feminists, whether believers or not, must concern themselves with the Bible and its interpretation because it still has great power in the lives of many wo/men.

In addition, it needs to be pointed out that feminists who have left biblical religions but have grown up in Western cultures have also internalized many biblical patterns and stereotypes. Western cultures are still permeated with the symbolism and values of the Christian Scriptures. In order to understand Western art, music, and literature one needs a certain amount of biblical literacy. Cultural ideologies and media stereotypes are still based on and derived from the Bible. Biblical texts and images fund the cultural language of hate against wo/men, against blacks, against homosexuals, against Jews, or against pagans.

The *biblical wo/men's studies* scholarship emerging in the 1970s saw wo/men both as subjects and objects of interpretation. However, the *wo/men's studies* approach also has been in danger of continuing the objectifying "wo/men in the Bible" genre or the Christian apologetic approach that in the face of feminist criticism proclaims either the Bible or Jesus as the liberator of woman. [23] This approach places the biblical text or Jesus in the center of attention rather than reflecting on the subjectivity and agency of wo/men. A radical feminist post-Christian or post-Jewish approach in turn has rejected the Bible as totally patriarchal and indicted those who still claim it as their heritage as "reformist," self-alienated, and co-opted by patriarchal religions.

These feminist hermeneutical debates of the late 70s and early 80s (see part I) presented challenges to articulate more fully a hermeneutical framework that was both critical and liberationist rather than apologetic and neoorthodox. My own work therefore sought to elaborate a different feminist model of critical interpretation.[24] Such a different feminist model, I argued, has first to place wo/men as citizen-subjects, as the *ekklēsia of wo/men*,[25] into the center of attention. In order to become feminist studies, I maintained, studies on *"wo/men in the Bible"* must recognize wo/men in religion as historical, cultural, the*logical, and scientific subjects and agents.

Biblical research and scholarship must be done in the interest of *all* wo/men and engender a radical democratic societal, cultural, religious, and personal transformation. The*logically, such an approach seeks to assess whether a biblical text reveals G*d as a G*d of domination and oppression or as a G*d of liberation and well-being and in what context the text receives its meaning. It understands "revelation" as what is put into Scripture by G*d "for the sake of 'our'—that is wo/men's—salvation." Utilizing an ancient Jewish hermeneutical insight, it seeks the Divine in "the white spaces" between the letters and words of Scripture.[26]

Such a research focus on wo/men as producers of critical knowledge requires a *double paradigm shift* in the ethos of biblical studies. A paradigm shift from a positivist-scientist, allegedly interest-free and value-neutral objectivist ethos of scholarship to a scientific feminist one on the one hand and a shift from an androcentric or better kyriocentric linguistically based cultural ethos to a critical feminist one on the other hand. It is a shift from a scientific positivist to a scientific feminist interpretation. *Finally*, such a reconceptualization of biblical studies needs to be interdisciplinary or transdisciplinary. It needs not only to integrate the insights of philology, classics, archeology, sociology, anthropology, ethnography, epistemology, and historiography but also to recognize the fundamental feminist criticism of these academic disciplines and their feminist reconceptualizations.[27]

THE ACADEMIC FIELD OF FEMINIST BIBLICAL STUDIES

Such a reconceptualization of biblical studies in critical feminist terms is necessary because the self-understanding of biblical studies as a positivist science cannot address the challenges raised by globalization. Central to the self-understanding of biblical studies, whether practiced in the academy, public discourse, or in religiously affiliated institutions, is the insistence on the scientific character of its research. By identifying as a scientific practice, biblical studies are determined by the theoretical assumptions that have shaped and governed positivist scientific discourse.

As I have pointed out in chapter 8, positivist scientific discourse seeks to produce objectivist and disinterested research in terms of quantitative methods, refinement of the technology of exegesis, archeological research, production of factual knowledge, anti-the*logical rhetoric, and the deployment of social-scientific models that are derived from cultural anthropology or quantitative sociology. The the*logical form of such a positivist attitude claims to be handing down the word of G*d as once and for all given, revealed truth. Both discourses, the positivist scientific and the positivist the*logical one, insist on such disinterested authoritative knowledge in order to maintain their public credibility and authority.

The discipline thus continues to socialize future scholars into a reifying methodological and allegedly value-free positivism and future ministers into biblicist literalism and the*logical positivism.[28] Biblical discourses in the public sphere are advocating either literalist biblicism or academic scientism. As long as this is the case, struggles for justice, radical equality, and the well-being of all will remain marginal in the discourses of the discipline. It is well known that biblical studies emerged on the scene together with other disciplines in the humanities that sought to articulate their discourses as scientific practices in analogy to the natural sciences. The feminist theorist Sandra Harding has pointed to a three-stage process in the emergence of modern science shaping and determining scholarly discourses, their presuppositions, and intellectual frameworks.

The first stage, according to Harding, consisted in the breakdown of feudal labor divisions and slave relations.[29] The second stage is exemplified in the New Science Movement of the seventeenth century that flourished in Puritan England and brought forth a new political self-consciousness with radical social goals.[30] Scientific knowledge was to serve the people and to be used for redistributing knowledge and wealth.[31] The third stage produced the notion of purely technical and value-neutral science. The progress that science represents is based entirely on scientific method. The institutionalization of science meant the separation of science's cognitive and political aims and the restriction of true science and scientists to the former.

Pure science, according to Harding, was characterized by atomism, the claim that nature's fundamental units are separate with no intrinsic connection. This model goes hand in hand with the political assertion that individual males are not bound to the group in which they are born but are autonomous individuals who form alliances by contract. It also goes hand in hand with value-neutrality, which captures what is real through impersonal, quantitative language; and method, understood as norms, rules, procedures, and scientific technologies. Scientific values are transhistorical human values; they are not particularistic, local, partial, or political. Historically and culturally specific values, emotions, and interests must be kept separated from depoliticized transcendental scientific practices.

Biblical studies as a discipline is located at this third scientific stage, which constructs a sharp dualism between science and the*logy, or scientific discourse and ideology, in order to prove itself as free from ideology. A series of structuring dualisms[32] and dichotomies between science and politics, history and the*logy, knowledge and fiction, past and present, rationality and faith, male and female, white and black, Caucasian and Asian, and so on, determine the Western scientific worldview. As a scientific discourse biblical studies thus participates in the discourses of domination that were produced by science.

For it is also at this third stage of the development of academic scientific disciplines that the discourses of domination—racism, heterosexism, colonialism, class privilege, ageism—were articulated as "scientific" discourses.[33] While previously discourses of colonization were developed on the grounds of Christian religion, now positivist science takes the place of religion and continues its work of hegemonic legitimization. The discourses of domination were formed as elite discourses that justified relations of ruling. Hence, "soft" academic disciplines such as history, sociology, and anthropology, in their formative stage, had to develop discourses of domination in order to prove that they also belonged to the "hard" sciences. Thereby academic social-science disciplines supported European colonialism and capitalist industrial development.

For instance, the nineteenth century professionalization of history fostered scientific practices advocating commitment to an objectivity above the critical scrutiny of such categories as class and gender, along with strict use of evidence, less rhetorical style, the development of archives, libraries, peer reviews, and professional education. Scientific historical discourses created an intellectual space inhabited by an "invisible and neutered I" that was considered as a "gender- and race-free" community of scholars. At the same time science was producing discourses of exclusion such as racism, heterosex-ism, and colonialism barring all wo/men and disenfranchised men from the professions and turning them into objects of research. As Bonnie G. Smith puts it: "Using women as the sign both of gender in its entirety (that is, women as the gendered other to the neutral man) and of all that was outside of history, the new scholars created a fantasy world of the Real, that is, of history. It was a world purged of gender (as well as class [and race]), sufficient unto itself in charting and defining significant human experience in the past, and redolent of the power such claims generated."[34]

American sociology in its formative years exhibits the same symptoms as scientific historiography. It was influenced by European anthropological discourses that emerged with imperialism, and understood colonized peoples as "primitives" who were considered to be more natural, sexual, untouched by civilization, and inferior because of their innate biological differences— for instance, their allegedly smaller brains. In the United States, Native Americans and African Americans were those who represented the "primitive" in sociological and anthropological scientific discourses. They were construed to be either violent or childlike or both. People who were nonwhite and nonmale were praised as "noble savages" or feared as "bloodthirsty cannibals" on biological and cultural grounds.

Asians, Africans, Native peoples, and white wo/men were viewed as childlike, a factor used to explain their supposedly inferior intelligence.

> White women and Blacks were also seen as more embodied, "natural," and controlled by their physical, biological essences. Both were viewed as having an inherent "nature" of some sort— for blacks violence, for White women passivity. Collectively, these comparisons generated a situation in which race and gender gained meaning from another, situated within economic class hierarchies that drew upon these ideas. . . . Remaining in the private sphere

of home and caring for the family would protect middle-class White women from the dangers of the public sphere that, with urbanization and industrialization, was increasingly populated by poor people, immigrants, Black people, and "fallen" women. . . . Thus social processes that created these categories in the first place, namely, restricting wo/men to the private sphere and racially segregating African Americans, could largely be taken for granted.[35]

To give an example from the use of biblical discourse: In an article entitled "The Use of the New Testament in the American Slave Controversy: A Case History in the Hermeneutical Tension between Biblical Criticism and Christian Moral Debate," J. Albert Harrill[36] has convincingly shown that the discourse on slavery has decisively shaped the development of historical-critical biblical studies. He argues that the abolitionist arguments during the American slave controversy pushed the field toward a critical hermeneutics and a more critical reading of the text in terms of an ethics of interpretation. The proslavery arguments in contrast "fostered a move to literalism emboldened by the findings of biblical criticism that the New Testament writers did not condemn slavery."[37] According to the plain literal sense of the biblical text Jesus and Paul did not attack slavery but only its abuse. Hence, the proslavery argument required a positivist literal reading of the Bible that was done in the name of biblical science. Moreover, the study of Shawn Kelley on *Racializing Jesus* also has shown how biblical scholarship has become racialized through the reception of the ideological frameworks of the Tübingen School and the philosophy of Heidegger via Bultmann,[38] whereas the works of postcolonial biblical interpretation[39] has underscored how such racialization has served colonial interests.

Consequently, critical global feminist biblical studies have to critically investigate the theoretical frameworks and scientific methods we adopt from malestream biblical studies. While some have argued that feminist biblical studies does not need to develop its own method, I would maintain that we not only should scrutinize traditional methods and their frameworks as to their emancipatory or concealing functions but also articulate feminist critical approaches, methods, and analytics.

Rather than reinscribing the disciplinary divisions between the*logical and scientific interpretation, between literary and historical methods, between sociopolitical and religious approaches, or between social-sociological and ideological–religious criticism, I have argued that critical feminist biblical studies must work for a paradigm shift that can overcome these dualisms by conceptualizing biblical studies as a rhetorics and ethics of inquiry and transformation.

CRITICAL AREAS OF DEBATE IN GLOBAL FEMINIST BIBLICAL STUDIES

The "field" of critical feminist interpretation is positioned *in between* globalization and localization, universality and particularity, isolationism and networking, disinterested academy and social movement, difference and differences, modernism and postmodernism. Hence, it is always in danger of dissolving these tensions of the "in-between" and struggles against global oppression and dehumanization by succumbing to competitive infighting and aggressive behavior against each other.[40] How we resolve the debates and disagreements in the following areas seems to me crucial for the future of global Christian New Testament studies.[41]

First: Insofar as feminist biblical studies have been accepted by the Western academy, they are in danger of becoming co-opted by its malestream scientific ethos. This has various ramifications, but the most important one in my view is the co-optation of feminist biblical studies through professionalization. Feminist students continue to be socialized into the hegemonic kyriocentric paradigm of the discipline while feminist faculty are forced to prove their academic excellence and good citizenship in terms of positivistic scientific standards.[42] For instance, I have met many young doctoral students across the world who were told by their advisors that if they want to do a feminist dissertation they needed first to critically deconstruct the allegedly intellectually naïve work of the first generation of feminist scholars. Then with the help of malestream theory—à la Barth, Foucault, Bourdieu, Derrida, Lacan, or Rahner and/or other hegemonic scholarship in the field (for example, archeological finds, form and redaction criticism, the method of the Jesus Seminar, or Social Scientific research on the Mediterranean)—they must reconceptualize the problem of their research so that they can produce acceptable "new" scholarship. It is therefore not surprising that many students do not seriously study feminist works and that young feminist scholars either repeat work that has been done without quoting it or even being aware of it or misconstrue it in such a fashion that the results of such previous feminist work are now claimed as their very own but in a kyriocentric key.

Second: According to Thomas Kuhn a new scientific paradigm can only emerge and rival the existing paradigms if it produces not only new knowledge but also new institutions.[43] If the rhetorical–emancipatory feminist paradigm of biblical studies should gain the strength to change the discourses of the discipline we need to search for ways of institutionalizing such emancipatory scholarship in the interest of dissident globalization. The present institutional locations of feminist biblical discourses in the academy, the church, and the media will not be able to promote justice, equality, and wellbeing as long as they remain beholden to the third stage in the development of science. The separation of academic feminists from feminist social movements and their problems and questions conforms feminist biblical studies more and more to the interests of the academy rather than keep us responsible to global movements for change.

A long time ago, the Australian feminist Dale Spender has shown that in the past four hundred years (and I would maintain throughout history) feminist ideas have been trivialized, silenced, and forgotten.[44] Consequently, the next feminist generation cannot learn from the thought of their predecessors but is compelled, so to speak, to reinvent the intellectual wheel again and again. As the historian Barbara Caine has shown, it is not just the dominant kyriarchal society and academy that fosters the forgetting of feminist knowledge. It is also every new generation of feminists themselves who finds it hard to recognize the work of their forerunners and therefore is compelled to distance themselves from the ideas of their predecessors in order to prove the novelty and creativity of their own ideas: "At the same time historians have to recognize that the frequent rejection of the term 'feminism'—and of any sense of connection with earlier feminists—by women who have embraced the notion of female emancipation indicates that women find it hard to establish trans-generational links or to set themselves up as legitimating or authoritative figures for each other or for future generations."[45]

Third: Another reason why a feminist paradigm shift from a positivist scientist to a critical-emancipatory scientific one has not yet been effective is the continuing reduction of feminist biblical studies to wo/men's or gender studies that work with an essentialized understanding of wo/man or retrace the dualistic Western sex-gender system but neglect to see racism, colonialism, class exploitation and poverty, ageism, nationalism, war, imperialism, and other forms of domination as crucial elements of wo/men's oppression. Insofar as feminist studies remain focused on sexual difference, wo/man, the feminine, and patriarchy as gender domination, on what I have called the ideology of the white Lady, we are not able to articulate and research the pyramidal intersectionality of domination that continues to reproduce ancient kyriarchal structures that still shape our lives and make wo/men and subordinated men second-class citizens.

Moreover, what Rey Chow calls "the differences revolution" has taken hold especially also in avant-garde feminist biblical studies. As long as difference is conceptualized, however, only in positivist, post-structural, linguistic terms that eschew all reference to actual experiences of oppression and sociopolitical struggles, difference is seen solely as positive and not also understood as an indicator of domination. As long as power is understood only as circulating horizontally and not also vertically in its oppressive force, the differences of kyriarchal oppression will either be positively romanticized or result in resentment and infighting among those on the margins of biblical studies.

Fourth: Structural change in biblical studies in my opinion is only possible if and when we create solidarity and alliances on the one hand among feminists of different social locations and on the other among all those in

biblical studies who pursue a critical rhetorics, politics, and ethics of emancipation and well-being for everyone. Religious communities and persons
face a theo-ethical choice: either they spiritually sustain the exploitation of
global capitalism or they engage the possibilities for greater freedom, justice,
and solidarity engendered by the technological market forces of globalization.
World-religions either inspire individuals and groups to support the forces of
economic and cultural global dehumanization or to abandon their exclusivist
tendencies and together envision and work for a feminist spiritual ethos of
global dimensions; either they advocate radical democratic spiritual values
and visions that celebrate diversity, multiplicity, tolerance, equality, justice,
and well-being for all or they foster fundamentalism, exclusivism, and the
exploitation of a totalitarian global monoculture. This ethical choice does not
reinscribe the dualisms created by structures of domination but struggles to
overcome and abolish them.[46]

Since nation-states are no longer in control of globalization, social political theorists such as Hardt and Negri have pointed out that it may be
more appropriate to understand globalization in terms of empire. Insofar
as the nation-state is replaced by multinational corporations, its globalizing
economic, cultural, and political forces form a polycentric empire.[47] The
danger of this shift from nation-state to international corporation is that
democratic government no longer can be exercised and the system of global
capitalism is not held democratically accountable. However such globalization
also presents possibilities for more radical democratization worldwide. It also
makes possible the interconnectedness of all beings and the possibility of
communication and solidaric organization across national boarders on the
basis of human rights and justice for all.

Insofar as transnational capitalism crosses all borders, exploits all peoples,
and colonizes all citizens it requires a counter-vision and dissident strategy
that Chela Sandoval has called "democratics," a strategy and vision that
has affinities with my own attempt to articulate the space of the *ekklēsia of
wo/men*[48] as a critical radical democratic space of interpretation. Sandoval
explains *democratics* as one of the methods of the oppressed in the following
way: "With the transnationalization of capitalism when elected officials are
no longer leaders of singular nation-states but nexuses for multinational
interests, it also becomes possible for citizen-subjects to become activists for
a new decolonizing global terrain, a psychic terrain that can unite them with
similarly positioned citizen-subjects within and across national borders into
new, post-Western—empire alliances. . . . Love as social movement is enacted
by revolutionary, mobile, and global coalitions of citizen-activists who are
allied through the apparatus of emancipation."[49]

However, I am somewhat hesitant to claim "love" as the sole revolutionary
force or to reduce "oppositional social action to a mode of 'love' in the
postmodern world." Although I am well aware that numerous American third-

world feminists have eloquently written about the power of love in struggles for justice,[50] I cannot forget the function of "romantic love" in the oppression of wo/men nor the anti-Jewish valorization of the "New" Testament "G*d of love" over the "Old" Testament "G*d of Justice." Democratics, in my view, must be equally informed by justice as Patricia Hill Collins has argued: "Justice transcends Western notions of equality grounded in sameness and uniformity. ... In making their quilts Black wo/men weave together scraps of fabric from all sorts of places. Nothing is wasted, and every piece of fabric has a function and a place in a given quilt. ... [T]hose who conceptualize community via notions of uniformity and sameness have difficulty imagining a social quilt that is simultaneously heterogeneous, driven toward excellence, and just."[51]

In this image of quilt and quilting for the making of justice the decoloniz-ing practices of a global democratics, of the *ekklēsia of wo/men*, and a critical feminist dissident global interpretation converge. To conceptualize feminist interpretation as such a critical quilting of meaning in different sociopolitical locations, I suggest, will enable us to articulate biblical visions of justice and well-being for all.

Notes

[1] See, for example, Janice Capel Anderson, "Mapping Feminist Biblical Criticism," *Critical Review of Books in Religion* 2 (1991): 21–44; Elizabeth Castelli, "Heteroglossia, Hermeneutics, and History: A Review Essay of Recent Feminist Studies of Early Christianity," *The Journal of Feminist Studies in Religion* 10, no. 2 (1994): 73–78. For Jewish feminist interpretations, see the work of Esther Fuchs, Ilana Pardes, Adele Reinhartz, Tal Ilan, Amy Jill Levine, Cynthia Baker, or Alicia Suskin Ostriker and many others. See also Esther Fuchs, "Points of Resonance," in *On the Cutting Edge*, ed. Jane Schaberg, Alice Bach, and Esther Fuchs (New York: Continuum, 2004), 1–20. For Muslim feminist hermeneutics, see Amina Wadud, *Qur'an and Woman: Rereading the Sacred Text from a Woman's Perspective* (Oxford: Oxford University Press, 1999); Barbara F. Stowasser, *Women in the Qur'an: Traditions and Interpretations* (New York: Oxford University Press, 1994); Asma Barlas, "Believing Women" in *Islam: Unreading Patriarchal Interpretations of the Qur'an* (Austin: University of Texas Press, 2002).

[2] Chela Sandoval, *Methodology of the Oppressed* (Minneapolis: University of Minnesota Press, 2000).

[3] For the problematic meaning of the term *woman/women*, see Denise Riley, *"Am I That Name?": Feminism and the Category of Women in History* (Minneapolis: University of Minnesota Press, 1988); Judith Butler, *Gender Trouble: Feminism and the Subversion of Identity* (New York: Routledge, 1990). My way of writing wo/men seeks to underscore not only the ambiguous character of the term wo/man or wo/men but also to retain the expression wo/men as a sociopolitical category. Since this designation is often read as referring to white women only, my unorthodox writing of the word seeks to draw to the attention of readers that those kyriarchal structures that determine wo/men's lives and status also impact that of men of subordinated race, classes, countries, and religions, albeit in different ways. The expression wo/men must therefore be understood as inclusive rather than as an exclusive universalized gender term.

[4] See Patricia Demers, *Wo/men Interpreters of the Bible* (New York: Paulist, 1992); Marla Selvidge, *Notorious Voices: Feminist Biblical Interpretation, 1500–1920* (New York: Continuum, 1996); Gerda Lerner, *The Creation of Feminist Consciousness: From the Middle Ages to Eighteen-seventy* (New York: Oxford University Press, 1993), and especially the work of Elisabeth Gössmann.

See Gössmann's biography *Geburtsfehler weiblich: Lebenserinnerungen einer katholischen Theologin* (München: Iudicium, 2003).

[5] In her book *Postcolonial Feminist Interpretation of the Bible* (Saint Louis: Chalice, 2000) and other writings, Musa W. Dube has pointed to the shortcomings of my writings when read from an anti-imperialist perspective. While I readily concede that my work, like all other work, is limited by my social location, it was difficult for me to understand why I have been singled out for such harsh criticisms. This was puzzling because Musa is well aware of the multiple possible readings of texts and concedes that the "theoretical articulations of *kyriarchy* and *ekklēsia of women* do go a long way toward counteracting imperialism, if followed" (quotation at 37). Reading the story of Musa's grandmother about the beautiful princess who was killed by the other girls of the village because they realized, "As long as Utentelazandlane is alive, no one will ever notice us," has shed light on this predicament. See Musa W. Dube, "Jumping the Fire with Judith: Postcolonial Feminist Hermeneutics of Liberation," in Feminist *Interpretation of the Bible and the Hermeneutics of Liberation*, ed. Silvia Schroer and Sophia Bietenhard (New York: Sheffield Academic, 2003), 60. I want to thank Dr. Dube for helping me to understand the power dynamics that were operating in this and other feminist academic conferences.

[6] *Kyriocentrism* is a name for the linguistic-cultural-religious-ideological systems and intersecting discourses of race, gender, heterosexuality, class, imperialism, and other dehumanizing discourses that legitimate, inculcate, and sustain *kyriarchy*, that is, multiplicative structures of domination.

[7] Alice Duer Miller, *Are Women People? A Book of Rhymes for Suffrage Times* (New York: Doran, 1915).

[8] See Christina Hendricks and Kelly Oliver, eds., *Language and Liberation: Feminism, Philosophy and Language* (Albany: SUNY Press, 1999).

[9] See especially the pathbreaking article by Satoko Yamaguchi, "Father Image of G*d and Inclusive Language: A Reflection in Japan," in *Toward a New Heaven and a New Earth: Essays in Honor of Elisabeth Schüssler Fiorenza*, ed. Fernando F. Segovia (Maryknoll: Orbis, 2003), 199–224. I hope that this article will engender more research on biblical translation and interpretation in non-androcentric language contexts.

[10] For the development of this argument see my book *Rhetoric and Ethic: The Politics of Biblical Interpretation* (Minneapolis: Fortress, 1999).

[11] Edward Said, *The World, the Text, and the Critic* (Cambridge: Harvard University Press, 1983), 4.

[12] Ann Brooks, *Postfeminisms: Feminism, Cultural Theory, and Cultural Forms* (New York: Routledge, 1997).

[13] See for instance Elizabeth A. Richman, "Separate and Equal?" *Lilith: The Independent Jewish Women's Magazine* 29, no. 1 (2004): 28–29, who confronts her mother's experience of discrimination with those of her own generation who allegedly have not lived through such experiences of inequality. However, I am doubtful that one can speak for an entire generation.

[14] See the very significant article by María Pilar Aquino, "The Dynamics of Globalization and the University: Toward a Radical Democratic-Emancipatory Transformation," in *Toward a New Heaven and a New Earth*, 385–406.

[15] See Christa Wichterich, *The Globalized Woman: Reports from a Future of Inequality* (New York: Zed, 2000); Ann-Cathrin Jarl, *In Justice: Women and Global Economics* (Minneapolis: Fortress Press, 2003); Marjori Agosin, *Women, Gender, and Human Rights: A Global Perspective* (New Brunswick: Rutgers University Press, 2001).

[16] The expression *malestream* articulates the fact that history, tradition, theology, church, culture, and society have been defined by elite men and have excluded wo/men. Frameworks of scholarship, texts, traditions, language, standards, paradigms of knowledge, and so on, have been and are elite male centered and elite male dominated.

[17] See the contributions of Gabriele Dietrich, "People's Movements, the Strength of Wisdom, and the Twisted Path of Civilization"; Bonna Devora Haberman, "'Let My Gender Go!' Jewish Textual Activism"; Marsha Aileen Hewitt, "Dialectic of Hope"; and Marjorie Procter Smith, "Feminist Ritual Strategies: The Ekklēsia Gynaikon at Work"; in *Toward a New Heaven and a New Earth*.

¹⁸Anna Marie Smith, *Laclau and Mouffé: The Radical Democratic Imagination* (New York: London, 1998), 58–59.

¹⁹See, for example, Musa W. Dube, ed., *Other Ways of Reading: African Women and the Bible* (Atlanta: SBL, 2001); María Pilar Aquino, Daisy L. Machado, and Jeanette Rodríguez, eds., *A Reader in Latina Feminist Theology: Religion and Justice* (Austin: University of Texas Press, 2002); Rosemary Radford Ruether, ed., *Gender, Ethnicity and Religion: Views from the Other Side* (Minneapolis: Fortress Press, 2002); and the articles by Vincent Wimbush, "In Search of a Usable Past: Reorienting Biblical Studies," and Ivone Gebara, "A Feminist Theology of Liberation: A Latin American Perspective with a View toward the Future," in *Toward a New Heaven and a New Earth*, 179–98 and 249–69. See also the significant work edited by Vincent Wimbush, *African Americans and the Bible: Sacred Texts and Social Textures* (New York: Continuum, 2000).

²⁰Virginia Woolf, *Three Guineas* (New York: Harcourt, Brace, Jovanovich, 1966).

²¹See my book *Sharing Her Word: Feminist Biblical Interpretation in Context* (Boston: Beacon, 1998), 50–74, and Kathi Kern, *Mrs. Stanton's Bible* (Ithaca: Cornell University Press, 2001).

²²The first wo/man who joined the SBL in 1894 was Anna Ely Rhoads, but the Society elected its first wo/man president only in 1987. In 1970 wo/men's membership in the SBL was only 3.5% of the overall membership according to Saunders, 103, with reference to Dorothy C. Bass.

²³For a critical discussion see my books *Jesus: Miriam's Child and Sophia's Prophet* (New York: Continuum, 1994) and *Jesus and the Politics of Interpretation* (New York: Continuum, 2000).

²⁴See also my article "Method in Wo/men's Studies in Religion: A Critical Feminist Hermeneutics," in *Methodology in Religious Studies: The Interface with Women's Studies*, ed. Arvind Sharma (Albany: SUNY Press, 2002), 207–41. Revised and reprinted in my book *Transforming Vision: Exploring Feminist The*logy* (Minneapolis: Fortress Press, 2011).

²⁵For a very perceptive contextualization of this feminist articulation, see Elizabeth Castelli, "The Ekklēsia of Women and/as Utopian Space: Locating the Work of Elisabeth Schüssler Fiorenza in Feminist Utopian Thought," in *On the Cutting Edge: The Study of Women in Biblical Worlds*, ed. Jane Schaberg, Alice Bach, and Esther Fuchs (New York: Continuum, 2003), 36–52. In *Feminist Biblical Interpretation in Theological Context: Restless Readings* (Burlington: Ashgate, 2002), 32–59 and 142–62. Jánnine Jobling discusses the concept of the *ekklēsia* of wo/men but chooses *ekklēsia* without the qualification of *wo/men* as her hermeneutical key concept in order to restrict the concept to the Christian feminist movement (143). In so doing she reinscribes the division between the Christian and the so-called secular women's movements that I sought to overcome with this radical, democratic, counter-kyriarchal image.

²⁶See, for instance, Naomi M. Hyman, *Biblical Women in the Midrash: A Sourcebook* (Northvale: Jason Aronson, 1997).

²⁷See, for instance, Nancy Sorkin Rabinowitz and Amy Richlin, eds., *Feminist Theory and the Classics* (New York: Routledge, 1993).

²⁸See Elisabeth Schüssler Fiorenza and Kent H. Richardson, eds., *Transforming Biblical Studies* (Atlanta: Scholars, 2010) for a critical discussion of graduate biblical education around the globe.

²⁹Sandra Harding, *The Science Question in Feminism* (Ithaca: Cornell University Press, 1986), 218, with reference to Edgar Zilsel, "The Sociological Roots of Science," *American Journal of Sociology* 47 (1942).

³⁰Harding, *The Science Question in Feminism*, 219.

³¹Wolfgang van den Daele, "The Social Construction of Science," in *The Social Production of Scientific Knowledge*, ed. Everett Mendelsohn, Peter Weingart, and Richard Whitley (Dordrecht: Reidel, 1977), 38.

³²For such structuring dualisms in Q research see the dissertation of Melanie Johnson-DeBaufre and her article "Bridging the Gap to 'This Generation': A Feminist Critical Reading of the Rhetoric of Q 7:31-35," in *Walk in the Ways of Wisdom: Essays in Honor of Elisabeth Schüssler Fiorenza*, ed. Shelly Matthews, Cynthia Briggs Kittredge, and Melanie Johnson-DeBaufre (New York: Trinity International, 2003), 214–33. For a comprehensive interpretation of Q scholarship, see Richard Horsley, *Whoever Hears You Hears Me: Prophets, Performance, and Tradition in Q* (Harrisburg: Trinity International, 1999) and Burton L. Mack, *The Lost Gospel: The Book of Q and Christian Origins* (HarperCollins San Francisco, 1993).

33See Ronald T. Takaki, "Aesclepius Was a White Man: Race and the Cult of True Womanhood," in *The Racial Economy of Science: Toward a Democratic Future*, ed. Sandra Harding (Indianapolis: Indiana University Press, 1993), 201–9; Nancy Leys Stepan and Sander L. Gilman, "Appropriating the Idioms of Science: The Rejection of Scientific Racism," 170–93, and Nancy Leys Stepan, "Race and Gender: The Role of Analogy in Science," 369–76.

34Bonnie G. Smith, "Gender, Objectivity, and the Rise of Scientific History," in *Objectivity and Its Other*, ed. Wolfgang Natter, Theodore R. Schatzki, and John Paul Jones (New York: Guilford, 1995), 59.

35Patricia Hill Collins, *Fighting Words: Black Women and the Search For Justice* (Minneapolis: University of Minnesota Press, 1998), 100–101.

36J. Albert Harrill, "The Use of the New Testament in the American Slave Controversy: A Case History in the Hermeneutical Tension between Biblical Criticism and Christian Moral Debate," *Religion and American Culture* 10, no. 2 (2000): 149–86.

37J. Albert Harrill, "The Use of the New Testament," 174.

38Shawn Kelley, *Racializing Jesus: Race, Ideology, and the Formation of Modern Biblical Scholarship* (New York: Routledge, 2002). For the rhetoric of blackness in antiquity and early Christianity see Gay L. Byron, *Symbolic Blackness and Ethnic Difference in Early Christian Literature* (New York: Routledge, 2002).

39For pathbreaking work in postcolonial biblical studies, see the work of Kwok Pui-Lan, Laura Donaldson, Musa W. Dube, Fernando Segovia, and R. S. Sugirtharajah. See also the contributions of Musa W. Dube, "Ahab Says Hello to Judith: A Decolonizing Feminist Reading," Kwok Pui-Lan, "Engendering Christ," Fernando Segovia, "Liberation Hermeneutics: Revisiting the Foundations in Latin America," R. S. Sugirtharajah, "The End of Biblical Studies?" and Richard A. Horsley, "Subverting Disciplines: The Possibilities and Limitations of Postcolonial Theory for New Testament Studies," in *Toward a New Heaven and a New Earth*.

40I do not want to be misunderstood: I do not want to stifle such critical debate but draw attention to its political location, which must be taken into account.

41The feminist academic rhetoric of difference and particularity, for instance, is no longer directed against elite white male and female scholars, not against "gender" or "white Lady" feminists, but against liberationist feminists and subaltern male scholars.

42See my article "Rethinking the Educational Practices of Biblical Doctoral Studies," *Teaching Theology and Religion* 6 (April 2003): 65–75.

43Thomas Kuhn, *The Structure of Scientific Revolutions* (Chicago: University of Chicago Press, 1962).

44Dale Spender, *Women of Ideas (And What Men Have Done to Them)* (Boston: ARK, 1983).

45Barbara Caine, "Women's Studies, Feminist Traditions and the Problem of History," in *Transitions: New Australian Feminisms*, ed. Barbara Caine and Rosemary Pringle (Sydney: Allen and Unwin, 1995), 3.

46I want to thank the anonymous reviewer of this article for her/his careful and perceptive reading and especially for drawing my attention to the possibility of such a misreading of such an ethical choice in terms of dualism.

47Michael Hardt and Antonio Negri, *Empire: A New Vision of Social Order* (Cambridge: Harvard University Press, 2000).

48For an excellent critical discussion of this concept see Jánnine Jobling, *Feminist Biblical Interpretation in Thelogical Context: Restless Readings* (Burlington: Ashgate, 2002), 32–60, 142–63.

49Chela Sandoval, *Methodology of the Oppressed* (Minneapolis: University of Minnesota Press, 2000), 183.

50Audre Lorde, bell hooks, Toni Morrison, Cornel West, June Jordan, Gloria Anzaldúa, Maria Lugones, Merle Woo, Alice Walker—to name just a few.

51Patricia Hill Collins, *Fighting Words: Black Wo/men and the Search for Justice* (Minneapolis: University of Minnesota Press, 1998), 248–49.